BRITAIN AND THE ORIGINS OF CANADIAN CONFEDERATION, 1837–67

98

Britain and the Origins of Canadian Confederation, 1837–67

Ged Martin
Director, Centre of Canadian Studies
University of Edinburgh

UBC PRESS / VANCOUVER

ISBN 0–7748–0488–2 (hardcover)
ISBN 0–7748–0487–4 (paperback)

Canadian Cataloguing in Publication Data

Martin, Ged.
  Britain and the origins of Canadian Confederation, 1837–67

  Includes bibliographical references.
  ISBN 0–7748–0488–2 (bound) — ISBN 0–7748–0487–4 (pbk.)

  1. Canada—History—Confederation, 1867.   2. Canada. British
North American Act.   3. Great Britain. British North American Act. 4.
Canada—Constitutional law.   5. Great Britain—Politics and
government—1837–1901.   6. Canada—Politics and government—
1841–1867.   I. Title.

FC474.M37   1995   971.04'9   C94–910310–1
F1032.M37   1995

UBC Press
University of British Columbia
6344 Memorial Road
Vancouver, BC V6T 1Z2
(604) 822–3259
Fax: (604) 822–6083

Published simultaneously in Great Britain by Macmillan.

Printed in Great Britain

Contents

Preface

'A book that needs apologies ought never to have been written.'[1] William Howard Russell's bold statement is a warning to authors who attempt to explain themselves in prefaces. The present study has passed through several incarnations and — perhaps more fruitfully — lengthy hibernations. The research upon which it is based has been supported successively by the British taxpayer (whose contribution to the funding of doctoral dissertations is too rarely acknowledged), then by research fellowships at Magdalene College, Cambridge and at the Australian National University in Canberra, followed by appointments as Lecturer in Modern History at University College, Cork and as Director of the Centre of Canadian Studies at the University of Edinburgh. I acknowledge with gratitude the support of them all, and thank in particular the Foundation for Canadian Studies in the United Kingdom, both for generous financial support to the Edinburgh Centre, and specifically for making it possible for me to take study leave for part of 1993 to complete this book. The Centre of Canadian Studies at Edinburgh has also enjoyed the support of various programmes of the Government of Canada, through the Department of Foreign Affairs and International Trade and the Canadian High Commission in London.

Over the quarter century, I have been helped by many people, not only in this research, but in my development as a historian and in the securing of my career. Most of these obligations of gratitude are of a private nature, and the one most important and necessary of them all, very deeply so. Prefaces should not be used to list one's friends in order of preference, and I intend to repeat my thanks to those who have helped me, personally and in private. Here I record appreciation to a small number among many friends and colleagues for immediate and direct support in the writing of this book: Don Beer, Phillip Buckner, Tony Cohen, Ronald Hyam,

Anthony Low, R. Peter Milroy, Barry Smith and Jim Sturgis. I thank also The Macmillan Press Limited for guidance in the production of this book, and the University of British Columbia Press for advice.

Thanks are gratefully expressed to the many Archives and Libraries acknowledged in my Notes. I thank all the copyright-holders of the various manuscript collections which I have been privileged to consult and to cite. Material from the Royal Archives is quoted by gracious permission of Her Majesty The Queen. All Crown-copyright material in the Public Record Office is published by permission of the Controller of Her Majesty's Stationery Office. I thank in particular Viscount Cobbold, the Earl of Clarendon, the Earl of Derby and the Trustees of the Broadlands Archive.

Over the years, I have published various articles and essays on British attitudes towards the future of British North America. While the present study represents a re-working of all earlier material, I have drawn upon previous publications, and again acknowledge with thanks the prehistory and provenance. Some essays have been published under the Macmillan imprint. 'An Imperial Idea and its Friends' appeared in 1986 in *Studies in British Imperial History: Essays in Honour of A.P. Thornton*, edited (with great forbearance) by Gordon Martel. '"Anti-imperialism" in the Mid-Nineteenth Century and the Nature of the British Empire' was published in 1975 in *Reappraisals in British Imperial History*, written jointly with Ronald Hyam. *History As Science or Literature: Explaining Canadian Confederation, 1858-1867* was published in 1989 in the Canada House Lecture series. I am indebted to the Academic Relations Officer, Michael J. Hellyer, for the invitation to speak, and to the Canadian Studies Projects Officer, Vivien Hughes, for the production of the text, and for much support and many kindnesses on the part of the Canadian High Commission in London. The Trustees of the Winthrop Pickard Bell Fund at Mount Allison University kindly invited me to contribute to their hospitable and prestigious lecture series in 1991, and the editorial labour of Terry Craig resulted in the publication of my contribution as *Faction and Fiction in Canada's Great Coalition of 1864* in 1993, from a revised text. One paper has enjoyed a promiscuous life unmerited by its own worth. In 1990, Acadiensis Press published 'The Case against Canadian Confederation, 1864-1867', as part of *The Causes of Canadian Confederation*, formally under my own editorship but actually owing much to the work of Phillip Buckner. Two other versions have appeared. One was in the 1990 collection, *From Rebellion to Patriation: Canada and Britain in the Nineteenth and Twentieth Centuries*, edited for the Canadian Studies in Wales Group by Colin Eldridge. The other version is in T.J. Barron et al. (eds), *Constitutions and National Identity*, published by Quadriga in 1993 as a tribute to G.A. Shepperson. I have also drawn upon four journal articles. 'Launching Canadian Confederation, 1837-1864' appeared in the *Historical Journal*, xxvii (1984). 'Confederation Rejected: the British Debate on Canada, 1837-1840' was published in volume xi (1982) of the *Journal of Imperial and Commonwealth History*. The *British Journal of Canadian Studies*, ii (1987), published 'Britain and the Future of British North America, 1841-1850'. 'Some Lost Confederation Initiatives, 1846-1857' appeared in its forerunner, the *Bulletin of Canadian Studies*, edited by the late Philip Wigley, in volume vi, 1983. I thank all these publishers and publications.

I am grateful to Drummond Street Reprographics for drawing the map, and to ASET for producing camera-ready copy.

The presentation of this study follows the recent trend of avoiding unnecessary capitalisation. Terms such as 'governor-general' and 'colonial secretary' were themselves shorthand versions of more complicated formal titles while, technically speaking, the office of 'prime minister' did not even exist in the nineteenth century. The Queen's representatives in the Maritime provinces were officially 'lieutenant-governors', acting on behalf of the Captain General and Governor-in-Chief based in Canada: I have referred to them throughout as 'governors'. Capitalisation has been used to indicate affiliation with formally constituted parties, such as 'Conservative', 'Bleu' or 'Whig', but the lower case to refer to looser political attitudes, such as 'tory' and 'radical'.

I have written out in full the abbreviations which Victorians sometimes used in their private correspondence but otherwise quotations have been rendered in their contemporary spelling and punctuation, avoiding the intrusive and superior '[sic]' as far as possible. The people who exercised political power in London in the mid-nineteenth century were under the impression that they were running a country called 'England'. For the purposes of the argument advanced in these pages, it is necessary to interpret 'England' and 'English' in quotations as meaning 'Britain' and 'British'. I have refrained from intruding correction except in one bizarre statement which claimed Glasgow for the southern

kingdom. I have, however, found it impossible to escape from one
aspect of Victorian political incorrectness. All the governors, every
colonial secretary, each and every legislator and at the very least
the vast majority of editorial commentators were male. The shrewd
comments of Frances Monck, even the pertinent queries of Queen
Victoria, not an acclaimed intellectual figure, are enough to confirm
that the nineteenth century wasted a vast amount of talent through
segregation of gender roles. None the less, that is how mid-
nineteenth century politics operated, and if I have sometimes
slipped into the language of a masculine debate, I can only plead
fidelity to the original.

'Reader, I think proper, before we proceed any farther together, to
acquaint thee that I intend to digress through this whole history as
often as I see occasion'.[2] It is tempting to continue this splendid
quotation from Fielding with even stronger endorsement, but I
content myself with warning that this book is also discursive. Since
1983, my career as a historian has been pursued in the cross-
disciplinary framework of Canadian Studies. Some of my most
productive teaching — to me, at any rate — has been at first-year
level, introducing undergraduates who were resolutely not
historians to the ways in which my craft might help them to
understand Canada. I have gained immeasurably from the pleasure
and the stimulus of participation in an interdisciplinary academic
community — especially through the British Association for
Canadian Studies. In this atmosphere I found myself thinking
about history as well as about Canada, and this will explain some
of the more irritating ruminations in this book. I thank all my
friends in BACS, while to the International Council for Canadian
Studies gratitude is owed both for the promotion of a world-wide
community of scholarship and for deeply valued recognition of my
own work at a time of discouragement.

I offer one further excursion into the prefaces of yesteryear. 'I
cannot claim that this book meets any conspicuous need,' wrote
E.M. Wrong in 1929, of his study of Charles Buller.[3] Such humility
would be suicidal in a modern academic, and I do not propose to
emulate it. Yet I should offer one disclaimer. I began doctoral
research in 1967, the year that most Canadians celebrated the
Centennial of Confederation and some, in Quebec, began to work
to break Canada asunder. This book appears in the mid-1990s, as
the issue of Quebec separation — now called sovereignty — is once

again to the fore. It would be utterly fallacious to read into the arguments advanced here some message for modern time. Perhaps the challenges which Canada has faced in the second century of Confederation have been a reminder that the country is the product not of destiny but of constant re-invention and human ingenuity. All I can say is that much of my work has been conducted at a distance, in parts of the world whose news media are famous for ignoring Canadian events. My affection for Canada is great; my appreciation of Canadian achievement enormous. Yet I am not a Canadian. I cannot expect to feel for Canada the emotions which it inspires in my friends who are its citizens. Most emphatically, it is not for me to pontificate about any possible relationship between Canada's past and its future. To argue that Confederation was not the obvious way forward for British North America in the 1860s is not to assert that it was the wrong course. Historians are by nature arrogantly judgmental, but nobody could get around the awkward truth that Confederation was sufficiently attractive to secure the support of enough British North Americans to bring about the adoption of a structure which has mutated and flourished for a century and a quarter. I hope that this re-examination of the origins of Confederation will be of interest and even of value to everyone who shares my enthusiasm for Canada, but there can be no profit in making the events of the 1860s a surrogate battleground for the challenges of the 1990s.

Ged Martin
Centre of Canadian Studies
University of Edinburgh
July 1994

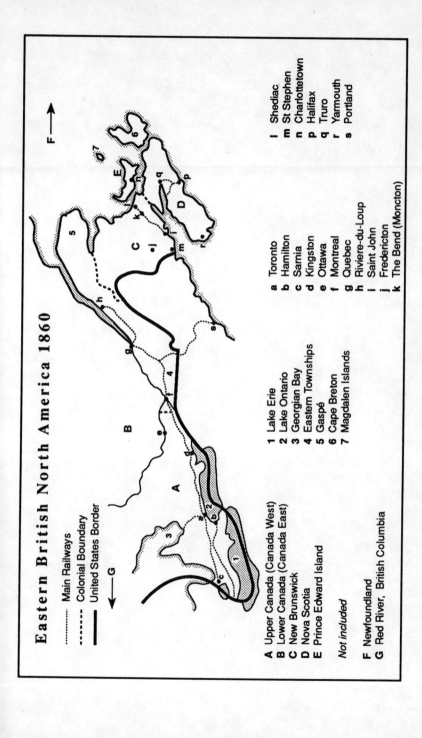

Eastern British North America 1860

········· Main Railways
– – – Colonial Boundary
———— United States Border

A Upper Canada (Canada West)
B Lower Canada (Canada East)
C New Brunswick
D Nova Scotia
E Prince Edward Island

Not included

F Newfoundland
G Red River, British Columbia

1 Lake Erie
2 Lake Ontario
3 Georgian Bay
4 Eastern Townships
5 Gaspé
6 Cape Breton
7 Magdalen Islands

a Toronto
b Hamilton
c Sarnia
d Kingston
e Ottawa
f Montreal
g Quebec
h Riviere-du-Loup
i Saint John
j Fredericton
k The Bend (Moncton)

l Shediac
m St Stephen
n Charlottetown
p Halifax
q Truro
r Yarmouth
s Portland

1 British North America on the Eve of Confederation

In February and March 1867, the British parliament passed legislation to unite Canada, New Brunswick and Nova Scotia into a single Dominion. The preamble to the British North America Act stated that 'such a Union would conduce to the Welfare of the Provinces and Promote the Interests of the British Empire'.[1] It is not always noted that Confederation passed through Westminster in the midst of the crisis of the Second Reform Act, the most divisive domestic political upheaval in the four decades between the repeal of the Corn Laws in 1846 and the defeat of Irish Home Rule in 1886. Yet the British North America Act was not passed in an imperial fit of absent-mindedness: the British were active participants in the process of Confederation, not mere onlookers. The main thesis of this study may be reduced to a single statement: between 1837 and 1867, the British came to favour the eventual creation of a union of British North America.[2]

Preliminary statements of this thesis have been summarised by one historian as meaning that 'while British support was essential for Confederation, it was circumstances within British North America which gave the British something to support'.[3] In fact, if British North America and its people are placed within the context of a wider Atlantic world, the British role may be seen to have been more dynamic. Even if viewed as mainly reactive, it is still necessary to explain why the British seem to have been so united in their response to the movement for political union of the provinces. Of course, a bare statement of the thesis is not enough, and its meaning is best explored by asking six questions of the text: who? where? what? why? when? and how? Who were 'the British'?

1

Where were they referring to when they talked of 'Canada' or 'British North America': were their perceptions and understanding of the provinces superficial or profound? What form of government did they believe might be appropriate to such diverse communities? Why did they feel that the provinces should be united? When did they envisage that a union might be brought about? How did they expect the process to occur? The answers to these questions suggest that the British were not simply spectators of a Canadian drama as they have so often been portrayed, but played an active and necessary role in defining and achieving the aim of Confederation.

The role of the British in the achievement of British North American union cannot be fully assessed without a wider examination of the way in which historians have predominantly explained the coming of Confederation in the 1860s. Here it is necessary to say something in defence of the notion that there is a shared corpus, a tendency to consensus, in the way in which historians have treated Confederation. It is argued in the present study that merely to meld words into phrases such as 'British pressure' does not in itself establish that the British had any leverage to contribute, and still less that any efforts they may have made were effective. It would be inconsistent to take such a position on the one hand while on the other simply hiding behind identically constructed allusions to scholarly consensus, interlocking explanatory packages and so forth. Above all, it would be pointed out that Canadian Confederation has attracted the attention of at least four historians of world rank, and that it is an unnecessary slight to their originality to shoe-horn them into a constructed and averaged viewpoint. The birth of the Dominion of Canada inspired a grandeur of imaginative empathy in D.G. Creighton, and a controlled passion of commitment in W.L. Morton. J.M.S. Careless and P.B. Waite combined sensitivity to the subtlety of the options facing British North America with a mastery of sources upon which the subsequent student can only draw with grateful respect.[4] To appear to lump such scholars together, and furthermore to cite them alongside the necessary simplifications of textbooks written for classroom use may seem both a scholarly discourtesy as well as intellectually pointless. Equally, a study which asserts that we should adopt a certain reserve in assessing the statements of the Fathers of Confederation should be wary of pouncing upon every eccentricity or passing error by individual historians as if to imply that each and every scholar who has considered the subject must embrace the same viewpoint.

It may also be objected that some of the works cited are now so dated that it would be kinder to leave them in the peaceful repose. For instance, A.R.M Lower's *Colony to Nation* first appeared in 1946, and even then went little further than 1939. Lower himself permitted its reissue in 1977 largely as 'a document in its own right'. His description of French Canadians as 'a feminine people' who should be wooed 'as a very womanly woman' was by the standards of 1946 a sympathetic attempt by an English Canadian to bridge the country's great internal divide, but it reflects stereotypes of culture and gender which would now be widely regarded as too embarrassing even to discuss.[5] Why, then, bother to consider Lower's assessment of Confederation? Overall, it may seem tempting to dismiss the notion of an inherited consensus of explanation and attitudes in the historical writing on Confederation as a straw target, lifeless, stuffed with shavings and far too easy to hit.

Yet it is possible to discern areas of predominant consensus and shared attitude in the way in which most historians write about major topics, in all countries and all centuries, and some of this — as Chapter Two discusses — has to do with methodological pitfalls in the craft of history itself. Take, for example, Canada's National Policy, the combined strategy of tariff protection and railway construction adopted in 1879 and seen by Creighton, and many others, as the natural fulfilment of the political union of 1867. In 1966, J.H. Dales attempted to strip the emperor's clothes from this national shibboleth. On the basis of quotation from five works, one of which he had perpetrated himself, Dales identified a 'historians' stereotype' which he attacked both for ignoring internal inconsistencies its package of arguments and for overlooking the 'awkward gap' of twenty years between the introduction of the policy and the results claimed for it. In positing a historical 'stereotype', Dales did not imply absolute and uniform orthodoxy. Indeed, he was specific in his praise for the way in which Lower impatiently brushed aside 'the standard patter'.[6]

A similar tendency to shared viewpoint — based on the repetition of inconsistent argument and unconvincing assertion — may be discerned in the way historians have discussed Canadian

Confederation. Commenting on three studies of the issue in New Brunswick and Prince Edward Island, Phillip Buckner found it 'difficult not to come away from these works with the impression that there was virtually no support for Confederation in the Maritimes, except for a handful of prescient individuals who had the imagination to accept the leadership of the more far-sighted and progressive Canadians'. This is a point of great importance for the present study, since a tendency among historians to exaggerate opposition to Confederation in the Maritimes has required a similar distortion to present the British as the countervailing force wheeled in to overcome bovine resistance. Buckner identified a tendency to patronise Maritimers as a common theme in the studies he criticised, even when written by scholars who were themselves natives of the region. He also found it significant that all three studies were products of the early 1960s. 'Since most Canadian historians were still influenced by the consensus approach, which minimized the significance of internal conflicts by focusing on the things which united Canadians ... they tended to downplay regional concerns and to interpret the making of Confederation as a success story of which all Canadians should be proud.'[7]

Thus it is possible not only to recognise originality and at the same time to honour grace and incisiveness in scholarly work, but also to point to shared assumptions which may colour and unwittingly distort the interpretation of a major episode. Since history is — or should be — written in multiple dialogue, it would indeed be surprising not to find both diversity and consensus, and the existence of the one does not invalidate the identification of the other. Here, the humble textbook may provide an illustrative role, since classroom texts usually represent a distillation and thereby to some extent a simplification of received opinion. Indeed, as the focus of historical scholarship in Canada has tended to shift to new and exciting themes in regional and social history, so the tried and true tale of Confederation seems to be squeezed into increasingly sparse outline. Thus the textbooks of yesteryear retain their place in any discussion of the way in which historians have treated the subject. Lower's structure for explaining Confederation was methodologically impressive, starting with the 'large factors' or long-term predisposing influences, and moving through intermediate causes to immediate circumstances and the role of personalities. Two shortcomings reduced the overall value of his interpretation. One lay in some of the insights which animated the structure he designed, and the other was his verdict that Confederation was a miracle.[8] However, those who teach history have a vested interest in assuming that its influence on those who study the subject lingers after they have completed their courses. In the Canada of the 1990s, both those who claim the country's system of government has failed and those who believe it can be renewed have appealed to the inspiring story of Confederation in the 1860s.[9] This will include an appeal to notions formed by adult citizens in earlier decades. It should be also noted that relatively little has been written on Confederation since the 1960s — itself a kind of testimony to the existence of a satisfactory historical consensus on the subject.

This study challenges a number of the elements which go to make up the generally accepted picture of the coming of Confederation. Briefly, the Union of the Canadas was not a political failure which had to be swept away in favour of the new British North American structure. It was anything but 'deadlocked' in 1864, although its politics had tangled into a short-term log-jam. One issue and one issue alone made its reconstruction overwhelmingly necessary, and that was the rapid population growth of Upper Canada, which rendered untenable the artificially equal representation of the two sections of the province in the Assembly. Some form of representation by population was virtually unavoidable, since Upper Canada was almost united in its demand, and English-speaking Lower Canadians were moving towards joining forces with them to resolve the issue once and for all. The Great Coalition formed in the province of Canada in June 1864 was by no means united in its determination to secure British North American union: the arch-enemies John A. Macdonald and George Brown attempted to seize each other not by the hand but rather by the throat. Brown aimed at trapping Macdonald into delivering a federation simply composed of Upper and Lower Canada, a cosmetic version of outright representation by population, but one which offered a measure of damage-limitation to Cartier and his French Canadian Bleus. Macdonald desperately needed the wider union for the exercise of his political talents of balancing and blandishment.

Confederation emerged as the solution in 1867 not because it was the right answer and inevitable destiny of the provinces. In reality, many of the arguments advanced for Confederation were

exaggerated and even downright misleading. It was not necessary
for the provinces to unite in order to build the Intercolonial railway,
which was in any case a project of doubtful utility. Confederation
had almost nothing to offer by way of improvement in local
defence, and was equally irrelevant to — if not diversionary from
— westward expansion. Arguments about interprovincial trade or
appeals to an emerging British North American nationality were
based on foundations too weak to provide credible historical
explanations. Of course, it is still possible to invert the argument at
each point, and conclude that Confederation was carried because
enough contemporaries saw sufficient prospect of personal gain in
any one of the individual arguments advanced to ignore
disadvantages or bogus claims and get behind the proposal. Yet
one reason why it was Confederation which triumphed, and not
any alternative framework which might equally have opened
opportunities, was because Macdonald exploited the fact that
British legislation would be required for the reshaping of the
province of Canada, and the British were committed to the wider
union.

Nova Scotians and New Brunswickers — even if reluctantly —
recognised that the time had come to accept a solution which the
British had long defined as an eventual target. Ironically, the
portrayal of Confederation as primarily the achievement of a far-
sighted Canadian coalition has actually required the interposition
of an imperial and imperious Britain to force a change of heart in
the Maritimes in 1865 and 1866. In reality, the imperial contribution
after 1864 was little more than bluff and hint, and by portraying the
British as the trump card against Maritime reluctance, historians
have not merely distorted the record of the mid-1860s, but failed to
appreciate the importance of the earlier British contribution in
defining the aim and clearing the way to the union of the provinces
in the years before 1864. It is necessary to move away from
mechanistic ideas of threats and 'pressure', towards a wider
appreciation of the position of the British North American
provinces within a context framed by the United States and shaped
by Britain, towards seeing Confederation not as a solution dictated
by the specific circumstances of the mid-1860s, but rather as a long-
maturing idea which came to blanket the political discourse of that
era because it could be argued — however spuriously and probably

with some degree of pardonable insincerity — that its time had come.

Chapter Two examines the interlocking explanation distilled from the predominant historical consensus about Confederation, and argues that the process of writing history may have imposed its own straitjacket on understanding. Chapter Three examines the origins and growth of British support for the idea of British North American union. Chapter Four asks who, where and what? Chapter Five explores the questions, where and when? Chapters Six and Seven discuss the fundamental issue, how? A reflective epilogue reverts to the role of an idea, and seeks to reconcile Canadian with imperial history. First, however, it is necessary to place British North America in its Atlantic context, to sketch the events preceding Confederation and to outline the way in which Confederation has usually been explained.

***

In 1861, the British railway entrepreneur, Edward Watkin, was glad to find that both the premier of New Brunswick, Leonard Tilley, and the colonial secretary, the Duke of Newcastle, shared his vision of a united transcontinental dominion in British North America.[10] To cite Watkin's enthusiasm as symbolic of the way in which an unofficial British observer could link the imperial government with provincial leadership is not to endorse the myth, which he created in his own autobiography, that he was the crucial progenitor of Confederation: at one time, Watkin made a regular appearance in accounts of the coming of Confederation, presumably to personify a sophisticated element of financial imperialism.[11] Latterly, he has been less visible, probably because it is no longer seemly for an Englishman to have played a key role in a Canadian national achievement, although he is probably the 'Edward Watkins' of a recent textbook.[12] More valuable to a stocktaking than Watkin's boosting of his own importance in the story of Confederation was his subsequent recollection that 'in 1861, this great idea seemed like a mere dream of the uncertain future'.[13]

However, though the future was opaque, it is possible to reconstruct something of the British North American present as it was in 1861, since most provinces imitated Britain in holding a census that year, and all dutifully submitted miscellaneous statistics for publication in London.[14] These statistics may not be perfect, but they are sufficient to demonstrate the position of British North

America as a vigorous but still comparatively small segment within a wider Atlantic world. In 1861, the eastern third of British North America was divided into five provinces, with a settler population of about three and a third million. Further west, the land was almost empty. Even by the end of the 1860s, there were barely 25000 settlers in the whole of British Columbia and at the Red River, while native populations probably numbered less than 100000. The North-West loomed large in the imaginations of some British North American leaders, but played almost no part in the events leading to Confederation.[15] For most practical purposes, British North America meant the Atlantic region, the St Lawrence valley and the settled areas to the north of the Great Lakes.

One province dominated British North America in 1861. Canada recorded two and a half million people, three quarters of the total. Moreover, Canada was growing fast: four years later, it was estimated to have added the equivalent of New Brunswick and Prince Edward Island to its population. Indeed, its rapid growth was imposing strains on its internal duality. The province had been created by the British in 1841 by legislating a union of the colonies of Upper and Lower Canada, which would emerge again in 1867 as Ontario and Quebec. The intention had been to use the English-speaking colonists to control the French, and since Lower Canada then had the larger population, Upper Canadian interests had been weighted by giving the two sections of the new province equal representation in the Assembly.[16] For a brief period, the two sections had been renamed Canada West and Canada East, but the old names soon resurfaced and here will be used throughout.[17] By 1861, Upper Canada (usually pronounced 'Up Canada'[18]) had pulled far ahead, with a shade under 1.4 million people, against the 1.1 million of Lower Canada. Around one fifth of the people of Lower Canada were of British or American origin: the French-speaking population probably fell just short of 900000 — enough for cultural survival, but too few to encourage any dreams of an independent state.[19] The remaining provinces were dwarfed by Canada. The three Maritime provinces collectively numbered half the population of Upper Canada, with a third of a million people in Nova Scotia, a quarter of a million in New Brunswick and a mere eighty thousand in Prince Edward Island. Newfoundland did not count its people in 1861, but there was little reason to think that its population had grown much since the previous census, in 1857, had reported 122000 inhabitants.

While the province of Canada overshadowed the remaining colonies of British North America, it looked a good deal less impressive when viewed within a North Atlantic context. To the south, the United States had enumerated over 31 million people at its census of 1860.[20] The raw figure was awe-inspiring, although in 1861 its full import could not be guessed since the great republic was embarking on a civil war which many thought would end in its disruption. Still, even fragmented, the numbers put British North America into a small perspective. The Southern States, seen by many as the gallant underdogs, had a white population of five and a half million, more than double that of the province of Canada, while Black slaves alone outnumbered all British North Americans. The twenty million people of the Northern States would soon show a frightening determination to fight for the Union cause, backed by an even more terrifying industrial might. The other external pole of the British North American world was Britain itself, where in 1861 the census counted 23 million people in England, Wales and Scotland, plus almost six million more in Ireland.[21] Certainly with nine times as many people living in the crowded British Isles as in all the British North American provinces combined, it is hardly surprising that the colonies not only remained dominated by Britain culturally and politically, but were content to be subordinate for purposes of defence and investment as well.

Comparative population figures help to explain the tiny part which British North America played in British affairs. A critic of Confederation warned the Canadian Assembly not to entertain inflated ideas of undertaking the defence of half a continent 'with a population less than that of the city of London'.[22] New Brunswick's governor Arthur Gordon was as usual exaggerating when he impatiently noted that his province was 'little exceeding in population an English manufacturing town', but it was true that there were more people in Liverpool, Manchester or Birmingham, and indeed in Dublin and Glasgow as well, than in New Brunswick. In the 1860s, Britain's great provincial towns were knocking on the doors of power, and it cannot be said that the politicians within were rushing to admit them. Colonies across a wide ocean could hardly be expected to have much more impact. The contrast became even more striking when towns were matched against towns. Montreal, by common consent the metropolis of Canada, was equal in population to Dundee, the sixteenth largest town in Britain. Toronto, the rising and ambitious centre of the upper province, was smaller than the Black Country town of Dudley, while Quebec ranked a shade ahead of neighbouring Wolverhampton. Saint John, the largest city in the Maritimes, had the same population as the Suffolk port of Ipswich. These comparisons are not intended to denigrate, but merely to stress the point that the Dundees and the Dudleys had little enough political impact inside Britain. Their equivalents overseas were almost invisible. In 1842, MPs packed the House of Commons to discuss the bribery of voters at Ipswich, because electoral corruption touched them all. When the colonial secretary attempted — with apologies 'that it might not excite much interest' — to follow the debate by introducing a measure for the government of Newfoundland, his words were drowned by the noise of MPs streaming from the chamber.[23]

British North American trade figures similarly illustrated the twin pulls of Britain and the United States. The provinces predominantly exported raw materials to Britain and the United States — the latter helped by the Reciprocity Treaty concluded in 1854 — and carried on very little trade among themselves. Canada sent 51 per cent of its exports by value to Britain in 1861, and 44 per cent to the United States. The rest of British North America accounted for under 3 per cent of Canadian export trade — and even then Canada had a substantial trade balance with the other provinces. Agricultural products and timber constituted by far the largest categories of exports from Canada. Fish, minerals and manufactures came well behind, each amounting to around 2 per cent of total exports. Unprocessed lumber tended to go to Britain, timber products and animals to the United States, which also absorbed most of Canada's barley. Flour and wheat exports were more evenly divided.

Each of the Atlantic provinces had its own distinct pattern of trade. Timber in various forms made up 70 per cent of New Brunswick's exports. Britain was the destination of two-thirds of its produce, with just under one-fifth going to the United States. Canada barely featured as a destination for New Brunswick exports, and even Nova Scotia took only 6 per cent of its total, although there may have been some under-recording here. Prince Edward Island alone had a trade pattern dominated by British

North America, feeding its neighbours with the corn and potatoes which accounted for two-thirds of its exports. Almost half of its exports went to the other provinces, but only the tiniest trickle found its way to Canada, while the United States was a large market. Fish accounted for two-fifths of Nova Scotian exports — mostly to the West Indies — with coal following at 10 per cent, then timber and a re-export trade in Caribbean sugar. In sharp contrast to neighbouring New Brunswick, Nova Scotia sent only 5 per cent of its exports by value to Britain, and its external trade was roughly equally divided among the United States, the other provinces and the Caribbean. Newfoundland's trading pattern was different again. Cod in one form or another accounted for 72 per cent of exports by value, and seal products — oil and skins — for 21 per cent. Two-fifths of Newfoundland exports consisted of dried cod shipped to Spain, Portugal and Italy, while Britain was the destination of a further third. Newfoundland did very little trade with the United States, while the rest of British North America was well-nigh invisible in its statistics.

British North American trade figures certainly do not suggest that in 1861 the provinces were in the process of economic integration as the precursor of political unity.[24] Nor would they constitute in any way a predictor of reactions to Confederation when the issue became a practical proposition three years later. By and large, the provinces did not trade with each other at all, and critics of Confederation in Canada argued that it was unlikely that they ever would, simply because they produced virtually identical products. The province which was most dependent on exports to its neighbours was Prince Edward Island, which doggedly refused to merge with them. Compared with Nova Scotia, New Brunswick was more than ten times as reliant upon the British market, yet it can hardly be argued that New Brunswick proved to be ten times more malleable to British wishes.

Yet the trade figures do offer some clues to the way in which the provinces would respond to the Confederation issue. For instance, they draw attention to the dominance of Halifax within Nova Scotia. In 1861 Halifax handled over half the external trade of the province. It is not surprising that there would be more support for Confederation in Halifax than in the rest of the province, for political union and improved communications might make the city the funnel for trade and the fulcrum of communications between

British North America and Europe. In the long run, the interests of Halifax were likely to be those of the province. Certainly Yarmouth, the centre of hardline resistance to union with Canada, ranked a poor third, handling less than 3 per cent of Nova Scotia's trade. The importance of coal in the Nova Scotian export trade is also striking, and once the end of Reciprocity threatened the United States market, it is understandable that eyes might be turned if not to Canada, then at least to any structure which might bring coal-consuming railways.

Once again, the overall importance of British North American trade needs to be assessed by placing it in a wider Atlantic context. The provinces accounted for around 3 per cent of Britain's total export trade, and supplied in return commodities which could for the most part be obtained elsewhere. By contrast, one-fifth of all British imports came from the United States, including four-fifths of the raw cotton which supplied Lancashire. 'Though with the North we sympathise,' sang *Punch* in 1861, 'it must not be forgotten that with the South we've stronger ties which are composed of cotton'.[25] Despite the steadily increasing obstacle of protectionist tariffs, the United States market remained very important to British industry. 'I leave you to judge how long your large towns would support you in a serious contest with their Customers,' Ashburton warned Howick in 1838.[26] The irony was that Britain was politically committed to the defence of the part of North America which was least valuable to it economically against a possible threat from one of its most important overseas markets. The problem did not greatly matter before 1861, since the British forces in Canada — small though they were — were believed to be superior to the minute United States army, and hence an effective deterrent. By the mid-1860s, a land war with the suddenly militarised United States had become unthinkable — and also terribly likely. From this ambiguity may be traced not the origin but certainly the fervour with which the British endorsed British North American union: Confederation might not provide the way out of an insoluble trap, but at least it was a step in some direction, even if an unknown one.

One final area of comparison is needed to set British North America into its Atlantic context, and this is perhaps the hardest of all to measure. Comparatively speaking, how rich were the provinces? An attempt at an international league table has been made by two American historians, R.W. Fogel and S.L. Engerman, as part of a controversial project to assess the economic effectiveness of slavery in the American South. Scoring the South at 100, they rated Canada, at 96, as the sixth most prosperous country in the world, behind Australia (144), the North (140), Britain (126) and Switzerland (100). Yet their figures are drawn from the post-Confederation period, and presumably involve an averaging of the diverse regions of the new Dominion.[27] Durham in 1839 had made much play with the contrast between the 'activity and bustle' of the United States and the 'waste and desolate' appearance of the British provinces.[28] Yet some of the perceived backwardness of the provinces was the result of their more recent settlement: for instance, if Upper Canada is compared not with the United States as a whole, but with neighbouring Ohio, Michigan and Indiana, its record of railway construction in the 1850s becomes more impressive.[29] Certainly by 1855, Sir Edmund Head could contrast the *'astounding'* prosperity of Upper Canada with 'the sort of sleepy look which pervades Lower Canada'.[30] The Maritimes, on the other hand, were thought of as poor and sluggish. There was certainly poverty in British North America, but there was comfort and prosperity too. What does seem clear is that British North America was capital-poor. Banks were small and funding for major projects would have to come from outside, and especially from the London money market.[31]

By 1861, all five provinces had achieved an undefined form of local self-government, in an imitation of the British parliamentary system which Dickens found like 'looking at Westminster through the wrong end of a telescope'[32] and Cobden 'inherently ludicrous', a travesty 'with its votes of Confidence, its cabinet Ministers, with a mock sovereign dismissing & sending for advisers, — & all about next to nothing.'[33] Party alliances were fluid enough in Britain, but in Canada, commented *The Times*, a politician 'sets about making a party as he would a salad'.[34] There were labels and allegiances, liberal, reform, Clear Grit, Rouge, conservative and Bleu, but they did not prevent politicians from forming alliances which were sometimes driven by personal ambition and feuds. Presiding over the whole was a governor appointed from Britain, in most cases more than the 'mock sovereign' derided by Cobden, but charged rather with a sensitive task of reconciling local and imperial priorities.[35]

In Canada, the British representative was styled 'governor-general', with the imperial functionaries of the Maritimes technically 'lieutenant-governors' subject to his sway. In practice, the connection was minimal, and for the Maritimes, the less cumbrous style of 'governor' is used throughout this study. Two ex-cabinet ministers, Durham and Sydenham, held office as governor-general of Canada during the crisis years 1838-41, but thereafter the post was held by a series of men who combined some measure of diplomatic, administrative or political experience at home with the financial need for exile in an unprestigious colony. Elgin, who held office from 1847 to 1854, was a Scottish peer who had briefly sat in the Commons. His successor, Sir Edmund Head, was an Oxford don turned administrator, of combined Kentish gentry and South Carolina loyalist stock. Head was succeeded in 1861 by Lord Monck, an Irish peer who had held minor office under Palmerston. For both Elgin and Monck, colonial service held out the attraction of a British peerage, since they were otherwise barred from sitting in the House of Lords.

Perhaps because of its sensitive proximity to the United States, New Brunswick also received socially and politically well-qualified governors between 1848 and 1866, although the last of them, Arthur Gordon, made up for relative lack of experience with a massive shortfall in humility, except in his dealings with the Almighty, to whom, in a much-derided official prayer, he styled himself 'thy servant Arthur'.[36] The actual power of a governor would greatly depend on his personality and local circumstances, but governors had a monopoly on official communications with the Colonial Office, often supplemented by unofficial access to influential figures in London as well.

Cobden was wrong in his scornful claim that British North American politics were 'all about next to nothing'. In Canada, the underlying issue by 1861 was the artificial equality of representation in the Assembly. Grand imperial plans of constitutional engineering had been undermined by the emergence in the 1840s of a system of internal self-government, by which the local affairs of the province were conducted by ministries answerable to the Assembly. Within the supposedly united province, the ministerial system which developed actually enshrined internal duality, partly because the two sections of the province continued to operate distinct legal systems. In a sharp variation from the British model, local ministries were usually led by co-premiers: LaFontaine-Baldwin; Hincks-Morin; Cartier-Macdonald.[37] By the 1850s, rapid immigration had tilted the population balance in favour of Upper Canada, and English-speaking reformers had begun to campaign for representation by population ('rep. by pop.' for short), a redistribution of Assembly seats and voting power which would place Lower Canada in a minority.[38] Alternatives were proposed by a Lower Canada politician, Alexander Galt, a Rouge though of independent leanings, who in July 1858 argued for the reconstruction of the province of Canada as a federation of two or three units, or for a federation of Canada with the North-West, or for a union of all the provinces.[39]

The ministry led by George Cartier and John A. Macdonald had emerged weakened from elections a few months earlier, but had apparently evaded the divisive question of selecting a permanent seat of government for the province (Canada, as a colony, could not aspire to a 'capital') by passing the choice to Queen Victoria. However, the Queen's compromise choice of Ottawa united supporters of other towns, and on 28 July the Assembly voted to ask Victoria to think again. Although undefeated on an issue of confidence, the ministry took the opportunity to resign the next day, thereby forcing the Reform leader, George Brown — who was also proprietor of the *Globe*, Upper Canada's most powerful newspaper — to shoe-horn his francophobic prejudices into an alliance with A.-A. Dorion and the Rouges. On 2 August, the Brown-Dorion ministry was sworn in. By taking office, the new ministers automatically vacated their seats in the Assembly, and had to return to their constituents to fight by-elections. As a result, an already weak combination went down to immediate defeat, and was forced to resign on 4 August following a refusal by the governor-general to call a fresh general election.

Now ensued an element of farce. The law required ministers to fight by-elections on first appointment to office, but it exempted those who accepted a new portfolio within thirty days of resigning an old one: Macdonald had carried the change the previous year to facilitate leisurely reshuffles. Consequently, by swearing themselves into entirely new posts on 6 August, the former Cartier-Macdonald ministers were able to retain their positions in the Assembly, since they had resigned their former offices only a week before.[40] On 7 August, they resigned their new posts and went back to their old ones: John A. Macdonald, formerly Attorney-General West, spent twenty-four hours as postmaster-general before reverting to the position for which his legal skills so well fitted him. So far as the law knew, there had simply been two ministerial reshuffles, both within the permitted thirty-day period. The Reformers remained saddled with the task of fighting by-elections to vindicate their right to hold offices from which they had been summarily ousted. They vented their anger by launching a private prosecution for perjury, claiming that Macdonald had 'insulted the Majesty of Heaven' by swearing to undertake an office which he knew he would abandon the following day. The courts ruled that Macdonald had only sworn to be a diligent postmaster for 'so long as he held the office', but on attempting to recover his legal costs, he found that the prosecution had been undertaken in the name of an undischarged bankrupt.[41] The 'double shuffle' was a squalid episode but one which — as will be argued in Chapter Two — does not merit all the indignation which some historians have poured upon it.

The Cartier-Macdonald combination emerged strengthened from this episode since they persuaded Galt to join them, adopting his policy of British North American union as their own. (This had the incidental advantage of making it less likely that Galt would be lured into alliance with Brown and Dorion, who were vaguely committed to some form of federal restructuring within Canada itself.) However, the Canadian federal initiative of 1858-59 made little progress. The other provinces were reluctant to be dragged into the problems of distant Canada, while the British government treated the whole matter with some reserve — a stance which requires further discussion, since of course it appears to conflict with the thesis of a developing British consensus in favour of a union of the provinces. None the less, the reconstituted ministry proved durable enough, although elections in 1861 once again shook its hold, as Upper Canada became increasingly insistent on securing what it saw as its rightful share of political power. One Reformer, William McDougall, even talked of 'looking below the border for relief'.[42]

The United States, however, provided not a solution but a shock. In November 1861, a Northern warship had stopped a British steamer, the *Trent*, on the high seas and arrested two unofficial

Confederate envoys who were on their way to Europe. The British were outraged and the two countries came close to war. Reinforcements were sent to the provinces, but were forced to make an epic journey across New Brunswick to reach Canada, since the St Lawrence was frozen and there was no rail link to the seaboard.[43] The crisis was resolved, but it seemed to point, first, to a reform of Canada's own local defence force, which was called with unconscious but appropriate irony, the 'sedentary' militia and, secondly, to extending Canada's Grand Trunk railway line eastwards to Halifax — a project which required a massive capital subsidy, since the Grand Trunk was almost bankrupt and the additional mileage was unlikely to generate much commercial traffic. Arguably, the real lesson of the *Trent* crisis was that Britain simply could not respond in time to defend the provinces against American attack, but in the short term, the militia and the railway were the main items on the political agenda, and historians have generally concluded that not only the politicians but the political system itself failed to respond to the challenge.

The Cartier-Macdonald ministry proposed a reform of the militia which was both extensive and expensive. On 20 May 1862, its bill was rejected in the Assembly. The British were outraged, their disappointment having been fuelled by over-sanguine private reports from the inexperienced governor-general, Lord Monck.[44] In London, both press and parliament accused the Canadians of failing to face reality, of falling down on their obligations. A new ministry was formed, headed by the Reformer, John Sandfield Macdonald, often known simply as 'Sandfield' to distinguish him among Canada's many Macdonalds.[45] His political principle was a primitive form of federalism called the 'double majority': the government would only take action if supported by a majority of members from Upper Canada and a majority of members from Lower Canada. His stance could variously be regarded as a recognition of basic duality, or as a blind abdication of all leadership.

At least there seemed some prospect of securing the 'Intercolonial' railway, as the line from Halifax to Quebec was coming to be called. In September 1862, the new ministry met representatives of New Brunswick and Nova Scotia to discuss how to apportion the construction costs. The British cabinet had reluctantly agreed in principle to guarantee a loan to finance the work. Two delegates,

L.V. Sicotte and W.P. Howland, were then sent to London for further discussions. There, to their dismay, they found that the chancellor of the exchequer, Gladstone, insisted that the loan be accompanied by a sinking fund, that is, that the provinces should take steps to repay the capital borrowed by annual instalments. The Canadians had of course hoped that the entire capital sum would fall due when the loan terminated, so that another generation of politicians would be left to face the task of repayment. Sicotte and Howland withdrew from the London negotiations, but managed to do so in a way which made a reasonable retreat based on lack of money appear as a discreditable lapse from uprightness and common courtesy.[46]

Sandfield's ministry ran into worse trouble the following session, when a private member introduced a bill to extend the degree of public funding to the separate schools of Upper Canada. The issue was apparently semantic but fundamentally sectarian. In Lower Canada, there were two parallel publicly-funded school systems, one Catholic, the other explicitly Protestant. In Upper Canada, there was officially a single system of public schooling. Protestants insisted that the Upper Canadian school system was non-denominational and open to all. Catholics retorted that it was really Protestant and unsuitable for their needs. Hence the development of separate (or Catholic) schools, which clamoured for a share of tax money. Upper Canadian opinion was predominantly opposed to any extension of Catholic privileges, but when the bill came to a vote, many members found it prudent to absent themselves, and the measure was imposed on the upper province by the votes of Catholic French Canadians. What became of the double majority if the principle could be pushed aside on such a sensitive matter? Sandfield replied that it did not extend to private members' bills.[47]

Not surprisingly, a resurgent John A. Macdonald was able to carry a motion of no confidence in May 1863, but narrowly enough to entitle Sandfield to take his case to the voters. The elections were hardly conclusive, although Upper Canadian feeling was hardening in favour of representation by population. Sandfield dropped Sicotte from his ministry, along with two Irishmen, Michael Foley and D'Arcy McGee, but failed to secure the compensating support of his Reform rival, George Brown, who had returned to active politics after a sabbatical business trip to Britain.[48] Both the colonial secretary and the governor-general began to hope that parties might be brought together in a strong government under a neutral leader.[49] Brown, on the other hand, approached the problem from the opposite end, arguing that the most prominent politicians should meet in conclave to review the options for the future of the province.[50] Meanwhile, Sandfield struggled on, to win a place in the folklore of Canadian politics as the premier whose ministry lacked even a 'drinking majority': its supporters dared not leave the chamber for a drink for fear that it would be defeated in their absence.[51] They were relieved from this onerous deprivation in March 1864 when Sandfield resigned, undefeated but unsustainable.

Lord Monck secured his elder statesman, but not the broad coalition the British had hoped for. Sir Etienne Taché agreed to come out of semi-retirement — he had dropped out of active politics in 1857 and sat in the Legislative Council — but he formed a ministry around the core of John A. Macdonald, Cartier and Galt which looked very like the combination defeated in 1862. However, the ministry was joined by Michael Foley and D'Arcy McGee, Sandfield's colleagues in 1862-63, notwithstanding the fact that Foley had earlier been characterised by John A. Macdonald as 'Lying Mike' and McGee as a 'ruffian'.[52] The new ministry offered a number of worthy policies, but it could not be said to be built around any overarching crusade for change: on representation by population, for instance, it had no policy at all. It was claimed that Foley had 'temporarily hesitated' on being invited to join, and 'insisted on knowing what the policy of the new Administration was to be'. John A. Macdonald slapped him playfully on the knee and replied, 'D--n it, Foley, join the Government and then help to make the policy.'[53] Parliament reassembled on 4 May 1864, and the new ministry duly went down to defeat on 14 June.

Brown had proposed his committee on the state of the province shortly before Sandfield's resignation in March 1864, but did not secure approval until mid-May. It proved to be unexpectedly harmonious, although this was partly because it also agreed to differ. At its first meeting, a veteran French Canadian, Joseph Turcotte, who had spoken of 'wading knee-deep in blood' to bar representation by population, astonished Brown by announcing that 'the war between Upper and Lower Canada must now cease'.[54] On 14 June, the committee reported in favour of reconstructing the province on federal lines, although it left open whether this should be British North American in scope or merely confined to the province of Canada. Consensus was still not complete, for three of the twenty members refused to sign the report, and these included Sandfield Macdonald, still wedded to the double majority, his namesake John A. on the grounds that a British North America should adopt the unitary structure of the United Kingdom. Significantly, however, Cartier parted company with his erstwhile ally to sign the report, thereby signalling that he was ready to respond to Brown's reported 'squinting' towards an alliance with the Bleus.[55]

After prolonged negotiations, Taché reconstructed his ministry in the form which became known as the Great Coalition.[56] Brown reluctantly entered, along with Mowat and McDougall, who had both served under Sandfield Macdonald. The Great Coalition is usually described as being committed to the achievement of a British North American union, a fair enough simplification since Confederation was to be its triumph, but in reality it had a dual aim: the union of the whole of British North America if possible, but the reconstruction of the province of Canada if the wider aim proved unattainable. Chapter Two argues that this divergent target was more significant than has usually been recognised.

On the face of it, during the closing months of 1864, the Canadians seemed to be leading a triumphant pageant along what Donald Creighton called 'the road to Confederation'. By useful coincidence, representatives of the Maritime provinces had planned to meet at Charlottetown in September to discuss a union among themselves. While with hindsight this may seem like a natural step towards Confederation, the meeting was in fact undertaken partly in reaction to the perceived bad faith of the Canadians at the Intercolonial negotiations of 1862. The Canadians did not actually gate-crash Charlottetown, but they were energetic in inviting themselves, and quickly won approval in principle for a union of all the provinces. A more formal conference followed at Quebec in October, where a series of resolutions was drawn up. This, the Quebec plan or scheme, became the basis of the eventual British North America Act. Throughout, the Canadians were the driving force, and the bonhomie of the two gatherings masked something of a take-it-or-leave-it attitude to the Maritimers, which soon ensured that neither Prince Edward Island nor Newfoundland would become founders of the new polity. It was the Canadian coalition which sent Brown as its representative to London in December 1864 to enlarge upon the proposals, and the year closed with enthusiastic expressions of support from both government and press in Britain.[57]

There were critics of the scheme in the province of Canada, and their cogency has been underestimated, but when the legislature debated Confederation in February and March 1865, it seemed clear enough that most French Canadians were acquiescent and most English Canadians enthusiastic about the opportunities it would offer.[58] Botched responses by local law-enforcement agencies to desperate raids by Confederate sympathisers from Canadian territory into the Northern States had once again inflamed cross-border relations, and Canadians debated constitutional change in an atmosphere of menace overshadowed by the awful prospect of a vengeful and victorious Northern army invading their province. In the Maritimes, however, a reaction seemed to set in. Joseph Howe was a giant among Nova Scotians, if sometimes a malign one. He emerged from his poor reward for a lifetime's voluble devotion to the empire, a roving post as a fisheries commissioner, to denounce the 'Botheration' scheme with characteristic bombast.[59] Charles Tupper, Nova Scotia's premier, remained committed to Confederation, but prudently refrained from pressing the issue in the Assembly. Worse still, New Brunswick's premier Leonard Tilley decided to go to the polls, and in March 1865 was soundly defeated.[60] The incoming New Brunswick ministry was by no means totally opposed to the union of the provinces — it too was a coalition laced with opportunism — but it seemed at first to be totally united in its dislike for the Quebec scheme. Confederation seemed to be at a standstill.

British North American politicians appeared to respond with a flurry of missions to Britain, and historians have tended to assume that if the principal players thought it appropriate to take their case to London, then the imperial factor must have had a crucial contribution to make. Macdonald, Cartier, Galt and Brown were the first off the mark: John A. himself immodestly styled them 'the big 4',[61] and Creighton dubbed their mission 'Appeal to Caesar'.[62] New Brunswick's A.J. Smith was quick to follow, and Arthur Gordon came home on leave, although in his case with the excuse that he had finally located a bride.[63] The British government made some threatening noises, including disapproving allusions to the problem of colonial defence.[64]

It seemed to work. In November 1865, the Smith ministry in New Brunswick began to fracture, with one member, R.D. Wilmot, converted to Confederation and another, T.W. Anglin, forced out for fundamentalist opposition. Charles Fisher won a symbolic by-election for the cause of Confederation, by the subtle device of promising not to raise the issue if he was elected. By the spring of 1866, Gordon had ousted Smith (something he was not really supposed to do) and both New Brunswick and Nova Scotia fell into line and passed resolutions accepting British North American union in principle. It was now the turn of the Maritimes to discuss the issue in a framework of fear. Demobilised Irish-Americans had proved a fertile recruiting ground for the Fenians, Irish nationalists who aimed to free Ireland by attacking British North America. They were no mean military force, as they proved when they invaded the Niagara peninsula in June 1866, but they were unable to maintain a long-term threat simply because there was a limit to the number of blind eyes the United States government could turn to their activities. Fenian schemes to attack New Brunswick conveniently preceded a second Confederation election in May 1866, and even more conveniently were conducted with minimal regard for confidentiality. For the Irish-born Timothy Anglin, New Brunswick's most fervent anti-Confederate, the Fenians were a disaster. It was not only paranoid Protestantism which came to equate opposition to Confederation with Fenianism: Catholic bishops also supported the constitutional change while damning the revolutionary threat. However, if the Americans showed only limited tolerance towards the Fenians, they vented their disapproval of the provinces by terminating Reciprocity: from St Patrick's Day 1866, British North American produce entering the United States would have to pay customs duties.[65]

The final stages of the road to Confederation led back to Britain. In the autumn and winter of 1866-7, Joseph Howe led a last-ditch campaign to persuade British opinion to grant a reprieve or at least a stay of execution to his province: an election would be due in Nova Scotia in 1867, and Howe hoped to repeat the New Brunswick experience and so block Confederation. Given the disturbed state of British domestic politics at the time, it is notable that Howe's campaign was so unsuccessful, especially as the delegates from Canada did not trouble to arrive until November. In December and January the final details were hammered out, and both the British North America bill and accompanying legislation to provide finance for the Intercolonial railway passed easily through a parliament which was tearing itself apart over changes to Britain's own system of government.[66]

There is admirable artistry in the way in which conventional historical accounts weave together the elements leading to Confederation. From the double shuffle onwards, the reader sees the crumbling of the existing Canadian Union through a series of sorry episodes, and watches it sink into helpless deadlock, as burgeoning Upper Canada demanded an additional share of power which stagnating Lower Canada could not concede. The *Trent* crisis introduces the element of external threat, and the defeat of the Militia Bill is presented as a further demonstration of the inability of the existing structure to rise to the challenge of British North American defence. Upper Canada's spectacular population growth also introduces another element, that of westward expansion. The demographic explosion of Upper Canada, where population trebled in twenty years, brought a sensation of impending land shortage, especially as new settlement ran up against the harsh rock of the Canadian Shield. By the mid-1850s, some Upper Canadians were casting covetous eyes on the largely empty western territories of the Hudson's Bay Company. By coincidence, a gold rush in the Fraser valley brought about the creation in 1858 of a Pacific coast colony, British Columbia, supplying a distant focus for expansionist vision. These vast western territories, it is sometimes asserted,[67] could only be absorbed through a wholly new, continental framework of government.

If some eyes in the province of Canada were looking west, others were drawn eastward, to the Atlantic seaboard, by means of the proposed Intercolonial railway. The 1850s were a golden age of railway construction, and by the end of the decade the province of Canada could boast the longest railway line in the world, running all the way from Sarnia in south-western Upper Canada, to Rivière-du-Loup, one hundred miles below the city of Quebec. In fact, length apart, there was not much to boast of about the Grand Trunk. It was widely associated with a lowering of standards of honesty in politics, and its commercial performance was poor: 'the Grand Trunk was, by 1860, virtually bankrupt'.[68] It ran parallel to one of the finest waterways in the world: in summer, it could hardly compete with the St Lawrence route on freight costs, and even for speed, let alone comfort, it had little to offer. Rivière-du-Loup was its eastern terminus mainly because the money had finally run out there. The Intercolonial fits into the explanatory package twice over: first, as a defence project, and secondly through the argument that such an eastward extension of the Canadian railway system could only be achieved if balanced by westward expansion to the prairies. Here again, the *Trent* crisis plays a vital role in the story, since the cameo of British troops sledging through the snowy interior of New Brunswick seemed to underline the defence argument for the railway. Moreover, the American Civil War also introduces an economic motive: Northern resentment at British North American sympathy for the South led to the termination of Reciprocity, and so forced the provinces to turn to each other. All in all, the moment was right for British North Americans to assert a sense of their own nationhood.

In summary, historians have presented five major reasons why Confederation came about in 1867 — with, of course, variation in emphasis and interpretation. The first was the need for defence against the United States, an argument which underlines the central role of the Intercolonial railway: 'a route for troops from one colony to another, if the Americans attacked'.[69] 'A federation of the British North American colonies could lead to the construction of an intercolonial railway, and to the organisation of a united colonial army'.[70] Secondly, the Intercolonial was also seen as a means of promoting trade among the provinces.[71] Thirdly, the end of Reciprocity provided a further motive 'for the colonies to look to each other, if only as substitute markets'.[72] This seemed to be 'a strong factor in Canada: a larger market had to be obtained somehow and if the United States would not provide it, perhaps the Maritimes would'.[73] Fourthly, Upper Canadians in particular wanted to annex the North-West, and it is asserted that a mere federation of the two Canadas 'could hardly have met the need for expansion'.[74] Lastly, the package is sometimes spiced with a delicate flavour of British North American nationhood, 'a nascent national feeling among English-speaking Canadians'.[75] 'In its emphasis upon expansion, national unification, and independence,' Creighton concluded, 'Canadian Confederation was a typical experiment in nineteenth-century nation-building.'[76] Perhaps this element has appealed to subsequent generations of Canada's historians, enabling them to draw retrospective comfort and inspiration in periods when their country's unity and identity has seemed under threat.[77]

These arguments for Confederation form not simply a series of individually cogent points, but tend to be fused together through the historian's trade of pattern-making into an interlocking package, in which elements are balanced, or traded off, one against another to create a watertight structure of explanation. Thus, according to Morton, 'Lower Canada could scarcely agree to the annexation of the north-west unless this were offset by guarantees of its historic rights in the new union, and by the adherence of the Atlantic provinces to the union to balance the indefinitely growing population of Upper Canada'. Furthermore, French Canadians and Maritimers would not accept 'the cost of building a Pacific railway unless that were matched by the building of the Intercolonial'. Where Creighton thought of the nineteenth century's nation-builders, Garibaldi and Bismarck, Morton was evidently inspired by its engineers, Brunel and Stephenson: 'Only a general union, balanced with all the care and precision of a cantilever, was practical in 1864'.[78] Perhaps the most elegant aspect of the interlocking package is the way in which it integrates nation-building with empire. Confederation is seen as the visionary initiative of the Canadian ministry, supported by a minority of far-sighted politicians in New Brunswick and Nova Scotia. When other Maritimers refused to recognise their destiny, the British are invoked as *deus ex machina* to force them to accept inevitability. The cumulative result constitutes a very attractive and satisfying scholarly analysis of the reasons for Confederation, one which appears to account for every element of a complex continental situation, neatly interweaving them all into a pattern which explains not simply why the provinces decided to unite, but why they decided to unite at a particular moment in the 1860s. It is, however, possible to suggest that the picture is too satisfying, and that in a number of respects it is open to challenge.

2 Canadian Confederation and Historical Explanation

The doubts expressed in this study about the explanation of Canadian Confederation have a great deal to do with the way in which history is written. Broadly, historians have two tasks, one of *description*, and the other of *explanation*. The first is obviously basic to the second: unless we know what happened, we cannot hope to understand the reasons for it. Yet description is not always a straightforward process, for it involves both reconstruction and selection. It is often impossible to reconstruct past events, simply because the evidence does not survive. There can also be the welcome complication that new evidence may be located which forces a challenge to accepted interpretations of certain episodes, as happened when additional archives became available throwing light on the British response to the Canadian proposal of British North American federation in 1858.[1] However, although lack of evidence is undoubtedly often a problem facing historians of Confederation, a more overwhelming hazard is that there is usually too much, and it is vital to select. The danger here is that the selection made may be influenced by the needs of the explanation adopted. To adapt Creighton's image of the 'road to Confederation', the historian is picking a route through a bewilderingly detailed map, and can be forgiven for tracing a thick line along the main highways and ignoring the side turns. Sometimes, it is not so much that the actual description has been inaccurate but rather that a particular kind of explanation has been fostered by omission in selection. If this may seem an accusation, then it is one which must be levelled at all historians, since every one of us is compelled to select.

27

One fundamental problem about explanation in history lies in the way in which the craft seems to straddle the scientific and the literary.[2] Superficially, historians set themselves the same task as experimental scientists, to establish causal connections which explain that *A* causes *B*. Thus the physicist may prove that a particle can crack a nucleus, a chemist that a drug can combat a dangerous disease and a historian that the need for a railway caused Canadian Confederation, and it is easy to assume that all three are engaged in precisely the same process of explanation. Yet, as Marwick has pointed out, 'there *is* a difference, and we all know there is a difference'. Physical scientists can go back to the laboratory and repeat their experiments, but 'the historian cannot call for a repeat performance of the past'.[3]

At one level, this may seem to make historical explanation totally futile, for since it is impossible to repeat the events of the 1860s in multiple variable combinations, it is also impossible to pronounce with certainty that Confederation would not have happened if there had been no American Civil War, and so on. There are commonsense reasons for sympathising with W.M. Baker's observation that if Confederation had not come about in the 1860s, 'it might have been postponed indefinitely',[4] but there is no experiment open to the historian to put the hypothesis to the test. Yet in other respects, this limitation forces historical explanation on to a superior plane, since historians must support their explanatory hypotheses by causal arguments, whereas the experimental scientist may simply appeal to statistical probability. A celebrated example is the discovery of penicillin by Alexander Fleming, who found by repeated experimentation that the drug killed an awesome array of bacteria. Yet Fleming himself had no idea *how* penicillin worked, and it was left to other scientists to account for its effectiveness. This did not prevent him from receiving both a knighthood and the Nobel Prize for Medicine.[5] Yet nobody would hail the historian who merely remarked that there seemed to be some sort of connection between Confederation and the Intercolonial railway: historical explanation requires the detailed elucidation of causal relationships, whereas the experimental scientist may simply appeal to mere repetition.

Occasionally, some historians betray the belief that they are practising the same techniques as experimental scientists by pronouncing general laws, sometimes expanded into vivid literary images. 'Nothing but a compelling necessity can reconcile self-governing provinces to the surrender of cherished rights to the exigency of a distant national state,' wrote Chester Martin.

> Like chemical reagents which are inert towards one another under normal conditions of pressure and temperature, the most disintegrated provinces may react in a national emergency with unpredictable responsiveness. That reaction at the time may be due to abnormal pressure and temperature but once it has resulted in organic federation, the product may be a permanent chemical compound capable of withstanding the stresses and strains of normal atmospheric conditions.[6]

Chester Martin's argument reflects the contemporary conclusion of the Irish journalist W.H. Russell in 1865, that 'the white heat of American strife' provided the moment for 'welding' the provinces together.[7] It could only be 'proved', in the scientific sense which the imagery implies, if it were possible to repeat the experiment by varying the temperature of the oven. The same problem arises with Waite's stimulating explanation of Confederation in terms of Newton's first law of motion: 'all bodies continue in a state of rest or of uniform motion unless compelled by some force to change their state'.[8]

Since mid-nineteenth century British North America can only be fully understood within the context of the overshadowing influences of the United States and Britain, it is easy enough to identify external forces which will 'explain' Confederation — if, that is, we are content to use Waite's hypothesis as the basis for its own proof. What cannot be 'proved' is that those forces and only those forces drove the provinces into union, since it is impossible to put past time into a bell-jar and repeat the events of the 1860s with a series of control experiments. Brebner acknowledged that it would be possible to 'put together a kind of algebraic formula or polygon of forces from the many external and internal elements which converged in pressure upon British North America to unite,' but he added sombrely that 'it would be an inexact thing at best'.[9] More generally, David Hackett Fischer has argued that the real problem is not so much that history itself is 'an inexact science' but rather that 'historians are inexact scientists, who go blundering about their business without a sufficient sense of purpose or procedure'.[10] Certainly some historians have tended to condemn the Canadian

Union in its last years as a violation of general laws of politics and human behaviour, sometimes without spelling out those laws, and invariably without applying the same standards to other periods of Canadian history.

The latent notion of historical explanation as a parallelogram of forces, or a Newtonian compilation of colliding pressures, is partly responsible for more fundamental shortcomings in the way in which Confederation has usually been explained. First, it creates a mental prison in which the reasons for Confederation are deduced almost entirely from the circumstances of 1864. This is not only a circular process in itself, but it is one which by its nature finds it difficult to take account of the importance of Confederation as a pre-existing vision of the destiny of the provinces. There is much to be said for taking as an explanatory starting point the *idea* of Confederation, and seeking to explain why this mental construct became fastened upon a set of circumstances to which it does not seem to have been a particularly appropriate response, rather than assuming that it was indeed the correct answer to the challenges of 1864 and then adopting an essentially descriptive strategy which supports that thesis. It is after all easy enough to find 'reasons' why British North American union emerged from the circumstances of 1864: the Fathers of Confederation certainly had few problems in presenting their solution as the answer to immediate challenges.

Secondly, the illusion of scientific proof violates Lady Bracknell's dictum that the truth is never pure and rarely simple. Many of the accounts of Confederation are altogether too neat and clinical. Historical explanation may be less satisfying but more convincing when it takes account of bluff and muddle, of ignorance and illogicality. These elements, as will be seen, lie at the heart of any discussion of the British role in the unification of British North America. At the very least, if historians wish to play at being scientists, they need to remember that constant and unceasing scepticism is the hallmark of the experimental road to understanding.

The damage which can be done by the illusion that history is a science is compounded by the seductive allures of its literary aspects. History is about words, both the words used by historians themselves, and those which they hail as 'evidence' from the mouths and pens of the people they study. Analysis is complicated by the process which social scientists call 'reification', the making of things by words. When B.A. Knox declares that from 1850 the establishment of colonial federations became 'an object of British policy', he invites us to assume that there was some such continuing entity which could be labelled 'British policy'.[11] On the other hand, writing of South Africa in the 1870s, C.F. Goodfellow more mildly characterised British support for a local federation as 'more of a hope than a policy'.[12] Knox's formulation is undoubtedly the more imposing, but Goodfellow's may be the more accurate. Canada's politicians find it difficult to put together a secure ministry. Does this amount to 'deadlock'? A colonial secretary sends minatory despatches to the Maritimes, hectoring them on the advantages of Confederation. Does this amount to 'British pressure'? Reification is a necessary shorthand — it is basic to the thesis of this study that Confederation had an independent existence as 'an idea' — but the shorthand may mislead.

Even more spectacularly misleading is the associated form of metaphor. Creighton used it in describing the Canadian mission to London in the spring of 1865 in a chapter entitled 'Appeal to Caesar'.[13] It conjures a splendid image of a metropolitan power both imperial and imperious, purple-robed and purple-faced, giving the thumbs down to the recalcitrant New Brunswickers. Unfortunately, the metaphor lacks depth. A Roman emperor faced with disobedient provincials would have sent in the legions and massacred every last one of them. Britain did not have that option in its dealings with New Brunswick: not even the swashbuckling prime minister, Lord Palmerston, would send gunboats against British subjects. The combination of a powerful metaphor with Creighton's beguilingly narrative strategy means that the real part played by the British in confronting the Maritimes is never fully confronted.

Much historical explanation — and not just of Confederation — is based on the combination of an affectation of scientific proof with the literary technique of assembling pungent illustrative quotation from contemporary sources. In this, it is easy to assume that the arguments used by the winners provide the key for understanding the reasons for their success. Thus the tale of Confederation can be unfolded in combined narrative form and explanatory function by quoting Macdonald and Cartier, McGee and Galt, a strategy which at one and the same time assumes that the contents of their speeches provide both evidence of their own motives and explanations for the triumph of their point of view. At first sight, this is an approach entirely appropriate to the conduct of public business in a society which, if not a full democracy in the modern sense, was at least governed through a liberal constitutional system based on discussion and majority votes. In fact, precisely because the key to all parliamentary government in an age of relatively loose party affiliations was the winning of majorities, the task of the successful politician was not principled advocacy but the assembling of coalitions.

In British politics, this lesson was learnt by Gladstone early in his career. As a young minister, he was charged with the responsibility of replying to a debate. 'Shall I be short and concise?' he asked his chief, Sir Robert Peel. 'No,' replied Peel, 'be long and diffuse. It is all important in the House of Commons to state your case in many different ways, so as to produce an effect on men of many ways of thinking.'[14] The demon of brevity rarely tempted the politicians of British North America. To put it simply, politicians and journalists were not engaged in providing source materials for future generations of scholars, but in winning support and discrediting opposition. It is utterly misleading for historians to assume that all the points in all the speeches can be fused together into a single, interlocking explanatory package. This is not how speeches are made, especially in debating chambers as intimate as the Assembly of the Province of Canada which, with just 130 members, was none the less the largest in British North America: different points are addressed to different interests, perhaps even to different individuals. At Westminster, Disraeli used to aim his remarks to the clock in the gallery, turning his back on the Speaker whom he was formally addressing, in order to speak to his own supporters behind him.[15] During the debate on conscription in November 1944, Mackenzie King actually turned his back on the opposition in order to dramatise an appeal for support to his restive backbenchers from Quebec.[16]

· Sometimes British North American politicians were consciously casual with the truth. At a banquet in Halifax in August 1864, shortly before the Charlottetown conference but with Confederation in the air, Joseph Howe proclaimed to a group of visiting Canadians that he had 'always been in favour of uniting any two, three, four, or the whole five of the Provinces'. Howe denied any inconsistency with his subsequent opposition to the

Quebec scheme, indignantly pointing out that he had risen to speak at ten minutes to midnight. 'Who ever heard of a public man being bound by a speech on such an occasion as that?'[17] Edward Palmer of Prince Edward Island was similarly charged with inconsistency for having spoken favourably of Confederation at a banquet in Toronto shortly before returning to damn it in Charlottetown. His defence was that to have discussed his own objections would have 'provoked a controversy that was not expected on such festive occasions'.[18] In assessing such sentiments, the challenge remains as it was defined by Francis Palgrave in 1843: the historian must be able to tell 'when the speech which makes the roof resound means nothing — and be equally able to find the expressive meaning of silence.'[19]

In fact, it is necessary to recognise that sometimes, in the task of assembling support, politicians uttered statements which they could not seriously have believed to be true. Could Sir Etienne Taché really have believed his often-quoted claim, in February 1865, that Canada had been 'bordering on civil strife' at the time of the formation of the Great Coalition the previous summer?[20] Selective description has obscured the derision which opponents poured upon his statement, not least because it contrasted oddly with his own ministry's recent throne speech which had thanked 'a beneficent Providence for the general contentment of the people of this province'.[21] Speaking at a banquet at Quebec City five months earlier, Taché had played down talk of the breakdown of the Canadian Union. 'We had been in political difficulties, no doubt ... but these difficulties were not so great — the body politic was not so sick and incurable as to make a remedy of no avail.'[22] Had he forgotten the atmosphere of the previous June? Did the full extent of the sectional crisis only dawn on him in retrospect? Or was it that there were delegates from the Maritimes at the Quebec banquet, and that they would hardly be encouraged to join Confederation if assured that it was necessary to prevent the people of Canada from killing each other? Similarly, Taché's warning that without a union of the provinces 'we would be forced into the American Union by violence, and if not by violence, would be placed upon an inclined plane which would carry us there insensibly' may be interpreted as evidence that Confederation was the vital protection against annexation.[23] Yet equally it may be evidence that there was general opposition to the incorporation of the province within the United States and that Christopher Dunkin was right in dismissing the argument that Confederation was 'a sure preventative of annexation to the United States' as one of the 'cheap and easy generalities' which were intended to obscure the practical weaknesses of the scheme.[24] Certainly it is curious that Taché should have formed a weak ministry — one which needed an inspiring policy objective — in March 1864, without a whisper of concern that Canada was on the verge of civil war, or sliding towards annexation.

Equally, it is hard to believe that Cartier was sincere in his linking of Confederation with British North American defence at a banquet in London in April 1865. 'Singly the two Canadas cannot defend themselves,' he announced, 'but if united with the Maritime Provinces, a perfect system of defence can be devised in connection with the mother country.'[25] Cartier was far too intelligent to believe that the militias of New Brunswick and Nova Scotia were the key to the continental power balance in North America. It is more likely that he appreciated that the British were uneasy and impatient about the vulnerability of Canada, and that he found it convenient to muddle the questions of defence and communications with that of political union. As he had told an audience at Halifax the previous autumn, 'Any one conversing with Englishmen, or reading the English papers, will see that the question which prevails there is the defence of the country'.[26] It is unlikely that Tilley, a champion of temperance, had been carried away by conviviality when at the same banquet he offered a preposterously simplified analysis of the difficulties of intercolonial co-operation as separate provinces. 'Now suppose we were all drawn together into one confederation, you would not meet with any of these difficulties. If you wanted to secure intercolonial free trade or an inter-colonial railway, then there would be no difficulty.'[27] Of course historians must beware of picking among the evidence, choosing only those items which suit their theories, but equally we should not abandon all our critical faculties. In fact, we pay greater respect to the dignity of the past if we conclude that the people we study were sometimes liars, if the alternative is to conclude that they were always fools.

In reality, even some supporters of Confederation were uneasy at the more extravagant arguments urged in its favour. The Toronto *Globe*, for instance, doubted the wisdom of Cartier's attempt to encourage the British to believe that Confederation would strengthen Canada's defences, since union 'will not add either to the valour of the people or to the military resources of the country'. Confederation was 'sought — not on the false pretence that it will make these Provinces more formidable in a military point of view — but for the purpose of securing good government and political harmony to the country'.[28] When a small-town newspaper argued the unfashionable case for joining the United States, the *Globe* replied that neither federation nor annexation, 'nor anything else, will make a merchant in Galt rich when he was poor before.... The sooner that idea is eradicated from the minds of the people, the better'.[29] If even the supporters of Confederation could feel uneasy about the arguments advanced in its favour, historians have an added responsibility to avoid the uncritical elevation of every contemporary debating point into a textbook explanation.

***

Historians who have welcomed the coming of Confederation have tended to portray the province of Canada as being 'on a downward spiral'[30] in the last decade of its existence. In fact, this condemnation rests upon a few episodes, exaggerated by selective description, and apparently based upon implied general laws of political behaviour which are usually waived in accounts of Canada's post-Confederation crises. Such sweeping condemnation distorts understanding of the likely options facing the province of Canada in 1864, while a verdict of supine, deadlocked failure renders it logically impossible to explain how a challenge as great as Confederation could be carried at all.

The seat of government issue, which triggered the 'double shuffle' crisis of 1858, was hardly the fault of the system of government, since Montreal had been deprived of its status nine years earlier because its citizens had rioted against the constitution. Regional rivalries within modern Canada plague the location of government projects and it was hardly surprising that the Assembly had found it impossible to choose among the competing and importunate candidates. If Britain itself had to choose its capital afresh, 'how would Lancashire fight for the Mersey, how loudly would Edinburgh proclaim the grandeur of modern Athens,' *The Times* sympathetically explained to its readers.[31] Canada's politicians were not taken in by the device of referring the choice to Queen Victoria[32] — and *The Times* was unduly stuffy in condemning the understandably disappointed protest vote as 'a poor specimen of the state of public morality in Canada'.[33] It is certainly not obvious that public morality would have been elevated by adding the still-more diverse regional interests which would come with a union of all British North America. As the Colonial Office official, Frederick Elliot, pointed out, Confederation would introduce politicians from other parts of British North America who although 'unavoidably less well informed on Canadian interests' would become 'the virtual arbiters of Canadian questions'. Since both Canadian parties would bid for their support, 'it needs but a moderate acquaintance with the habits of legislative bodies in North America, to anticipate the extravagant race into which contending politicians would enter for gaining the favour of their distant colleagues. All manner of expensive and questionable public works would be embarked in solely for political objects'.[34] Elliot may have been a pessimist, but he would also prove to be something of a prophet.

Many historians have condemned the double shuffle, although some seem to have been embarrassed by the fact that the villains of 1858 would soon emerge as the nation-building heroes of 1864-7. Consequently, they have placed the blame not upon the players but rather on the game itself: to Morton, the episode was 'a further symptom of the rapidly developing organic disease of the Union'.[35] 'People of all political hues began to wonder how workable was a union that depended upon trickery for its continuation', a recent textbook pronounces, without identifying the doubters.[36] Perhaps nineteenth-century Canadians were less squeamish than twentieth-century academics. There was nothing illegal about the double shuffle, and for all its tawdriness it barely ranks with the blatant attempt by the Meighen government in 1926 to ignore the irksome by-election rule altogether, let alone with the tactics used by the St Laurent government during the notorious Pipeline debate in 1956. The most appropriate verdict is surely that of a contemporary official in Britain, who merely commented on 'the general air of lunacy which hangs over the whole proceedings'.[37]

If Canada's historians wish to demand high ethical standards of their past leaders, so be it. They might, however, be consistent in their outrage. Lower condemned the double shuffle as 'sharp practice'[38] but was oddly unabashed by evidence that a great deal of money was spent to persuade New Brunswick voters to accept Confederation in the election of 1866. 'Bribery is a form of consent,' he remarked, 'and the alternative to consent is force.'[39] For most historians, Confederation was inevitable. For some, it was evidently also an offer which could not be refused. There seems to have been less indignation showered upon the far more spectacular affair of the Pacific Scandal of 1873, in which Macdonald was forced to resign in the face of charges that he had granted the contract for the transcontinental railway to the man who had funded his election campaign the previous year: much may be excused a politician who could plead the defence of nation-building.[40] 'A fair verdict would be "Not Guilty but don't do it again!"', jested Lower.[41]

Historians have been virtually unanimous in their condemnation of the next episode in the indictment, the defeat of the Militia Bill in 1862. They have shared the outrage felt by contemporary British opinion at the apparent insouciance of Canada's politicians in the face of the continental crisis of the American Civil War. Political rivalry, said Lower, 'was so bitter as to cause party advantage to be placed before public necessity'.[42] Certainly, the defeat of the Militia Bill cannot be regarded as a glorious episode — war with the United States had after all seemed frighteningly close just six months earlier — but some of the condemnation rests upon highly selective description of the circumstances and the implied assertion of questionable general laws of political behaviour. First, there was no guarantee that the proposed force of 30000 trained militia would actually make the province secure. At the battle of Shiloh a month earlier, the combined Union and Confederate casualties had totalled over 23000 — and the two sides continued to fight, with 186000 men in two entirely different armies clashing in the eastern theatre in the Seven Days' Battles where there had been 39000 casualties by the end of June. It was not so much that 'Canadians had not as yet become very excited over the alleged danger of the great new military machine which the North was building up',[43] but rather that some of them hesitated to adopt a response which might be inadequate and perhaps also provocative.[44]

Secondly, few historians stress that the Militia Bill of 1862 contained a contingent element of conscription: if a district failed to contribute enough volunteers for training, the shortfall would be made good by a draft, a degree of government intervention which was regarded — then and subsequently — with great suspicion by French Canadians.[45] Canada's historians have generally judged the conscription crises of the twentieth century in terms of the handling of the susceptibilities of Quebec rather than the imperatives of military needs. W.L. Morton, for instance, judged the Union Government of 1917 to be 'gravely mistaken' in imposing conscription on Quebec, for 'a majority on fundamental issues is not enough. At bottom, Canada must be governed by concurrent majorities of French and English.' This particular scientific law of Canadian government asserts precisely the principle that Confederation was supposedly intended to sweep away, as Morton himself elsewhere acknowledged in condemning Sandfield Macdonald's double majority principle as 'a political impossibility in Canadian politics'.[46]

Thirdly, the Militia Bill would have imposed the enormous additional cost of a million dollars a year for training, increasing overall provincial expenditure to about twelve and a half million dollars a year, with revenue, on the other hand, estimated at a little over seven million dollars. When the Assembly threw out the Militia Bill, it was not necessarily refusing to accept responsibility for the defence of Canada, but rather demonstrating that it lacked confidence in the flagging Cartier-Macdonald ministry to undertake the task. With a shrewd innuendo, Joseph Howe regretted 'that the late Government elected to fall on the Militia Bill, and that their opponents were good-natured or unskilful enough to let them'. A good deal of misunderstanding in Britain, Howe believed, would have been prevented had the critics passed a formal resolution stating 'the reasons for which they turned the ministers out'.[47]

There is certainly no scientific law of history requiring free assemblies to respond positively to crises in defence policy by spending money on a lavish scale. The British were hardly qualified to uphold any such principle. In 1847, in response to a panic fear of French invasion, Lord John Russell's ministry had proposed a major and very expensive training programme for the militia, which would have involved raising income tax from sevenpence in the pound to one shilling. The House of Commons mutinied, and Russell ingloriously withdrew the scheme. 'The chances of invasion seemed preferable to the addition of fivepence on the income tax.'[48] Russell's government never fully recovered from this retreat, although it struggled on for another four years, until it was fatally weakened in December 1851 when Palmerston was forced to resign over a foreign policy issue. Palmerston quickly took his revenge —

his 'tit-for-tat' as he elegantly styled it — by defeating Russell's Militia Bill of 1852, an episode which Goldwin Smith inconveniently recalled in the general atmosphere of outrage at the Canadians ten years later.[49]

Given the extent of military unpreparedness which would be revealed by the disasters of the Crimean War, it might be thought outrageous that any political system could make defence issues the sport of faction. In fact, Palmerston continued to be the dominant figure in British politics, and while organic reform might have seemed imperative and overdue, even a mild instalment was delayed until after his death in 1865. Equally, the shortcomings of Canadian politicians in responding to the invasion threat in 1862 hardly bear comparison with the handling of the next major defence issue in Canadian history, the inglorious exercise in indecision known as the 'naval question' which straggled on inconclusively between 1909 and 1912. In 1909, the Liberal government under Laurier and the Conservative opposition agreed on a bipartisan naval policy, but the two parties then quarrelled over the interpretation of what they thought they had agreed. In 1912, the newly elected Conservative government pledged Canada's word to meet the cost of three modern battleships for the Royal Navy — only to have its naval policy blocked by the unelected Senate, which was dominated by members who owed their appointments to the rejected Liberal government. As a result, instead of the Dominion fleet of eleven ships envisaged by Laurier, by 1914 the Royal Canadian Navy consisted of two superannuated British cruisers, one stationed at each end of the country, and it was the Japanese navy which undertook the protection of Canada's Pacific coast in the First World War. One study of the period has called the episode 'a petty, vindictive, partisan shambles' and 'an embarrassment to the nation, if not its leaders',[50] but a recent textbook has preferred to praise Laurier for 'an important assertion of Canada's autonomy *within* the British Empire'.[51]

In comparative context, then, the rejection of the Militia Bill of 1862 violates no law of necessary response to defence crises. The needs of the explanation have distorted the historical task of description by omitting to explore in much detail the motives of those who opposed the measure. In fact, selectivity in description has created even more misunderstanding of events after May 1862. Readers of the textbooks are by and large left to conclude that little was done to reform the Canadian militia and that consequently Confederation was the answer to the problem of continental defence. The first contention is untrue, and the second implausible. In April 1863, the new premier, Sandfield Macdonald, introduced his own measure to reform the militia. It was opposed by the ousted Conservatives, who succeeded in forcing an election.[52] To move a no-confidence motion over militia reform four days after the bloody battle of Chancellorsville might not seem a responsible gesture of opposition, but the knowledge that John A. Macdonald would become a nation-builder just around the corner acquits him of any censure: Morton seems almost admiring of his 'keen partisan purpose'.[53]

To put the matter simply, it was praiseworthy for John A. Macdonald, soon to become the leading Father of Confederation, to delay militia reform by challenging a ministry in 1863, but outrageous of Sandfield Macdonald, who would soon oppose Confederation, to use militia reform as a means of ousting a ministry in 1862. That the continental crisis and the effective power of the Northern armies were both far greater in 1863 than in 1862 has been irrelevant to the value judgements. As a result, legislation was delayed until October 1863, when Sandfield secured passage of a measure to provide for a trained volunteer force of 35000 men. In June 1864, the Taché ministry introduced a 'traditional and rather political'[54] bill designed to tighten up the act of 1863. It was never debated, since the ministry fell the very next day, to be replaced by the coalition which launched Confederation.

At this point, the question of militia reform virtually vanishes from most textbooks, and has to be reconstituted from specialist studies. In 1865, a British officer, Colonel Sir Patrick MacDougall, took charge of training, bringing the effective strength in the province of Canada to 25000.[55] Arguably, the end of the American Civil War made the militia more important: a small citizen force could have done little to block Grant and Sherman, but it was the appropriate defensive response against bands of Fenians, rarely more than a thousand strong, while disorganisation in militia ranks at the battle of Ridgeway in June 1866 demonstrated a continuing need for training. However, if Confederation was indeed intended to strengthen British North American defences, the new political system hardly shone in its muted response. Cartier's Militia Act of 1868, which mainly consolidated existing forces, was based on

Sandfield Macdonald's 1863 legislation, although it sought to place the militia more firmly under political control, thereby adding to patronage opportunities.

Soon afterwards, the much-praised Colonel MacDougall was eased out of office. His downfall came when he attempted to cashier a prominent Conservative MP, Colonel Mackenzie Bowell, who had publicly criticised a superior officer and claimed immunity as a form of parliamentary privilege.[56] The unscathed Bowell continued his career as a Tory packhorse, serving for many years as Grand Master of the Orange Order and as Minister of Customs, thereby securing both sectarian and patronage support for the Conservatives. In 1882 he took a major part in the gerrymandering of Ontario ridings known as the 'hiving of the Grits' and in 1894 he began a brief term as one of Canada's least distinguished prime ministers. Thus had Confederation enabled Canada to escape from 'the cul de sac of petty politics'.[57] Meanwhile, the British pulled out their garrisons altogether and, as late as 1874, the young nationalists of Canada First could still call for an 'improved militia system, under the command of trained Dominion officers'.[58] The dismal story can be baldly summarised: the only politician who did much for the militia was the abused Sandfield Macdonald, and his reforms were achieved in the face of partisan opposition from those very politicians who were to launch the new Canada a year later. Textbook accounts highlight the defeat of the Militia Bill of 1862, but thereafter description lapses into utter silence, creating the impression that the old province of Canada could achieve nothing, and that Confederation was the miracle solution.

The failure of the intercolonial railway negotiations of 1862, and the Upper Canada separate schools dispute of 1863, are further examples of episodes which were inglorious in themselves but hardly evidence of a bankrupt political system.[59] The problem in the railway talks was Gladstone's insistence that the provinces make an annual repayment of the capital sum borrowed. Most British North American projects were planned on the basis of present funding and future re-financing: Confederation itself was one of the biggest buy-now-pay-later ventures of them all. It would have been difficult for any government which had inherited such an awesome budget deficit from its predecessors to meet Gladstone's condition. The real failing of the Canadian delegates in

1862 lay in the furtive manner of their refusal, which provoked disgust from the British and resentment among the Maritimers. Even Morton admitted that while the behaviour of the Canadian delegates 'seems to have been distinctly reprehensible, their position under the circumstances appears at least defensible and probably inevitable'.[60] Nor is it beyond all doubt that Gladstone's motives derived from 'his characteristic moral fervour'.[61] He had been an obtuse opponent of Canadian self-government, was openly sympathetic towards the Southern States, and may even have been attracted to the idea of bringing the Civil War to a close by handing over Canada to the North as compensation.[62]

It would only be fair to pronounce a structural condemnation on the province of Canada for the outcome of the Upper Canada separate schools dispute of 1863 if it could be proved that Confederation resolved the perennially controversial question of minority schooling. In practice, the British North America Act normally made it possible for Ottawa politicians to avoid repetitions of the imbroglio of 1863, since Section 92 placed education under provincial control. However, the divorce was by no means absolute since Section 93 gave the Dominion parliament power — and arguably the Dominion government the duty — to impose remedial legislation. Hence Canada was subjected to controversies over Catholic schools in New Brunswick in the early 1870s and again in Manitoba in the 1890s, with subsequent echoes when the new prairie provinces were created in 1905, followed by calls for intervention on behalf of French-language education in Ontario after 1912. In many respects, Confederation offered the worst of both worlds: Section 93 created an expectation of protection but in practice the Manitoba episode proved it to be a 'dead letter'.[63] To say this is not to condemn Confederation, but rather to recognise the intractability of an issue which brings into conflict the rights of parents, the needs of children and the claims of rival religious groups.

The real significance of the failure of the Intercolonial Railway talks and the passage of the Upper Canada Separate Schools Act may lie in the more fundamental need which some historians have felt to denigrate Sandfield Macdonald. The teleological approach to the explanation of Confederation requires the downward-spiralling province of Canada to hit rock-bottom, for the dawn of 1864 to be immediately preceded by a very dark night. Thus Sandfield is portrayed as the nadir. In reality, it is by no means clear that he was so bad: the man whom Careless called a 'temperamental, stiff-necked individualist'[64] was described by Goldwin Smith — no indulgent observer of Canadian public life — as 'a thoroughly good fellow, and honest'.[65] Morton is particularly hard on the 'pawky Highlander', an 'unabashed mediocrity' whose real offence was that he aimed 'to prolong the life of the [Canadian] Union' and so delay Confederation.[66]

This is not to claim that Sandfield Macdonald was a great statesman, but rather to suggest that he seems to have been judged against an unstated law about political leadership which emphatically is not applied in later phases of Canadian history. 'His solution for any difficulty was, first, to hope that it might disappear,' wrote Morton disapprovingly, 'and second, to deal with it by some expedient inspired by the pressure of the last moment.'[67] The description might be applied word-for-word to Mackenzie King, 'the consummate master of opportunity' as Morton called him, with evident approval. 'Few men by doing so little had accomplished so much.'[68] The implied law of political leadership used to condemn Sandfield is one deduced from the need to explain Confederation as the sweeping away of a political system sunk in its own irrelevance. A longer-term view of Canadian history might suggest that the country functions best under consensual styles of leadership. By general agreement, Canada's most successful leaders have been prime ministers like John A. Macdonald, whose evasion of difficult issues gained him the nickname 'Old Tomorrow', and Mackenzie King, of whom F.R. Scott once wrote that he would never do anything by halves that could be done by quarters. Sandfield Macdonald has been condemned for attempting to govern in a style that kept Mackenzie King in the saddle for a quarter of a century.

It is tempting to suggest that if Sandfield Macdonald had not existed, the historians would have been obliged to invent him. In fact, it may well be that the Sandfield of the textbooks has indeed been invented, to form a contrast with the hero of Confederation, the man of visionary principle, his namesake, John A. Macdonald. Yet when it fell to John A. to select a premier to act as his satellite in the new province of Ontario in 1867, on whom did his choice fall? Joseph Pope, who knew 'Old Tomorrow' well, recounted that Sir John A. Macdonald 'came to the conclusion that John Sandfield

Macdonald was just the man to undertake the task'[69] — and this despite the fact that Sandfield had been one of four unregenerate Upper Canadian members who had opposed Confederation to the very last minute. By and large, historians have spared themselves the embarrassment of having to explain Sandfield's appointment: in four books dealing with the period, D.G. Creighton managed never once to mention who it was that his hero designated as premier of the largest province in the new Dominion.[70] To have confronted the question might have been to be forced to recognise that, regrettably, Confederation involved something less than a crusade by high-minded nation-builders against the petty and unprincipled mentality of the parish-pump. Rather, it was one further stage in a steady process of forging political alliances which often crossed the notional allegiances of party warfare.

Perhaps to dramatise his indictment of an entire political structure, Lower resorted to a literary form of guilt-by-association, alleging that 'the political situation of the [Canadian] Union brings to mind the France of the Third Republic', which 'like Canada under the Union, was in constant political crisis because it could get no government with a chance to endure until it had worked out its policies'.[71] The parallel was absurd: in the last years of the Third Republic, no ministry could match the longevity of the Cartier-Macdonald combination between 1858 and 1862.[72] In any case, the party systems of interwar France and mid-Victorian Canada were fundamentally different: the former was riven by class and ideological conflict, while in the latter, the art of government was coalition-building on the middle ground. Having unfairly implied that the province of Canada was a French farce, Lower then proceeded to declamatory denunciation, condemning the Canadian Union for eight general elections and at least ten premiers in twenty-seven years. It will come as little surprise to learn that his arithmetic was faulty: the Union lasted for twenty-six years and there were fourteen premiers.[73] As most of these were in fact co-premiers, the record compares favourably with the five years from 1891 and 1896, when Canada had no fewer than six prime ministers, on the eve of a decade which would be one of the country's rare periods of exploding prosperity. By contrast, Canada had just three prime ministers between 1921 and 1939, years of prolonged economic depression and public discontent. Yet again, the scientific law implied in the breathless condemnation does not stand up to examination.

The kernel of Lower's charge is that by 1864, the Canadian Union had effectively broken down. 'Two elections and four ministries in three years! Everyone recognized it was impossible to go on.'[74] Lower's formulation may be traced back to a statement in the pioneering political chronicle published in 1881 by J.C. Dent: 'Four different ministries had been condemned within little more than two years,' he wrote. 'The state of affairs seemed hopeless, for the constitution itself was manifestly unequal to the task imposed upon it.'[75] Dent's verdict in turn bears the mark of an editorial in the *Globe* on 18 June 1864, which sought to defend its owner, George Brown, for entering into coalition negotiations with his foes. Not surprisingly, it argued that Canada required an entirely fresh political start, and it reviewed the hopelessness of recent events to conclude: 'Four Administrations condemned in the short space of two years — and what hope was there of any satisfactory change in this state of things?'. Lower's contribution lay mainly in the addition of an exclamation mark, in which he was followed by Careless in his authoritative biography of George Brown: 'Four ministries within two years! A constant succession of political crises, an inability to get even ordinary parliamentary business done'.[76] Thus was an exercise in special pleading silently converted into a historical explanation.

It is hard to see why the Canadian Union was politically bankrupt simply because it had held general elections in 1861 and 1863, and now faced the prospect of a third in 1864. There is no scientific law which states that frequent general elections must lead to fundamental change. Britain held three in less than two years between 1922 and 1924; Ireland endured three within eighteen months in 1981-2.[77] In Canada there were three successive and equally inconclusive elections within as many years between June 1962 and November 1965. A Royal Commission into the state of the nation did warn that 'Canada, without being fully conscious of the fact, is passing through the greatest crisis in its history', but — Quebec separatists apart — nobody seemed to have 'recognized it was impossible to go on'.[78] Once again, description has been dressed up as explanation, and explanation has drawn upon an imaginary scientific law of political behaviour.

In fact, the province of Canada had prospered under the Union. As Joseph Perrault pertinently asked: 'have we not reason to be proud of our growth since 1840, and of the fact that within the past twenty-five years, our progress, both social and material, has kept pace with that of the first nations in the world?'[79] Similarly, Christopher Dunkin preferred to stress the positive achievements of the Union, scornfully rejecting the claim that the people of Canada had got

> into such a position of embarrassment among ourselves, are working our political institutions so very badly, are in such a frightful fix, that, never mind what the prospects of this particular step may be, it must positively be taken; we cannot help it, we cannot stay as we are, nor yet go back, nor yet go forward, in any course but just this one.[80]

Some even doubted that there was a very close correlation between political stability and the health of the body politic. James O'Halloran feared being 'legislated to death' at the hands of those who believed that 'even the grass cannot grow unless it is regulated by an Act of Parliament.'[81] Henri Joly mockingly agreed 'that all these changes must have been very unpleasant for the different ministers who have succumbed under them' but pointed out that the five million dollar deficit of 1862 had been replaced by a surplus. 'If all these changes of ministries had not taken place,' Joly added sarcastically, 'it is impossible to say how large the deficit would have become by this time'.[82]

Most fundamentally of all, there is a massive logical inconsistency in the claim that after allegedly failing to confront the various challenges which lay within its proper sphere, the province of Canada suddenly managed to convert itself into the corner-stone of a new nation. There is surely something curious in the way that politicians condemned for having 'drifted spellbound' were suddenly capable of becoming statesmen who 'seized this transient opportunity with boldness and decision and used it to weld the scattered communities with a population of less than 4000000 into a nation whose dominion should extend from sea to sea.'[83] Historians have variously stated that the rejection of the Militia Bill was 'symbolic of the total collapse of the existing constitutional structure' and that 'the fabric of Canadian politics crumbled' with the defeat of Taché's ministry in June 1864.[84] It is hardly surprising that two historians have solemnly pronounced that Confederation was a miracle.[85] It is hard to see what other explanation could be offered in the circumstances.

Crucial to the argument that the Canadian Union had failed is the claim that in June 1864 it had finally reached deadlock. This pervasive and commanding metaphor has a long pedigree. 'Parties were nearly equally balanced, the wheels of government had nearly ceased to move,' George Brown claimed in September 1864, adding 'a dead lock was almost inevitable'.[86] A quarter of a century later, Goldwin Smith reacted sourly to the glorification of the 'Fathers of Confederation' with the sneer that 'its real parent was Deadlock'.[87] Not only was the phrase adopted by the textbooks — 'hopeless deadlock', 'the famous state of deadlock'[88] — but mysteriously it also became bracketed with its own solution. One textbook refers to 'deadlock in the Canadian legislature and the formation of a coalition to seek a solution', as if nothing were more natural than to link the two. 'The deadlock that virtually paralyzed the union government,' another states blandly, 'provided the necessary push for change.'[89] In a bound, Jack was free.

The reconstruction of the province of Canada had indeed become necessary by 1864, for one overwhelming reason: it was impossible to maintain the existing structure, with its artificial equality of representation between the two sections, in the face of Upper Canada's rapid population growth and increasingly insistent demand for a larger share of political power. The province had reached not deadlock, from which by definition escape is impossible, but should rather be thought of as caught in a log-jam, in itself a far more appropriately Canadian image.[90] By the middle of 1864, several of the logs were ready to shift, and movement of any one of them would remove the blockage. It was not the impossibility of obtaining some form of representation by population which confronted the politicians, but rather its overwhelming likelihood.

One of the confusions encouraged by the 'deadlock' metaphor has been a tendency to elide a confrontation between the two sections of the province with one between its two communities, as if Lower Canadians were identical with French Canadians. Ormsby, for instance, wrote that representation by population 'could never be acceptable to Lower Canada for it was a direct threat to French-Canadian interests', while Creighton described it as 'a revolutionary reform which French Canada would never accept willingly and English Canada could hardly impose by force'. Morton took the confusion even further, writing that 'Upper Canada wanted ... freedom from the French majority [sic] in domestic matters'.[91] In reality, far from commanding a majority, in 1865 French Canadians held no more than 49 out of the 130 seats in the Assembly.[92] Two questions arise. Was it possible for English-speaking members to force through a redistribution of seats according to population? Were there signs by 1864 that this was going to happen?

Far from being impossible of achievement, representation by population was both permissible and indeed likely. When the British parliament passed the Union Act in 1840, it had ordained that any change in the distribution of ridings must require a two-thirds majority of the whole Assembly — a provision which entrenched the equal representation provision but obstructed even minor boundary changes. In a little-noticed move, the British parliament abolished the entrenchment provision in 1854, making it possible for a simple majority of voting members to carry representation by population.[93] In theory, this would mean that if the Upper Canada members united to demand justice for their section, it would require the support of just one Lower Canadian representative to secure them victory. Sir Edmund Head had foreseen this as early as 1857. 'The only solution of the difficulty will be the chance that the district of Montreal, and the English population about it and in the townships, may be got to side with Upper Canada and thus turn the scale in favour of that section, which ... must prevail.'[94]

Of course, this did not mean that a snap vote would suddenly give Upper Canada additional seats in the Assembly: any such proposal would require detailed legislation, with all the opportunities that process would present for the obstructive skills of experienced politicians, and might perhaps be delayed in the Legislative Council, Canada's upper house, which has been little studied by historians. Ultimately, no doubt, the majority would have its way. What might force politicians to draw back and seek another solution was not the impossibility of redistributing the balance of legislative power within the province, but rather the consequences of victory in a head-on confrontation between Upper Canada and the French. As Chester Martin was almost alone in observing, 'the real peril was not "deadlock" but what lay beyond'.[95]

Were there signs that the clash was imminent? There had been 49 Upper Canada members — out of 65 — in support of representation by population in 1861. The number fell back to 43 a year later, but in the wake of the general election of 1863, George Brown predicted that the Upper Canadian representatives would be 'almost unanimous' in support of representation by population, fortified as they were by the results of the 1861 census.[96] Brown was prone to be unduly sanguine in crediting what he wanted to believe, but there are indications from other, less enthusiastic, quarters that change was inescapable. When Taché formed his ministry in March 1864, representation by population was declared an open question: not even an alliance predominantly made up of Conservatives and Bleus would pledge itself to resistance. In February 1865, John A. Macdonald flatly told the Assembly that 'if some such solution of the difficulties as Confederation had not been found, the representation by population must eventually have been carried ... it is certain that in the progress of events representation by population would have been carried'.[97] Joseph Cauchon had opposed British North American union in 1858, but now he warned readers of his *Journal du Québec* that Lower Canadians of British background were tiring of the unending struggle in which they could not be expected to share the passionate commitment of their French Canadian neighbours, and were privately making it clear that they would put an end to the confrontation by switching sides.[98]

Of course, the historian must produce evidence to confirm the jeremiads of Macdonald and Cauchon, for politicians and journalists were capable of appealing to bugbears to frighten others into accepting a course of action they had determined upon for perhaps entirely different reasons. The doom of equal representation was announced in a little-noticed vote on 14 March 1864, although the debate in which it occurred is well-known, for it was the first appearance of George Brown's 'famous resolution for a select committee on federation'.[99] An amendment was moved by Joseph Perrault calling in extreme terms for a return to entrenchment, so that the equal representation of the two sections would remain inviolate forever. It was rejected by a massive 82 votes to 25. As Brown had predicted, Upper Canada was virtually unanimous in rejecting Perrault's amendment. 'Only one Upper

Canadian voted for it', the *Globe* noted. No fewer than 54 registered their opposition.[100]

Far more significant was the presence in the 'No' lobby not just of fourteen Lower Canada English representatives, but of an equal number of French members. The message was clear. Faced with the prospect that the Lower Canada English would join a united Upper Canada block to force through representation by population within the existing provincial structure, the more far-sighted French Canadians were offering the dominant section a choice of collaborators, with the implication of alternative and more easily achieved compromise solutions. Why else should they have bothered to vote against a private member's proposal which was obviously going to be defeated? Eight Bleus and six Rouges were signalling that not only was the log-jam on the point of breaking, but also that they were offering a near-united Upper Canada a choice of three potential groups of Lower Canadian collaborators in carrying change. Under those circumstances, it made sense for George Brown to abandon his tenuous links with the Rouges, bypass the English-speaking minority and deal direct with the Bleus, the largest party in the lower section. Why should the Bleus suddenly rush to assist in their own defeat? Their basic priority would be to conduct an exercise in damage-limitation in the face of an unstoppable shift of power towards Upper Canada. First, by co-operating, they could mitigate the extent of their defeat. Ontario eventually secured 82 seats, as against Quebec's 65, based on a straight population comparison. From the French point of view, it might have been worse: had Upper Canada chosen to dictate an allocation based either on registered voters or on adult males — either of them closer to the representational philosophy of the era — the imbalance between sections would have been greater, since the combination of a high birth rate in French Canada and a heavy immigration of young adults into the upper province had created significantly different demographic profiles. However, a more important consolation prize was the hope of trading off the predominance of the upper province, within a legislature covering both the Canadas, in return for a measure of local autonomy within a bivalved federation. This consideration draws attention to the fundamental but usually under-stressed importance of the idea of a federation confined to the two Canadas as a central policy plank in the formation of the Great Coalition.

The politician most likely to be marooned by the rising tide of irresistible constitutional change was John A. Macdonald. The tendency to portray Confederation as the ideal solution to Canada's problems has obscured his nimble flexibility and impudent pertinacity in adjusting, surviving and ultimately triumphing between 1864 and 1867. As Hodgins has pointed out, 'John A. Macdonald entered the last parliament of the province of Canada, the one that was to make his name immortal, with only a remnant of supporters'.[101] Macdonald's principal title to a tenuous hold on power lay in his alliance with the solid block of Bleus from the lower province, plus his consequent ability to lure wayward Reformers with the bait of office. A shift of political power towards Upper Canada would devalue the relative strength of the Bleus while leaving him with little claim on the gratitude of his own section. It is sometimes argued that French Canada needed to bring the Maritimes into a union in order to counterbalance the power of Upper Canada. In reality, as some critics objected,[102] French Canada had no motive for uniting with any more English-speaking Protestants than was absolutely necessary. It was Macdonald who desperately needed Confederation. His talents of political management required a steady supply of 'loose fish' for the building and re-building of political alliances. Where better to go for loose fish than the Maritimes? The immediate background, then, to the negotiations which produced the Great Coalition in June 1864 was not one of immovable deadlock, but rather of a log-jam in which all three of the Lower Canada logs were about to remove the blockage by shifting position. For the English-speaking community in the lower province, outright representation by population would be the most attractive form of change, since they would remain securely under an English-speaking, commercially-oriented government.[103] The Rouges, condemned by the Church to minority status within Lower Canada, also had some incentive to prefer a province dominated by secular-minded Upper Canadians: Dorion talked of conceding at least a token additional seat and perhaps as many as half a dozen.[104] It was the Bleus, the majority group within Lower Canada, and the most tenacious in defence of the conservative culture of French Canada, who had the major interest in securing control over their local affairs by collaborating in restructuring the province in some form of federation.

One historian has effectively summarised the true implications of the events of June 1864. 'If Macdonald could not stem the tide of votes to reform and "rep. by pop.", his career would end,' concludes Desmond Morton. 'Cartier could now foresee a political battle his *Canadiens* could not win.' The logic of the situation pointed to talks between Macdonald and Brown. 'The bibulous opportunist and the self-righteous autocrat hated each other. They might also use each other.'[105] Although a detailed record of the negotiations has been in print since 1882,[106] by and large the Great Coalition has been portrayed as a ministry 'whose purpose would be to inaugurate discussions leading to a general confederation of all the British American provinces'.[107] In fact, the talks opened with Brown agreeing that British North American union was a good idea and one which 'would come about ere long, but it had not yet been thoroughly considered by the people; and ... there were so many parties to be consulted that its adoption was uncertain and remote'. He pressed instead for 'parliamentary reform, based on population, without regard to a separating line between Upper and Lower Canada', and fell back on federation of the two Canadas, with provision for subsequent extension to the whole of British North America.[108]

Some degree of selectivity is of course necessary in the writing of history if we are not to be drowned in the cacophony of past disputes, and it would be fair enough to eliminate Brown's initial doubts as a blind alley if the Great Coalition had indeed committed itself to the wider union and pursued it with single-minded unity. It did neither. After extensive negotiations, agreement was reached pledging the introduction of 'a measure next session for the purpose of remedying existing difficulties by introducing the federal principle into Canada, coupled with such provisions as will permit the Maritime Provinces and the North-West Territory to be incorporated into the same system of government'.[109] If these terms meant anything, Brown had trapped Macdonald, depriving him even of his celebrated weapon of procrastination. None the less, Creighton declared victory on behalf of his hero, John A. Macdonald, dismissing the 'verbal formula' as a sop to Brown's 'last vain attempt' to insist upon the federation of the two Canadas. Despite the 'alleged compromise', there was 'no doubt that the coalition would be committed to an immediate attempt to seek a general federation'.[110] So it was — but the key word was 'immediate'. Macdonald was staking everything on being able to persuade the Maritimes, more or less from a standing start, to join a continental union.

In the event, the massive gamble would come off, but Brown was never fully convinced of its feasibility, and the march down the road to Confederation can only be fully understood by taking account of the tempting availability of the alternative route of a purely Canadian federation. It was not that Brown was against Confederation. It was merely that he had not advanced much beyond his earlier position that it was unlikely to come about. 'We will be past caring for politics when that venture is finally achieved,' he had written in 1858.[111] Several historians have described the grand scene in the Assembly on 22 June 1864 when the new ministers announced that they had set aside their animosities to work for a fresh start in British North America. None appear to mention that Brown sounded oddly noncommittal for a Father of Confederation. He talked of it as a matter which the new ministry would study in detail and discuss with the Maritimers and with the imperial government. He modestly claimed that he was not ill-informed on political matters — he was, after all, proprietor of Upper Canada's mightiest newspaper — 'but I am free to confess that I am not so well informed as to all the bearings on the question of a union of all the British North American Provinces, that I could at once pronounce a final opinion on that question'.[112] It was a barely coded signal that he did not take the wider option very seriously. The *Globe* spelt out the message: 'Efforts are to be made to induce the Lower Provinces to join the confederation, but the success of the scheme, as far as Canada is concerned, is not to be contingent on their assent'.[113]

Brown made the position brutally clear at Halifax in September 1864, telling the Maritimers, 'we have not come here to seek relief from our troubles for remedy of our grievances is agreed upon and come what may of the larger scheme ... our smaller scheme will certainly be accomplished'.[114] 'Now is the time, or we may abandon the idea in despair,' Macdonald told the delegates at Quebec the following month, for 'if we come to no decision here, we Canadians must address ourselves to the alternative and reconstruct our Government. Once driven to that, it will be too late for a general federation.'[115] 'We are *not going to be tied to Lower Canada*, for twelve months more', Brown told Arthur Gordon.[116]

In the circumstances, it is hardly surprising that Macdonald was reported to be drinking heavily during the Quebec conference,[117] nor that he should testily refer to Tilley's electoral defeat as 'New Brunswick revolting against the Confederacy'.[118] Dorion was prompt to challenge the ministers to act on their promises after the setback in New Brunswick. 'The Administration could not give a pledge that they would carry the Confederation of all the provinces, but they could pledge, and did pledge themselves to bring in, in the event of the failure of that scheme, a measure for the federation of Upper and Lower Canada.'[119] Brown was unperturbed at the apparent collapse of Confederation. 'If it fails after all legitimate means have been used,' he wrote to his wife, 'we will go on with our scheme for Canada alone.'[120] When Taché's sudden death forced the reconstruction of the ministry in August 1865, Brown would only accept the notional presidency of Sir Narcisse Belleau on condition that the increasingly powerful Macdonald repeated the commitment to introduce the smaller federation, now in the session of 1866, 'should we be unable to remove the objections of the Maritime Provinces'.[121]

Further rifts appeared during a by-election campaign in October 1865, with the *Globe* insisting that Upper Canadian demands for reform be satisfied 'without waiting indefinitely for the accession of the Lower Provinces'.[122] When Brown resigned in December 1865, he trailed a thinly disguised offer of coalition to Cartier: 'if you stick to the compact you made with me when Sir Narcisse came into government ... you will have my best aid in carrying the constitutional changes we were then pledged to'.[123] As Creighton recognised, the phrase 'constitutional changes', rather than 'Confederation', was a 'pointed reminder of the agreement that, even if confederation failed, "justice" must be done to Upper Canada'.[124] Actually, the Confederation tide was already turning in the Maritimes, as Brown well knew from his recent visit, and his decision to resign over Galt's handling of Reciprocity negotiations in Washington may have been a temporary sacrifice designed to win friends in Nova Scotia and New Brunswick. Certainly his reported conversation with the Nova Scotian Liberal (and anti-Confederate) William Annand, in which Brown pleaded that it was 'too bad that at this period I should be obliged to throw myself into the hands of our opponents to carry this measure'[125] sounds like a politician seeking to build a post-Confederation alliance.

Neither Macdonald's need to involve the British nor the responses of New Brunswick and Nova Scotia can be fully understood without an appreciation of the continuing dual policy of the Great Coalition. Maritimers objected both to the take-it-or-leave-it attitude of the Canadians, and to the apparently cynical way in which the lower provinces were being used as a cover for the solution of purely Canadian problems. In a passionate denunciation of both Canadian politicians and their constitutional nostrum, the New Brunswick ministry complained in July 1865 of

> the eagerness with which they seek to force its immediate adoption upon unwilling communities, for they are well aware that, did the plan avowedly contemplate only the separation of the Canadas, it would be impossible even speciously to present it to the Imperial Government as in any manner a scheme of union. [126]

The New Brunswick critics, it will be argued, were right to perceive that British preferences played a part in swinging the balance between the smaller and the larger union.

***

There is, of course, another way of accounting for the events of the mid-1860s, and that is one which argues that Confederation happened because it met the needs of the time. Thus it may be claimed that only Confederation could bring the Intercolonial railway and its accompanying commercial benefits. Confederation alone could strengthen the defences of the provinces, in the face of Britain's imminent abandonment of its commitment to protect them against the United States. Only through a framework of wider union could the urgent task of westward expansion be undertaken. Confederation was an expression of and a step towards a new British North American nationality. Moreover, the arguments pointing to Confederation constituted in their totality, something greater than a mere shopping list of sectional priorities, for when melded together — both at the sordid level of political trade-off, and on the elevated plane of historical explanation — they fused together as the arch of Morton's cantilever. It is an attractive explanation, but one which is open to a good deal of doubt. [127]

The Intercolonial railway was in many ways the centrepiece of Confederation: certainly it is one of the few engineering projects ever to have been written into a country's constitution. [128] In the event, Confederation and the Intercolonial did become part of a package, but it was by no means necessary that this should be so. There is no scientific law which proves that communications projects linking different jurisdictions require political union. Canada had completed a railway into the United States in 1851, without seeking annexation to the Republic. Similarly, many New Brunswickers were keen to join their railway system but not their province to the United States. The provinces had rejected a British hint in 1862 to link the Intercolonial with Confederation.[129] Nor was Confederation necessary to secure British financial backing to borrow the capital required to build the line. The British government had agreed in principle to underwrite the loan in 1862. All that remained was for the provinces to agree on the terms of repayment, and for parliament at Westminster to pass the validating legislation. The colonial secretary, Edward Cardwell, brilliantly played a weak hand when it became clear that parliament might prove uncooperative, implying that Confederation was the price the provinces must pay to secure confirmation of the promise, but George Brown was on firm ground in assuring the Canadian Assembly in 1865 that 'the money has already been found for the Intercolonial Railway', for the British offer of a guarantee meant that 'the money is ready at a very low rate of interest, whenever required'. Consequently, Henri Joly was able to give a resounding negative to the question, 'is Confederation necessary in order that we may build the Intercolonial railway?'.[130] Since the British offer of a guarantee had a time limit which would expire in 1867, it is equally plausible to argue that a bid for Confederation in the mid-1860s was an unnecessary complication.

The commercial case for the Intercolonial was twofold: first, it would provide a winter outlet for Canadian exports to Britain independent of the United States, and secondly that it would stimulate interprovincial trade. So far as the Maritimes were concerned, the prospect of capturing Canada's export trade did little to make the project attractive to the region as a whole. 'In New Brunswick,' Tilley confessed, 'they say: all the trade is to be carried away from that Province towards Halifax.'[131] This was one reason why Saint John was lukewarm towards Confederation, and indeed throughout New Brunswick, as Tilley found to his cost in the 1865 election campaign, there were votes to be lost as well as votes to be won over the actual route of the railway. 'Mr Tilley, will you stop your puffing and blowing and tell us which way the railway is going?'[132]

Nor was the argument for an additional outlet to the ocean particularly attractive to Upper Canadians. Tilley had found 'a strong feeling against the Railway' in 1863, 'because they have two outlets in winter, New York and Portland, and a third in summer by the St. Lawrence'.[133] Canadian exports to Britain mainly consisted of low-value bulk commodities, chiefly timber, flour and grain. It was far more likely that these would be carried by water than by rail. The Toronto merchant William McMaster pointed out that Upper Canada millers were already reluctant to use the much shorter American lines during winter because railway freight charges were 'so expensive that they find it to be for their advantage to pay interest, storage and insurance on their wheat and flour until the opening of the navigation'.[134] Opponents of Confederation argued that a barrel of flour shipped over a thousand miles from Toronto to Halifax 'would be nearly eaten up in expenses'.[135] It is true that James Ferrier warned the Canadian Assembly that the existing lines through the United States were seriously congested, but we should not overlook the fact that Ferrier was a director of the Grand Trunk.[136] Even Galt had openly admitted in 1858 that he did not 'for a moment pretend to say that Canada would use the Intercolonial Railway for her trade while shorter and cheaper lines exist'. It would only become an acceptable outlet — although still an inconvenient one — 'if at any time a different trade policy were to be adopted by the United States or war were to break out'.[137] John A. Macdonald was equally blunt in telling the citizens of Halifax in 1864 that the Intercolonial 'would be of comparatively little commercial advantage to the people of Canada. Whilst we have the St. Lawrence in Summer, and the American ports in time of peace, we have all that is requisite for our purposes'.[138] By 1864, as will be argued, it was unlikely that the Intercolonial would be of any use at all in time of war with the United States.

It seemed to many even less likely that any extensive internal trade would develop between the province of Canada and the Maritimes. Lower used bold metaphor to portray the Maritimes at a crossroads of economic destiny. 'Oceanic forces towed the Maritime colonies out to sea; continental forces split them in two.' In fact, continental forces from the St Lawrence valley were too weak even to chip the Maritimes. As a Saint John newspaper put it, 'the Canadians are a people with whom we have little or no trade'.[139] Nor was any likely to develop, simply because the two sections produced the same staples. 'Let us not ... be lulled with fancies of the great commercial advantages we shall derive from a Confederation of these provinces,' warned Eric Dorion. 'With regard to timber,' said Henri Joly, 'the Gulf provinces have no more need of ours, than we have of theirs.'[140] When George Brown told the Assembly that 'the addition of nearly a million of people to our home consumers' was an overwhelming argument for Confederation in itself, he may have been aiming merely to make the roof resound.[141]

Even if there was a mutual commerce to develop, it did not require political union. 'What hinders us from having free trade with the Gulf Provinces?', asked Henri Joly.[142] This may have been an embarrassing challenge for those Fathers of Confederation who had been members of the previous ministry, formed in March 1864, which had pledged itself to the pursuit of intercolonial free trade without a whisper of an idea of political union. Indeed, Morton was so perplexed at the failure of any grand policy initiative to emerge from the ministerial negotiations of March 1864 that he consoled himself by describing the aims of the short-lived government as 'a program containing all the elements of a federal union but union itself'.[143] Morton had failed to catch the expressive meaning of silence: as recently as March 1864, nobody seemed to think it necessary to go for Confederation in order to secure intercolonial free trade. Independently of the movement for Confederation, the provinces began to co-operate on commercial matters through the Confederate Council on Trade.[144] A charitable verdict on the virtual invisibility of this intercolonial body in most historical studies of the period might be that its existence was unimportant. An uncharitable verdict might suggest that its existence was inconvenient to an explanatory package predicated on the overwhelming necessity of political union to secure all good things.

While intercolonial free trade and political union were not inextricably linked, there was a necessary connection between Confederation and a common external tariff. For high tariff Canada, Confederation would actually mean a reduction in customs duties to appease the free-trading Nova Scotians — a step devoutly wished by the British[145] — although when the compromise rate was imposed in Nova Scotia at the end of 1867 it was still onerous enough to increase popular feeling against Confederation to fever pitch.[146] The tariff question had two important implications, neither of which strengthened the arguments for Confederation. First, at a time when money was being 'scattered on all sides in handfuls'[147] to win support for the scheme, the largest province was actually about to reduce its chief source of revenue. This provoked fears both in Canada and especially in the Maritimes that political union would have to be paid for by direct taxation — taxes either on property or on goods and services — something which a visiting journalist disapprovingly noted was regarded by 'the British colonies generally throughout North America ... as the greatest evil which can befall a community'.[148] Conversely, the smaller provinces faced the prospect of paying more in import duties but losing all control over the way in which they would be spent. The Maritime provinces derived the majority of their revenue from customs duties. Thus when George Coles objected at Quebec that if Prince Edward Island surrendered control over customs to a central government, 'she would have no revenue left to carry on the business of the Province', he was stating a simple fact and should be acquitted of the charge of adopting 'the obstructionist tactics which were to characterize the Island's attitude' during the Quebec conference.[149]

The combination of large-scale expenditure commitments with a planned reduction in the major source of revenue hardly squares with the claim that political union would enable the provinces to establish a stronger credit base and so attract new investment. 'We cannot borrow without telling tales of our condition, resources and expectations, that will in the end be found out to be lies,' warned Christopher Dunkin.[150] Furthermore, while the new Dominion tariff was sufficiently burdensome to stimulate secessionist feeling in Nova Scotia, it was not in itself explicitly protectionist. In the long sweep of hindsight, Creighton may have been right in concluding that in 1879, that is, twelve years after Confederation, 'the Dominion of Canada completed its programme of national unification with the National Policy of Protection',[151] but it would be misleading to assume that Confederation was intended to create a closed national market in 1867. Even if a fortress British North America had been planned in trade terms, the Maritimes could hardly have offered rich pickings. George Brown made the best of it: Confederation, he told the Canadian Assembly, would 'give us the control of a market of four millions of people', but his own newspaper inconveniently pointed out that 'in a British North American Federation ... about four-fifths of the people would be Canadians'.[152] As consumers, the half-million people of the Maritimes barely qualified as a substitute for Reciprocity with the 31 million people of the United States.

Central Canadian manufacturers did indeed make inroads into the Maritime market by the early 1870s,[153] but this represented only a tiny fragment of total British North American trade — certainly not enough to be regarded as a pivotal factor in the creation of Confederation. For instance, in 1861, the total value of agricultural equipment manufactured in the province of Canada just exceeded $400000 — equal to less than 1 per cent of the province's $42 million export trade, which was overwhelmingly made up of primary produce. Even in 1871, Ontario remained largely rural: its largest city, Toronto, had only 56000 people out of a provincial total of 1.6 million.[154] The Intercolonial railway, which was not completed until 1876, was only one factor encouraging the development of trade within the new Dominion. Most goods were shipped by Gulf steamer to Pictou, using rail freight merely for local distribution.[155] By 1878, the Intercolonial had cost a staggering $36 million. In 1881, it managed to break even on its operating costs for the first time.[156] Given the troubles of the Grand Trunk in the years preceding Confederation, it would be hard to conclude that the problems of the Intercolonial came as any great surprise. At the time of the *Trent* crisis, *The Times* had wondered why the Grand Trunk had not been connected to Halifax 'by a branch line', showing a typical metropolitan inability to grasp the sheer scale of British North America. Its answer, however, was sound: the cost would be 'exceedingly large' and 'far in advance' of actual needs. 'We need not say what has been the fate even of the Grand Trunk line, and the Halifax line would have even fewer chances of success. In short, the railway must have been constructed principally, if not solely, against the contingencies of war, and principally at the public expense.[157]

By the 1860s, the 'contingencies of war' had become a highly convenient argument to secure the public funding without which the commercially marginal Intercolonial was unlikely to be built. While it is hard to see how a railway which was not completed until 1876 could be presented a decade earlier as an insurance against the threat of imminent invasion from the United States, it was none the less argued that the Intercolonial would make possible the despatch of British reinforcements to the interior of Canada in the event of an impending conflict with the United States. This notion was riddled with implausibilities, and was much derided by the critics of Confederation. Even if British troops could cross the Atlantic in time to be of use — the quickest reinforcements during the *Trent* crisis had arrived four weeks after news of the incident had reached London[158] — it was 'ridiculous' to imagine that the Americans would sit by while convoys of potentially hostile troops lumbered along hundreds of miles of railway line close enough to their own border to be sabotaged. The New Brunswick stretch of the Intercolonial might be diverted away from the United States frontier, but once it got into Lower Canada, it would have to pass through a narrow corridor of British territory on the south shore of the St Lawrence, little more than twenty miles from the state of Maine. As Dorion pointed out, 'a railway lying in some places not more than fifteen or twenty miles from the frontier, will be of no use whatever, because of the readiness with which it may be attacked and seized.' Far from being a lifeline, the railway would be a 'trap' which would require another army to defend it.[159] According to the journalist, W.H. Russell, the Grand Trunk itself ran some stretches so close to the border that 'trains could be fired upon from American territory!'.[160] To cap it all, any route through northern New Brunswick and eastern Lower Canada would have to cross an inhospitable terrain which had one of the highest rates of snowfall in British North America. Robert Lowe claimed that 'owing to the severity of the climate and the desolate regions through which it passes', the Intercolonial 'must be closed during a large portion of the year, and yet this is the line ... to be constructed especially to enable troops to be brought up from Halifax to Quebec, when the St. Lawrence is closed!'.[161] In the Canadian Assembly, James Biggar was even more comprehensive in dismissing the project. 'Looking at it from a military point of view, it is well known that part of the proposed line would run within twenty-six miles of the American frontier, and that any communication could be cut off at any moment by an American army; and that as a commercial undertaking it could never compete with the water route during the season of navigation; and in winter it would be comparatively useless on account of the depth of snow.'[162]

What of the wider argument that Confederation would add to the defence of British North America? 'It was a natural impression,' Goldwin Smith later wrote, 'although some saw through the fallacy at the time, that the political union of the Provinces would add greatly to their force in war.'[163] Indeed, this equation was ruthlessly exploited to bolster the arguments for Confederation. 'Look around you to the valley of Virginia,' McGee cried to those who doubted the necessity for union, 'look around you to the mountains of Georgia, and you will find reasons as thick as blackberries'.[164]

For perhaps the classic attempt to establish a logical interconnection between Confederation and defence, it is necessary to turn to the often-quoted memorandum drafted by Britain's chancellor of the exchequer, W.E. Gladstone, on 12 July 1864. Gladstone was opposed to expenditure on a programme of fortifications in Canada, arguing that no effort by Britain could defend the provinces against the overwhelming force of the United States. In fact, 'nothing can defend them except the desperate energy of a brave, self-relying population, which fights for hearth and home'. British North America should be 'detached, as to their defensive not less than their administrative responsibilities, from England', in order that the Americans would cease to see the provinces as a threat. Consequently, 'the true aim of all our measures at this important juncture should be to bring the people of the British North American Colonies ... as nearly to a national sentiment and position as their relation to the British Crown will permit.' Far from spending money on fortifications, 'efforts should be made, without delay, to ascertain whether it is practicable to establish a Federation or Political Union of these Colonies'.[165]

Read out of context, Gladstone's arguments proved — to Creighton at least — 'the essential connection between Canadian defence and British American reorganization'.[166] Unfortunately, the context spoils the picture. First, Gladstone was by no means typical of British opinion, and certainly not of government opinion, in his wish to evade responsibility for the protection of the provinces, however terrifying might be the prospect of a war in their defence. Secondly, his memorandum was written not in the abstract, but in the light of news published in the London press the previous day of the formation of a Canadian ministry pledged to attempt some form of union.[167] It was not intellectual deduction but arithmetical subtraction that inspired Gladstone's argument: he was dedicated to economy and grasped at any straw to oppose expenditure, especially in a province which he neither understood nor viewed with much favour.

Macdonald claimed that one of 'the great advantages of Confederation is, that we shall have a united, a concerted, and uniform system of defence',[168] but opponents pointed out that there was no necessary connection. 'We do not need Confederation to give us that unity which is indispensable in all military operations — unity of headship,' argued Henri Joly. 'A commander-in-chief will direct the defence of all our provinces.'[169] Even the Duke of Newcastle, a colonial secretary very sympathetic to Confederation, had concluded in 1862 that 'none of the objections which oppose it seem to impede a union for defence'.[170] As for Gladstone's vision of British North Americans desperately fighting for hearth and home, few notions aroused so much hostility in the various colonies as the fear that their forces would be marched off to fight somewhere else — especially in the Atlantic provinces, where the Militia Bill episode of 1862 created a belief that they would be expected to shoulder the responsibility which Canadians themselves had shirked.[171] In Prince Edward Island, there were fears that the militia would be 'drafted for slaughter' in defence of Upper Canada,[172] while in Newfoundland, Charles Fox Bennett pictured the island's youth 'leaving their bones to bleach in a foreign land', a phrase he was to refine in the 1869 election campaign to a celebrated reference to 'the desert sands of Canada'.[173]

Opponents of Confederation pointed out that no change in the system of government could alter the basic fact that three million British North Americans would face ten times as many Americans should war break out. 'With Confederation, neither the number of men in the several provinces, nor the pecuniary resources now at their disposal, will be increased.'[174] John S. Sanborn could not understand how 'the people of New Brunswick could be expected to come up to Canada to defend us, and leave their own frontier unprotected'. It was far more likely, said Dorion, that Canadians would have to go down and defend New Brunswick against invasion from New England. As one Fredericton paper put it, in or out of Confederation, New Brunswick could no more resist an American invasion than a fish could walk up a beanpole.[175] Since it was 'generally admitted' that neither Canada nor the Maritimes could resist an American invasion, James O'Halloran asked how it could be denied that 'by adding the frontier of the Lower Provinces to that of Canada, and by adding the force of those provinces to our own, there will not be the same defencelessness as at present?'.[176] Joining with the Maritimes, said another, 'was like tying a small twine at the end of a long rope and saying it strengthened the whole line'.[177] The young Wilfrid Laurier described the claim that Confederation would provide a defence against the United States as like being 'armed with an egg-shell to stop a bullet'.[178]

It is hard to believe that the Fathers of Confederation took their own arguments very seriously. 'The British Provinces, separated as at present, could not defend themselves alone,' said Cartier, 'and the question resolved itself into this: shall the whole strength of the empire be concentrated into Prince Edward Island, or Canada, as the case may be, in the event of a war with the United States — or shall the provinces be left to fight single-handed, disunited?'[179] There is something comical in the notion of the entire military strength of British North America defying an American invasion from the strongpoint of Prince Edward Island. Henri Joly sardonically suggested that the Americans be offered free transportation for their armies on the Grand Trunk Railway, on condition that they agreed only to attack British North America in one place at a time.[180] James O'Halloran suggested that Newfoundland and Prince Edward Island be towed up and sunk in Lake Ontario to create a more compact and defensible British North America.[181]

There is reason to suspect that the Fathers of Confederation played the defence card in the hope of gaining support for Confederation by discrediting their opponents. They were not seriously worried that Britain would desert its North American provinces, and except for a few brief war scares — one of which conveniently coincided with the setback of the New Brunswick election of 1865 — they did not really expect an attack by the United States. At Halifax in 1864, Macdonald spoke of 'forming an effective body of militia, so that we shall be able to say to England, that if she should send her arms to our rescue, at a time of peril, she would be assisted by a well disciplined body of men'.[182] 'When we had organized our grand defensive force, and united for mutual protection' said Cartier, 'England would send freely here both men and treasure for our defence.'[183] Although, in his mid-winter mission to London, George Brown privately reported 'a manifest desire in almost every quarter that, ere long, the British American colonies should shift for themselves',[184] none the less he felt able to assure the Canadian Assembly soon afterwards that he had not met 'one public man, of any stripe of politics, who did not heartily declare that, in case of the invasion of Canada, the honor of Great Britain would be at stake, and the whole strength of the Empire would be unhesitatingly marshalled in our defence'.[185]

Brown was right. Confederation did nothing to reduce Britain's commitment to the defence of the provinces. 'There is not a foot of territory in all these hundreds of thousands of square miles which would become less English than now, so long as the Queen's representative is head of the Federation,' objected Nova Scotia's governor, Sir Richard MacDonnell, 'nor is there any obligation in regard to these Provinces which now devolves upon Britain that would be diminished by their being thus huddled together into one heterogeneous assemblage.'[186] The prime minister, Lord Palmerston, refused even to discuss 'whether our North American provinces are to be fought for or abandoned'.[187] The foreign secretary, Lord Russell, advised the British minister in Washington in 1864, that if the Americans had any thoughts of annexing the provinces, 'they must look to a fight with us'.[188] It was not that the British sought a quarrel with the United States. When Seward, soon to become Lincoln's secretary of state, told the Duke of Newcastle in 1860 that Britain would never go to war for Canada, he received a sharp warning. 'Do not remain under such an error. There is no people under Heaven from whom we should endure so much as from yours.... But once touch us in our honour and you will soon find the bricks of New York and Boston falling about your heads.'[189]

Sir Frederic Rogers, of the Colonial Office, felt that 'nothing can be more provoking than to be obliged (if we are obliged) to fight the United States in the place and manner which are most disadvantageous to ourselves, for a colony which is no good to us and has no real care for us'. Yet Rogers did not wish his country to duck its responsibility to fight for Canada, 'for England would not be great, courageous, successful England if she did'.[190] Even the politicians sometimes identified as closet separatists recognised the reality of the British commitment to defend the provinces. 'If

Canada desires to be British, and to fight for British connection as men fight for their country', Gladstone wrote in 1865, 'I do not think we can shrink from the duty of helping her.'[191] This is not to deny that many British observers, looking to the far future, expected that the tie would gradually be modified and eventually might disappear altogether. Hence *The Times* could greet the Quebec scheme with the prediction that 'it may be that such a Government will be only a state of transition, marking the passage of British America from colonial tutelage to national independence'. Yet it was surely cavalier of Creighton to omit the first seven words of that quotation and so portray the sentiment as one of firm prediction that the provinces would soon break away.[192] As late as 1879, the foreign secretary, Lord Salisbury, could refer to the 'solid and palpable fact that if they are attacked England must defend them'.[193]

What was at issue was not *whether* Britain would defend the provinces, but *how*. The Crimean War of 1854-6 had demonstrated that the British army was ill-organised to fight as an expeditionary force far from its home base. It had also accelerated the process of reducing the size of British garrisons in British North America: the admittedly acerbic Lord Grey told the 1861 parliamentary enquiry into colonial defence that the main function of the peacetime garrisons at Kingston, Quebec and Halifax was to prevent vandalism.[194] 'He who attacks Canada declares war against England, and will call down on himself all the might of England', *The Times* pronounced in 1861, adding, 'but in the matter of her own fields and cities Canada's duty is to defend herself'. Four years later, the message was reiterated in still bleaker form: 'Canada can best be defended by attacking her assailants and forcing them to relinquish their hold.'[195]

The British were determined not to be trapped into a war of attrition in the interior of Canada. By 1865, British defence experts favoured withdrawal to a few heavily fortified bases, concentrated at Halifax, Quebec and Montreal, and retaliating against any American invasion by blockading and shelling the seaboard cities of the United States. Hence Newcastle's warning to Seward that the bricks of New York and Boston would fall about his head. In such a conflict, Britain would lose one-eighth of its export market, run the risk of massive social distress in Lancashire, which depended on American cotton, of insurrection in Ireland and of opportunistic attacks on its interests elsewhere in the world. An Anglo-American war was almost unthinkable — almost. 'I have a horror of war and of all wars one with the United States because none would be so prejudicial to our interests,' wrote Lord Clarendon at the time of the *Trent* crisis, 'but peace like other good things may be bought too dearly and it can never be worth the price of national honour.'[196] The horror of such a war was itself a deterrent. 'The injury to our own trade of burning New York & Boston would be so serious that we ought to be nearly as reluctant to do it as to destroy Liverpool & Bristol,' wrote Newcastle not long after his confrontation with Seward, 'but they know we must do it if they declare war and what would be injury to ourselves would be ruin to them.'[197] Hence the predominant confidence among provincial leaders that the Americans would not in the last resort go to war. As George Brown assured the Canadian Assembly, 'such a war as one with England would certainly be, is the last they are likely to provoke'.[198] Even Creighton had to admit that in the Colonial Office memoranda of 1864, 'there was no connection drawn between federation and defence, and no suggestion made that the former would promote the effectiveness of the latter'.[199] Lord Monck's niece was probably unconsciously reflecting the way the two questions initially ran in parallel when she wrote that 1864 was 'an interesting year to be in Canada, between the Confederation business and seeing whether Canada is able and willing to defend herself, or rather to be *on the alert* in case of danger'.[200] It was only in 1865, as Confederation ran into trouble, that its proponents sought to fuse the two together.

What, then, are we to make of the frequent invocations of 'a new nationality' to be created in British North America as a result of Confederation? The sentiment was too often expressed and too loudly cheered to entitle any historian to dismiss it as inconvenient froth, even though James O'Halloran grumbled at 'cleverly drawn abstractions and sophistries — such as new nationalities — union is strength — a great empire'.[201] Joseph Howe thought it irresponsible: 'every young fellow who has had a taste of the license of camp life in the United States' would be tempted to 'have a fling' at 'this guy of a "new nationality"'.[202] 'Nationality' evidently did not mean 'nation-state', but rather equality with England, Scotland and Ireland — hence the hankering for the style 'kingdom'. The desire for status was evident in Cartier's confident prediction that a united British North America 'will have to be erected into a Vice-Royalty, and we may expect that a member of the Royal Family will be sent here as the head'.[203]

At its simplest level, references to a 'new nationality' may simply have been a pre-emptive rhetorical strike against the objection that British North America contained too great a diversity of cultural and national groups to work effectively as a union. 'Objection has been taken to the scheme ... because of the words "new nationality",' Cartier admitted, explaining away the reference by claiming it merely meant that 'when we were united, we would form a political nationality with which neither the national origin, nor the religion of any individual would interfere'.[204] Taché neatly combined the appeal to a future common identity with ethnic stereotypes, which hugely entertained the diners at a banquet in Quebec, and were recorded by a journalist in the third-person form which was the conventional method of press reporting at the time. Taché looked to 'a fraternal era' in which 'the cool-headed and persevering Englishman might be drawn closer to the warm-hearted and generous Irishman, to the keen, persevering and economical [laughter] — they should reserve their laughter as he had not finished the sentence — the persevering and economical son of Caledonia, and the gay and chivalric offspring of old Gaul,' all of them 'blended together in one grand people'.[205] Such sentiments were regularly received with 'Enthusiastic cheering', but so too were those which firmly repudiated any wish to loosen British North America's tie either with Britain or with the Crown. Hence John A. Macdonald's loudly cheered peroration, challenging the Canadian Assembly 'to embrace the happy opportunity now offered of founding a great nation under the fostering care of Great Britain, and our sovereign lady, Queen Victoria'.[206] Yet to some, the term was plainly irrelevant. 'I cannot see that the Federation of these provinces has anything of a national phase in it,' concluded Thomas Scatcherd. 'When you speak of national existence, you speak of independence; and so long as we are colonists of Great Britain we can have no national existence.'[207] It was a phrase which made the roof resound, for Confederation as new nationality was vastly more inspiring than Confederation as hotchpotch.

The appeal to 'nationality' was also a useful rhetorical device in presenting what might otherwise seem the ramshackle marriage of unequal stranger provinces as part of the spirit of the age. 'Why is one policy to be established for Italy and Germany and another for the Provinces of British North America?', Cardwell challenged in the House of Commons.[208] Cardwell was a disciple of Peel, and was here surely acting on his master's dictum of stating a case in as many different ways as possible. A recent analysis by a team of political scientists has examined such matters as trade relations within the provinces, the degree of integration of élites and the extent of newspaper coverage of each others' affairs, to reach the conclusion that 'Canada must be viewed essentially as a political unit that had become amalgamated without necessarily achieving integration'. Another way of putting it might be to say that John A. Macdonald was not Bismarck (and the application of the nickname to Peter Mitchell is testimony mainly to the verbal ferocity of New Brunswick politics).[209] 'The authors of Confederation once appealed to the spirit of nationality,' the impatient young men of Canada First would complain a decade later. 'Now some of them tell us that their object was limited and they set the forest on fire only to boil their own pot.'[210] Even a quarter of a century after Confederation, the wily Macdonald sensed the electoral advantage of insisting that he intended to die a British subject.

The belief that Confederation was necessary for westward expansion seems largely based on the misleading mythology of deadlock: Lower Canadian politicians 'knew that annexation of the West would end forever the equality that then existed, and since they were half the power of the House ... annexation of the West to the United Province of Canada was simply impossible'.[211] In fact, the Lower Canadian metropolis of Montreal had interests in the West too, as Cartier showed in the alacrity with which he welcomed the British Columbians in 1870. If it is accepted that representation by population was actually on its way, then there would soon be no political barrier — only financial ones — to prevent the incorporation into Canada of some portion of the western territories, as had been envisaged by the British parliamentary enquiry of 1857. Under those circumstances, the Canadian government could have prepared to take responsibility for the small but turbulent community at the Red River free from the preoccupations of Nova Scotian discontent which arguably distracted its attention with unhappy results in 1868-9.

The fact that the Fathers of Confederation contemplated any form of westward expansion tends to confirm the suspicion that they did not seriously expect a desperate war for survival against the United

States, however much they may reasonably have feared that the existing vacuum of real authority in the heart of the continent represented a threat to stability. Critics asked how provinces which feared their inability to defend a frontier fifteen hundred miles long, could possibly take on one of four thousand miles, embracing an area 'as great as the continent of Europe'.[212] Dorion thought it 'a burlesque to speak as a means of defence of a scheme of a Confederation to unite the whole country extending from Newfoundland to Vancouver's Island, thousands of miles intervening without any communication'.[213] In fact, the Fathers of Confederation did not intend to rush westward. Resolution 69 of the Quebec scheme merely promised that improvements in communications with the North-West would 'be prosecuted at the earliest possible period that the state of the Finances will permit',[214] a formula which one critic sourly interpreted as meaning that the region was 'hermetically sealed'.[215] George Brown was pushing Toronto's interests in the prairies, but he described the a proposal for the eventual admission of British Columbia to Confederation as 'rather an extreme proposition'.[216] Macdonald affected to doubt even the value of the prairies, claiming in 1865 that the West was 'of no present value to Canada', for the province had 'unoccupied land enough to absorb the immigration for many years'.[217] Allowance must be made for the fact that he was writing to Watkin, who had a major interest in the Hudson's Bay Company, from which Canada would have to buy those western lands, yet subsequent history would bear him out: as late as 1891, 60 per cent of the two million people of Ontario lived on farms. This is not to deny that there was 'a sense of spatial limitation'[218] impending in Upper Canada from the mid-1850s, when the last cultivable wild lands were auctioned, but the notion that the whole province was bursting at the seams and ready to explode westwards is exaggerated, as the subsequent slow development of Manitoba confirmed.

If westward expansion was not envisaged as a major immediate task for the new Dominion, what becomes of the argument that it was 'traded off' against other demands in the Confederation package? In February 1864, C.J. Brydges, manager of the Grand Trunk, thought he had convinced Brown 'that nothing could be done about the Northwest without the Intercolonial', preferably as part of a more general political deal.[219] At first sight, this was a classic example of what was supposed to be wrong with the old system where, as the thoughtful London journal, the *Saturday Review*, had complained 'every local job which was ever perpetrated in the interest of one division of the nominally united colony (and there have been an abundance of such transactions) had to be balanced by a corresponding piece of extravagance for the benefit of the other'.[220] In fact, the Quebec resolutions placed the Intercolonial firmly before the West, promising action on the former 'without delay' while vaguely consigning the latter to a more prosperous future. According to Morton, Brown and his supporters wanted to build a Pacific railway, but Lower Canada and the Atlantic provinces would not agree to this unless it was 'matched by the building of the Intercolonial'.[221]

The truth was far more complex, too complicated for a simple bargain of the kind Morton imagined. Brown was identified by some with a railway to the Pacific,[222] but the *Globe* would subsequently pour scorn on the promise to rush a line across the continent. Toronto's interest in the West had been stimulated by the completion, late in 1855, of a railway to Georgian Bay, with the inviting prospect of access, via the Lakehead, to the prairies.[223] Hence the Quebec resolutions spoke not of a railway but vaguely of improvements in communications, which might include canal locks and wagon roads. Edward Watkin was an enthusiast for a transcontinental railway, but the logic of the Grand Trunk's orientation — west-south-west deep into the extremities of Upper Canada — pointed to an extension which would reach the Hudson's Bay territories by way of Chicago and the American Midwest. In 1872, Brydges flatly refused to tender for the Pacific contract, insisting 'that railways from Fort Garry around the north shore of Lake Superior and Lake Nipissing could not be built except at a frightful cost, when built could not be worked successfully in winter, and if it could be worked would have no traffic to carry upon it'.[224] If anything, the Grand Trunk sought extension in both directions, which is a very narcissistic form of trade-off. The route eventually selected for the Canadian Pacific actually suited Montreal interests most of all, by funnelling traffic into the Ottawa valley.

The other half of the trade-off is also open to question. One argument for the Intercolonial — though certainly an exaggerated one — was that it would provide an additional outlet for Upper Canadian trade, in which case Upper Canada was very smartly trading off something which Upper Canada wanted. Nor was Lower Canada united in a desire to see the Intercolonial built. Tilley had found in 1863 that the Intercolonial was unpopular in Lower Canada precisely because many French Canadians feared that its construction would 'lead to the Union of the Provinces, and the destruction of their power and influence'.[225] One of the most fundamental logical weaknesses of the whole approach of the interlocking package is that it assumes that controversial projects may be made more palatable by being paired with other controversial projects. This is not necessarily the case. Moreover, one section's gain might be seen as another's loss. Macdonald flatly announced in Halifax that 'as a commercial enterprise', the Intercolonial would be of little value to Canada, in order to stress to the Nova Scotians that so far as the Canadians were concerned, the railway 'can only be built as a means of political union for the Colonies'.[226] This in turn meant that its costs would fall generally on the taxpayers of British North America, three-quarters of whom lived in the existing province of Canada. Thus Canada, which had undertaken to meet five-twelfths of the cost of the project in 1862, would actually shoulder roughly double its earlier share. Galt rightly told the Maritimers that they would have 'the best of the bargain', but the admission did not make the project any the more popular among its critics in Canada itself.[227]

Much the same may be said of the argument that French Canadians accepted the predominance of Upper Canada only on condition that the Maritimes joined 'to club with the weaker combatant to resist the big fighter'.[228] It is unlikely that this argument could have been particularly attractive to Maritimers,[229] nor does it seem to have struck deep roots in French Canada, and for good reason.[230] First, French Canadians were not in a strong position to make terms. Secondly, what they needed for cultural and political survival was a guarantee of autonomy within their own unit of a federal system. As Joseph Cauchon admitted, a federation of the two Canadas could have proved just as effective in this as the wider union.[231] The problem was that it was Confederation which the politicians ensured was actually on offer. As Dorion insisted, it was not a true confederation in the sense of entrenching local autonomy: John A. Macdonald actually hoped that the provinces would wither away and become 'absorbed in the General Power' although, as he hastened to add 'it does not do to adopt that point of view in discussing the subject in Lower Canada'.[232] New Brunswick and Nova Scotia were predominantly anglophone and Protestant provinces: Archbishop Connolly pungently insisted that Nova Scotia had the most anti-Catholic school laws in the world, while New Brunswick schools would spark one of the first constitutional rows in the new Dominion.[233] As good politicians, Cartier and Taché followed Peel's dictum, and sought to present their case in as many ways as possible to appeal to as many viewpoints as possible. Yet it was not really very convincing to argue that French Canada should link its fortunes to those of any more English-speaking Protestants than was absolutely necessary: 'we shall have forty-eight members in the Federal Parliament against one hundred and forty of English origin,' warned one Rouge. 'What could so weak a minority do to obtain justice?'[234]

The interlocking argument for Confederation existed, if at all, because the proponents of Confederation said it existed. When at the Quebec conference, R.B. Dickey of Nova Scotia mildly suggested that the provinces might 'have those advantages we look for without legislative and administrative arrangements', he was simply ignored.[235] Similarly, an expression of hope by the Chairman of the Quebec Board of Trade 'that if we did not obtain a political union, we should at least have a commercial union' was firmly squashed by Charles Tupper. 'I fail myself to understand how the commercial union ... is ever to be realized, except in connection with a political union.'[236]

In effect, most historians have asked 'why did British North America adopt Confederation as the answer to the problems of the mid-1860s?'. Once it is assumed that Confederation was embraced as a logical deduction from contemporary circumstances, the task of explanation seems relatively straightforward: it is merely necessary to identify the challenges facing the provinces, note how supporters of Confederation argued that it would solve those problems, and deduce from the fact they carried the day that a satisfying explanatory package may be distilled from their evidence. In many respects, Confederation was not the most obvious answer to the continental challenges of 1864. Indeed, if the overwhelming priorities were the need to secure a larger market, better communications and to put an end to the threat of American invasion, the obvious solution — certainly by 1865 — would have been to seek annexation to the United States. Even if the provinces had preferred union among themselves, the logic of overwhelming American economic and military power pointed to Confederation on United States terms, under United States protection. Indeed, Joseph Howe feared that such would eventually be 'the hard terms of its recognition as a separate but not independent state'.[237] In seeking to account for the union of British North America, we should remember that it was a union of British North America as part of the British empire. It might be argued that the mid-1860s was a very unwise moment at which to risk provoking American opinion with talk of a new, British, monarchical nationality on the northern flank of the United States.[238]

The question needs to be re-phrased to ask instead: 'why was it *Confederation* and not some other solution which dominated the British North American response to the challenges of the mid-1860s?'. This formulation inverts the relationship between the problems and the answer, asking instead why an idea which was not an immediately obvious solution came to dominate discussion of the future. It may be placed alongside a similar inversion of a standard question recently posed in an important re-interpretation of the response of Maritimers to Confederation, which asks 'not why were so many Maritimers opposed to Confederation but why so many of them agreed so easily to a scheme of union that was clearly designed by Canadians to meet Canadian needs and to ensure Canadian dominance'.[239] This approach focuses attention on 'the long years of germination of the idea of British North American union'.[240] It also requires clarification of the role of the British, who were more than benign spectators but less than imperial Caesars.

***

The politics of Canada's Great Coalition can only be understood in terms not simply of the duality of its policy aims, but of Macdonald's almost desperate need to keep alive the option of the union of all the provinces rather than be forced into taking action to create a purely Canadian federation. In this, the British factor was vital. At the very least, involving the British would give Macdonald the precious gain of time: communications were slow, and so too were the processes of contemporary government. There was too the added bonus that the British were virtually united in their enthusiasm for uniting all — or as many as possible — of their North American provinces. Whether that enthusiasm would translate into the historians' reified shorthand of 'pressure' was another matter. However, there was one crucial role which rested with the British, and the British alone, and that was legislation.

In 1872, Macdonald offered his own explanation for his success in outwitting George Brown. 'The great reason why I have always been able to beat Brown is that I have been able to look a little ahead, while he could on no occasion forego the temptation of a temporary triumph.'[241] John Willison put it in slightly different terms. 'Brown had the temper of an agitator and the outlook of a reformer. Macdonald had genius for government.'[242] In terms of Canadian politics and the negotiations of June 1864, Brown had out-manoeuvred Macdonald: if Confederation faltered, legislation would be introduced the following session to re-structure the province of Canada on federal lines. The *Globe* was firm in announcing that 'Parliament will ... be asked to carry out the principle as regards this Province, while those who are beyond the control of the Canadian Parliament will be taken in whenever they are willing to come'.[243] The context suggests that the *Globe* had Canada's parliament in mind. The local legislature had the power to introduce representation by population, but could it legally turn the province into a federation? The *Globe* talked of a constitution,[244] but by definition a constitution would involve amendment of the Union Act of 1840, and that would mean legislation at Westminster. When *The Times* greeted Confederation as long overdue but disapproved of the impropriety of a colonial ministry attempting to dictate a solution 'on principles to which no colony has the power to give effect', the *Globe* was both surprised and offended by the novelty of the notion.[245] His visit to London in December 1864 left Brown still convinced that the British were a mere legislative convenience: 'if we insist on it, they will put through the scheme just as we ask it'.[246]

This was not entirely true, even of Confederation, the solution which did command British support. Edward Cardwell, the colonial secretary, made clear that 'the ultimate decision would be reserved for the Imperial Parliament'.[247] Cardwell's attitude reflected a combination of an innate metropolitan sense of superiority with a sound concern for his own political position. In 1858, he had come close to unseating a Conservative government by proposing a censure motion on its handling of the crisis in India, and it was in his interests to walk carefully in case they repaid the compliment by alleging that he had lost control of Canada. From a civil servant's point of view, as Frederic Rogers recalled, the 'constant presence' of the House of Commons in Cardwell's mind was 'a terrible nuisance' but none the less as a minister, he 'had a fine instinctive sense of what "would do"' in dealing with the Commons.[248] The House, he told Brown, would never pass a scheme which would not work.[249]

It is impossible to say how the British might have reacted to a request for enabling legislation to permit the transformation of the province of Canada into a two-headed federation as a cosmetic cover for representation by population. No request for such legislation ever came from a Canadian ministry, and in all the vast bulk of British official and private correspondence, speeches and articles on British North American affairs in the mid-1860s, nobody seems to have considered the eventuality. It is however possible to suggest that the British government might have been reluctant to co-operate and that the House of Commons might not have been acquiescent in its consideration of such a proposal.

The ageing prime minister, Palmerston, was annoyed when a young backbencher asked him what legislation was planned for the session of 1864. 'We cannot go on adding to the Statute Book ad infinitum,' he insisted, '... we cannot go on legislating for ever.'[250] Westminster was not a highly tuned machine for manufacturing laws. Parliament normally rose in July to take a vacation lasting until the following February: even if Tilley had won in New Brunswick in 1865, it is unlikely that a bill to unite the provinces would have seen the light of day until the following year. Even George Brown recognised that British preferences imposed some limitations on the future of the province. He had dismissed the extreme option of seeking outright repeal of the Union in 1859 by asking: 'Will the British go for it?'.[251] Furthermore, and most awkward of all, colonial questions sometimes became surrogate battle grounds for British political issues. It was part of the folklore of politics that Burke had quarrelled with Fox over the French revolution in 1791 during a debate on the government of Quebec. The ensuing split among the Whigs had kept their party out of office for the best part of four decades. In the 1830s, Canadian questions had been complicated by the confusion between colonial legislative councils and the House of Lords in Britain. In the early 1850s, settlement of the controversial problem of the Canadian clergy reserves had been delayed because of sensitivity over the established position of the Anglican Church at home.

At just the time when Canada's politicians began negotiations for the Great Coalition — and the timing may not be entirely coincidental — Gladstone had brought parliamentary reform back to the centre of the British political stage with a startling if opaque statement on 11 May 1864 which seemed to open the way for a broad extension of the right to vote.[252] With Palmerston approaching his eightieth birthday, a period of political instability seemed likely, as British politicians attempted to grapple with the challenge of Reform by forming alliances and seeking solutions exactly as their Canadian counterparts were attempting to do in response to the demand for representation by population. At least one Canadian politician was aware of the likely implications. Sir Narcisse Belleau warned in February 1865 that there was 'no time to lose' in securing legislation from Westminster, given 'the age of the premier of England, and the uncertain position in which his cabinet would stand if he should die'. Letellier de St Just poked fun at the idea of rushing through a fundamental constitutional change simply 'because the Prime Minister of England is old'.[253] Still, Belleau's grasp of the probable unravelling of British politics may help to explain his otherwise surprising nomination as compromise premier in succession to Taché in August 1865 — at a time when George Brown was re-asserting the claims of the alternative policy of Canadian federation.

The Reform question had two main aspects. The predominant issue was obviously the extent of the right to vote, which was held by only a minority of the adult male population. The other, which is sometimes overlooked, was the distribution of representation. Considerable anomalies had survived the surgery of 1832, and 'the map of representation remained much as it had been in Stuart England'.[254] The Norfolk market town of Thetford, with 4000 people and 200 voters, elected two MPs; so did Liverpool, with 400000 people and 17000 voters. 'Too little weight is given to the growing parts of the country,' Walter Bagehot had complained in 1859, 'too much to the stationary'.[255] He might have been commenting on the Canadian Union, where George Brown underlined the parallel by consistently applying the term 'Parliamentary Reform' to Upper Canada's demands.

In the event, British politicians agreed in 1867 to a broad extension of the right to vote in the towns, but tacitly agreed to a severely curtailed redistribution of seats. The under-represented industrial areas of the Midlands and the North of England gained just sixteen seats in a House of 658. Only after a cross-party revolt were the four largest cities granted a third member. To put the matter simply, it did not matter how many people voted in Liverpool and Manchester if Liverpool and Manchester only returned three MPs apiece. The entire difference between Canadian and British political culture may be captured in a single comparison: prior to 1867, Upper Canada was virtually united in indignation at being deprived of the 27 members its population seemed to warrant. *After* the redistribution of 1867, it has been calculated that the metropolis of London remained under-represented, in terms of population, by no fewer than 63 seats.[256]

Thus while it is impossible to say how any British government would have responded to a request to create a federation of Upper and Lower Canada as a means of providing representation by population, the expressive meaning of silence would suggest a marked lack of enthusiasm. The Duke of Newcastle had privately condemned the double majority principle as *'retrogression* with a vengeance' in 1862.[257] Cardwell flatly refused to consider introducing legislation for anything short of Confederation in 1865, thereby cutting the ground from under Tupper's diversionary manoeuvre to revive Maritime Union in 1865.[258] Representation by population could be swallowed within the larger framework of Confederation because British North American union embodied a long-cherished British aim. Even so, a British minister was at pains to assure the House of Commons that 'the constitutional difficulties of Canada ... were no more the cause of the proposal for the union of the provinces than the divorce of Henry VIII was the cause of the Reformation'.[259] It seems safe to suggest that no British politician would have relished going to the despatch box to ask parliament to endorse representation by population in Canada and risk stirring a revolt based on the protest that what was good for Upper Canada should also be granted to urban Britain.

Ultimately, the response of British ministers and legislators, had George Brown's policy triumphed over that of Macdonald and his allies, can only be the subject of speculation. What is clear is that the British gave their full support to the wider aim of Confederation once it came on to the practical agenda in 1864. Canadian ministers were fêted, with George Brown himself becoming the first colonial politician to be treated as a Canadian statesman, a welcome which did at least something to reinforce his support for Confederation. New Brunswick opponents were snubbed, Nova Scotian malcontents isolated and ignored. Through a stream of despatches and homilies, both official and unofficial, the British ensured that Confederation could not be dismissed as a dead option.

Yet their practical leverage was very small. A great power did not have the option of threatening to abandon small provinces to the mercies of a rapacious rival. The British government could barely command even the power of polite bribery: they had already set the outline terms for securing access to capital for the construction of the Intercolonial railway back in 1862. Least of all, Creighton's metaphor notwithstanding, could they throw Caesar's legions into the battle for British North American union. They could not even send Lord Palmerston's gunboats to shell the coasts of the recalcitrant Maritimes. Yet in order to explain why Confederation happened in 1867, we need to shift emphasis away from its abstract merits as a solution — for these have undoubtedly been exaggerated — towards the crucial context of pre-existing British support. Between 1837 and 1867, British opinion came to favour the creation of a regional union in British North America. Chapter Three examines how that consensus developed. Chapter Four asks who? where? and what?: defining the 'British', reconstructing their understanding of British North America, and examining their ideas about structures of government. Chapter Five asks why? and when?: dissecting the motives behind British enthusiasm for a union of the provinces, and seeking to reconstruct the time-frame they envisaged. Chapters Six and Seven ask the crucial question, how?: dividing the consideration into the decades before 1864 and the actual era of Confederation.

3 The Origins of British Support for Canadian Confederation

The fact of British support for the union of British North America between 1864 and 1867 is so much a part of the accepted background of the story of Confederation that it is easy to overlook that in some respects, the extent and unanimity of British backing was surprising. While some historians have demonstrated that there had been interest in the possibility of British North American union for earlier decades,[1] others have deduced the reasons for British support for the initiative of 1864 largely from the contemporary circumstances of the American Civil War.[2] This is another example of the way in which the nature of the causal argument may have been influenced by our knowledge of the outcome: in 1864, Britain backed Confederation, therefore the American Civil War provides the explanation. It is reasonable enough to see American events as the context within which the British response to Confederation was formed, but the causal deductions do not necessarily follow.

1864 was the year when it gradually became clear that the North was going to win the Civil War. It was also the year when Northern opinion, already angry at European sympathy for the South, was further inflamed by the French adventure in Mexico, complete with a comic-opera Emperor. All in all, 1864 might well have seemed a highly unpromising year in which to launch not simply a union of the British North American provinces, but one which evidently intended to remain under the sovereignty of Queen Victoria and the protection of the British empire. Pro-Southern opinion in Britain, which naturally had to downplay the role of slavery in bringing about the war, held firmly to the belief that any federal system of government contained within itself the seeds of disruption — or even that the sheer size had made the United States unwieldy. 'That it must become overgrown, and then fall to pieces, was assumed from the time when it was first seen to be growing', complained the *Daily News* in 1864, 'and any misfortune which might happen to it was sure to be regarded as the fulfilment of the prophecy.'[3]

'Divide and rule' had seemed to be a more consistent thread in British policy towards colonies of settlement in the two decades immediately before 1864. Two new colonies had been carved out of New South Wales and two semi-autonomous settlements launched in New Zealand, while on the Pacific coast of North America, British Columbia had been established in 1858 as a separate colony alongside Vancouver Island. In backing Confederation, then, the British were acting in some degree against the pattern of their recent colonial policy. Their endorsement of Confederation in the mid-1860s was not necessarily dictated by a contemporary response to the circumstances created by the American Civil War. Rather, the British role in Confederation drew on support for a union of the provinces which had evolved through the previous thirty years.

The thesis may be summarised in a single sentence: between 1837 and 1867, British opinion came to favour the eventual creation of a regional union in British North America. This statement requires extensive discussion and clarification, which is best secured by asking six simple questions: who? where? what? why? when? and how?[4] Who were 'the British' whose opinion can be thus generalised? Where was their British North America: did they have a sound grasp of geographical realities and problems, or had they located their transatlantic provinces in the realm of fantasy? What structures did they have in mind when they talked of regional unions? Why did they favour some form of unification of the provinces? When did they expect a union to come about? How did they envisage that a union of self-governing dependencies would be formed?

Before discussing these questions in the chapters which follow, it is necessary to outline evidence for the contention that an overall British sentiment in support of the union of British North America developed from the middle of the 1830s onwards. While the interest was by no means constant, the fact that it arose on almost every occasion when British North American issues were intruded into domestic politics is in itself an indication of the latent tenacity of the idea. The cyclical or intermittent nature of speculation actually demonstrates the steady growth of its appeal: British North American union was a controversial proposal in the late 1830s — at least as an immediate option — but by 1849, support had become general across the whole spectrum of British political opinion. Individual proposals were criticised, sometimes in strong terms, but gradually a sentiment prevailed that even if the union of British North America was not practicable at the time, it was something which would and should come about in the years ahead. However inchoate, ill-informed and superficially analysed that sentiment might be, it still deserves to be ranked as one of the most basic causes of Canadian Confederation.

Proposals for a union of British North America can be traced back to the late eighteenth century, but by and large these appealed to colonial tories and drew upon a loyalist tradition which dated back to the period before the American War of Independence.[5] One notable exception to this categorisation was the Scots radical Robert Gourlay, the 'banished Briton' whom the colonial élite deported from Upper Canada in 1819 as a trouble-maker.[6] These early proposals met with little encouragement on the British side. The Nova Scotian J.B. Uniacke was told in 1826 that the colonies were 'tranquil' and the British government would not 'agitate the question'. Gourlay hoped to persuade the prominent radical Henry Brougham to adopt his policy but, as Upton pointed out, he hardly helped his cause, first, by attempting to horse-whip Brougham and then by publishing a revised scheme for British North American federation from an asylum.[7] It was the crisis of the 1830s, the absence of tranquillity in the colonies, which led some British policy-makers to a cautious examination of federal structures as a possible means for solving the contradictions between imperial supremacy and local autonomy.

In January 1837, the cabinet adopted a scheme drawn up by James Stephen, permanent under-secretary at the Colonial Office, which its author accepted pointed 'to a new Congress on the North American Continent' by convening an annual meeting of representatives of the four mainland provinces, thereby using the three English-speaking colonies to check the French.[8] This project had already been abandoned by the time rebellion broke out in the two Canadas at the end of 1837, since Stephen himself had to warn that Upper Canada and Nova Scotia were no longer politically reliable, thereby rendering highly unattractive the prospect of an annual meeting of their delegates with the discontented Lower Canadians.[9] It was presumably the irruption on to the Nova Scotian political stage of the young Joseph Howe which caused Stephen to have second thoughts. There is some irony that Howe, who failed to stop Confederation in 1867, should have unwittingly blocked its shadow predecessor three decades before. The fact that federation was advocated in the House of Commons by the radical MP John Arthur Roebuck, agent at Westminster for the Lower Canada Assembly, was perhaps another reason for pausing.[10] Federal schemes were attractive to the British because they seemed to provide a local buffer against the assertiveness of French Canada: Roebuck's personal enthusiasm was a complication.

Yet when Lower Canada exploded in rebellion at the end of 1837, there was a surprising breadth of interest in the possibility of a general federation. While the outright union of Upper and Lower Canada seemed the most direct and effective way of diluting French discontent, several London newspapers thought it 'better to unite federally all the provinces' or, better still, sweep away all the 'petty administrations' and have 'one Governor-General'.[11] Lord John Russell, one of the most active ministers in Lord Melbourne's dispirited cabinet, consulted a former governor, Sir James Kempt, on the feasibility of a general union.[12] Stephen and his principal ministerial ally, Lord Howick, revived the idea of a 'Federal body' (the term 'Federal authority' was edited out at draft stage),[13] and even Melbourne, never an activist prime minister, professed himself 'ready to consider this scheme of a general Congress of all the provinces'.[14] There were already signs that the innocent visionary enthusiasm of the British was running ahead of British North American reality. 'The era for such a fabric has not yet arrived', a colonial correspondent warned in *The Times*,[15] while Kempt apparently convinced Russell that federation was ruled out by difficulties of communication between Canada and the Maritimes, coupled with problems of apportioning revenue among the various levels of government. Melbourne's open-mindedness on the question of British North American federation did not last long. 'It is at once giving to these Provinces the Constitution of the United States, & leaving the people nothing to do but ship off your

Governor & elect a President,' he told Howick early in January 1838.[16]

The Melbourne cabinet attempted to compensate for its own inability to grasp issues by devolving the formation of policy on to its High Commissioner, Lord Durham, who was sent to Canada with emergency powers in 1838. 'On my first arrival in Canada,' Durham later recorded, 'I was strongly inclined to the project of a federal union.'[17] Durham's own preference was to create a central Assembly, elected by the 'better class' of all six colonies.[18] He made some large promises to influential colonists to win their support,[19] and summoned the intercolonial convention which Howick and Stephen had proposed. Support for the idea was not universal. In Upper Canada, R.B. Sullivan found it 'difficult to understand' how a federal government could be prevented from challenging Britain's ultimate control over the colonies. His cousin, Robert Baldwin, more bluntly described federation as 'worse than useless' unless intended as 'a preparatory step' to full independence.[20] From New Brunswick, Sir John Harvey warned of 'a decided indisposition' in the Maritimes to become involved with Canadian problems, while the more enthusiastic Sir Colin Campbell of Nova Scotia acknowledged 'that the Lower Provinces would not willingly come into that measure'.[21] None the less, on 13 September 1838, Durham was able to notify the Colonial Office that deputations from Nova Scotia and Prince Edward Island had arrived in Quebec to discuss 'a general arrangement for the future government of the North American Provinces'.[22] The meeting was cut short by the drama of Durham's resignation on learning that he had been over-ruled in London in his attempt to transport leaders of the rebellion out of the province without trial. Charles Buller claimed at the time, perhaps optimistically, that the Maritimers had 'entered warmly' into the project, but later admitted that discussions with them had 'pointed out various difficulties in the details of a general union' and 'raised great doubts' about the chances of its acceptance.[23]

British reactions to Durham's scheme were mixed. The *Globe*, a London evening newspaper, was the first to publish news of the project, which it praised for ensuring the principle of representative government while providing safeguards against parochial feuding. The Conservative *Morning Post* was untroubled by the fact that the scheme was 'clearly of Washington origin', but the reactionary *Morning Herald* damned the surrender of sovereignty to a democratic assembly 'upon the shoulders of which some O'Connell or Papineau would soon clamber into the president's chair, without the awkward necessity of much fighting'.[24] Melbourne, who had entertained similar fears, was by now suspicious that Durham was merely seeking a glamorous but temporary solution whose inevitable collapse he would blame on the mistakes of others.[25] Another influential critic was Edward Ellice, a former cabinet minister and election manager for the Whig party, whose views on British North American issues were filtered through his financial interests in seigneurial property and the fur trade. He was regarded as the source of an attack in the Whig *Morning Chronicle* which superciliously concluded that British North American federation 'must be the invention of some Utopian anxious to amuse the world'. The plan was comprehensively dismissed as unnecessarily complex, a surrender to the French, and a pointless attempt to link the Canadas with provinces with which they had as much in common as with New South Wales.[26]

The slight prospect of an immediate move towards British North American union disappeared with the collapse of the Durham mission. By June 1839, Russell could claim that British North American federation 'has been at present abandoned by its proposers' and a year later, Melbourne thought it 'unnecessary to dwell upon it'.[27] A similar retreat may be observed in the thinking of Lord Durham. In October 1838 he wrote of the necessity and convenience of 'some Government that might regulate all matters of general concern to the two Canadas and the other Provinces of British North America'.[28] By the time of his *Report on the Affairs of British North America* in January 1839, he could still argue that Lower Canada should be united with 'one or more of the surrounding Provinces', but general union was now identified as a development for the future.[29] Buller claimed Durham had embraced the immediate union of Upper and Lower Canada 'much against his inclination' in response to a second Lower Canadian uprising at the end of 1838. Yet even Buller became convinced that 'the argument against federal Union is that it does nothing to obtain the main end which we ought to have in view', which was 'keeping Lower Canada quiet now, & making it English as speedily as possible'.[30] As Durham himself wrote, 'the period of gradual transition is past in Lower Canada'. When Howick attempted once again to persuade the cabinet to endorse his scheme for a federation designed by an intercolonial convention, Russell damned its complexity. 'Such a monster in politics was never yet seen, such a provision for confusion was never yet created.'[31]

The evidence would not justify an assertion that an enthusiastic and united British consensus in favour of the union of British North America had emerged by the end of the 1830s. The Prime Minister, Melbourne, was highly suspicious, and his opposition was shared by two cabinet colleagues who were to become his ultimate successors, Russell and Palmerston, who would each hold office for the last time during the mid-1860s. However, it should be noted that the Union of the Canadas was adopted less for its merits but rather because it seemed to present an immediately available solution to the pressing problem of controlling French-Canadian discontent. As Gladstone put it, if it were asked 'what measure would be most expedient for the settlement of the government of the Canadas, it might be susceptible of doubt whether the union of the two provinces was in the abstract the best measure that could be adopted'. Lord Ashburton backed the Union of the Canadas because 'nobody seemed to have any other plan to suggest', while Lord Ellenborough pungently noted that it was being proposed 'not because it is just, or wise or safe, but because it is said to be necessary "to do something"'. 'It was not that the measure was not open to reasonable objections,' commented the *Examiner*, '... but it was felt that, such as it was, it was the only plan practicable; and that if it were rejected, no other could be substituted'.[32]

By implication, such statements demonstrate that the wider union of British North America had ceased to be seen as a practical option by 1839. None the less, there were indications that the idea of a union of all the provinces had lodged itself on the longer-term agenda. Despite his role in a press attack on Durham's policy of general federation, Edward Ellice exerted his backstage influence to press the cabinet to adopt a federal structure for the Union of the Canadas. Ellice proposed that the district to the south-east of Montreal, where he owned the seigneurie of Beauharnois, should become a separate unit within the Canadian federation, thus demonstrating a thread of consistency — the single-minded defence of his own interests against French Canadian majority rule — through his various positions on Canadian affairs. In February 1839 he held out the incentive that if 'a larger federative union of the North American provinces is contemplated', his purely

Canadian federation 'affords every facility, and certainly opposes fewer obstacles to it than an immediate union'.[33] Charles Buller continued to believe that 'the uniting of the two provinces would be followed by the union of all the other provinces'.[34] The opposition leader, Sir Robert Peel, stated in April 1840 that he would have preferred 'that the government of our entire North American colonies might be under one supreme control' in a federal structure.[35] Lord Ellenborough also favoured 'a point of Federal Union which should give the semblance of a State to the British Colonies in North America' and believed that federation would 'ultimately be necessary'.[36] British North American union had slipped into the background, but the idea still attracted politicians as diverse as the radical Buller, the maverick Ellenborough and the Conservative Peel.

Despite Peel's interest, and the fact that he was prime minister between 1841 and 1846, the first half of the following decade saw at most only a few ephemeral and unimportant British speculations on the subject of British North American union.[37] Few wished to unscramble a political settlement carried with so much time and difficulty through parliament in 1839 and 1840. In any case, the early years of the Canadian Union were characterised by controversy and division, and Peel himself took a gloomy view of the future of Britain's relations with the province. In 1840, an informed source had commented on Peel's 'great anxiety to get rid of the Canada question, while still in Opposition'. By May 1842, as the major political crisis of Sir Charles Bagot's governorship was unfolding, Peel was arguing that if 'the British party' could not in fact control Canada, as the policy of Union had envisaged, 'very frank language' would be required about the value of continuing the political connection. The link with the Maritimes, on the other hand, should be retained 'for their geographical position makes their sea-board of great importance to us'.[38] It is not hard to detect in this the spirit of the boundary concessions of the Ashburton Treaty, signed shortly afterwards, by which plausible British claims in northern Maine were conceded, thus reducing the corridor between New Brunswick and Lower Canada to the narrow neck which would later make the proposed Intercolonial railway so vulnerable to American attack. A sentiment which contemplated breaking the link with Canada while retaining the Maritimes was certainly not conducive to the encouragement of a union of all the provinces.

British North American union began to return to the agenda after the Whigs returned to office under Russell in 1846, thanks to the incoming colonial secretary, the former Lord Howick, who had recently inherited the family title to become the third Earl Grey. General changes in colonial policy favoured the re-emergence of the issue, but these should not be overstressed. Peel had been ousted in the crisis caused by the repeal of the Corn Laws, which pointed to a general concession (or imposition) of free trade as colonial policy.[39] Recent historical debate has cast doubt upon the extent to which free trade and colonial self-government were necessarily intertwined,[40] but it is still probably fair to conclude that once Britain ceased to require close control over colonial tariffs, potential spheres of autonomy were opened, which not only fostered an increased measure of local self-government but also pointed to areas requiring regional co-operation. At a practical level, free trade and local responsible government would revive the question of wider union by 1849, because a section of 'the British party', outraged at losing both its preferential trading access to Britain and its monopoly of local power, began to threaten annexation to a United States.[41]

Grey had to tread carefully. He had twice resigned from office in the 1830s, and in December 1845 his opposition to the return of Palmerston to the Foreign Office had given Russell a perhaps-not-unwelcome reason for abandoning an attempt to form a ministry when Peel first attempted to resign. Grey's motives in 1845 had been laudable, for he had feared that the bellicose Palmerston would be a dangerous minister at a time when war with the United States threatened over the Oregon boundary. Grey, one commentator noted 'lays down excellent principles, but ... at inconvenient times' and as a result, the term 'crotchetty' was frequently applied to him. His aristocratic rank was not matched by equivalent social skills: 'he *looks* morose, even at times ill-tempered'. Hence political stands he had taken on high principle were easily viewed as acts of lordly arrogance. 'He scorned to be an apprentice, but rather regarded himself as one of the master's family, ready to be taken into the firm when the time came.'[42] A shy man, he had in fact been wounded by the general condemnation of his conduct in December 1845, and it was tacitly specified that in taking office the following year, he would play as a member of Russell's team. Furthermore, Russell, who had a tendency to inscribe his personal achievements on to tablets of national greatness, made it clear that in his opinion Canada had been 'saved' by the Union of 1841 and by the administration of his close ally Lord Sydenham as its first governor-general.[43] A sympathetic observer urged Grey to take account of 'those infirmities of our race which make the perfect practical application of abstract propositions, however true they may be, a great difficulty, if not an impossibility'.[44] The advice would prove applicable to his continuing enthusiasm for the union of British North America.

The senior official at the Colonial Office, James Stephen, agreed that it would be 'eminently useful' to have a central co-ordinating body for the North American colonies, the more so as the concession of increased autonomy in matters such as tariffs and postal services created areas in which co-operation would be useful. To Stephen, the creation of any kind of co-ordinating body was 'pregnant with an innovation of far deeper importance' for, once established, it would extend its control into other spheres.[45] Consequently, Grey urged the colonies to consider forming an association on the lines of the German *Zollverein* to discuss trade matters.[46] He also encouraged the newly appointed governor-general, Lord Elgin, to travel through the Maritimes and urge the case for federation on his way to Canada. Grey was 'very anxious' to hear Elgin's views on the possibility 'of doing anything in the way of effecting a closer union' of the British North American provinces, since he was convinced 'that there is nothing more important to their interests & also to ours'.[47] Elgin, however, dwelt on the 'inconvenience and danger of treating such Subjects in the Abstract' and bluntly told Grey in his theoretical discussions the colonial secretary never mentioned 'the greatest of them all', the inadequacy of 'the materials with which I have to work in carrying out any measures for the public advantage'.[48]

Elgin's great political strength lay in his ability to manage people, and he did not regard the politicians he found himself managing as nation-builders. Nor did he consider federation in itself to be a particularly useful project. He did not seem disappointed to find 'little feeling' in its favour in Canada.[49] British opinion seemed equally apathetic in 1847. Buller seemed alone in urging Elgin and Grey to work towards 'the larger views embodied in Lord

Durham's Report' and unite the provinces 'into a compact and powerful community'.[50] *The Times*, however, remained 'anxious that the time should not be precipitated which is to give the harbours of Nova Scotia or the banks of Newfoundland to a hostile republic or rebellious federation.'[51] Grey accepted some of Elgin's practical criticisms of the utility of federation, but consoled himself with the thought that 'short as the tenure of office generally is while one holds it one ought to act as if it were to be permanent or as if ones successor was likely to carry forward the policy one has begun'.[52]

If the idea of British North American union as a consistent if long-term aim could cheer Grey in his discouragement in 1847, it was the events of 1849 which seem to have clinched the wider British endorsement of regional union. A controversy over the Lower Canada Rebellion Losses Bill in the first half of the year culminated with an emphatic decision by the House of Commons not to intervene in an internal Canadian issue, a decision which carried with it a tacit acceptance that the boundaries of colonial self-government were certainly undefined and probably very elastic.[53] The United States had emerged from the Mexican War and had not yet plunged fully into the paralysing internal controversy over slavery which would bring threats of disunion a year later. 'The Union is no longer a cluster of independent states,' *The Times* commented in January 1849, 'it is an empire dominating over a continent and giving laws to a world.'[54] The 'childish threats' of annexation aroused as much exasperation as fear in Britain, but Canadian discontents revived discussion of British North American union.[55]

In May 1849, first in a book and then in a parliamentary debate, Roebuck drew on his proposals of a decade earlier to argue that Britain should take steps to render the creation of a British North American confederation 'not only probable but certain'.[56] His efforts succeeded more as an exercise in publicity than in the formation of practical policy, securing a cautiously favourable response in a range of newspapers, including some which had condemned British North American federation a decade earlier. The *Morning Chronicle*, now the organ of the moderate Conservative Peelites, and the Protectionist *Morning Herald* were agreed that federation was not a new idea. Liberal newspapers were enthusiastic in their support.[57] Russell recalled the warning he had received from Sir James Kempt eleven years earlier, and made a fundamental point which Roebuck had managed to overlook, that any British North American union would require colonial consent.[58] The parliamentary under-secretary, Benjamin Hawes, ignored a Colonial Office brief on the disadvantages of Roebuck's scheme and assured the House that far from being hostile to the federal principle, the government planned to introduce it for the Australian colonies.[59]

It was the danger that the Canadian tories would opt for annexation to the United States which converted both *The Times* and the Prime Minister to the idea of British North American union. On 6 August, *The Times* reported that the idea of federation was popular in Upper Canada. That same day, Russell wrote to Grey advocating what the colonial secretary significantly called 'the old idea of forming a federal union'.[60] Four months earlier the prime minister had declared himself 'against uniting Canada with Nova Scotia, & New Brunswick' — the position he had held in 1839.[61] He had been noncommittal on the subject when speaking in Roebuck's debate in May, and had given 'only a general reply' when the Canadian tory leader Sir Allan MacNab had urged the federal option on him in July.[62] It was the convention of the tory British American League, at Kingston, which finally changed Russell's mind. The combination of the 'pressing danger' of annexation with the prospect of the colonial consent which he had insisted would be requisite convinced him that it was 'necessary to take into immediate consideration the state of British North America'.[63]

Grey replied cautiously that it would be 'for the present at least premature' to press for a British North American federation, simply because of the lack of 'sufficient common interests to form the ground work', while in the absence of a rail connection between Halifax and Quebec, it would be 'practically very difficult if not impossible' for a central authority to operate.[64] However, he also used Russell's initiative to reopen the question with Elgin,[65] who had in fact already concluded that tory talk of a federation was an insincere compromise dangled by annexationists to wean those who remained loyal to Britain from their allegiance.[66] In any case, Elgin continued to believe that a colonial federation would be both useless and weak. 'I am rather coming round to your view', Grey had to admit. On the other hand, the submersion of the provinces into a legislative union seemed 'hardly practicable'.[67]

In 1850, the government abandoned its outline scheme for a federation of the Australian colonies, and Grey's attempt to link the colonies of South Africa in 'some system which may combine distinct government in merely local affairs with general government for general purposes' barely survived the drafting stage in January 1851.[68] These were to be the last echoes of the Howick schemes of the 1830s to create federal frameworks for colonies at an early stage of their constitutional development. British North America had already passed the point where such imperial engineering was possible. In September 1849, Grey had been able to assure the suspicious Canadian finance minister Francis Hincks that 'no measure sufficiently definite and practical for serious consideration has yet been suggested'.[69] When the Canadian Assembly debated British North American federation two years later, Grey neutrally commented that it was 'perhaps a very good project but a very large one'.[70] A similar conclusion had been reached by New Brunswick's governor, Sir Edmund Head, who had been interested in 'Lord Grey's view of a Zollverein' and its development into 'a federal union or quasi federal union for specific purposes of these Provinces'.[71] In September 1849, Head believed that while federation 'would be practicable ... it would require great consideration & care in framing'. Consequently, his 'speculations' were unlikely to lead anywhere, and his friend, Grey's cabinet colleague George Cornewall Lewis, agreed that federation was 'not a likely event'.[72]

When Grey optimistically hoped that his 'policy' would be carried forward by his successors, he probably did not foresee that in the seven years after he left office, no fewer than nine ministers would hold the seals of the Colonial Office. 'It might be expected that all unity of management would thus be lost,' commented Lord Stanley, as he himself passed rapidly through 14 Downing Street in 1858. 'But the excess of the evil works its own cure: for the real management of ordinary business falls into the hands of the permanent officials (Merivale and Elliot) who being able and sensible men, manage it well, though without responsibility.'[73] Key phrases here are 'ordinary business' and 'without responsibility': lack of ministerial continuity made it difficult either to respond to or to launch major policy initiatives. While Sir Edmund Head in New Brunswick applied his considerable intellect to analytical memoranda on British North American union,[74] the question once again slipped into the background so far as imperial policy-making was concerned.

After 1850, however, it may be argued that the idea of British North American union was sufficiently well established to reappear whenever an issue involving the future of the colonies came to the fore. In 1853, for instance, *Fraser's Magazine* deplored the separation of Canada from the Maritimes, regretting that the strength of British North America was 'frittered away in separate colonies ... when it should be one large dominion, with one Governor-General, and one capital city for the seat of government'. (The choice of the term 'dominion' was a lucky hit.) The *Morning Chronicle* criticised the provinces for failing to pursue common interests, 'as if isolation, instead of federation, were the object they had in view'. The *Standard* re-published an article from the *Quebec Chronicle*, which it called 'another brilliant anticipation' of the subject. In 1854, Gladstone's friend J.R. Godley concluded that uniting British North America was a far more important aim for Britain than 'curbing the power of Russia' in the Crimean War.[75] The *Morning Herald* proclaimed itself a supporter of British North American union. When Gladstone made a public speech on colonial issues in 1855, *The Times* demanded to know whether he would 'form the colonies into confederacies'. 'Before long it is probable that all British North America will be under one government,' it casually remarked in 1857. *Blackwood's Magazine* that same year complained that it was 'annoying and disgraceful' that 'no attempt has been made to establish a federal bond of union' joining the provinces.[76]

As it happened, an attempt had been made, but so discreetly (as well as unsuccessfully) that it left almost no mark on the historical record. The Duke of Newcastle had begun the first of two spells at the Colonial Office in December 1852, when Whigs and Peelites had temporarily united in a coalition headed by Lord Aberdeen.[77] *The Times* was moved to exclaim, 'what a career of public utility lies before them!' In colonial affairs, it specified, 'the moment is one of critical interest, for the maintenance of our connexion with Canada'.[78] Newcastle was a high-minded Peelite who had been a diligent opponent of many aspects of Grey's policies, notably those relating to the settlement of Vancouver Island. His endorsement of the aim of British North American federation is thus testimony of the developing ministerial consensus which Grey himself had hoped for. Six months after Newcastle's appointment, Sir Edmund

Head submitted a confidential report on the problems of government arising from the small size of the New Brunswick legislature. The Colonial Office clerk with immediate responsibility for British North American affairs, Arthur Blackwood, often displayed a bureaucrat's caution in the face of proposals for change, but he commented that 'the real & only remedy' for the problems Head had described lay in a 'general consolidation of the British North American Provinces into one Government'. Newcastle agreed that 'the consolidation of the provinces into one Government will eventually be found the surest, if not the only, remedy, for this and other evils attaching to these small assemblies', although there were 'many considerations of too much importance to be even touched upon' in an official answer.[79] Shortly afterwards, Newcastle minuted that it would be 'impossible ... to postpone much longer some steps for providing against dangers from *within & without*' the Hudson's Bay Territories.[80] On the other side of the continent, it was becoming harder to refuse the demand for responsible government in Newfoundland, especially as it had just been granted to Prince Edward Island and despite the warning of the island's governor that Newfoundland would become 'a misruled papal diocese'.[81] There was every reason for Newcastle to seek a solution at British North American level.

By the close of 1853, when Elgin returned to Britain on leave, Newcastle was convinced that the 'remedy' for the various problems of the provinces lay in a general union. 'Eight years ago,' he informed the cabinet early in 1862, 'I believed this remedy to be possible, and I asked Lord Elgin to return to Canada for the purposes of attempting to carry it into effect'.[82] The *Spectator* had carried a news item to that effect as early as September 1853,[83] and reports in the Canadian press were taken sufficiently seriously for Francis Hincks, the leading Upper Canada minister, to lobby against the scheme he had already objected to in 1849.[84] Newcastle made a more muddled reference to the episode in November 1863. Arthur Gordon, the brash young governor of New Brunswick, had annoyed Newcastle by praising his own efforts to encourage a union of the Maritime provinces. Newcastle rebuked him for his presumption, adding that

it has been constantly agitated for more than ten years and more than once has appeared quite as near being accomplished as it does now. In 1853-4 I thought the question ripe and actually asked poor Elgin to return and take a new lease of the Government of Canada for the purpose of accomplishing the further union which would be the consequence.[85]

Elgin was dying in India, and Newcastle's health was in such 'a precarious state' that he was not expected to live six months.[86] Certainly, his memory gave way in the last months of his life and confusion may already be apparent in his rebuke to Gordon, but it is probably also evidence that Newcastle saw Maritime Union as a step to fusion with Canada.

It is hard to decide what form of historians' shorthand best describes the 1853 episode: Newcastle's 'federal initiative' or, more colloquially, his 'bid to unite the provinces'? Newcastle asked Elgin to return to Canada and take undefined steps 'for the purposes of attempting to carry it [intercolonial union] into effect'. Elgin, who was not a wealthy man, was chiefly concerned to secure re-appointment or alternative employment, and he became extremely angry at Newcastle, convinced that the duke, his one-time friend, was playing 'a cunning game' to oust him from the colonial scene.[87] Rogers would later note that Newcastle could seem indecisive in the appointment of governors,[88] but on this occasion it is possible that he was stalling on Elgin's re-appointment in order to force him into a promise of support for a wider union of British North America. Elgin, who was convinced that the real constitutional change required was some form of imperial federation,[89] perhaps felt that he could discharge Newcastle's wishes by returning to North America to negotiate a trade treaty with the United States on behalf of all the provinces, a triumph which he achieved in the Reciprocity Treaty of 1854. Newcastle was soon to become deeply involved in the administrative problems of the Crimean War, transferring in June 1854 to the newly created War Office. One of his last acts at the Colonial Office was to name Sir Edmund Head as Elgin's successor. It was the first time since 1828 that a governor from the Maritimes had been promoted to the post of governor-general of Canada. Head was a very able functionary, but his appointment broke a quarter-century tradition of preferring British to British North American political experience in the selection of a governor-general. No doubt Canada under responsible government had passed the stage where a threat of war could make the selection of a military governor appropriate, but the scholarly Head was not an obvious choice to preside over a major province in wartime. It is possible that in Newcastle's eyes, Head's principal claim to promotion lay in his thoughtful assessments of the advantages and problems of British North American union. (Conversely, when it again fell to Newcastle to appoint a governor-general during his second term at the Colonial Office, in 1861, he passed over and apparently offended Manners Sutton of New Brunswick, who possessed similar experience but was opposed to a union of provinces.)

If Newcastle's aim in sending Head to Canada had been to carry forward the cause of British North American union, it did not bear immediate fruit. In fact, during his first three years in the province, Head drew back from his previous advocacy of general federation, pleading as his reason for abandoning his earlier enthusiasm 'a knowledge of Canada more accurate than I then possessed'.[90] He provoked an outcry among French Canadians by incautiously attributing the astonishing prosperity of Upper Canada to the superior virtues of the Anglo-Saxon people,[91] but he did perceive that the rapidly tilting imbalance of population within the province, which would eventually open the way to Confederation, was in the short term shifting the centre of gravity of Canadian interests further away from the Maritimes.[92] In forwarding an unofficial proposal for colonial union to London in January 1856, he added a terse comment. 'There are few persons to whose minds this scheme has not presented itself in some shape or other — I have myself reflected on it a great deal and I cannot say that the difficulties surrounding it have diminished in proportion to the consideration which I have given it.'[93] Later that year he told the colonial secretary, Henry Labouchere, 'I do not now believe in the practicability of the federal or legislative Union of Canada with the three "Lower Colonies". I once thought differently but further knowledge and experience have changed my views'.[94]

In the Colonial Office, there was also a sense of marking time in the mid-1850s. In 1855, J.H.T. Manners Sutton, Head's successor in New Brunswick, reported that his province sought quasi-diplomatic representation in Washington, describing it as an example of the way in which 'every opportunity is eagerly seized of taking a step in the direction, which may be supposed to lead to the union of the British North American Provinces, and to what might be called an alliance with, rather than dependence on, the Mother Country'. Herman Merivale, Stephen's successor as permanent under-secretary, commented that the move 'points to federal union'. Merivale had succeeded Stephen as the senior civil servant in the department seven years earlier, but this seems to have been the first occasion on which he had referred to British North American union. However Merivale dismissed a proposal by C.D. Archibald, the British consul in New York, for a union of the provinces as a viceroyalty, condemning 'the restless vanity and ambition of one man' for latching on to an issue which was apparently seen as both important and sensitive.[95] It seems that the British were wary of falling into the trap of acting on the basis of marginal or transient support for general union within the provinces. In 1855, the New Brunswick town of St Stephen brought the 'prospective Union of the British North American Provinces' into its campaign for rail links to the hinterland. Russell, who briefly returned to the Colonial Office during the political upheavals of the Crimean War, described their sentiments as 'a very natural wish, but premature'.[96] In 1857, the Nova Scotian ministry authorised delegates it was sending to London in order to discuss the Intercolonial railway to enter into talks on British North America union as well, along with mining and immigration. 'These gentlemen will have plenty to do,' Arthur Blackwood drily noted, as he listed 'Consolidation of the British North American Provinces' last in the list.[97]

The longest serving colonial secretary in the mid-1850s, Henry Labouchere, held office for just over two years, from November 1855 to February 1858. There has been a tendency to regard him as an undynamic minister, perhaps because he is one of the few for whom no private papers survive. After Labouchere had left office, Merivale claimed him as a latent supporter of British North American union. 'Mr Labouchere's view was, not that it was a thing to be urged from this side, but that we ought to be prepared for its proposal & rather encourage it than otherwise.' There was an element of special pleading in this, as Merivale attempted to reassure an anxious minister, Sir Edward Bulwer Lytton, that Head had not gone beyond his instructions in endorsing British North American federation in the aftermath of the double shuffle.[98] However, in the amicable cross-party atmosphere of mid-Victorian politics, Lytton could have checked Merivale's statement with Labouchere himself. The accuracy of its general spirit is confirmed by a letter which Labouchere wrote in 1857 to the foreign secretary,

Lord Clarendon, in which he criticised a proposal to introduce colonial MPs to the British House of Commons. 'A closer union between our North American Provinces would be another matter,' he wrote, adding that he would be 'very glad' to see the Maritimes 'united into one Colony — but am afraid that things are not yet ripe for such a measure'.[99]

The source of this enthusiasm for a union of the three Maritime provinces was probably a memorandum by Head which seems to have formed the basis for private discussions when the governor-general returned to London on leave in 1857. The decision of the Nova Scotian ministry to include the question of general union in the mandate of their delegates to Britain that year appears to have influenced Head in his arguments for Maritime Union. 'Such a step would not in any way prejudice the future consideration of a more extensive union either with Canada or Newfoundland', should the British government and the colonists wish it.[100] Thus Maritime Union could be seen not merely as a desirable reform in its own right, but as a stage in a longer-term timetable towards the union of British North America. 'Even those who look to a more extensive union of the North American colonies might conceive it to be a stepping stone towards that end.'[101]

Sir Edmund Head's temporary retreat from espousal of British North American union was based on two assumptions which the events of 1858 were to shake. The first was his belief that 'the separation of the St. Lawrence from the Lakes is not to be thought of for a moment'. The second was his conviction that Canada was 'tolerably well satisfied with her own form of Government'.[102] In one respect, however, Head was well aware that the Union was not working smoothly. While he regarded as 'theoretically absurd' the notion that Canadian ministries required a majority in each section to hold office, he had accepted as early as 1856 that 'in practice it must be looked to' and his label of it as 'a quasi-federal question' suggested that he already saw a possible way out.[103] The political crisis of 1858, which Merivale in London feared as heralding 'a general break up of Lord John Russell's united Canadian Republic',[104] was interpreted by Head as posing the challenge 'whether the Union was not *federal* rather than legislative in character' in the first place.[105] It could not be allowed to fail outright, for 'to give up the Union is to efface all the brightest hope of future greatness for this country'. Consequently, 'the next —

indeed the only hope — would be the formation of some government on a still larger scale more or less like a federation which shall gather up the reins & control the St Lawrence as well as the Western & Eastern waters.'[106] In short, 'all the objects which Lord Sydenham aimed at might be equally served by a general Union of the colonies'.[107]

Thus the inconsistencies in Head's pronouncements on British North American federation between 1855 and 1858 are less profound than might appear. However, it was not simply colonial circumstances which steered Head back to his earlier federal course, but encouragement from London. Accounts of the Canadian federal initiative of 1858 have referred to the doubts which the proposal encountered from the colonial secretary, Sir Edward Bulwer Lytton, who held office for a twelve-month period from June 1858 in a minority Conservative government headed by Lord Derby.[108] Brief though the ministry proved to be, Lytton was in fact its second colonial secretary, but the three-month preliminary tenure of office by Lord Stanley, Derby's son, left little mark on the historical record, largely because his personal papers only became available for study in the 1970s. The story which they have revealed once again demonstrates the inter-relationship between explanation and partial description — or rather, in this case, an expressive silence.

Historians were only vaguely aware of Stanley's interest in British North American federation. They could hardly be blamed for this, since the knowledge was kept from Lytton himself through a crucial period of his response to the double shuffle crisis. The gap in the overall record meant that Lytton's doubts were emphasised and the British accordingly portrayed as opponents of federation. As will be discussed in Chapter Six, Lytton's concern centred more on the important question of the mechanics rather than the aim of a federal initiative. His opposition was not so much to a union of the British North American provinces as to the political embarrassment to an obviously weak government of appearing to lose control of an important sphere of imperial policy, even to a colony as obviously unique as Canada. However, the interpretation of Lytton as an outright opponent of Confederation has made the 1858 episode seem like the scientific control experiment for 1864. In 1858, there was no American Civil War and there was no British 'pressure' for change. Both were obviously part of the story by 1864-5, and so the comparison with 1858 was enough to 'prove' that the American Civil War and the support of the British were crucial to the success of Confederation in the 1860s.

In reality, the complications of 1858 concerned means rather than ends, and the inconclusive outcome does not contradict the claim that the British were by this time looking to an eventual regional union in British North America. Indeed, it was the very attraction of that target which placed the item on the transatlantic agenda, and a chapter of accidents which created the impression of doubt. In February 1858, Palmerston's Whig ministry had fallen, and Derby formed his second minority Conservative government. After much heart-searching, his son, Lord Stanley, went to the Colonial Office. Stanley was a strange person. Disraeli, whom he hero-worshipped, referred to him as 'Young Morose'. At root, he seems to have been a victim of a clash fairly common in the Victorian aristocracy, between father and eldest son, and his romantic passion for a woman fifteen years his senior suggests a need for parental affection.[109]

If dynastic loyalty made Stanley a member of his father's party, inner revolt may have influenced him to embrace progressive ideas largely alien to the Conservatives. In 1855, when Palmerston had attempted to recruit Stanley to his cabinet, *The Times* had argued that 'the entire discrepancy of sentiment and opinion' between his views and those of his party made his departure from the Conservatives 'an event sooner or later absolutely certain', although it was in fact to be delayed for over twenty years. However, if he was both personally and politically an oddity, he was also seen as 'certainly by far the most promising member of the House of Commons of his age',[110] and in the 1860s was widely seen as a possible coalition prime minister, and was even rumoured to be a candidate for the throne of Greece. His own ambitions were more modest, and at one time he dreamed of becoming governor-general of Canada.[111]

Unusually for an aristocrat of his generation, Stanley had visited British North America, and soon after his return in 1848 had become an enthusiast for the admission of colonial MPs to the British House of Commons — a project often associated with some form of Confederation in this period.[112] In 1852, he had held his only previous ministerial post, as under-secretary at the Foreign Office at the time of the fisheries dispute with the United States —

the episode which had stung his hero Disraeli into denouncing the Maritime provinces as 'wretched Colonies' which were 'a millstone around our necks'.[113] His background and experience may thus explain why he described British North American union as something 'often considered in a speculative point of view' although, when asked to define his attitude in 1858, he found it 'new to me, &, I believe, to most English public men, in the practical form which it now seems likely to assume'.[114]

The 'practical form' consisted of no more than a series of resolutions which Galt announced in the Canadian Assembly on 8 March 1858, calling for a re-division of the Canadas and the establishment of a British North American federation.[115] The unsuccessful motion of a backbencher would not normally have been of great moment, and Head's private request for guidance from the new ministry on the question tends to confirm Merivale's subsequent statement that 'Mr Labouchere particularly requested him to take it in hand, when he ... was last in England'.[116] Head's letter, which was sent through Merivale, does not survive, but Stanley's reply implies that Head expected the question of wider union to be raised in 'one or more' of the colonial legislatures, implying that he had taken seriously the expression of support the previous year from Nova Scotia.[117] Perhaps it was the suggestion of a more-or-less concerted move which tempted Stanley to a positive response. Grey in 1851, Russell in 1855 and Labouchere in 1857 had all reacted cautiously to motions, petitions or resolutions within individual colonies. There may also have been a simple element of inexperience in Stanley's reaction. He had at first attempted to limit his support for his father's ministry to an under-secretaryship, which he believed would have freed him from responsibility for cabinet decisions — a curious attitude to collective accountability in government.[118] Responding to Head in his early months in office, he may not have fully realised that cabinet ministers must be cautious in the expression of private opinions. On the other hand, if he placed Head in the awkward position of receiving encouragement without the assurance of support, he did at least leave his endorsement in writing, whereas Labouchere, as Merivale had to confess, did not record his request for action at all.

Stanley's letter to Head on 7 April 1858 was a wide-ranging discussion of the advantages and problems of a union of the British North American provinces, the latter in his opinion indicating a solution on federal rather than unitary lines. The salient point, from the perspective of establishing the existence of a British consensus, is that Stanley assured the governor-general that there was 'nothing in the idea of federation' to which he would object from an imperial point of view.[119] Replying on 28 April, Head admitted that he had 'formerly thought that a federal government could be established without much difficulty, but experience has increased my estimate of the importance of the task & the obstacles to its successful execution.' None the less, he seemed to assume that a concerted move was imminent, even predicting that the Maritimes 'would meet any proposal of the kind with gladness'.[120]

By the time the letter could arrive in Britain, a new ministerial crisis had ensued, caused by the resignation of Lord Ellenborough from the Board of Control, the ministry for India. As is argued in Chapter Six, Ellenborough's resignation — for unfairly and indeed cruelly censuring India's harassed governor-general, Lord Canning — would not only overshadow the British response to Sir Edmund Head's endorsement of British North American federation in August, but would also determine that the ministerial strategy concentrated on the question of means rather than ends. The immediate effect of Ellenborough's resignation was to remove Stanley from the Colonial Office. For two weeks, politics stood still while the Conservatives attempted to woo Gladstone for the vacant post, but at the end of May Derby admitted defeat and transferred his son to the Indian portfolio, with the gruff and ungracious comment, 'there is no help for it'.[121] Stanley was thus plunged into the responsibility of attempting to govern a sub-continent, half the world away and in the final stages of the vast upheaval of the Mutiny. He could be forgiven for temporarily forgetting about the union of British North America.

Stanley's successor, Sir Edward Bulwer Lytton, thus entered the cabinet without any ministerial apprenticeship of any kind. He was better known as a romantic novelist than as a politician, and he looked the part. Galt found him 'rather deaf' (a handicap which understandably added to his fear of attack in the House of Commons) but described him as 'an exceeding agreable [sic] man, though odd & eccentric in his appearance, his hair long and disheveled, a sandy moustache & beard'.[122] Frederic Rogers was struck by Lytton's 'lean, narrow face, and hurried theatrical, conscious kind of ways'.[123] He was in poor health, and throughout the remainder of 1858 'contended against much physical pain & suffering' before offering the first of a series of attempted resignations.[124] Lytton worked very hard at his job, producing 'perfect volumes by way of minutes' and then amusing Rogers by assuring him that one of the great maxims of life was 'to write as little as possible'.[125] He also attempted to discharge much of his responsibilities from his country mansion at Knebworth in Hertfordshire, where J.R. Godley found him frantically drafting despatches in the middle of the night.[126] To add to his sorrows, Lytton had been estranged from his wife for years, and she campaigned against him in the by-election made automatic by his appointment to office (a circumstance which perhaps coloured his reaction to the 'double shuffle' device employed by Macdonald and his allies to dodge similar electoral inconvenience). Lytton no doubt over-reacted in securing the committal of his wife to an asylum, from which she was soon released, enabling her to circulate descriptions of her husband's marital practices which even the amoral Disraeli found strong.[127] Lytton sought promotion to the House of Lords to avoid a repetition of his humiliation at a general election, and was hurt when Derby bluntly indicated that marital disharmony was not a qualification for a peerage.[128]

When news reached London at the end of August that Canada's reconstructed ministry had advised the governor-general to approach the other provinces to discuss the union of British North America, it was received not by an imperial Caesar resolutely opposed to Confederation, but by an inexperienced and insecure minister, desperately afraid that his own vulnerability would be exploited to oust an already-weak cabinet. The reluctance of the British government to endorse the Canadian federal initiative of 1858 had far more to do with concern at the means employed than opposition to the end envisaged. The Colonial Office clerk, Arthur Blackwood, found the news of the new Canadian policy 'very startling' and asked whether Sir Edmund Head had been authorised 'to initiate the discussion of a federal union'. Merivale attempted to defend Head, but Carnarvon, the parliamentary under-secretary, was also uneasy. If federation was 'not entirely a gratuitous proposal' but stemmed from previous discussion, he would be satisfied, but if it represented a new development, Head ought to have warned the British government of 'his intention of bringing forward this important matter, already more than half impressed with the mark of his own concurrence'. Lytton was agitated and angry. The proposal had 'caused the greatest displeasure' and it was 'absolutely necessary to administer a reproof' to the governor-general for his 'great indiscretion'. [129]

This does not sound like evidence of a British consensus awaiting the moment to enforce its support for the emergence of a regional union in British North America. In fact, although Lytton continued to feel that Head had not kept him properly informed, the storm over the way in which the Canadian ministry had announced its initiative soon sunk in its own teacup. Part of the reason for Lytton's strong reaction lay in the alarm expressed by the Prince Consort.[130] Merivale quickly quietened such concerns through the sensible move of asking Stanley if he could throw any light on Head's apparently sudden initiative. Stanley happily produced the correspondence which India's crisis had apparently swept from his memory.[131] The eventual circular despatch to the North American provinces was important enough to require royal approval, and Lytton had to tread warily in its wording, asking Victoria's husband to 'condescend to notice' that he was anxious to dispel 'the impression that Her Majestys Government were disposed to initiate, or pointedly to countenance, the notion of Federation'.[132] Furthermore, Lytton did have some reason to fear criticism in the House of Commons. The *Canadian News*, for instance, a London-based weekly digest of British North American events, confidently announced that Head would never have adopted a federation policy 'without the fullest assurance that it had been considered in the Imperial councils',[133] while in Newfoundland it was assumed that so important a proposal 'originated with the British Government'.[134] It would be embarrassing for an untried minister to have to report to parliament that the first he had heard of the matter had been the news of Head's speech outlining the policy of the Cartier-Macdonald ministry. At least one Canadian politician, well experienced in the instability of minority government, was wholly understanding of the position of his British counterparts. 'They cannot *command* a majority in the House of Commons,' Galt explained, 'and it thus makes them timid in deciding any policy, and naturally inclines them to put off what can ever be postponed.'[135]

In the circumstances, it is the mildness of Lytton's comments on the aim of federation itself which should be emphasised. The union of British North America, he wrote, 'may be wise or not', but it was a matter requiring a cabinet decision, after 'the most anxious deliberation'.[136] He quickly decided that — whatever he might tell Albert — it would be 'injudicious' for any British government to take an open stand against a colonial move in that direction. The existing Union 'will not be long tenable' and Confederation — the term was coming into shorthand use — was 'one of the most obvious solutions of the serious problem' posed by the insecure Canadian constitutional structure. In any case, it soon became clear that the Canadian ministry had under-estimated the practical obstacles and regional jealousies which lay in their path. If the British government maintained a 'reserve', the project would either 'fail from its inherent difficulties' or emerge in a form which would enable the British 'insensibly & quietly to strip it of danger & harmonize it to Imperial policy'. Lytton's way of escaping from an awkward predicament was to acknowledge the importance of the subject, but to insist that by the same token it belonged to the imperial sphere of responsibility.[137]

While the British press did not take extensive interest in the proposal for federation — no doubt to Lytton's relief — there are further signs that the idea was widely accepted. *The Times* a year earlier had taken the prospect more or less for granted. In reporting the first stages of the double shuffle crisis, it predicted that the existing Canadian Union would soon be swept away in a sectional upheaval, and asked whether the solution might 'possibly be found in a federation of all the British Colonies in the North-East of America'. By September, *The Times* was pronouncing on the destiny of British North America, albeit in grave and archaic tones. 'These settlements have arrived at a point which seems to render such an union, for the sake of their commercial and material interests, highly desirable.' While regarding the idea of intercolonial union 'with more favour than hope', *The Times* was convinced that the provinces shared so many common interests and were divided by such minor barriers 'that it seems impossible to conceive a measure in principle less liable to objection'. It was certainly significant that *The Times* should have specifically welcomed 'the proposition thrown out by the Governor-General in his speech proroguing the Canadian Parliament', while pointedly passing over any irregularity in its genesis.[138] Its editor, J.T. Delane, had rebuffed Disraeli's initial blandishments and denounced the Derby ministry as a national penance for the sin of ousting Palmerston, whom he regarded as a personal friend. At the end of May, a frustrated Disraeli had caused a sensation by counter-attacking, branding leading newspapers as 'place-hunters of the cabal' — his term for the opposition — adding that 'once stern guardians of popular rights simper in the enervating atmosphere of gilded saloons'.[139] The decision of *The Times* not to exploit ministerial embarrassment over the Canadian federal initiative may therefore be taken as powerful evidence that by 1858, the British consensus in favour of British North American union soared above even the most virulent partisanship. The *Spectator* was more inclined to see the idea of federation as a party-political dodge, but the *Morning Herald* and *Morning Post* were favourable, perhaps out of a desire not to embarrass a Conservative government at home. When the Canadian ministers arrived in Britain at the end of September, Galt was able to report 'that all the press of the country is in favour of my favourite scheme of Confederation'.[140]

The Canadian ministers strongly argued that the 'very grave difficulties' of the Canadian Union made federation a natural way forward for both imperial and colonial interests. Galt begged Lytton to 'avoid expressing any opinion hostile to the Confederation' and — like Taché seven years later — bluntly alleged that anybody who blocked the union of British North America was tacitly helping the cause of annexation. Galt even secured permission to draft a despatch which would embody Lytton's reservations about the way the issue had arisen while indicating general support for the aim.[141] Lytton did not follow Galt's advice, but there was an evident wish to avoid an open breach and — as Chester Martin noted — he showed 'genuine interest' in Galt's ideas.[142] When Edmund Head offered to trundle out his favourite weapon, the memorandum, Lytton replied that while

it would be unadvisable for the Mother Country to offer any opposition to a declared & unequivocal desire on the part of the British North American Colonies — a desire growing spontaneously out of their wants & interests, to enter into practical negotiations for legislative or federal union — on the other hand I consider it would be unwise in Her Majesty's Government to do anything to encourage or force on such a project.[143]

Lytton finally opted for a circular despatch addressed in confidence to the governors of all the provinces, to guard against what Manners Sutton called 'the dangerous excitement which in these Provinces always accompanies a protracted discussion on constitutional questions of importance'.[144] By this means, the federation question was successfully postponed. Lytton's attempt to damp down the issue in 1858 certainly demonstrates that nobody had seriously addressed the problem of how dependent provinces might take the initiative to shape a project of imperial significance. It is not evidence of a British block against the aim of a union of the provinces as such.

In June 1859, the Derby ministry was finally ousted, and seven years of relative political instability in British politics brought to an end by the effective fusion of Whigs and Peelites into a Liberal ministry — even if its unity was in part dependent upon the determination of its prime minister, Palmerston, that neither its unity nor its liberalism should be unnecessarily tested by reckless innovation.[145] The Duke of Newcastle returned to the Colonial Office. His association with the failures of the Crimean War had dented his prestige: his staff wondered at the story that Sir Robert Peel had seen him as his ultimate successor as prime minister, and at least one ambitious colleague detected a decline in the duke's 'vigour of administration'.[146] Yet Newcastle remained a politician of standing, garbed in ducal aura and knowledgeable in matters colonial. So far as attitudes to the future of British North America were concerned, it quickly seemed as if the Lytton interlude had never happened. Under pressure from Galt, the gruff 'reserve' of 1858 was soon explained away: British insistence on imperial control of any movement towards federation was evidence of the importance, not of the undesirability, of the aim, and in any case, the British government would be happy to respond to a colonial initiative.

In October 1859, Merivale recalled that Head's experience of both Canada and New Brunswick had convinced him 'that the best prospect for the so called Lower Provinces was an Union between them (legislative, as I think, and not federative) to the *exclusion* of Canada with which a subsequent *federal* union might or might not be formed'. Newcastle agreed:

I believe it would be beneficial in itself, and so far from being an impediment to any future Union with Canada it would place such a measure on a more just footing by rendering it more nearly a union of equals instead of appending three weak Provinces to one strong one and *swamping* the divided interests of the former by the united influence of the latter.

British North American federation would follow Maritime Union, but Newcastle did not believe that the time had arrived 'to take any active steps for bringing it about'.[147] None the less, he read Head's resurrected memorandum on Maritime Union 'with great interest' in the early months of 1860.[148] Although the cause of British North American union seemed to Merivale to have been set back because 'the politicians of Canada have rather injured the prospects of the whole scheme by using it for their own political purposes',[149] Newcastle presumably expected further moves towards Confederation from across the Atlantic. In January 1860, he refined the position of the British government, disclaiming any intention of initiating a movement towards a union of the provinces, but equally offering an assurance that Britain would not stand in the way.[150] There was perhaps an element of rosy exaggeration in Watkin's subsequent statement, that by 1860 the Duke of Newcastle agreed that the union of British North America was 'the necessary, the logical result of completing the Intercolonial Railway and laying the broad foundations for the completion of such union of a railway to the Pacific'.[151] However, at about this time it seems that Newcastle was sufficiently interested in the question of intercolonial union to remove from the official files the memorandum on the subject drafted in 1849 by T.W.C. Murdoch.[152] Moreover, in 1860 he became the first colonial secretary to visit the provinces while holding office, escorting the young Prince of Wales on a state visit. Both the memorandum and the tour perhaps tended to increase the duke's natural tendency to see problems rather than opportunities: he was to report to the cabinet in 1862 that his visit had further convinced him that 'minor measures' had to precede a general union.[153] A proposal in 1861 from the Canadian government for an assimilation of British American tariffs prompted Elliot to comment that most people

who have reflected on the subject, are rather favourable to the idea of a legislative union among the Lower Provinces, — some (of whom I should not be one) are even favorable to a union of the whole of the Provinces, &, none, I believe, would consider it wise for this Country to put itself in direct and avowed opposition to that object, if it should be generally sought by the colonists themselves.

Two years later, Elliot's views were unchanged: Maritime Union was desirable and should be encouraged but 'to promote, — or foster the discussion of, — their Incorporation with Canada is far more doubtful'.[154] Elliot's determination to see Maritime Union as a one-step programme only underlines the fact that Newcastle, cautious though he was, saw it as part of a wider move towards the general union of British North America. This, he insisted in 1860, 'is what must eventually be brought about and may be hastened by events arising out of the condition of the rest of the Continent'.[155] Yet he could reassure the suspicious Manners Sutton in 1861 both that intercolonial union lay in the future and that the provinces, not Britain, must take the lead in bringing it about.[156] In June 1862, he succeeded in finding a formula which urged the provinces into action while still reserving the ultimate role to the imperial power.[157]

Just as our understanding of the events of 1858 has been greatly enhanced by the discovery of the private papers of Lord Stanley, so the reconstruction of a memorandum by Newcastle throws light on his attitude to British North American union in 1862.[158] The document was drawn up as a submission to the cabinet early in 1862, and argued in favour of a British guarantee of a loan for the construction of the Intercolonial railway. Newcastle was locked in combat with the chancellor of the exchequer, Gladstone, who — in the words of the exasperated though financially very interested Watkin — 'thought spending money, or taking risks, however slight, a kind of crime'.[159] The subsequent history of Newcastle's memorandum is a reminder of the vulnerability of archival material. In 1879, fifteen years after his death, there was a major fire at Clumber, the family's Nottinghamshire stately home. Remarkably, books and pictures were removed from the blaze, but a Sèvres vase fused into glass and Newcastle's private papers were only rescued as bundles had begun to char. Oddly enough, it was Gladstone, Newcastle's executor, who undertook the work of salvage, reporting that as many as thirty thousand documents had been 'thrown about everywhere'. He was tempted 'to destroy the whole mass', rather than risk the escape of sensitive material.[160] In these circumstances, it is not surprising that Newcastle's 47-page memorandum remained in disarray. Somebody certainly attempted to re-assemble it at some stage, for the first few pages were re-numbered in another hand, but the rescue was quickly abandoned. Perhaps it was Gladstone who made the attempt, and perhaps he did not wish to be reminded of days when he had clashed with the man who had once been among his closest friends.

Newcastle included in his memorandum four areas of imperial interest which favoured the construction of the Intercolonial. One of these, the improvement of postal services, he admitted to be 'minor'. He saw the Intercolonial as a means of facilitating British trade, by securing 'our access over British ground to our most important Colony, as well as to the whole of the vast Western region which must yearly become more and more important to us as it fills with an ever increasing population of producers and consumers'. The third argument of Newcastle's argument was defence, and drew heavily on the inconveniences encountered in reinforcing the provinces during the *Trent* crisis. 'With a Railway ... we should wait & watch the turn of events, confident in our power of rapidly and surely reinforcing the troops in Canada in case of necessity.'[161] Newcastle's argument for an Intercolonial railway may have contained an element of special pleading. The previous summer, he had put up a stiff and successful resistance to military pressure for precautionary large-scale reinforcements to be sent to British North America to signal to the Northern States that Britain took its responsibilities in the provinces seriously.[162] Newcastle's stance may in turn have been influenced by his bruising experience as War Minister during the Crimean campaign, since there was more than a hint in his opposition of a notion that such matters were too important to be decided by generals.[163] The *Trent* crisis came a few months later, and Newcastle seems to have sought to convince himself that it was the absence of a railway, rather than the lack of adequate garrisons, which constituted Britain's weakness.

Each of these arguments, in fact, was little more than a preliminary to political considerations, and Newcastle was ready 'to rest my case upon this fourth and last head'. He recognised that the Intercolonial railway was not a project to be assessed merely in the present. 'Indeed no one can fairly judge the question who looks merely to the wants and wishes of the moment and does not look beyond immediate results into the great future of our North

American Colonies.' Isolation weakened the provinces, leaving Canada 'practically cut off from Europe during six months out of the twelve', while the 'poor & petty Dependencies' of the Maritimes were 'incapable of running the race of competition' with frontier regions of the United States. 'Statesmen have looked for a remedy of this state of things and they have naturally thought they found it in a union, either legislative or federal, of all the North American Colonies.' This was the project which Newcastle had asked Elgin to take up eight years earlier, but experience of the difficulties involved had 'convinced me that though this is the object to be aimed at', it would have to be the culmination of a phased programme. 'The Lower Provinces will not accede to the wishes of Canada for a federal union because they justly fear that their individual interests would be swamped by the powerful combination of the two Canadas.' Maritimers were however aware of their own weakness, and might overcome 'local jealousies' to form a union of their own 'if there were not the great physical obstacles of want of intercommunication'. A railway 'interlacing them from North to South' would prepare the Maritimes 'when thus combined into one Province for that more important union with Canada which as a British object ought in my opinion to be always kept in view'.

More generally, Newcastle accepted that 'Canada cannot for ever — perhaps not for long — remain a British Colony. Upon this Railroad in my opinion depends in great measure her future destiny.' Without a rail link to the seaboard, the province of Canada could not become an independent state, but would eventually be absorbed into whatever structure emerged from the Civil War to the south. 'But with the railroad made and the union with the Lower Provinces effected she would become to us a strong & self-reliant Colony so long as her present relationship with the Mother Country continues'. When separation eventually came, Canada would be 'a powerful and independent Ally and a most valuable, I believe an essential, makeweight in the balance of power on the American Continent'. The upheavals of recent years 'have warned politicians not to prophesy' but all the same 'I cannot imagine an object more clearly marked out for a British Statesman to aim at than to secure the continued separation of Canada and the United States and the eventual foundation of a powerful State out of the disjointed and feeble British North American Provinces.'

Newcastle's vision of the future went still further. He forecast that the heavy burden of taxation caused by the American Civil War would lead to the further secession of the West, which would make the inland states even more dependent upon the St Lawrence after losing control of the Mississippi. 'A continuous line of Railway through British Territory from Chicago to Halifax would be a most valuable bond of amity between us and them', and one which would ensure both 'good behaviour on their part' as well as good prospects of making the railway 'a paying concern'.

Finally, Newcastle permitted himself 'a still deeper dive into futurity'. Railways spanning the entire continent would come far sooner than most observers predicted, 'if time is measured by the life of Nations', and the Intercolonial would play a major part in influencing the route to be taken from the Atlantic to the Pacific. The choice for Britain would be 'whether it shall give us over our own territory a free and clear passage across America (and thus in fact around the world) or leave us at the mercy of probably two or three more separate Republics, one or other or all of which may often be in hostility to us'.[164]

Within a few months, as will be argued in Chapter Five, the rapidly unfolding North American crisis had begun to shorten the time horizon. The defeat of the Militia Bill in Canada provoked an outcry in Britain, and the vexed issue of defence became increasingly intertwined with that of federation. True, in the angry debates in the House of Commons, nobody linked the two subjects, but commentators as various as Goldwin Smith and Anthony Trollope espoused the idea as a gradual means to the dissolution of the colonial tie. Goldwin Smith believed that the provinces were 'plainly destined to form a united confederation'.[165] Trollope felt that if Britain's object 'be to keep the colonies, then I should say that an amalgamation of the Canadas with Nova Scotia and New Brunswick should not be regarded with favour by statesmen in Downing Street', but if such narrow ideas of imperial power 'are now out of vogue with British statesmen, then I think that such an amalgamation should receive all the support which Downing Street can give it'.[166]

One British statesman who wholeheartedly agreed was Russell, now very much an elder statesman, and whose role as foreign secretary brought him once again to consider the future of Canada which he had first debated half a century earlier as an undergraduate.[167] In June 1862, he drafted a letter to Newcastle urging that the British government should make a 'public recommendation' of 'a Federal Union of the British North American Provinces' to Canada, New Brunswick and Nova Scotia. This was 'the plan long ago contemplated & then found impracticable' to which, 'more than twenty years ago', Sir James Kempt had 'objected naturally enough on the ground of the difficulty of communication'. Russell envisaged a federal system, in which French Canadians 'would find themselves always outvoted by the colonists of British descent', while each 'state' would have 'an Assembly for local purposes' but forbidden to meddle with questions of defence or tariffs — the latter being required to pay for a combined 'Federal force' of regular and militia troops. In return for a 'perpetually binding' agreement limiting import duties on British goods to a ceiling of 15 per cent, the British government would 'at once' guarantee the loan necessary to construct the Intercolonial. 'The Federal Province might be constituted in such a manner as to form a loyal constitutional State subject always to the British Crown.'[168]

The destruction wrought by the Clumber fire makes it impossible to be certain that Russell actually sent this letter, but the balance of probability is that Newcastle was aware of the views of his cabinet colleague. In 1861, the Nova Scotian Assembly had passed a generally worded resolution designed to explore British policy towards the federation of British North America. It was not until May 1862 that the resolution was forwarded to London, and there is some reason to suspect that — as in 1857 — the Nova Scotians believed that they would help the prospects of securing funding for the Intercolonial by making polite noises about a project known to be popular in Britain. Newcastle now decided that Maritime Union need not necessarily precede Confederation. 'I would not discourage the larger scheme,' he wrote, 'but I would give the Colonists to understand that the movement must come from them though I am well inclined to enter heartily into any well-considered plan which has the concurrence of all the Parties concerned.'[169] As will be discussed in Chapter Six, no trace of heartiness permeated the resulting despatch of 6 July 1862, but it was none the less to prove an important document in facilitating the negotiations of 1864.

***

The evidence, then, points to the development of a British consensus, if often a latent one, in favour of a regional union of British North America. 'Everybody pretty well agrees that this is the best chance for Canada,' the *Spectator* remarked in August 1862.[170] Does this simply bring us back to Buckner's statement that 'while British support was essential for Confederation, it was circumstances within British North America which gave the British something to support'?[171] A key point here is that some of the evidence for a British consensus in favour of eventual Confederation comes from statements by observers in the provinces themselves, who noted — not always with approval — that metropolitan enthusiasm appeared to be well ahead of colonial reality. 'The idea of uniting all the British North American Provinces is said to be a popular one in London,' William Lyon Mackenzie observed in 1850.[172] Francis Hincks in 1853 felt that 'up to this time the scheme of Union has had more support among Eminent British Statesmen than in any other quarter.' Hincks believed that a British North American federation would be a disaster for imperial interests, but he conceded that it 'might possibly be carried if British influence were thrown in the scale in its favour'.[173] The Nova Scotian P.S. Hamilton, on the other hand, a strong enthusiast for legislative union, was encouraged by the thought of British support. 'An opinion prevails in British America that many of the leading statesmen of Great Britain are more desirous than otherwise that a union of these Provinces take place.'[174] Galt was similarly encouraged by favourable press comment on Confederation in 1858.[175]

By the 1860s, well-informed British North Americans knew that the British favoured the creation of a regional union in British North America, and awareness of British support and potentially of British influence can hardly have been absent when the Great Coalition decided to include Confederation among its aims in 1864. The next step in the discussion is to clarify the argument by defining what (and who) is meant by 'the British', and examining their perceptions of the constitutional structures which would be required and the extent of their knowledge of the provinces they hoped to see amalgamated. Chapter Four does not go so far as to conclude that in matters of imperial constitutional engineering, ignorance was bliss — if nothing else, the British can hardly be accused of foolhardy intervention — but it does suggest that hazy knowledge widely diffused had some far-reaching implications for metropolitan ideas about the future of British North America.

4 The British and their Perceptions

Who were 'the British' who desired to see Confederation brought about? How far did they appreciate the realities and challenges of British North America? What did they mean when they used terms like 'federation' or 'union'? This Chapter asks who? where? and what? as a preliminary to looking at the crucial questions of motive and means — why? when? and how?[1] In each of these discussions, a good deal of vagueness will be encountered — ignorance about the province of Canada and especially about the rest of British North America, imprecision in the use of terms, generalised and simplistic assumptions about the utility of an intercolonial union. Historians like to define and are expected to provide neat and, above all, logical explanations. Yet Confederation may be better understood through a blurred focus. Imprecision, even outright fuzziness, is an essential part of understanding British notions about their North American provinces.

This imprecision is encountered at the outset, in attempting to define that most basic term, 'British'. What is meant by references to 'British policy' or 'British support'? Who were these 'British'? Imperial historians have tended to use a shorthand form, 'the Colonial Office', an unhelpful compound exercise in reification, since it assumes not merely the existence of coherent policies, but their origin in an administrative super-brain or think-tank.[2] As already noted, Goodfellow's description of British support for South African federation in the 1870s as 'more of a hope than a policy' is a helpful caution against the casual over-use of that loaded word.[3] Certainly the mid-Victorian Colonial Office was not an immediately obvious location for a ruthlessly long-sighted policy machine. Its cramped building at 14 Downing Street was condemned in 1839 as beyond repair. Reconstruction was considered in 1858, and in 1860 the Duke of Newcastle hoped that the building would fall down at night: he was certain that it would fall sometime. Not until 1876 was the 'commonplace brick house' demolished. The cellars were so damp that fires had to be kept burning year-round to preserve the despatches stored there.[4]

William Baillie-Hamilton, who joined the office as a young man in 1864, was quickly disillusioned in his hopes of becoming 'an active participant in some of the most important and delicate ideas of State', and regarded much of the longhand copying work of the junior clerks as 'a singularly elaborate waste of time'.[5] 'The staff is in its lower departments ineffective ... whilst in its higher branches it is so overtaxed as to be quite unequal to its work', Carnarvon complained in 1866.[6] The clerks were certainly not overtaxed: their working day began at noon and officially ended at 5.30 in the afternoon. Around the time of Carnarvon's plaint, bored junior officials established a fives court in an empty attic, but their exertions threatened the stability of the building and they took instead to playing darts, improvised from pen-nibs tied with the celebrated red tape.[7]

In the circumstances, it may seem surprising that so many historians have discussed imperial relations in the mid-nineteenth century in terms of the activities of 'the Colonial Office'. A major reason, of course, was that contemporaries themselves abused 'the great house at the bottom of Downing-street', in the demonology of the mendacious controversialist Edward Gibbon Wakefield.[8] Henry Taylor, for fifty years a key official, felt a certain pride that 'England was probably the only country in Europe' which could house an important government department in a building 'less like a centre of State affairs than a decent lodging-house',[9] but Charles Buller conjured a very different picture of dispirited colonists dejectedly waiting to lobby for redress of barely comprehended grievances in '*the Sighing Rooms*', with their 'old and meagre furniture ... tables covered with baize, and some old and crazy chairs scattered about'.[10] The obscurity and seediness of the premises made the Colonial Office an easy target. 'Should the authority which extended from pole to pole be hid up three pairs of stairs in a *cul-de-sac* in Westminster?'[11] When Sir William Molesworth attacked the Colonial Office in 1850, *The Times* cautioned that he was assaulting a 'fabulous monster',[12] while George Cornewall Lewis gravely concluded that critics exploited the unpopularity of the Colonial

Office 'to attribute to its influence what are in fact the evils inherent on dependence'.[13] Even a governor-general could slip into the trap of referring with airy disapproval to 'the Colonial Office (in which phrase I understand you to be comprehended)', as the Duke of Newcastle wrote in rebuke to Lord Monck.[14]

Modern historians have perhaps been inclined to embrace this shorthand reification of 'the Colonial Office' partly because it is undoubtedly a convenient simplification, but also because in the late nineteenth and early twentieth centuries, there was an active and academic bureaucracy at the heart of the empire. Historical debate over the nature of British imperial policy-making for almost forty years has been greatly influenced by the brilliant but largely undefined concept of an 'official mind', at one and the same time the distillation of inherited experience and an independent determining cause of events in its own right.[15] This concept may be helpful in explaining how the British suddenly came to occupy much of the African continent in the 1880s, but it is less illuminating, when applied in the surrogate form of 'the Colonial Office', to the mid-nineteenth century. It is true, for instance, that mid-century officials, like the mandarins of a later generation, debated their responses by means of 'minutes'. These solemn-sounding documents were less impressive than they might sound. In most cases, the first step in minuting a document was to fold over the corner of its last page to make a triangle within which comments were scribbled. The process was apparently introduced in 1836, and the degree to which it was encouraged depended to a great extent upon the personality of successive ministers: Grey in the late 1840s seems to have been the first to create an atmosphere within which senior officials felt able openly to voice what were often grumbles and prejudices about governors and their colonies. The practice became so well established that at the time of Confederation, an embarrassed minister had to break the news to Joseph Howe that it was impossible to return the last page of a document which he had submitted because it had been covered with comments.[16] However, there is no correlation between the subjects minuted and any intrinsic importance in the issues involved. Questions of style and precedence drew far more comment than issues of policy: Herman Merivale once raised the question of whether it was correct to use the term 'predecessor' to describe somebody who was still alive.[17]

Much of the unpopularity of the Colonial Office can be attributed to its association with James Stephen, the stiff and upright under-secretary from 1836 to 1847, Charles Buller's 'Mr Mother Country'. Even Russell, whom Stephen admired, could privately joke that Stephen's great fault was 'that instead of being Under-Secretary *for* the Colonies, he was Under-Secretary *against* the Colonies'.[18] Stephen was mortified by the frequent public attacks upon him, as he noted sardonically in his diary in March 1846 when he met with Gladstone and Lyttelton, respectively colonial secretary and parliamentary under-secretary, and his senior colleague, T.F. Elliot, to discuss land regulations for South Australia, 'forming thus in fact the much abused "Colonial Office" in the full manifestation of all its imputed ignorance, oppression folly & so on.'[19] Although he began his career as a lawyer and ended as Professor of History at Cambridge, Stephen had no illusions of a Colonial Office masterplan. 'It would be a very arduous task to vindicate the best of our Colonial schemes of Government on the principles of political philosophy,' he wrote in 1836. 'All that be said for them is, that they are as good as Parliament will sanction, and the Colonists will accept.'[20] Stephen at least felt that the Colonial Office had to go through the motions of responding to problems. 'To do nothing is indeed easy,' he wrote in 1836, 'but to determine that nothing shall be done, is impossible.'[21] His political masters did not always agree. In handing over the seals of the Colonial Office in 1839, Lord Normanby advised Lord John Russell that some problems 'might by postponement dispose of themselves — a process to which you will find after a little practise many Colonial questions are not unapt to yield'.[22] Heroically, in view of his workload, Stephen did attempt to work with Lord Howick in designing a 'forecasting Policy' for British North America in 1836-7, one which involved preparing the way for federation.[23] In December 1837, Howick encouraged the prime minister, Lord Melbourne, to discuss the idea of British North American federation with Stephen in person, but warned that the meeting would be 'rather a severe trial of your patience for he has not a good manner of communicating his opinions'.[24]

Stephen's venture into anticipatory policy-making was not to be repeated, and officials made remarkably little contribution to the shaping of British policy in the coming of Confederation. Even T.W.C. Murdoch and T.F. Elliot, who had actually visited Canada, were marginal participants, perhaps not least because each had seen the province at a time of constitutional upheaval: Elliot as secretary to the Gosford Commission in the mid-1830s, Murdoch as secretary to Sir Charles Bagot in 1842. Certainly, although Elliot noted in 1848 that the rapid increase of Canada's population was 'most remarkable', he either failed to appreciate the extent to which the province had changed, or regarded its rapid growth as additional reason for responding with alarm to deft Canadian moves to seize the initiative for constitutional change after 1858.[25] Murdoch did prepare a memorandum on the subject in 1849, probably to brief the parliamentary under-secretary Benjamin Hawes at the time of a Commons debate on John Arthur Roebuck's scheme for a British North American federation. Although insisting that it was 'beyond our province to offer any opinions upon it' because 'such a measure must be discussed and decided upon purely political grounds', Murdoch nonetheless conveyed a disapproval which Hawes managed to ignore.[26]

While Colonial Office staff fended off ambitious inventors, soothed correspondents who felt that railings should be built at Niagara Falls and dealt with various correspondents who were either in lunatic asylums or (so officialdom thought) should be confined to them, much of the real policy-making was carried on through another channel: that of a quasi-official private correspondence with the governor-general of Canada. Herman Merivale, Stephen's successor, strongly supported this method of communication, advising incoming ministers in 1852 that because of the 'anomalies' of responsible government, 'the institution itself being scarcely tried as yet', the best form of 'unreserved communication' between colonial secretary and governor-general was 'not by despatch either public or private, but by letter'.[27] Newcastle, soon after taking office, informed Lord Elgin in Canada that he understood 'that whilst Lord Grey was Colonial Secretary it was your habit to correspond privately with him on most subjects connected with Government and that in consequence the Official Despatches were less frequent from Canada than from most other far less important Colonies'. Elgin promptly undertook to supply unofficial reports 'over & above that contained in formal despatches'.[28] As Merivale explained to Lytton in 1858, 'the official correspondence is *intentionally* meagre and defective' since an official record of metropolitan views of Canadian public affairs 'would probably sever the slight connexion between us and Canada without delay'.[29]

Yet even Merivale had to admit that the system was 'by no means free from objection', the more so if an incoming minister was personally unacquainted with the governor-general or if party allegiances were a barrier between them. Sydenham hoped that the Whigs would hold on to power for the whole of his term as governor-general, telling Lord John Russell that if a political opponent came into office, he would not feel that he could 'discuss matters with the Secretary of State on equal terms as if I was still his Colleague in the Cabinet'.[30] Unluckily, the Whig government fell at just the moment when Sydenham died from the effects of a riding accident, creating a double caesura. Lord Stanley, the new colonial secretary, reported to Peel that Sydenham had 'communicated, if at all, privately with Lord John, of which correspondence we have hardly a trace'.[31] Elgin joked that should Grey resign, his successor 'will have little idea of what is going on unless you let him see my private letters to you'.[32] No wonder that Stanley pointed out in 1849 'that private correspondence is the private property of the Secretary of State' which he would take with him when he left office.[33] His son did just that on transferring from the Colonies to the India Office in 1858, with awkward results.

The existence of a quasi-official private correspondence between colonial secretary and governor-general is an important element in understanding the British role in the coming of Confederation. The system almost became institutionalised: outgoing ministers often made available recent letters to their successors, and on the change of ministry in 1866 Lord Monck asked the incoming under-secretary, his friend C.B. Adderley, for a long-range introduction to the new minister, Lord Carnarvon, explaining that he had found great advantage 'from having been on terms of private intimacy with both my previous masters'.[34] Such private correspondence shifted the focus of policy-making further from officials towards their political masters, and probably made it much easier for an interested prime minister to undertake close supervision of British relations with Canada. The correspondence between Grey and Elgin, for instance, is well-known thanks to its publication in a scholarly edition, but less evident is the extent to which the correspondence was triangular, with at least sixteen traceable examples of Grey forwarding the governor-general's reports to

Russell — an arrangement of which Elgin himself may not have been aware.[35]

Perhaps more important, private correspondence between the colonial secretary and the governor-general offered one way of breaking the technical impasse which inhibited the launching of a political initiative for the union of the British North American provinces. Grey unsuccessfully urged Elgin to take steps to push the issue to the fore. Stanley in 1858 was if anything too positive in encouraging Sir Edmund Head to seize an opportunity to get federation on to the agenda.[36] One of the factors working against the ill-fated federal initiative of 1858 was that it came at a moment when the confidential channel between colonial secretary and governor-general had temporarily broken down, with Stanley too harried by the crisis of the Indian Mutiny to remember to pass on his earlier correspondence and Lytton too new and insecure in office to have established his own lines of communication. There were frequent changes in the post of colonial secretary between 1852 and 1858, at a time when Sir Edmund Head was in political terms the least distinguished, although by no means the least able, governor-general between Bagot and Confederation. As a result, Head 'got into a way of writing his narration of events in the form of long private letters' to the civil servant Merivale, although his close friendship with George Cornewall Lewis gave him a direct line to an influential figure who was a cabinet minister from 1855 to 1858.[37]

The apparent breakdown in the private correspondence between colonial secretary and governor-general may explain why no serious attempt was made to press the issue of British North American union in the mid-1850s. However, such judgements must be tempered by realisation that not all personal archives have survived. Given that such private correspondence was by its nature widely dispersed, historians have in fact been remarkably well served by the material available. A major exception is the gap of just over two years from late 1855 to early 1858, for some part of which it seems likely that Head and Labouchere were in direct contact. What can be stated with certainty is that by the time Monck was partnered first with Newcastle and then with Cardwell, the link was working efficiently, so much so that Monck sought its continuation when the political see-saw brought a stranger into office in 1866. It may be going too far to claim that a continuous quasi-official correspondence between colonial secretary and governor-general was a necessary precondition for the launching of a Confederation initiative, but it would seem difficult to deny that such a link was vital if a governor-general was going to be successful in emulating 'a man riding two horses in a circus',[38] by reconciling his imperial role with his Canadian responsibilities.

If the existence of a near-continuous and quasi-official private correspondence removes the location of policy-making further from officialdom, it also widens the question of the definition of what is meant by the term 'British'. If ministers rather than civil servants determined the responses to events which presumably constitute 'policy', then we need to seek for the origins of their ideas in a broader context of opinion-formation. The phrase 'British opinion' may be sustained on the basis of three defensible hypotheses. The first is that opinion emerged from an inter-related network of comment in the press and certain influential periodicals, which also provided a platform for the discussion of official reports and some of the vast flood of pamphlets which characterised the period, all reciprocally connected with parliamentary debates, which collectively constituted a forum for the discussion of ideas. Secondly, it may be argued that certainly between 1832 and 1867, the years of the First and Second Reform Acts, politics in Britain continued to be dominated by a minority of the population at the apex of a social pyramid, who constituted not so much a twentieth-century idea of a 'ruling class' but rather something closer to Edmund Burke's view of a Britain in the hands of those whom one scholar has identified as the 'political nation' of the eighteenth century.[39] Not even the two-party system of Whigs and Tories, Liberals and Conservatives should obscure the essential truth that the political nation of the mid-nineteenth century was agreed on almost all fundamental matters, and even on many peripheral ones — which explains why even though the Liberal Irish peer Lord Monck had never actually met the Conservative Berkshire landowner Lord Carnarvon, he could feel reasonably sure that that once in direct contact, they would share the same general policy aims. Thirdly, the British frankly knew little about their empire in general and their North American colonies were no exception to this ignorance. Sketchy perceptions of British North America actually made it easier to subscribe to vague hopes for their destiny: hence the paradox that British opinion was almost certainly more enthusiastic about the prospect of Confederation for two decades or more before 1867 than was the case in British North America itself, where politicians knew at first hand the magnitude of the problems of scale and diversity which would have to be overcome.

The survival of such a vast amount of both personal and official correspondence from the mid-nineteenth century is in some sense misleading, for it tends to obscure the extent to which the free flow of ideas moved through two other channels — at a basic level through personal conversation and at a much higher level through newspapers and reviews, the two processes combining in the case of Canada to create the outline of notions and prejudices which constitute 'British opinion'. The overwhelming majority of the conversations are utterly lost to us; the enormous bulk of newspaper files would defy even a lifetime of research. One of the great advantages of a correspondence like that between Elgin and Grey was that it took place between men separated by thousands of miles of ocean, who had necessarily to commit to paper not merely their day-to-day opinions but discussions of the assumptions behind them. Yet even the Grey-Elgin correspondence rested upon previous personal discussion. 'You know we settled that you were not to be merely nominal Governor General,' Grey wrote, 'but to exercise substantial authority over the Lower Provinces.'[40] Elgin presumably knew exactly what the colonial secretary meant, but we do not.

The scraps of evidence which survive are often tantalising. James Stephen shared a cab from Paddington Station to Piccadilly with, of all people, Charles Buller, one day in 1846, 'talking chiefly of Canada'.[41] What exactly did they discuss? Perhaps nothing very profound, given Stephen's taciturnity and his antipathy to his fellow-passenger. One spring day in 1852, the Duke of Newcastle unexpectedly found himself sharing a railway carriage with Edward Watkin. The two men talked about American affairs, of 'slavery, and the possibility of a separation of North and South'. It is not unlikely that in such a context they also discussed the future of British North America, but Watkin's evidence does not go beyond a recollection that they were travelling 'probably between Rugby and Derby'.[42] Given that such conversations took place, perhaps fairly frequently, among influential British figures who generally possessed no profound knowledge of British North American reality, it would not be surprising if they frequently turned to the superficially attractive idea of federation as the all-purpose solution to a colonial anomaly. It may well be that the possibility of federation also formed part of the staple conversational fare with visiting colonials, if only for lack of alternative topics, and this may explain why so many British North American politicians were convinced of the strength of British support for the idea. When Edward Knatchbull-Hugessen greeted the prickly Liberal Edward Blake in the early 1870s with the words, 'Well I hope our friend Sir John Macdonald is getting along all right', he dropped a brick the size of a boulder, but the real significance of the story is that even a junior minister at the Colonial Office (albeit one whose hobby was writing children's fairy tales) was not richly endowed with conversational gambits on Canada.[43]

Opinion, whether informed or half-ignorant, emerged from a primeval cloud of comment in newspapers, parliamentary speeches and pamphlets. Cornewall Lewis, in his 1849 essay, *The Influence of Authority on Matters of Opinion*, identified two reasons why the press was 'one of the principal guides of public opinion'. The first was that leading articles acquired an *ex cathedra* status from their anonymity, which gave far greater weight to any pronouncement than could possibly come from even the most distinguished of named columnists.[44] As a young barrister, Frederic Rogers eked out his income both by working as a free-lance leader-writer for *The Times* and by dining out at the tables of fashionable London hostesses. While in preparing a leading article, Rogers might have considered and discarded various approaches, he was surprised by the extent to which conversation at fashionable social gatherings would consist of the rehashing of phrases he himself had committed to print in fleshing out and polishing the viewpoints of his employers. Understandably, he found it

amusing, to see how mere commonplace views on this or that subject, were taken for granted at dinner parties for the next week or so. ... They *talked* my article, as if there was no other point in the debate than that which I had selected, and no other conceivable opinion but that which I had, perhaps doubtfully, adopted.[45]

It is hardly necessary to suggest that such dinner table opinion was dominated more by the majesty of *The Times* than by the ingenuity of young Mr Rogers, nor should it be surprising that ministers took care to ensure that *The Times* formed a central part in the 'British' response both to the launching of Confederation in 1864 and to the outfacing of New Brunswick in 1865.[46]

Lewis based his second reason for the influence of the press on the argument that each journal acquired 'an authority extrinsic to the mere anonymous effect of the arguments or opinions which it circulates' by virtue of being identified with a particular political party or philosophy. He pointed out that this made the relationship between the press and public opinion a two-way process, since the need for circulation tempted newspapers to 'seek to render their opinions acceptable to a large number of purchasers, and thus they often follow, as well as lead, public opinion'.[47] From the point of view of Canadian issues, it is the first half of the point which needs to be emphasised: few newspaper readers in Britain could have been expected to have well-defined views on British North America themselves — but if they felt themselves to be Conservatives, they would read a Conservative newspaper, which would tell them what a Conservative should think about Canada. The fact that the *Morning Post* in 1838 or the *Morning Herald* in 1849 could pronounce favourably on British North American federation may not in itself be of great historical significance: there are few things as ephemeral as a daily newspaper. It is rather the fact that support for British North American union can be traced, not consistently but none the less often unexpectedly, in such ultra-tory newspapers which underpins the argument for a broad 'British' consensus favouring an eventual regional union of the colonies.

The leading article was all the more influential because mid-nineteenth century newspapers did not carry front-page headlines: the leader both reported and commented on current events. This strengthened the inter-relationship between speeches, pamphlets and editorial comment. Many pamphlets were printed mainly for the purpose of stimulating press comment: few succeeded, and when the abolition of the Newspaper Stamp Duty in 1855 encouraged the launching of new newspapers and reviews, the craft went into rapid decline.[48] Speeches delivered by leading politicians outside parliament were not necessarily aimed at their immediate audiences who, like the yokels of Trollope's East Barsetshire as they listened to Mr Daubeny, were 'wont to extract more actual enjoyment from the music of his periods than from the strength of his arguments'. What counted were not even the newspaper reports of the speech the following day, but rather 'the next day the leading articles, in which the world was told what it was that the Prime Minister had really said'.[49] Richard Cobden conducted a long-running battle against this practice, aimed especially at *The Times*, whose management he accused of not only hiding behind 'a strict *incognito* towards the public' but interposing a distorting filter between orator and readers.[50]

Public speeches by major figures purely devoted to colonial subjects were so infrequent that other motives must be suspected. Gladstone's celebrated sense of duty no doubt led him in November 1855 to outline his views on 'Our Colonies' to the Chester Mechanics Institute, but it may not have been coincidence that the post of colonial secretary was vacant and Gladstone himself was out of office and apparently drifting between parties.[51] (*The Times* handled the speech roughly, charging Gladstone with avoiding committing himself on the important issue of colonial federation: he had merely contented himself with 'adorning commonplace ideas by clear arrangement and well-chosen language'.[52]) As its grandiose nickname, 'the fourth estate', implied, the press was probably at its most powerful while parliament was in session, for speeches at Westminster provided a vast and immediate flow of copy for editorial comment which could in turn stir up further parliamentary debate. When *The Times* expressed doubts about Sir Edmund Head's handling of the political upheaval of 1858 — although supporting the idea of federation itself — Merivale calmed the agitated Sir Edward Lytton with the reassurance that 'all this will have passed over, & be forgotten, long before Parliament meets'.[53]

Because newspapers are ephemeral, historians must be on guard against reading too much into a single statement in a single issue. Even *The Times*, the mightiest and most read of London journals, was 'famous for its versatility and inconsistency'.[54] Several points may be made here in reference to British press discussion of Confederation. Coverage of the issue was mainly reactive: the union of British North America would be discussed, if at all, in the context of some form of crisis in Canada — the Maritimes were rarely mentioned.[55] By the 1850s, at least, such references were invariably in favour of an eventual union: the significant historical point lies not with the individual references, which in themselves may have carried little weight, but in the cumulative evidence of an overall pattern reflecting a general consensus. There were occasions when British North American issues, such as the 1837 rebellions and the clergy reserves, became entangled with party battles in Britain, and the whole question of Protection versus Free Trade had implications for the colonies. However, by and large, the question of intercolonial union had no partisan overtones. As Lewis argued, it seems reasonable to assume that subscribers to newspapers chose those journals which most closely reflected their beliefs and prejudices on major issues. 'People talk of the war in Spain, and the Canada question,' observed the Duke of Wellington in 1838. 'But all that is of little moment. The real question is church or no church.'[56] When journals which ferociously upheld the claims of the established Church shared with those which wished to tear it down a desire to see the British North American provinces united, it is fair to speak of a 'British' viewpoint.

There can be no doubt that *The Times* dominated the daily press. Even in 1840, a disgruntled rival could damn it as 'the misleading journal of Europe', and from then until the abolition of the Newspaper Stamp Duty its circulation steadily climbed, dwarfing all its London rivals.[57] '*The Times* is very powerful, and it has got a great hold upon the public mind, and, when once this sort of power is established, it is difficult to undermine it,' Charles Greville wrote disapprovingly in 1855.[58] Lord Clarendon, who was to be one of its victims, more succinctly concluded that it was 'a well-known fact' that *The Times* 'forms or guides or reflects — no matter which — the public opinion of England'.[59] In Clarendon's formulation, the shaping of opinion could be a two-way process, but *The Times*, increasingly arrogant in the consciousness of its power, talked far more than it listened. Occasionally, as in 1851 when it attacked the Hungarian patriot Kossuth, *The Times* received 'a slap in the face' by unexpectedly running counter to public sentiment. Cobden complained at the 'absurd position' of so complete a dictatorship over public opinion exercised 'by one newspaper, that it requires a periodical revolt of the whole people to keep the despot in tolerable order!'.[60] Stanley thought the only post to carry so much power as the editorship of *The Times* was that of governor-general of India; for Anthony Trollope, the effective comparison was with the Tsar of Russia. For Lord Shaftesbury, there was no earthly power which could match *The Times*. 'Millions on Millions of Christian people should meet to "pray down" that paper,' he wrote in 1855, 'and implore God to stop its wicked course.'[61] Not surprisingly, the influence of *The Times* was recognised across the Atlantic. Abraham Lincoln jocularly remarked that it was second only to the Mississippi River in its power.[62] 'The Canadians have been taught to look upon *The Times* as an exponent of the feelings of the British people,' complained a critic.[63] Joseph Howe warned his fellow Nova Scotians 'that making war upon *The Times* is altogether fruitless labour'.[64] When Sir Richard MacDonnell announced that he never read *The Times*, Frances Monck wondered 'how they could entrust any Government to him!'.[65]

However, the enormous power of *The Times* did not mean that other publications were altogether without influence. Abraham Hayward was an interested party when he argued in 1853 that it was 'an error to measure utility by circulation', since he was lobbying political friends to ensure that his own *Morning Chronicle* was given the same access to news stories as its mighty rival, which happened to be their critic. 'Every one of the leading papers is read at all clubs and reading rooms' and effective articles were 'reproduced in the provincial papers, or worked up anew in the shape of speeches'.[66] Disraeli invested much of his time and his supporters' money in attempting to establish a weekly review, the *Press*, on behalf of the Conservative party. In 1854, a year after its launch, he optimistically claimed that it had 'very much affected opinion, has been referred to in both Houses of Parliament' and 'given a tone and cue to the country's journals'.[67] Access even to a minor publication could thus become a ticket of entry to a collective press debate. As Mitchell's *Newspaper Press Directory* put it, the circulation of the London press was 'great — very great numerically — and like a pebble thrown into a stream, the eddies of its intelligence reach far and wide.'[68]

However, the consensus which an old-fashioned tory condemned in 1874 as 'the vulgar prejudice which is nowadays dignified by the name of "Public Opinion"'[69] was moulded by a relatively narrow band of publications. In 1852, the essayist W.R. Greg complained that ministers and MPs 'draw their information from the same *set* of organs, and look at the world through spectacles, different, indeed, in power and colour, but all proceeding from the same workshop.' They were 'insensibly moulded by the gossip of the clubs' and weighed the articles of the Whig *Edinburgh Review* and its Tory rival, the *Quarterly*. They 'listen anxiously to the language of *The Times*, and are not wholly without concern about the articles in the

Morning Chronicle, the *Morning Post*, and the *Daily News*. But beyond these they seldom go.'[70] The list could be disputed: the *Morning Post*, for instance, was diplomatically described by Mitchell's *Newspaper Press Guide* as containing 'just as much of politics as may inform, without distracting', although the impression that it spoke for Palmerston gave it some standing.[71] The *Morning Chronicle* was already in terminal decline, as the Peelite party for which it attempted to speak dwindled towards absorption by the Whigs. In the following decade, the repeal of the Newspaper Stamp Duty enabled some voices to break in — notably the *Saturday* and the *Fortnightly*.

None the less, Greg's general point may be accepted: effective 'British' opinion was moulded and expressed within a limited range of journals. While Mitchell could insist that it was one of 'the vulgar errors of the day' that the provincial press was dwarfed in importance by the metropolitan journals, Greg in 1852 listed the two leading newspapers from the North of England, the *Leeds Mercury* and the *Manchester Guardian*, among those which fell outside the magic circle, 'wide as their circulation, and great as their influence is among the miscellaneous and the middle classes'.[72] The spread of the railways and the rise of another innovation of the Steam Age, the mechanised printing press, added to the nation-wide dominance of the London newspapers. No longer was it true that in the provinces, 'the London newspaper circulates chiefly in exchange rooms, and places of business'.[73] Few pieces of evidence so poignantly capture the hopelessness of Joseph Howe's campaign to block Confederation in Britain than his jubilant report in November 1866 that the capture of the *Hampshire Independent* had given a 'brave lift' to the Nova Scotian cause.[74] If the middle classes and the provinces could exercise little input into the process of forming opinion, the chances of the working classes having a worthwhile say were correspondingly less. Nor is there much evidence of working class political interest in colonial topics, which is perhaps surprising in view of the attractions of emigration to the poor. Attempts by Chartists and radicals in January 1838 to mount a campaign in support of the Canadian rebellions met with little success. At Lambeth, a working man argued that the fighting in Canada would be over before parliament could meet, and time was better spent discussing the grievances of working people. An authentic working class voice 'occasioned some confusion' when it intruded into an oration on Canadian politics by Joseph Hume at a radical meeting in Westminster a few days later. 'Go put your head in a bag', it shouted.[75]

In one sense, this definition of 'British' has a narrowing effect, by recognising that the shaping of opinion was largely confined to an élite. However, their attitudes and opinions seem to have been largely shared at other levels of society. While Chartists were inclined — when they considered Canadian affairs at all — to look favourably upon annexation to the model of republics, other groups on the fringe of political influence seemed on the whole to have embraced élite notions regarding the destiny of British North America. The Nonconformist *Eclectic Review*, for instance, designed its own scheme for British North American federation in 1838, projecting a voluntaryist utopia upon distant colonies.[76] In that sense, the absence of any well-developed alternative vision of the future of British North America, based on class or sectarian conflict, makes a definition of 'British' attitudes derived from relatively narrow sources potentially a broad one as well: many ideas and attitudes in Victorian Britain filtered outward and downward from the élite through the wider Burkean political nation. That was, after all, how British politics operated between the Reform Acts of 1832 and 1867.

This potential inclusiveness of the definition of 'British' opinion could indeed be still further broadened. It is tempting to characterise the participants in mid-nineteenth century imperial affairs as either 'British' or 'colonial', but the distinction may be less rigid than the convenience of discussion would imply. Thus John Arthur Roebuck is labelled 'British', while George Brown is 'Canadian'. Yet Roebuck had been educated in Canada, Brown lived in Scotland until he was eighteen: the label refers to their sphere of operation in adult life, not necessarily to the formation of their basic identities or loyalties. Raw census figures in particular tend to disguise the extent to which Upper Canada was peopled by the British-born: W.H. Russell noticed the change in accents as he travelled overland from Buffalo to Toronto.[77] True, by 1861, almost two-thirds of the population of Upper Canada had been born in the province, with less than 30 per cent coming from Britain. Upper Canada had a high birth-rate, and immigrants were more strongly represented in the adult age-groups: significantly, almost half Upper Canada's legislators on the eve of Confederation were

British-born.[78] The remarkable appeal by the Irish-born Bishop Rogers urging the Catholics of New Brunswick to support Confederation ('Do we owe nothing to the Mother that bore us?') suggests that neither ethnicity nor the nineteenth-century shorthand habit of calling the motherland 'England' excluded those of Irish background.[79] The language and discourse of colonial politics included the native-born as well, as shown by Joseph Howe's protestations of his British-ness, two centuries after his ancestors had left an Essex village for Massachusetts Bay.[80] Even Cartier on one occasion claimed that a Lower Canadian was an Englishman who spoke French, although it may be appropriate to bear in mind that he was speaking to Queen Victoria at the time.[81]

Obviously, it would be much harder to demonstrate just how far a specific idea, such as British North American union, was so transmitted, but there are some indications of a two-way traffic. It was the debates of the British American League at Kingston in 1849 which sparked one of the earliest indications of a general British acceptance of the eventual aim of Confederation. The resolutions of Galt the backbencher in March 1858 stimulated Stanley into the expression of interest which undoubtedly encouraged Sir Edmund Head to allow federation to come on to the political agenda in August, thus triggering the British press consensus in its favour which so encouraged Galt the minister later in the year.[82] More direct interchange was provided by the various governors, at one and the same time imperial officials but imbibing at least some of the outlook of the communities over which they presided. Thus Elgin in his British capacity was supposed to lobby for intercolonial union, but in his capacity as a Canadian official he discouraged the notion. Edmund Head's views wavered as he shifted from stagnant New Brunswick to dynamic Canada. One contemporary figure almost defies categorisation. John Hamilton Gray was born in Charlottetown in 1811. His father was a Scottish-born Loyalist, who sent the boy to Britain for his education as a teenager. He spent the next twenty years as an officer in the Seventh Dragoons, mainly in India and South Africa. In 1852 he retired to the family estates on Prince Edward Island, but returned to active service overseas during the Crimean War. In 1856 he settled permanently on Prince Edward Island, and in 1863 he became premier. The following year he led the Island delegations at the Charlottetown and Quebec conferences. Should Colonel Gray be classified as a British army officer, or a Prince Edward Islander? Gray himself would perhaps have refused to see any conflict between the two. Certainly when he spoke 'warmly, but briefly, in favor of Confederation' at a banquet in Saint John in September 1864, his remarks contained a revealing statement. 'He had, before leaving England, in order to take up his residence in the land of his birth, resolved to use his influence in favor of this measure, and he hoped to see it effected in his lifetime'.[83] True, he was not an initiator of the movement towards Confederation, nor did his own province become a founder member. On the other hand, he had been almost alone in arguing for the wider federation when the Assembly had discussed Maritime Union in 1863,[84] and if he was selected to preside over the Charlottetown meeting chiefly because he was premier of the host province, it must also be noted that the chair placed no obstacles in the way of the visitors from Canada. A central purpose of this study is to demonstrate and discuss the nature of metropolitan British support for Confederation. In addition, it may be at least suggested that there is no necessary barrier preventing those who intended to die British subjects on one side of the Atlantic from subscribing to and sharing views shaped by those who had been born British subjects on the other.

The difference was that the British North Americans were aware of the problems which any form of union would involve, whereas their British cousins in the homeland were 'horribly ignorant'[85] of the provinces, and consequently came to underrate the obstacles to unification. Their ideas about the form which a colonial union might take were also imprecise, although by the end of the 1850s the imprecision had managed to generate a circle-squaring notion of a union which would somehow combine the flexibility of federation with the strength of centralisation. Thus in both areas, knowledge of British North America and understanding of the technicalities of federal government, the very ignorance of the British became harnessed to their growing enthusiasm for the union of the provinces.

When H.S. Tremenheere complained in 1852 that 'neither Canada in particular, nor the British North American provinces generally, are appreciated as they ought to be by the people of England', he appears to have had in mind Herman Merivale, the senior official at the Colonial Office.[86] The fact that the provinces were so far away played a role in the general level of ignorance, 'distance producing,

in some respects, the effects of time'.[87] A transatlantic crossing of
15½ days in 1837 could be described as 'a most extraordinary rate
of sailing'.[88] Steamships were more reliable, if not always much
faster: Monck called an eight-day crossing in 1866 'a capital
passage', while Howe the same year thought 7½ days from Halifax
to Cork 'charming'.[89] The excellent Mancunian Mrs Wilson in *Mary
Barton* knew that Canada was far away — 'beyond London a good
bit I reckon; and quite in foreign parts'.[90] A combative Scotswoman
led a protest movement on a transatlantic steamship, persuading
other passengers that Canada really lay to the south of Britain, and
that the captain was steering in the wrong direction. The sight of
icebergs convinced the malcontents that the captain was actually
aiming to win the reward offered for the discovery of Sir John
Franklin's expedition lost in the Arctic.[91]

Examples of male ignorance are equally abounding. When J.W.
Williams came out from England in 1857 to a bishopric, he 'knew
nothing of Canadian geography' and could name only three towns
in the province. Williams was no ignoramus. He was a
schoolmaster, a devotee of the writings of Swift and — unusually
enough for a man in holy orders — an enthusiastic reader of
modern fiction.[92] Even Howick, one of the few British politicians to
take an intelligent and consistent interest in British North America,
once confessed to his journal a 'painful sense' of his ignorance of the
geography of the colonies.[93] Two colonial secretaries, the father and
son Lords Stanley, had actually visited British North America as
young men, and the Duke of Newcastle toured the provinces while
in office in 1860, under the unusual circumstances of an official visit
by the young Prince of Wales. As already noted, the visits to
Canada by two Downing Street officials, Elliot and Murdoch, may
actually have been counter-productive, since they failed to adjust to
the fact that their experience had rapidly become out of date.
Against this general lack of first-hand understanding of the
provinces within the élite must be placed the unquantifiable
influence of naval and military officers who had served in British
North America. One measure of the severity of the *Trent* crisis was
that battalions of the élite Guards regiments (including one from
the Grenadiers) were despatched to Canada, for colonial service
was normally reserved for lowlier units in the hierarchy of military
prestige. Joseph Howe believed that it was the experience of
Guards officers which convinced 'the higher classes' that the

Canadian border was 'indefensible', thus leading to the subtle although illogical conclusion that Confederation would somehow resolve the problem of the inherent military vulnerability of the provinces.[94]

There were specific aspects to this general ignorance which influenced the British consensus of support for intercolonial union. The first was an inability to grasp the sheer scale of British North America. When Russell suggested to Canada's governor-general Poulett Thomson that he should visit Halifax to solve a Nova Scotian political row, he was chided for seeming to believe that the provinces were 'as near to each other as Downing Street to the Parks'.[95] Arguing in 1858 for a union of the provinces, *The Times* baldly stated 'they are not divided by any great natural feature'.[96] 'A glance at the map is sufficient to show that some sort of union between these communities is essential for their protection', claimed the *Saturday Review* in 1864.[97]

One indication of British ignorance of internal distance was the way in which the idea of British North American union could even grow to span the whole continent. In May 1849, the *Morning Herald* — hardly a publication which actively welcomed new ideas — expressed its astonishment at the idea of 'a railway through our North American colonies, from Halifax, across the Rocky Mountains ... to a point at the mouth of Frazer's River — only 4000 miles in length' and costing one hundred million pounds. 'Had we not had such a scheme positively submitted to us we could hardly have believed that a sane individual could have seriously entertained such a monstrous absurdity.'[98] Others were less astonished. The *Sun* noted that 'intelligent men are beginning to argue for the formation of a trunk railway connecting the Atlantic and Pacific' and even Lord Grey was 'far from thinking these schemes so wild as they sound'.[99] By August 1849, the *Manchester Guardian*, in favouring colonial federation, could add that it 'embraces, in the scope of its ultimate design, all the vast territory which we hold from the shores of the Atlantic to the Pacific'.[100] Stanley in 1858 thought a federal union might 'ultimately' stretch as far as Vancouver Island, although Head believed that 'for a long time to come' it would be too remote for inclusion, and *The Times* spoke of a union of 'North America East of the Rocky Mountains'.[101] Watkin recalled that by 1860, the Duke of Newcastle believed that a Pacific railway and transcontinental union would go hand in hand.[102] Newcastle's memorandum on the Intercolonial in 1862 steered clear of the political question, but bluntly stated: 'Those who have not watched events in the vast Continent between VanCouvers Island and Canada will hardly be prepared to believe how soon ... there will be a direct communication between the Atlantic and the Pacific'.[103]

The *Westminster Review* sounded more realistic in 1866 in arguing that it was 'impossible to fix any probable time at which the extension of the new confederation of British America to the Pacific will be practicable'.[104] (In fact, British Columbia joined just five years later.) What is striking is not that there should have been voices of caution and disbelief, but that the idea of transcontinental communications and a political union from the Atlantic to the Pacific should have been apparently so easily accepted by so many in Britain: on the face of it, the *Morning Herald*'s offer in 1849 to arrange 'free entertainment for life' in a lunatic asylum for promoters of a transcontinental railway was, if cruel, at least understandable.[105] One likely explanation is suggested by the fact that these ideas seem to date from 1849: British North America was seen as a mirror image of the United States, which had just succeeded in leaping the continent to California. Far from being an obstacle, the fact that little was known of the Pacific coast of British North America merely meant that inconvenient reality could be kept at arm's length. 'What most of us know of these ultra-occidental regions may be summed up in a few words,' *The Times* admitted in 1858 — and even that information came largely from the novels of Washington Irving.[106] The imaginative leap to the Pacific incidentally minimised en route the difficulties which might otherwise have been anticipated in the settlement of the prairies, 'these barren tracts' as Hawes called them when Roebuck wished them to form part of a British North American federation in 1849.[107] Nine years later, *The Times* termed the region 'an American Siberia',[108] but Sir Edmund Head could none the less argue that 'one great recommendation' of federation was 'that it will thus admit of extending westward the body of our North American colonies'.[109]

The British knew equally little of the Maritimes. 'If an Englishman thinks of North America at all, he divides it between Canada and the United States,' Joseph Howe claimed in 1854. 'Except in some sets and circles, chiefly mercantile, you rarely hear of Nova Scotia,

New Brunswick, Prince Edward Island, or Newfoundland.'[110] His statement was confirmed by the *Saturday Review*. 'Of all the districts on the face of the earth there is none of which we in England know so little as of the thriving provinces of New Brunswick and Nova Scotia,' it admitted in 1865.[111] Even the description of the Maritimes as 'thriving' suggested a lack of hard information: official witnesses giving evidence to the 1861 parliamentary enquiry on colonial defence described them as 'poor Colonies'.[112] Arthur Blackwood of the Colonial Office believed that those Englishmen who had actually heard of Nova Scotia and New Brunswick usually thought they were parts of the United States.[113] Newfoundland seems to have been a little-known mystery.[114] 'Where are the Magdalen Islands?' Merivale enquired in 1854.[115] 'Prince Edward Island is out of the way of those who travel for pleasure, and not much in the way of those who travel for business,' wrote a Scottish visitor in 1865. The vacuum was filled by often-preposterous analogies from the homeland. 'Prince Edward's Island is to be the Isle of Wight of British North America', the *Saturday Review* informed its readers in 1864.[116]

The only spot in the entire Atlantic region to be relatively well-known in Britain was Halifax, probably because it was one of the most important military stations outside Europe, as well as a key point in Britain's world-wide network of naval bases, 'one of the sound eye-teeth of England', as the *Examiner* called it in 1864.[117] The Nova Scotian capital may even have been better known than its Yorkshire namesake: the MP for Halifax told the Commons in 1858 that a remittance addressed to his firm had been posted in Plymouth, and sent across the Atlantic — before eventually reaching its correct destination, with the untampered banknotes a testimony to Bluenose honesty.[118] Unfortunately, there is also evidence that many in Britain believed Halifax already to be part of Canada,[119] as would be expected on the basis of Joseph Howe's assumption of a division of the whole continent into two. Consequently, while at a British North American level, ministers and officials had to work within a wider context of opinion, however diffuse, to some extent they had a freer hand when dealing with the Maritimes. So long as they did nothing which might provoke a backlash of public protest — an unlikely development as Joseph Howe discovered in 1866 — they could cautiously urge steps towards a union of the Maritimes and eventually a link with the province of Canada. Moreover, events from 1865 onwards demonstrated that a British public opinion which vaguely assumed that Nova Scotia and New Brunswick were already part of Canada would be slow to sympathise with Maritime reluctance to be absorbed into Confederation.

One other aspect of contemporary British perceptions of the British North American provinces needs to be stressed. British opinion, formed among an élite, saw the colonists as social inferiors. 'Across the Atlantic we have two or three millions of labourers and small farmers, with scarcely a gentleman or a good income among them,' *The Times* remarked in 1844. At the age of fifteen, in 1845, Arthur Gordon dreamed of going to Canada, despite the fact that emigration was 'generally thought of as a last resort for people who have ruined themselves at home'. Gordon confidently expected his social eminence to sweep him to political leadership in the colony, a fantasy which may help explain his subsequent frustrations in New Brunswick.[120] His idea did not catch on. In 1858, Arthur Blackwood counselled against encouraging two young gentlemen who wished to settle in Canada. 'Laborers, or small farmers are wanted — not persons, who have received the education which a Barrister in this Country would probably give his Sons.'[121] This social disdain for British North America was not simply part of an overall distaste for the colonies. A sizeable middle class emigration in the 1850s did much to overlay the perceived convict origins of the Australian colonies. Joseph Howe helped found the British North American Association in London in 1862 because 'for every one person that you meet who knows anything accurately about North America, there are ten who have either returned from or read something of Australia'.[122] Macdonald, indeed, told the Quebec Conference that one of the reasons for Confederation would be to force the British take their North American provinces as seriously as they took Australia.[123] In 1860, *The Times* could remark that 'the people who have left the shores of England for the Antipodes are more thorough representatives of the mother country than the generality of immigrants to America, coming, as the former do, from a wealthier and more completely English class'.[124]

The equation of 'Englishness' with a good income is revealing. In 1869, an MP told the Commons that 'there was hardly a gentleman in that House who had not a friend or a relation in New Zealand'.[125]

The statement was probably an exaggeration, but it certainly could not have been made about New Brunswick, whose immigrant population contained a substantial Irish Catholic element, nor even about Upper Canada. When *The Times* remarked in 1856 that 'if you want to see the "British subject" in his most essential form you must go to Canada West', there was a clear implication that the opinion-formers who read Britain's dominant newspaper would find the experience more akin to a visit to the Zoo than to a family reunion.[126] Allowance must be made for the disillusionment of the Nova Scotian lobbyists opposed to Confederation at their failure to gain a hearing from Parliament in 1867, but there was some point to William Garvie's disgust when 'country gentlemen who could not maybe point out Nova Scotia on the map' crowded into the House as it moved from consideration of the British North America Bill to debating a dog tax which would affect those who kept fox hounds. 'It showed they considered Colonists as beings as little related to them as the inhabitants of some nameless Chinese mud village.'[127]

This sense of social superiority is important both in interpreting British perceptions of the provinces, and in assessing the British role in the carrying of Confederation. Disdain for colonial politicians was a commonplace in the correspondence of ministers and governors, especially in relation to the Maritimes. In New Brunswick, Arthur Gordon assured Gladstone, 'to be a member of the Assembly is a proof that a man is uneducated and is not a gentleman'.[128] The two Nova Scotian giants of the era, Howe and Tupper, were not held in high regard. The former, Lord Grey commented to Sir Edmund Head, 'has a little too much of what your neighbours call *smartness*', while Head's successor, Manners Sutton, more bluntly dismissed him as 'a very pernicious Individual'.[129] Tupper — the only Father of Confederation to have attended a British university — was damned by Gordon as 'a man possessed of but very moderate abilities, considerable obstinacy, and a very large share of vanity'. Elliot recalled 'ample evidence' that Tupper was 'very wrongheaded and intemperate'.[130]

Such explosive condemnations were less frequently directed at the politicians of the province of Canada, although Elgin bluntly told Grey that the greatest barrier to launching British North American union lay in the quality of the local politicians. Colonial politics, a London newspaper commented in 1864, operated 'at the level of a town council in Lancashire';[131] this was not intended as a compliment. Lytton accepted as a matter of course that corruption was 'the natural consequence of Democracy' in Canada.[132] Howe indignantly countered such sneers with the reminder that there were MPs who had bribed their way into the Commons, and peers who had used their power to block legislation to force railway companies to pay exorbitant sums to cross their lands.[133] The written record of official dealings with the provinces, with its punctilious use of polite forms — 'gentlemen', 'My dear Sir' — only rarely captures the slight reserve with which such terminology was almost certainly used, but it is possible to detect in private correspondence an irony in the use of such terms as 'Prime Minister' and 'Honourable', a designation which in Britain was reserved to the children of members of the House of Lords. Colonial Office officials devoted much time to limiting the use of such titles, and not even the passage of Confederation could shake the Duke of Buckingham in his refusal to allow members of the newly created Canadian Privy Council to be granted the equivalent style of 'Right Honourable'. It would, he commented, be 'inconvenient' if Canadian politicians gradually gained a social rank equivalent to that of English statesmen.[134]

Chapter Seven argues that assessments of 'British pressure' in the carrying of Confederation should be made against this background of an evident social gulf between metropolitan and colonial politicians. Head believed that 'the presence of an English gentleman acting as Governor' could be 'a wholesome check' upon the corrupt tendencies of colonial politicians.[135] George Brown and John A. Macdonald were both sons of Scots who had emigrated because their business affairs had failed: in Peter Brown's case, only a plea of naive incompetence could clear him from a charge of massive fraud.[136] The difference between their backgrounds and those of Palmerston, the Irish peer, or Carnarvon, the English earl, would have been palpable in face-to-face dealings. Occasionally, a colonial ego was mishandled: Francis Hincks, who had begun his career as a clerk in Belfast, took offence in 1852 when his reception at the Colonial Office fell short of recognising his position as the Queen's confidential adviser in her Canadian province.[137] His hurt feelings were assuaged by his appointment in 1856 as a colonial governor, and much fuss was made of the fact that he was the first colonist to qualify for such an imperial appointment. There was less stress on the awkward truth that there was not a great deal of well-qualified competition for Barbados and the Windward Islands. However, the great strength of the imperial factor in dealing with British North American politicians was not so much the exercise of patronage as the opportunity to patronise. Between 1864 and 1867 the social resources of the 'higher classes' — right up to the Queen herself — were harnessed to ensure that visiting colonial leaders were left in no doubt that those who supported Confederation would bask in glory, while those who did not would find the stately homes closed to them, and the drawing rooms a minefield of disapproval.

The social gulf between British and Canadian politicians contributed to metropolitan ignorance of colonial politics. 'It is the misfortune of the sort of connexion we keep up with British America that we seldom hear anything about it, unless it be something unpleasant,' *The Times* remarked in 1854. 'Had we really much to do with these provinces ... Canadian, or Nova Scotian, or Newfoundland politics would be familiar to all of us; and, when debates at home were getting rather dull, we might fill up the void with examples of Canadian eloquence or intrigue.' In fact, Canadian crises burst upon the British scene at intervals, and 'we only hear of these provinces as we do of Mount Etna, that is, when there is an eruption.... For nine days at the outside — sometimes only for nine hours — a Canadian topic may be said to occupy the public attention, and people begin really to think they know something about Canadian affairs, and are interested in them.' Invariably, the subject would fade just as quickly 'and it will be a twelvemonth before any body remembers there is such a place as British America'.[138]

By the 1860s, this combination of social superiority and overall ignorance had spawned a further element in the prevailing British attitude to the provinces: one of annoyed disapproval directed against Canada in particular. The two prime irritants were the Canadian tariff of 1859 and the Militia Bill affair of 1862. The tariff increased import duties on British manufactured goods, prompting the merchants of Sheffield into a protest that American goods were gaining a market advantage in a British colony. Galt, Canada's finance minister, replied with devastating contempt, dwelling on factual errors in the complaint and pointing out that as Sheffield managed to compete with American goods in the United States market, they could hardly be suffering any disadvantage in

Canada. Rather, he ingeniously claimed, the Canadian tariff actually made British imports cheaper, since the proceeds went to improve Canada's canals and develop its railway network, thereby cutting delivery costs.[139] In the Colonial Office, Chichester Fortescue commented that Galt 'does treat the Sheffield gentlemen rather contemptuously',[140] and indeed Galt was to be equally tactless in a speech at Manchester on colonial defence in September 1862.[141] In fighting for the guarantee for the Intercolonial in 1862, Newcastle complained to Monck that he had to combat 'the unfortunate influence ... exercised by your high tariff on British Manufactures both in the Cabinet and amongst the Public'.[142]

However in the early months of 1862, this was as yet an undercurrent in public feeling towards Canada. *The Times* dismissed Goldwin Smith's campaign against the connection with Canada as the kind of wild idea which surfaced from time to time, to receive 'almost as much favour as the projects for general disarmament or for equalizing the political rights of the sexes'. Even among 'those who once had misgivings as to the policy of retaining Canada, nine out of ten are by this time convinced of their error' and ready to help the province either in 'maintaining her allegiance to this country' or working towards eventual separation. The *Trent* crisis, in short, had 'strengthened the bond' and Canada seemed set fair to accepting her own share of responsibility for defence through militia reform. The defeat of the bill came as a shock: *The Times* found the news 'difficult to read without emotion of some kind'. Within a short time, it had declared itself against any funding for the Intercolonial ('The money will be thrown away') and ominously announced that 'the present appears to us a proper time for plain-speaking about the future relations between England and her more advanced colonies'.[143] Newcastle sourly assured Monck that his ministers had 'succeeded in *producing* on this side of the water a feeling which two months ago had no other existence than in their imaginations and in the clever but eccentric brain of Goldwin Smith'.[144]

Two years later, a Scots Liberal MP, R.S. Aytoun, successfully moved in the Commons for the production of Galt's reply to the Sheffield manufacturers.[145] Its publication revived resentment at exactly the moment news arrived of the formation of the Great Coalition: *The Times* commented on the two events in the same leading article, welcoming the political development but damning the financial heresy.[146] Aytoun's move may have been coincidental in timing and the product of a purely personal interest in colonial matters: he supported Confederation but attacked the Intercolonial guarantee.[147] Equally, it is possible that there was collusion with Cardwell, recently appointed to the Colonial Office and drily Peelite on matters of colonial trade and finance: somebody, after all, must have informed Aytoun that the contents were worth publishing. In 1865, *The Times* combined anger with contempt: 'if our existing contract with our American provinces is worth one half-penny in the open market of the world, the Colonists will insist upon ... the substitution of another contract which shall not be worth that one halfpenny to us'.[148]

Compilations of sentiments of this kind were for long held to justify the description of the 1860s as an era of 'anti-imperialism'.[149] The sentiment cannot be denied, but an alternative collage of quotations can equally establish that it was a decade of deep and even atavistic pride in empire. The crucial point was that, at most, 'anti-imperialism' was no more than a sentiment, and not a formative influence on policy. It did not prevent the British from continuing to envisage British North American union as the future destiny of the provinces, and this would not be dented by subsequent protests from the Maritimes that they were being handed over to the politicians of Canada. In 1864, the *Examiner* seems to have been alone in associating the move towards union with the Militia affair of two years before: 'To the volunteer humbug has succeeded the Federation ditto'.[150] Rather, even when denouncing Galt's effrontery in 1862, the *Saturday Review* had supported his call for a union of the provinces in the belief that Confederation would foster a breed of politicians to replace those who judged 'the profoundness of their policy by the depths to which it was warranted to dive into the pockets of British taxpayers, and by the refinements by which it could irritate and injure British trade'.[151] Indeed, the combination of general ignorance of Canadian affairs with a low estimation of colonial politicians made it possible to create a more-or-less instant mythology at the time of Confederation explaining why constitutional change had become 'an absolute necessity'. The *Westminster Review* assured its readers in 1865 that government after government in Canada was forced to confess itself unable to control parliament; and resignation followed resignation, and election succeeded election, with no other effect than to increase the embarrassment. The result was that sectional majorities, firmly united, impeded legislation, and assailed each other with every weapon that strong sectional differences place at the disposal of political factions.[152]

As argued in Chapter Five, the British did not support Confederation as a means of forcing independence upon the provinces. Some of the sharpest expressions of irritation were testimony not of a British intention to abandon a dangerous imperial commitment to defend the provinces, but rather an expression of frustration at not being able to escape from the obligation.

In the last resort, then, British policy towards the provinces would not be the product of irritation and anger. However, the politicians of British North America would have been foolhardy not to take some account of those sentiments. The harsh words and plain speaking of 1862 left an enduring mark on Canadian attitudes. Twenty years later, J.C. Dent wryly remarked that while, thanks to their distance and ignorance, 'Englishmen have always been conspicuous for shooting wide of the mark where Canadian affairs are concerned', the tone of the English press in 1862 'struck a blow at Canadian loyalty from which it has never fully recovered'. Canadians felt they had 'received a series of unmerited slaps in the face'. Loyalty remained their predominant characteristic, 'but it is a sentiment of radically different stripe from that which animated us during the discussions arising out of the *Trent* affair' and any observer of Canadian opinion 'will admit that a change first began to be apparent during the summer of 1862'.[153] Thus it was that the British were able to imply in 1865 and 1866 that without Confederation, there would be a question mark over both the Intercolonial loan guarantee and the willingness of the British to protect the provinces.

One of the more positive aspects of the overall simplification of British perceptions of British North America was that the provinces were almost invariably seen in the context of their giant neighbour, the United States. Literary travellers who crossed the Atlantic tended to include Canada as a sub-section of their accounts of the United States: press reports often came by way of New York, and were published as an addendum to American news. However, while the United States context was appropriate to a fundamental appreciation of British North America's potential role in the world, it could also at times dominate. It was G.M. Grant who later said that Canadians 'understand current events and the social life of England from the illustrators of *Punch* more truly than from the columns of *The Times* or the *Morning Post*'.[154] Certainly in the era of Confederation, Canadians would have been able to learn from the coverage of the London satirical weekly just how small a place they occupied in the British political firmament. Between 1861 and 1865, one quarter of its weekly political cartoons referred to the American Civil War. The gladiatorial combat of North and South perhaps lent itself to caricature, but the editorials of *The Times* showed a similar concentration. By contrast, *Punch* ignored British North American affairs, summarising Confederation in a couplet notable both for awkward scansion and doubtful accuracy: 'Our Scotia Nova and our Brunswick New/ Would unite with Canada, which they shall do'.[155] 'We listen with open ears to the faintest rumour of a cabal that threatens to cripple or depose one of Lincoln's Generals,' *The Times* admitted in 1863

...but who is Minister, if any, at Quebec or any other seat of British Government in America, we none of us know. If we knew to-day we should forget tomorrow, and if we saw the startling announcement of a new Ministry ... we should refuse to read the three important lines, and skip them for the news from the Rappahannock.[156]

The way was open for generalisation and stereotype to supply the place of detailed understanding. Lord John Russell objected to discussions of Canada's destiny 'as if a million & a half of people were like one man, who wished for British rule, or were against it'.[157] *The Times* convinced itself that Canada and the United States were separated by 'a great difference in manners and sentiment, far greater than what now distinguishes many European States'.[158] It even went so far as to picture Canada as 'nothing more than England reformed, with the addition of an unlimited supply of land, an advantage that even the most utopian reformers never ventured to dream of'.[159] Pessimists sketched a rival picture, of a people 'republican in character, feeling and institutions, to an extent of which the people of this country are by no means aware'.[160]

These stereotypes, whether optimistic or pessimistic, tended to assume that the provinces were inhabited an English-speaking population. In the 1830s, French Canadians were, understandably enough, seen as actual or potential enemies, 'a perverse faction of ill-intentioned foreigners', as *The Times* called them in 1837, whose demands 'were manifestly not means of redressing wrongs, but of inflicting them — that is, of dismembering the British empire'.[161] A decade later, James Stephen could still refer to 'the French and Roman Catholic Population, distinguished chiefly by their bigotry in Religion, their ignorance in Politics, and their antipathy to the English Race'.[162] By the end of the 1840s, such attitudes were increasingly overlain by a more benign notion of French Canadians. *The Times* now professed itself 'anxious to believe that the French Canadians are a simple, quiet, and orderly race', even if they were 'neither very enlightened nor very shrewd, nor yet very fond of the Anglo-Saxons'.[163] The shift in perceptions was partly a by-product of the success of responsible government in creating a partnership between Canada's two communities. It helped, too, that Catholic and peasant Ireland was quiescent for a decade and a half following the Famine of the 1840s, for French Canadian discontents had frequently been equated with disturbance among the Irish. It was undoubtedly also convenient that, despite occasional war scares, Britain and France managed to remain at peace, and even fought side by side in the Crimea. Perhaps most useful of all was the fading memory of the French Revolution. Sarcastic references to 'the happy days of the Directory and Robespierre' could perhaps still stir chilling memories in 1837,[164] but they seem to have disappeared a decade later. In any case, the Canadian French had 'skipped the revolution',[165] and when the British thought of them at all, it was as 'a quiet sort of people',[166] '*old* french'.[167] As Richard Cobden wrote in 1865, 'the Lower Canadian Frenchman is left the same amiable thoughtless ignorant happy person he was in 1750'.[168] Neither stereotype stood in the way of British hopes for a union of British North America. If the French were hostile, union would outvote and control them. If they were docile, they could be caged within their own local unit of a wider federation and peaceably left alone to drift.

***

What kind of regional union did the British wish to see created in their North American provinces? Once again British perceptions obstinately defy clarification, requiring the historian to recognise that the attractiveness of union lay partly in a comprehensive vagueness. In strict theory, the choice was straightforward. 'It is scarcely necessary to dwell on the distinction between a Legislative and a Federal Union,' an anonymous New Brunswick anti-Confederate told readers of *The Times*. 'In the former there is one supreme Legislature, and one only; in the latter there is, indeed, one central Legislature, but it is not supreme, for sundry petty local Legislatures surround it'.[169] In theory, both the Canadian Union and the United Kingdom itself were unitary systems, and the United States the classic model of a federation. In practice, the distinction was blurred. When Durham argued that 'the experience of the two Unions in the British Isles may teach us how effectually the strong arm of a popular legislature would compel the obedience of the refractory population', he probably had Ireland rather than Scotland in mind. However, he saw the terms of the Union of 1707 as a precedent for the maintenance of distinct French Canadian institutions within a legislative union.[170] By 1844, a correspondent of the *Colonial Gazette* was arguing that the Canadian Union could only function 'in that federal spirit' which had characterised the Union of England and Scotland.[171] The ambiguity was underlined by Sir Edmund Head when in 1858 he defined the kernel of Canada's political problems as 'whether the Union was not *federal* rather than legislative in its character'.[172] To add to the confusion still further, by the late 1840s the United States was behaving more and more like 'a youthful empire'.[173] The British, having no direct experience of a federal system of government, were imprecise in their vocabulary: the Halifax newspaper editor P.S. Hamilton complained that the integration of British North America was usually described 'as a *Federal* Union, but without any reason being given for the application of that epithet'.[174]

A further complication was the basic fact that the British North American provinces were colonies within the British empire. A colonial federation could not be a precise parallel to the United States unless it ceased to be colonial. In the late 1830s, before responsible government had enlarged the sphere of colonial autonomy within the Empire, there were considerable practical objections to any attempt to insert a mezzanine tier of regional government between the imperial parliament at Westminster and the colonial assemblies. Despite his own sympathy for the idea,

Durham recognised that it might produce 'a weak and rather cumbrous Government ... the greater part of the ordinary functions of a federation falling within the scope of the imperial legislature and executive'.[175] T.C. Haliburton demanded to be told from where a federal government would draw its powers. 'If from Parliament, you cease to control these countries, and they become independent; if from the Local Legislatures, you annihilate them.'[176] 'There is no vacant or unoccupied ground for their sphere of action', pointed out Henry Bliss, New Brunswick's agent in London.[177]

Stephen and Howick attempted to meet these concerns by designing a structure which would fall short of a full system of federal government, beginning with an intercolonial convention which — in Stephen's words — would 'regulate those matters in which the provinces are jointly concerned'.[178] Howick found this 'very like a scheme of mine', in which a 'Federal body would supply that bond of connection between the different provinces which has hitherto been found only in their common subjection to the domination of the Parent State'.[179] Palmerston refused to accept an evolutionary approach to an undesirable end, predicting that Howick's intercolonial convention 'would in fact become a Sovereign as well as a Constituent Power, and whatever it recommended must be done'.[180] Russell also pointed out that in every federation, 'the federal power is the supreme power' and concluded that 'with a neighbouring Congress at Washington, will not the federal body aim at the authority now held by the Mother Country?'.[181]

Howick, by now the third Earl Grey, revived his scheme in 1846 for 'if not exactly a federal Union of the British provinces at all events some connection among them for certain objects of common interest'.[182] Elgin did not share his enthusiasm. 'A congress without foreign relations, armies navies and ambassadors would be a very insipid concern.'[183] Echoing Haliburton, he predicted that a colonial federation 'can hardly fail to become either a nuisance or a legislative Union'.[184] His objections even seem to have made some impression upon Sir Edmund Head, for whom in the abstract federal systems had an almost mathematical attraction. Recognising that a federal legislature 'might employ its spare time in mischievous agitation', Head suggested short sessions or biennial meetings as remedies.[185]

To its enthusiasts, federation squared the circle by combining all the advantages of union with those of local autonomy. A London newspaper described federation in 1838 as providing 'all the advantages of a representative government, while it guards against the mistakes and occasional effects of personal collisions to which small communities are exposed'.[186] A quarter of a century later, Goldwin Smith preached federation to the British North American provinces in the same magic formula. 'It may give them at once the peace of great Empires, the active intelligence of small communities, the mutual education and discipline of a cluster of independent nations.'[187] Enthusiasts for legislative union rejected such notions as naive. Henry Bliss was convinced that anyone who studied the theory and practical operation of the American constitution 'must find the former an absurdity and the latter an accident'. The provinces should demonstrate 'a profounder comprehension of political science' by rejecting the United States model and showing 'a worthier preference for the institutions of their parent country'.[188] However, Elgin regretfully concluded in 1847 that 'until the Provinces are connected by Railway, a legislative Union between them would be hardly practicable'.[189] When Francis Hincks attempted to dissuade Newcastle from pressing ahead with moves towards federation in 1853, he described legislative union as 'the only proposition that I think should be entertained for one moment and yet it is precisely the one which would be most difficult to carry'.[190]

Federation would be weak and quarrelsome, legislative union ideal but unattainable. British vagueness about the nature of federal systems provided the germ of a solution to a dilemma which in strict logic was insoluble. Why not combine the two? An anonymous pamphleteer in 1838 suggested that the provinces be united under 'one really general government', but with the provincial legislatures retained 'for merely local purposes of administration' until communications improved.[191] Durham's supple intellect also favoured the combination of legislative union with provincial assemblies exercising 'merely municipal powers' as part of 'the gradual transition of the Provinces into a united and homogeneous community'.[192] Grey found the hybrid a useful compromise between his own preference for a loosely federal structure and Elgin's belief in full interprovincial fusion. When Elgin complained that the limited size of the Canadian Assembly made ministries vulnerable to small factional defections, Grey concluded that the eventual remedy would be 'a Legislative Union of all the Provinces coupled with an improved municipal organisation'.[193] By 1849, he was looking to a 'very much strengthened system of Municipal organisation' to replace the colonial assemblies.[194]

In fact, there was an element of intellectual justification lurking behind these apparently pragmatic attempts to straddle two opposed systems. As Sir Edmund Head noted in 1858, any attempt to create a British North American union 'should, as it were, start from the fact that all the provinces are under the same sovereign — not from the assumption that each is a separate state possessing individual & independent rights'. Head did not intend to override the provinces, but to draw attention to

the technical difference between a subordinate government & a municipal body with large powers.... The former possesses all the rights not *expressly* taken away — the latter holds only the rights which are *expressly* given.... however large the powers left to each local Government should be, it ought, in essence, to be assimilated into a strong municipal body than to a Provincial Government properly so called....[195]

Head's analysis was elaborated by *The Times* in its discussion of the 1858 federal initiative. The United States was a federation of sovereign states, each consenting 'to delegate to a central authority a portion of its sovereign power, leaving the remainder, which is not so delegated, absolute and intact in its own hands'. This was a precedent which

cannot possibly be followed in its principle or details by the British colonies ... each of which, instead of being an isolated sovereign State, is an integral part of the British Empire. They cannot delegate their sovereign authority to a Central Government, because they do not possess the sovereign authority to delegate.

Whereas the motto of the United States was 'E pluribus unum', the motto of a united British North America might be inverted to 'Ex uno plura'.

The first steps towards a Federation of the American colonies would thus be to form them all into one State, to give that State a completely organized Government, and then to delegate to each of the colonies out of which that great State is formed such powers of local government as may be thought necessary, reserving to the Central Government all such powers as are not expressly delegated.[196]

It is tempting to see in this the kernel of the thinking behind the division of powers between the Dominion and the provinces laid down in Sections 91 and 92 of the British North America Act, for Section 2 specifically declared that Canada, New Brunswick and Nova Scotia 'shall form and be One Dominion', while Section 5 proceeded to divide that Dominion into four provinces.

It may not be entirely coincidental that the term 'Confederation' appears in at least some of the discussions of 1858. Head referred to 'the future confederation (or whatever it may be called)' in April 1858, in the same paragraph as his discussion of their common subordination to the Crown.[197] By September 1858, Lytton was using the term more freely. In a letter to the prime minister, Lord Derby, 'Confederation', with a capital 'C', occurs five times, while 'a Confederation', capitalised, and 'a confederation', in lower case, each appear twice. The abstract and capitalised usage may imply a sense of the process of uniting the provinces — which Lytton wished to keep under firm imperial control — rather than the form of union which would emerge, but the meaning was easily transferable from the one to the other.[198] After 1861, 'Confederation' probably gained from the reassuringly anti-Yankee aura of the Southern Confederacy, but there is much to be said for Waite's conclusion that 'the prefix "con" seemed to contemporaries to strengthen the centralist principle rather than to weaken it'.[199] Without such a pre-existing mental distinction, it is surely unlikely that the British would have so enthusiastically welcomed a scheme for an apparently federated union of the provinces at a time when the American Civil War seemed to have discredited federal government. Cardwell's reaction to the formation of the Great Coalition in July 1864 bears this out. He wrote to Monck

I was a little startled when I head the word *Federation*, for Federal Government has not risen in public estimation recently either in America or in Europe. But if I correctly understand what your advisers are likely to propose it will not be *Federation* in the real meaning of that word but *union* of many municipalities under one

Supreme Legislature. This will exclude altogether the States-rights question which has broken up the United States.[200]

As he waited for news of the Quebec conference, Cardwell's chief fear was that adoption of a loose structure 'would run British North America upon the rock on which the [American] Union has gone to pieces'.[201] In assuring an agitated Arthur Gordon that 'it signifies little what name is employed', Cardwell insisted that 'we all agree in favouring a complete fusion, not a federation'.[202] In fact, the colonial secretary was far from indifferent to the significance of terminology. In his concern to elevate the central power, he even deleted the word 'federal' from a draft despatch — a far cry from Howick's watering down of 'federal authority' to 'federal body' three decades earlier, to make the prospect seem less alarming.[203] Sir Fenwick Williams, acting as governor of Nova Scotia, urged Cardwell to resist any attempt 'to expunge the word *Confederation* in the Imperial Parliament'.[204] In a confidential despatch in September 1866, Monck regretted 'that the designation "Federal" was ever applied to the proposed Union'. The technical error of classification was in itself 'a matter of small moment' but there was a danger that 'the use of this word as descriptive of the intended Union is calculated to direct into a wrong channel the minds of persons who have not very carefully considered the terms of ... "The Quebec Plan", and mislead them as to the intentions of those who prepared that scheme.' In fact, 'almost the only feature common to this plan and any instance of "Federal" Union' was the existence of a parallel system of central and provincial governments. Quoting Madison on the nature of federal government, and stressing the delegation of authority to a central body by sovereign member states, Monck proved by reference to the Quebec resolutions 'that so far from the word "Federal" being an apt designation of such a form of government its general meaning conveys an idea the direct contrary of ... the intent of the Quebec plan'.[205] At the Westminster Palace Hotel conference in December 1866, the delegates obligingly substituted 'Confederation' for 'federation' as they amended the Quebec resolutions.[206]

Over a thirty-year period from the middle of the 1830s to the 1860s, a consensus grew in Britain that the destiny of their North American provinces lay in some form of regional union. At the time of the Canadian rebellions, general union was rejected, by most as a practical option, by some as desirable aim. When the question of the future of the provinces came to the fore again a decade later, support for eventual federation or unification was much more widespread, and by the middle of the 1850s it seems to have been a commonplace in the British world view. This is certainly not to claim that British opinion was continuously obsessed with the vision of Confederation: even when British North American issues forced themselves upon metropolitan attention, they were not always discussed in the context of an eventual union of the provinces: disputes over Rebellion Losses, the fisheries, the Clergy Reserves and — most notably of all — colonial defence, could be carried on with little or no reference to the possibility of an eventual union of the provinces. Indeed, the cyclical nature of upsurges of interest may in itself have been important in the steady growth of its acceptance: thus Russell, sharply critical of Howick's enthusiasm for federation in 1839, could implicitly plead changed circumstances in embracing the same plan in 1849. Similarly, Palmerston, who had opposed British North American federation in 1838, and the elder Stanley, who (between 1841 and 1845) was the only long-serving colonial secretary never to show the slightest interest in the possibility, were the prime ministers whose governments endorsed Confederation between 1864 and 1867.

Yet the doubts, even the opposition, of individual British politicians do not detract from a claim of overall 'British' support for an eventual union of the provinces. By the mid-1860s, not a single significant voice was raised in opposition to Confederation, thus demonstrating that a consensus had developed among the political élite, a shared view of the future of British North America which formed part of the world view of those politicians, journalists and writers who constituted the political nation which held power between 1832 and 1867. Arguably, their agreement influenced ideas about their destiny held in the provinces themselves, partly because mid-nineteenth century British North Americans were part of a wider 'British' world which responded to and shared ideas from the homeland, but also — and perhaps more crucially by 1864 — because colonial politicians were well aware of the extent of British commitment to the target of unity, an awareness which may have helped to shape their own response to the challenges facing their provinces.

That British enthusiasm for the union of British North America ran well ahead of support for the project in the provinces themselves need cause no surprise. Unlike the colonial populations which had to contend with the problems of distance and primitive communications, who knew at first hand the realities of local particularism and cultural pluralism, the British seem to have been happily unaware of the obstacles to their transatlantic dream. Perhaps the most charitable characterisation of the British approach is that they painted with very broad brush strokes, sketching a vision of British North American union which gave little attention to detail. More bluntly, ignorance of colonial reality, coupled with an assumption of superior worth and wisdom over colonials, enabled the British to brush aside practical difficulties. Ignorance, muddle and vagueness are awkward elements for the historian, since historical explanations seek to weave together precise factors into logical patterns. Yet central to any understanding of the existence of a prior British consensus in favour of Confederation is the realisation that British support rested in large measure upon ignorance, not unmixed with arrogance. Perhaps it was a natural corollary that British arguments and motives for uniting the North American provinces were more impressive for bold simplicity than for either logic or detail. It is these aspects of British opinion which are considered in Chapter Five.

5 Motives and Expectations of the British

British motives for endorsing an eventual regional union in British North America were marked by the same features that characterised their overall perceptions of the provinces: a few bold outlines, but much fuzziness of detail. Broadly, there were three main reasons why British opinion favoured a union of British North America: better government, preparation for eventual independence, and the creation of a barrier against the United States. The three types of argument were interconnected, for if intercolonial union created a more efficient system of government, the provinces would be better prepared to stand alone in the world and resist the temptations of annexation to the United States. However, this superficially convincing package of reasons for Confederation masked the fact that the arguments were in fact free-floating in a sea of illogicality, in which several basic assumptions were never explained, if only because they were rarely questioned.[1] These broad notions in favour of British North American union were formed prior to the outbreak of the American Civil War: indeed, if anything the war itself discouraged speculation on the subject, with the result that the British were to some extent taken by surprise when the Great Coalition adopted Confederation as one of its policies in June 1864. It was a pleasant surprise, and arguments for uniting the provinces which had been formed in earlier and calmer times were by and large carried forward in its support, their very familiarity probably discouraging too close an examination of logic and consistency.

It was not immediately obvious that a larger colonial state would be governed with greater honesty or effectiveness than a series of small ones, and Joseph Howe was surely entitled to protest against the assumption that the tone and standard of Nova Scotian public life would be raised by association with the public men of Canada.[2] Certainly the implication behind the assumption was that any union of British North America would be highly centralised, enabling wiser and more ambitious leaders to act on a larger stage. This ran to some extent counter to the emerging compromise idea that an intercolonial union would have to embody the federal trappings of regional sub-assemblies, which would presumably be correspondingly less attractive theatres for political leadership — a prospect which was to alarm some of the thoughtful Maritime critics of the Quebec scheme.

Arguments which equated British North American union with better government also saw some form of Confederation as a framework for the increasing devolution of practical authority to the provinces — thus enabling them to sustain a degree of independence. Here again, there were elements of confusion, since there was some ambiguity as to whether a union of the provinces was a step towards greater autonomy within the empire, or the means by which increasingly self-governing dependencies could alone sustain themselves independent of Britain. Here, it must be noted, part of the confusion lies with posterity. The late twentieth century has a precise notion of 'independence', having witnessed the collapse of several empires and the emergence of new states into the international community. We should not rush to assume that mid-nineteenth-century writers used the term in the same precise way, envisaging such processes as the formal transfer of sovereignty, the bold declaration of nationhood or the midnight flag-raising ceremony that have characterised the emergence of new national states in modern times.

When the mid-Victorians talked of the 'independence' of Canada, they usually had a much looser definition in mind, as their frequent invocation of parent-and-child imagery underlined.[3] Indeed, it is worth recalling that Canada — like Australia and New Zealand — finds it hard to select a single emotionally satisfying point at which the country achieved its independence.[4] The imprecision is of course largely explained by the overshadowing proximity of the United States, and the belief that Confederation would prevent annexation has to be identified as the central and consistent motive behind British support for the union of the British North American provinces. Yet for all its stark simplicity, this argument also lacked logical underpinning. It was assumed that a union of the provinces would create a common front against the United States, ignoring the possibility that it might foster previously latent tensions and so create precisely the kind of instability which would encourage American intervention, perhaps even render it unavoidable. Prior to the outbreak of the Civil War, the relationship — if any — between the political union of the provinces and their military and naval defence was rarely if ever explored. It is vital to take this vacuum into account when attempting to explain how Confederation and colonial defence became intertwined questions in 1865. Furthermore, although intercolonial union was seen as a talisman against the incorporation of the provinces into the United States, British opinion rarely took the prospect of immediate annexation very seriously, even when it surfaced as a distinct possibility in 1849.

To some extent, the contradictions inherent in British arguments for intercolonial union were disguised within a comfortably long time-frame of expectation: hence this Chapter asks not merely 'why?' but 'when?'. Until the American Civil War accelerated all expectations, British North American union was seen as a natural but eventual, perhaps even remote, development. Consequently, assumptions about the relative military strength of the United States and the British empire derived from the realities of the 1840s and 1850s were projected into a relatively distant future. When the balance of force on the North American continent changed so quickly and so dramatically in the first half of the 1860s, Confederation appeared attractive partly because it was associated with earlier assumptions of intercolonial strength and resistance to annexation. The crucial element on the British side was not to be found in any of the specific arguments for uniting the provinces, but rather in the sense among policy-makers, notably the Duke of Newcastle, of a sudden foreshortening of the future, which converted Confederation from a misty hope to a practical option — not so much as a means to improved defence, which in the face of United States might was probably impossible, but rather as a substitute political gesture, capable of seeming to be a positive response precisely because it drew upon an earlier collection of arguments and assertions which portrayed the union of British

North America as in itself a guarantee of salvation from the United States.

A consistent theme was the belief that an intercolonial union would develop a more dignified political culture. Peel in 1838 believed not only that 'their union would add to the strength of each' but would also 'tend to elevate them in the scale of civilisation'.[5] Durham described federation with the same morally improving verb: 'a scheme that would elevate their countries into something like a national existence'. He was 'inclined to attach very great importance to the influence which it would have in giving greater scope and satisfaction to the legitimate ambition of the most active and prominent persons to be found in them.'[6] Russell's conversion to federation in August 1849 was similarly prompted by his wish to give the colonists 'something to look to, which shall be above and beyond the miserable party struggles in which they have been so long engaged'.[7] 'A wide field for ambition & distinction in the "Federal" Legislature would be open to the inhabitants of all the associated colonies,' wrote Sir Edmund Head in 1851, '& the "High Court" would probably gather round it an able & efficient bar.'[8] Drawing upon his experience of the Maritimes, Head assured Stanley in 1858 that 'they govern themselves badly because there is no public opinion to act as a check on public men & on public measures'. Even if a central government did not itself impose checks upon local peculation, 'their misconduct would be made known to the larger community, not directly interested in the question'.[9] *The Times* put the point more positively, predicting that 'with higher objects of ambition and greater chance of obtaining renown and consideration in the eyes of the world, the standard of public capacity might be raised', leading to the emergence of politicians capable of governing with 'those qualifications for the task which we fear have not always been found in the responsible Governments to which the destiny of our fellow-subjects across the Atlantic have been intrusted'.[10] Writing in the 1880s, Edward Watkin combined this type of argument with the myth of a deadlocked province heading for civil war. 'The cure for this dangerous disease was to provide, for all, a bigger country — a country large enough to breed large ideas.'[11]

While this line of argument was both pervasive and attractive, some doubted its validity. In a memorandum in 1849, the Colonial Office official T.W.C. Murdoch took account of claims that British

North American union would moderate party conflict 'by bringing a more extended public opinion and more varied and independent interests to bear on Colonial politics', and that the devolution of major responsibilities to a central legislature might encourage 'more extended and liberal views in the members'. None the less, he remained doubtful whether able colonists could be recruited to public life.[12] Lord Grey, who saw the construction of a railway from Halifax to Quebec as 'an indispensable preliminary' to political union, attempted in 1849 to divert Russell's arguments in that direction, by pleading that funding for the project would 'answer your purpose of giving the Colonists something to look to beyond their mere party struggles' since it would be 'an object in which they are all deeply interested for which the Colonies might begin to act together'.[13]

As additional spheres of responsibility were handed over to the provinces — especially with the advent of free trade in 1846 — Grey and Stephen believed it would be 'eminently useful' to have some form of central decision-making in British North America.[14] Others were less enthusiastic: as Elliot pointed out in 1858, while federation would give the provinces a point of contact for the pursuit of common interests which they lacked, it would equally provide them with a point of collision which was also happily absent. In any case, he stressed the virtual absence of common interests between Canada and the Maritimes. Only 'barren symmetry' would be achieved by harmonising tariffs among provinces where there was almost no trade.[15] By 1861, however, the Canadian government saw advantages in moving in that direction, if only as a consequence of Reciprocity with the United States.[16] Similarly, the notion that federation would create a larger stage for would-be colonial statesmen held few attractions for the politicians of the province of Canada. Elgin agreed that Maritimers might be tempted by 'the prospect of having a larger scope for the exercise of their talents and influence',[17] and a decade later Mulgrave agreed that in Nova Scotia, enthusiasts for federation argued that it 'would place within their grasp, prizes more worthy of their ambition, than any offices to which they could aspire, in their own Province'.[18] To say the least, there was some conflict here between assumptions based on ambition and those which assumed disinterested high-mindedness. Head privately observed that 'the most striking defect' in the politics of New Brunswick was 'the want of honest & efficient public opinion in money transactions',[19] but were standards any higher in Canada? 'Depend upon it,' wrote Joseph Howe, 'our manners will not be much improved by association with Canadian politicians.'[20]

The empty generality of the 'better government' argument may be illustrated by the virtual absence of discussion of two aspects of intercolonial union which surely ought to have been obvious: its cost and its implications for relations between English- and French-speaking colonists. 'Canada is terribly in debt', *The Times* reported in 1863,[21] but it does not appear that economy was seen as an incentive for the union of the provinces. Head in 1852 flatly stated that a federal system 'would not be a cheap Government',[22] and even in the case of Maritime Union, which was intended to eliminate administrative duplication, he felt that any reduction in costs would be 'a secondary matter'.[23] In fact, British politicians actually hoped that the wiser counsels to be fostered by the larger colonial stage would incline British North America towards what Stanley in 1858 called 'a sound and liberal system of Finance'[24] — for even former Protectionists were now converts to the cause of free trade. 'Surely if your new advisers wish to form a great Country north of the United States they will not seek to do so on the exploded principles of Protection,' Cardwell wrote to Monck in July 1864.[25]

It does not appear that the British ever sought to explain how the additional costs of the two levels of central and provincial government could be met if revenue from customs duties was to be reduced. Equally clearly, they did not envisage the use of tariff protection to encourage the growth of internal British North American trade. Francis Hincks in 1853 suspected that another kind of economy motivated British politicians to 'devise some plan by which the burden of defence may be thrown on the Colonies, and they imagine that this can only be effected by a large Combination'. If the British wanted to cut their military costs in British North America, they should simply reduce their garrisons. 'England must declare that the time has arrived when the Colony should be able to defend itself, and that it is their intention to withdraw the troops without delay.'[26] In reality, it would not be so easy for the British to abandon their commitment to Canada without seeming craven. The key point, however, is that colonial union and colonial defence could be argued as entirely distinct subjects, and indeed the garrisons were reduced in the years which followed. Overall, the mid-Victorian passion for economy does not seem to have intersected at all closely with the pervasive British assumption that a union of British North America would be better governed.

As described in Chapter Four, British perceptions of French Canadians, although imprecise, tended to shift in the later 1840s: what had been seen as the fifth column of a hereditary enemy became something like the political equivalent of a Krieghoff painting. This change in perceptions helped to resolve the conflict between legislative union, ideal but practically unattainable, and federation, possible but undesirable in permitting a potentially dangerous element of local autonomy to the French. In December 1836, James Stephen had drafted a scheme for a partition of Lower Canada into English- and French-speaking areas, to be governed by a commission drawn from both provinces.[27] In January 1837, he broadened the proposal to create a commission consisting of five members from each of the four mainland colonies. This would come into operation as soon as fifteen members had been appointed, but its quorum would be eleven. It was not necessary to point out that Lower Canada could neither boycott nor control the new structure.[28] When news of the rebellions reached London in 1837, Russell was persuaded by Sir James Kempt that it was impractical to think of 'summoning the British colonies to redress the balance of the French'.[29] Howick continued to toy with intercolonial structures, arguing that English-speaking colonists would feel less hostile to concessions to Lower Canada if made through a body which they controlled, thereby protecting themselves against 'the asserted anti-commercial spirit of the legislation of the French'.[30] Sir George Arthur was also anxious that a federal authority should be strong enough to protect Upper Canada from French Canadian interference with its commercial interests.[31] J.A. Roebuck, London agent for the Lower Canada Assembly, ingeniously pleaded to Lord Melbourne that 'if England fears the French Canadians, the way to balance their power is by means of a federation of the Colonies'.[32]

Roebuck's advocacy of federation confirmed its suspect status: while he seems to have been captivated by the vision of British North American union almost for its own sake, he did admit to Durham that he saw federation as a 'subsidiary purpose' to the restitution of representative government in Lower Canada.[33] The second wave of uprisings, late in 1838, made this unacceptable to the British. Melbourne concluded that 'we can never suffer the French to govern or to have much influence in Lower Canada again'.[34] This in turn pointed to an immediate legislative union of the two Canadas. Even Charles Buller, an enthusiast for general federation during the Durham mission, accepted by February 1839 that federation in any form was ruled out by the urgent need to subdue Lower Canada. Buller believed that 'an English Assembly would be much more rigorous in repressive measures than a Governor & Council',[35] thus reflecting what the Upper Canadian R.B. Sullivan called the 'fallacy' of assuming 'unanimity of purpose among the whole British party'.[36] Fallacious or not, the assumption of communal confrontation was enough to rule out the immediate adoption of British North American federation in the late 1830s, precisely because it was the form of government which would accommodate French Canadians.

Soon after his arrival in Canada in 1847, Elgin took comfort from the refusal of the French to join the faltering Conservative ministry by noting that it would be easier to work for a union of the provinces if they were in opposition.[37] Two years later, when the British American League revived the strategy, a correspondent of *The Times* reported that as 'an union of all the provinces ... would place the French party in a minority, it would of course meet every opposition from them'.[38] Elgin, by now presiding over a successful communal partnership, was utterly without sympathy.[39] So far as the union of British North America was concerned, French Canada virtually dropped out of sight. Even Roebuck in 1849 was writing of a 'powerful, increasing, and really English federation', although he did conclude that the French Canadians 'would form a great item in the federal union I have proposed'.[40] Few projectors were as meticulous as Sir Edmund Head, yet in his 1851 memorandum there is a suggestion of afterthought in the mention of the 'incidental advantage' that federation would place distinct French Canadian institutions — especially those relating to land tenure and the Church — in the hands of their own local legislature 'whilst, in all that concerned the relation with Great Britain, the French interest would be in a minority in the "Federal" Government'[41] — an incentive which also appealed to Russell in 1862.[42] Stanley in 1858 sought reassurance that Lower Canada 'would go on peaceably and in the right direction' as a reconstituted

French-majority province, but the fact that Galt was the chief campaigner for federation was the best answer to any such fears.[43] Overall, by the 1850s, the French dimension had almost disappeared from British thinking about a future union of the provinces.

While the implications of intercolonial union for fiscal responsibility or communal harmony went almost without discussion in Britain, the steady widening of the sphere of colonial autonomy gradually undercut the objection that a federal government would have little to do but occupy itself in making mischief. The federal schemes of the late 1830s had envisaged control over a limited range of areas, some of them minor — communications, quarantine, postal services, currency and the collection of customs duties.[44] The introduction of free trade widened the scope for colonial tariff policies. By 1849, Roebuck had added taxation, legislation covering copyright and naturalisation, the chartering of universities and establishment of prairie settlements.[45] Galt in 1858 specified lighthouses, fisheries, Indian affairs and control of public lands as responsibilities devolving upon a federal government.[46] When Nova Scotia's governor Lord Mulgrave rehearsed the old argument in 1858 that a colonial federation could control little more than posts, currency and tariffs, his despatch was annotated in the Colonial Office to add railways, waterways and a Supreme Court.[47]

Increases in the sphere of colonial autonomy, especially if they required a measure of intercolonial co-operation, were associated with the possibility of political union. Thus James Stephen in 1846 and Nova Scotia's governor Sir John Harvey in 1849 saw first, moves to transfer control of postal services from British control and secondly, exploratory talks to harmonise tariffs as steps — perhaps even immediate steps — towards constituting some form of colonial federation.[48] By no means all officials welcomed the implications of the link between British North American union and the widening sphere of autonomy. Elliot in 1858 feared that public discussion of the issue 'must be expected to branch into numerous collateral topics, and the wisest man may be unable to foresee what will be the ultimate opinions and feelings to which it will give rise'.[49] Manners Sutton had warned in 1855 that a New Brunswick proposal to send an envoy to Washington was part of a wider assertiveness.[50] Like Elliot, he viewed the Canadian initiative of

1858 with misgivings. 'All British North America is fermenting, and unless care is taken some bottles will burst,' he reported, 'but I hope to keep the New Brunswick cork in its right place.'[51]

Such statements touch on the much wider question of the relationship between intercolonial union and the possibility of British North American independence. This raises again the extensively debated issue of 'anti-imperialism' in mid-nineteenth century Britain, referred to in Chapter Four: did the British seek to get rid of their colonies?[52] It would be easy enough to accept the obvious logic behind statements such as Henry Warburton's verdict of 1838 that 'emancipation was as natural an event in the history of the colonies as death to an individual'.[53] 'Would it not be a safer and more politic conduct for English interests to keep all these colonies separate?' Roebuck asked rhetorically in 1849. '*They* would be happy and well-governed — and *we* should be secure in our dominion.' His answer was that independence would come anyway, and that it made sense to lay federal foundations in order to prepare for a national existence. However, when Roebuck confidently asserted that nobody disputed 'the assertion, that our provinces in British North America must soon be independent,'[54] he might equally have added that nobody seemed to have any clear notion — or at least anything like a modern concept — of what was meant by the term 'independence'. 'Independence is the hope of the colonies,' *The Times* stated in 1865, in language which strikes an immediate chord in the post-imperial late twentieth century. Yet it completed the sentence with the words, 'independence in its present form or, if it must be at some distant day, formal, literal, and absolute self-government,' thereby inverting two concepts from the era of European decolonisation. *The Times*, indeed, could even write that 'Prince Edward Island enjoys independence', which suggests a very broad band of meaning for the word.[55]

In fact, the mid-nineteenth century knew of only two processes by which transatlantic colonies had separated from their European homelands, and by far the most notable of these involved violent uprising and a war of liberation. 'The final separation of those colonies might possibly not be of material detriment to the interests of the Mother Country,' Melbourne reflected in 1837, 'but it is clear that it would be a serious blow to the honour of Great Britain, and certainly would be fatal to the character and existence of the Administration under which it took place.'[56] Two subsequent prime ministers feared that the consequences of losing the provinces would extend far beyond political defeat. 'The loss of any great portion of our Colonies would diminish our importance in the world,' wrote Russell in 1849, '& the vultures would soon gather together to despoil us of other parts of our Empire, or to offer insults to us which we could not bear.'[57] Palmerston in 1861 refused to 'think loss of our North American Provinces a light matter, or one which would not seriously affect the position of England among the nations of the world. It would lower us greatly, and if reputation is strength, would weaken us much'.[58] No government would welcome, still less hasten, a violent rupture with the British North American provinces. Britain, Spain and France had all suffered the loss of transatlantic territories in expensive and humiliating warfare. Only Portugal had peaceably separated from its empire, thanks to the creation of a separate Brazilian monarchy, which lasted until 1889.

Schemes for British North American union sometimes included the idea of a royal viceroy — even from projectors as unlikely as Gourlay, McGee and Cartier. Queen Victoria herself was interested in a Canadian monarchy.[59] The attraction of these schemes was that they personalised the widely used language of parent and child relations between Britain and its colonies, which even some contemporaries regarded as obfuscating. The *Saturday Review* in 1862 wrote that 'almost universal as the notion of an ultimate severance between England and her colonies has become, we believe that it depends much more on the loose analogy of the paternal relation than on any sure grounds of experience or rational conjecture'.[60] In fact, the image of a continuing blood link could mean that even so major a development as Confederation did not necessarily point to complete separation. 'We do not say that even then our connection must cease,' wrote the *Leeds Mercury* in 1865, 'or that our relative places as mother country and colony must necessarily come to an end. But the relation must be that of a mother to a daughter of full age and independent means.'[61] Anthony Trollope returned from his North American tour of 1861 convinced that Britain should welcome a colonial federation as a 'child-nation'. 'There is, I think, no more beautiful sight than that of a mother, still in all the glory of her womanhood, preparing the wedding trousseau for her daughter.... So is it that England should send forth her daughters.'[62] Thirty years after Confederation,

Kipling caught this notion of Canada's status in an expressive couplet picturing Canada as mistress in her own house but still a dutiful daughter to her imperial mother.[63] Even Goldwin Smith, usually cited as the quintessential British anti-imperialist of the 1860s, was imprecise in his use of the term 'independence', and implied that 'the sympathy, deeper and surer than any political connexion, which unites all men of English blood' would survive the departure of a British governor-general. Smith envisaged common citizenship between Britain and a united British North America.[64]

The imprecision in the definition of colonial independence may be illustrated by Russell's angry response in 1850 to comments made by Elgin on a speech made by the prime minister, in which he had told the Commons that at some distant day, colonists might say: 'The link is now become onerous to us — the time is come when we can, in amity and alliance with England, maintain our independence'.[65] Elgin deplored this 'sting in the tail' and — probably without realising that Russell would be shown his comments — censured 'the habit of telling the Colonies that the Colonial is a provisional existence'. Instead, they should be encouraged 'to believe that without severing the bonds which unite them to Great Britain they may attain the degree of perfection and of social and political developement to which organized communities of freemen have a right to aspire'. In keeping with this aim, Elgin foresaw that 'the time may come when it may be expedient to allow the Colonists to elect their own Governors ..., England withdrawing all her forces except 2000 men at Quebec & being herself represented in the Colony by an Agent — something like a Resident in India'. This, in Elgin's view, would not constitute independence from Britain.[66] In a letter so angry as to be almost illegible, Russell exploded that 'because I say that a time may come when the two countries may amicably dissolve their ties, he turns round, & holds me up as encouraging separation.... at all events any thing would be better than an *elective Governor* & an English Garrison of 2000 men. Better blow up Quebec & all our fortifications in Canada!'[67]

At most, the connection between colonial federation and the path to full independence was seen as one involving lengthy transition. Stephen had not only accepted in 1836 that his plan for a twenty-member commission drawn from the four mainland provinces would develop into a colonial congress, but argued that 'this is one of the great recommendations of the measure', although not one to be trumpeted publicly:

> It would not be difficult to show that the time must arrive when some such Body may be required to facilitate the relaxation, if not the actual abandonment of a rule, which, in the nature of human affairs, cannot be very protracted, and for many obvious reasons, Canadian independence yielded to a Central Body of this kind, may be said to be the Euthanasia of the present Constitution.[68]

A year later, he warned against 'acting on the assumption that between colonial dependence, & national independence, there is no resting place or middle point'. An intercolonial convention would permit the 'silent substitution' of what he confusingly called a 'federative union' — between Britain and the provinces, not among the colonies themselves — in place of 'dominion on the one side, & subjection on the other'.[69] It was this kind of argument which Russell found too sophisticated, predicting that a British North American congress would emulate its American counterpart and break with Britain altogether.[70] Yet even in the late 1830s, Russell foresaw the possibility that 'at a fit time' in the future, the provinces might be 'formed into a separate and distinct state, in alliance, offensive and defensive, with this country'.[71]

By 1849, he saw that time coming closer: 'the British North American Provinces would soon be strong enough to form a state of themselves, but if in strict alliance with this country, I do not think that result ought to alarm us'.[72] The concept of independence could thus be stretched to cover a form of junior partnership. Others espoused intercolonial union without predicting separation. Durham professed himself

> so far from believing that the increased power and weight which would be given to these Colonies by union would endanger their connexion with the Empire, that I look to it as the only means of fostering such a national feeling throughout them as would effectually counterbalance whatever tendencies may now exist towards separation.[73]

A former colonial official, C.R. Ogden, summed up his scheme for a colonial federation in 1850 with the slogan, 'Colonial Independence, under the Flag'.[74] Sir Edmund Head in 1851 argued that a federal union would bind the provinces together 'until as time advanced ... they might if they did separate be ready to assume as a whole, the bearing of a powerful and independent State', but he refused to 'consider it impossible that the connection should be maintained for an indefinite period'.[75] Lytton was alarmed by the potentially separatist implications of the Canadian initiative of 1858, but consoled himself that rivalries among the provinces 'would make them dislike the idea of any native Presidential authority', so that British interests might continue to be protected, not by Elgin's resident agent but by 'a statesman of great skill & acuteness, & above all with the invaluable gift of conciliation' continuing to serve as governor-general.[76]

It was not until the very eve of Confederation that any serious attention was given, even unofficially, to the question of just how Britain and Canada might 'amicably dissolve' their ties. In 1865, Lord Bury proposed what might be termed a sleeping treaty, an advance agreement between Britain and 'The New Nation', as he termed the projected union of British North America, which could be invoked by either side, to give a year's notice of separation, thereby obviating the danger of quarrelling over details at a time when relations had already become sufficiently strained to make full independence attractive. Bury had served as personal secretary to Sir Edmund Head (whom he apparently disliked) and may have been spelling out the implications which he saw as latent in the federal initiative of 1858. Perhaps more significant was the fact that he had married the daughter of Sir Allan MacNab, whose confidence in the durability of Canada's British connection seems to have been reduced after the introduction of self-government. Bury also proposed that no separation would be permitted in the immediate aftermath of the American Civil War, or at any time of danger in North America — recognising that this restriction entrenched the very responsibility 'from which many persons now desire to escape'.[77]

The alternative scheme of 1865 was put forward by a skilled parliamentary draftsman, Henry Thring, who drew up legislative machinery through which any self-governing colony might seek legal independence by passing addresses through both houses of its local parliament, with two-thirds majorities at an interval of three months.[78] Thring's scheme had the drawback of providing for the imposition of conditions upon independence, without any guarantee that they could be enforced after separation. Bury's approach was equally flawed in failing to realise that precisely because colonies were legally dependencies, they could not conclude binding treaties. However, Bury and Thring did at least try to tackle the technical question of colonial separation, which is more than can be said of any politician or government official. Newcastle responded angrily in 1861 when Palmerston referred slightingly to 'some supposed theoretical Gentlemen in the Colonial Office who wish to get rid of all Colonies as soon as possible', firmly assuring him that 'if there are such they have never ventured to open their opinions to me — and if they did so on grounds of peaceful separation I should differ from them as long as Colonies can be retained by bonds of mutual sympathy and mutual obligation'.[79]

In assessing British attitudes to the future of the imperial relationship with Canada at the time of Confederation, it is important to grasp that the relationship between federation and colonial independence was vague, and not universally accepted as an inevitable linkage. Moreover, statements of hostility to the colonial connection may be matched by equally influential declarations of pride in Britain's imperial role.[80] By the mid-1860s, it would be impossible to deny that there was a rising sentiment in Britain which was at least reconciled to the likely ending of the political link. George Brown in December 1864 was disturbed to encounter 'in some quarters evident regret that we did not declare at once for independence'.[81] Joseph Howe was equally dismayed to find in March 1867 that 'the almost universal feeling appeared to be that *uniting the Provinces was an easy mode of getting rid of them* ... and the sooner the responsibility of their relations with the Republic is shifted off the shoulders of John Bull the better'.[82] Special circumstances may partly explain the strength of the feelings the two men encountered. Brown's visit to London coincided with a low point in British-American relations, and he was sure that the sentiment he encountered sprang 'from the fear of invasion of Canada by the United States, and will soon pass away with the cause that excites it'.[83] Howe undoubtedly encountered public men who were blunt in disabusing him of any hopes that Nova Scotian opposition to Confederation would meet with a sympathetic hearing. He was, for instance, optimistic of gaining the support of Laurence Oliphant, a backbench MP who had served as Lord

Elgin's private secretary during the negotiation of the Reciprocity Treaty in 1854. Oliphant bluntly declared 'that Confederation would have his support because it would take these Provinces off England's hands, on which they were a useless and dangerous encumbrance'. Shortly after, Oliphant actually settled in the United States, becoming for some years the spiritual slave of an American mystic.[84] He may not have been wholly typical of contemporary British thinking. Given the degree of British resentment against the Canadian tariff, and the depth of real concern over the quagmire of British North American defence, it is surely significant that Confederation was seen as no more than a contingent and speculative step towards future separation. The formal link between Confederation and independence, so attractive to historians, was conspicuous by its absence.

In one sense, it is not at all surprising that Confederation was accompanied by speculation in Britain about the possibility of British North American independence. Unlike most political developments in the provinces, their plans to unite attracted extensive and overwhelmingly favourable attention in Britain, where commentators were agreed in regarding it as an important step. This presumably implied that it must be an important step in some particular direction. While a few enthusiasts already cherished the dream, later to flower as 'Imperial Federation', that a united British North America would take some share in the overall running of the empire, they were mainly confined to uninfluential and minor figures, such as the Christian Socialist J.M. Ludlow — although Frederick Bruce, the British minister in Washington, championed the idea which his brother, Lord Elgin, had argued for in earlier decades.[85] If British North America was taking a step forward, and if there was little prospect of the empire reconstituting itself into a global super-state, then it seemed to follow that in some sense, Confederation was a step towards independence — whatever that might mean. *The Times* caught this in its comments on Cardwell's published despatch approving of the Quebec Resolutions.

It is true we are not actually giving up the American Colonies — nay, the despatch ... does not contain the slightest hint that such a possibility ever crossed the mind of the writer; but yet it is perfectly evident — there is no use in concealing the fact — that the Confederation movement considerably diminishes the difficulty which would be felt by the colonies in separating from the mother country.

'It is not so much a step towards independence,' concluded the *Saturday Review*, 'as a means of softening the inevitable shock.'[86]

There was one ineluctable problem about this prediction: the colonies did not show the slightest sign either of seeking separation, or of recognising its inevitability. 'The colonists advance with excessive timidity to whatever has the appearance of ultimate independence,' noted the *Westminster Review*, puzzled that 'they seem to be wholly unconscious that they are framing a confederation which is to form a stepping stone to this final end.'[87] Some were sardonic in their interpretation of continuing colonial loyalty to Britain. The vision of British North America's future held by the Canadian ministry, according to the *Saturday Review* in 1865, was 'that of a single united and substantially independent Federation, enjoying unlimited loans at 3 per cent on British credit, for the construction of railways and canals, and the maintenance of their land and sea defences.' Financial considerations dictated Canada's expressions of loyalty, 'for the unanswerable reason that they have got no money to spend'.[88] Annoyance with the Canadians was understandable, but it had no practical outlet: as Frederic Rogers and Lord Bury had separately recognised, national honour made it impossible for Britain to abandon its commitment to British North America at the very moment when national interest suggested that its continuance could be suicidal. In the mid-1860s, there was no alternative but to make the best of British North America's insistence upon continuing membership of the empire. The *Edinburgh Review* was philosophical. 'Retainers who will neither give nor accept notice to quit our service must, it is assumed, be kept on our establishment.'[89] As *The Times* had reminded Goldwin Smith in 1862, 'the Colonists have rights as well as ourselves'.[90] *Punch* probably came closer to the general public sentiment when it mistranslated Carnarvon's Latin peroration on the British North America bill to assert that newly confederated Canada was 'quite welcome, we are sure, to stand under her great Mama's big umbrella'.[91]

The roots of British support for Confederation in the mid-1860s must be sought, not in a contemporary desire to find a means of making British North America leave the empire, but rather in the consensus of preceding decades that only through some form of union among themselves could the provinces be enabled to defend their separate identity against the pressures and temptations which would incline them towards becoming part of the United States. Duty and interest coincided in the discharge of national trusteeship towards the North American provinces, Head argued in 1851. Duty required Britain 'so to govern these Colonies as to fit them gradually for an independent existence if the tie with the Mother country be severed', while interest dictated 'that such an independent existence should be given them as will not allow them to swell the strength and influence of the United States'. British North American union was the answer. 'That they should maintain their independence singly is hardly conceivable;' Head wrote in 1851, 'that they should do so if formed into one compact and United body does not seem absurd'.[92] In 1853, he predicted that 'Canada will never be annexed to the United States if we give her freedom enough ... & foster her own sense of self importance'. Canadians would find no attraction in sinking the level of 'slave catchers to the United States ... especially if any sense of *united interest* in all the British Provinces can be created. Whether Canada belong nominally or not to England is comparatively immaterial.'[93]

The desire to prevent the incorporation of British North America into the great transatlantic republic appears as the most consistent and basic element behind British support for a union of the provinces. As early as 1784, Robert Morse had predicted that a united British North America might be 'made a formidable rival to the American states'.[94] 'A forecasting Policy', wrote Stephen in April 1836, 'would appear to suggest that provision should be deliberately, though of course unavowedly, made for the peaceful and honourable abdication of a power, which ere long it will be impossible to retain, and for raising up on the North American Continent a counter poise to the United States.'[95] Roebuck in April 1837 similarly urged parliament to act 'wisely and with forethought' in creating a new 'federal republic' to 'check and control' the northward expansion of the United States.[96] As the mouthpiece of the Lower Canadian Assembly, it no doubt made tactical sense for Roebuck to stress this aspect of British North American affairs, but his subsequent campaign in 1849-50 suggests that he had been sincere in returning, early in 1838, to advocating the uniting of the colonies into 'one compact body' as a preparatory step to their independence as 'a northern confederacy, balancing and controlling the powers of the United States'.[97] Lord Brougham also wished to 'balance the colossal empire of the United States' by uniting British North America into 'an independent, flourishing, and powerful state', while the radical Henry Warburton feared that they would fall 'separately into the possession of their great neighbour'.[98] Durham also thought that a general union of the provinces 'might in some measure counterbalance the preponderant and increasing influence of the United States on the American Continent'.[99] These sentiments were not confined to reformers and radicals, who might be expected to have been the least hostile to American institutions, but were also shared by some Conservatives, even in the 1830s. 'Would not the consolidation of a British North American Union be a good check on the growth of United States superiority?' asked the *Morning Post* in October 1838.[100]

When British North American union was next widely discussed, in 1849, Roebuck renewed his advocacy of a 'new confederation' to act as 'a counterpoise to the gigantic empire and influence of the United States', which had expanded as a result of the Mexican War so that its 'mighty wings seem as if about to be unfolded, and then to overshadow the whole of that vast continent, of which already she has acquired but too large a portion'.[101] *The Times* asked whether it would 'be impossible to devise such a Government — whether Royal, Imperial, or Republican — as, by consolidating the three North American provinces, would erect a huge breakwater between us and our nearest rival?'[102] Russell's conversion to the idea of federation in August 1849 was similarly motivated. 'The pressing danger is that of annexation to the United States to which I could never give my consent.'[103]

Perhaps the most striking assumption in Russell's statement was his confidence that British consent would in fact be required for such a change. Five years later, the population of the United States had overtaken that of Great Britain and British national confidence had to cope with the shock of colliding with the imponderable bulk of Russia in the Crimean War. The colonial enthusiast J.R. Godley summed up a number of insecurities in an alarmed comment:

the Statesman must be blind who does not see that *the* great peril which overshadows the future of the civilized world lies in the vast power and progress of the United States, coupled as their gigantic material resources are with unbounded energy and inordinate ambition. To raise up to this over-weening power a rival on its own continent, would be a work far more valuable and important to England than the curbing of the power of Russia. Such a rival as British America would be to the United States, necessarily inferior in power, would for its own sake be a faithful ally to England, for on England's friendship and support her existence would depend. If, on the other hand, the British American States remain disunited, they must be annexed one by one to the mammoth republic.[104]

A union of the provinces would of itself check American expansion — a crucial assumption behind the equation of the 1860s that Confederation would somehow solve the problem of colonial defence — while the adverse balance of forces would compel British North America to lean on imperial protection. Left to themselves, the provinces would fall like dominoes to the great republic.

The strength with which such sentiments were expressed requires some discussion and explanation. The provinces of British North America were, after all, the shreds and patches of a continental empire, the bulk of which had been lost in a costly and humiliating war of national independence barely half a century earlier. Why should the prospect of losing what was left to the United States appear as anything other than a tidying-up which would finally close a mistaken chapter of British history? In many respects, the very fact that the American War had been so obviously the product of mistaken policies prompted succeeding generations to some determination to do better in their remaining provinces. Moreover, under the old imperial trading system, British North America played a useful dual role, as a supplier to the British islands in the West Indies, and as an alternative source of timber to the Baltic, which few could forget had been closed by Napoleon in the last throes of the great struggle against France. While Cobden, in what Russell condemned as his 'narrow view', insisted that 'under the *régime* of Free Trade, Canada is not one whit more ours than is the great Republic', habits of thought died hard even after 1846. For strategic reasons, protective duties on colonial timber lingered on until the 1860s, and it was widely assumed that the continuing colonial connection ensured that British manufacturers would have favourable terms of entry into the Canadian market. Russell comforted himself with the belief that 'No Canadian or Australian

Lowell can be fostered for the sake of colonial protected manufactures', a reference to the town which symbolised the New England cotton industry.[105] These illusions seemed to be dispelled by the Canadian tariff of 1859.

In the mid-twentieth century, the years of a perceived 'special relationship' in which the British persuaded themselves that they played the role of civilized Greeks to the raw American Romans, there was some tendency among British historians to stress the values and interests which had linked the two countries throughout the nineteenth century. One scholar even argued that since 'biological inheritance of racial characteristics is plainly a fact ... there is no clear proof that it does not operate in the sphere of national character and even psychology'.[106] While nineteenth-century British commentators did not forget that the two peoples 'had been rocked in the same cradle', they also perceived a steady dilution of the blood link by foreign immigration: war with the United States, W.H. Russell concluded in 1861, would be 'unnatural', but less so than in 1776 and 1812.[107] The imagery of an extended family made it easier to explain how the passage of time reduced mutual sympathies. 'An unaccountable cross has crept into the American breed,' *The Times* lamented in 1860, 'and we hardly know ourselves when we look at our second cousins.' Indeed, it concluded that climatic factors were differentiating the 'bold, hardy, manly' British North Americans from their neighbours, whose 'brains are made restless and whose nerves are irritated by an almost tropical sun'.[108]

When an anglophile New Englander reminded a British friend that 'we must not confound the *State*, that is the political organization of the State, with the *People*', he identified an important source of British concern.[109] It was precisely because the United States combined democratic institutions with the energies of Anglo-Saxon people that it was so capriciously dangerous, both to British world power and to British domestic institutions. 'Not one man in a thousand cares whether the Canadians prosper or fail to prosper,' said Phineas Finn, Trollope's fictional under-secretary for colonies, in describing British public opinion. 'They care that Canada should not go to the States, because — though they don't love the Canadians, they do hate the Americans.'[110] A colleague explained Palmerston's suspicion of the Americans by remarking that 'he was launched into public life when the feeling of the whole country was bitter against them as rebellious colonists, and no man quite gets rid of his early impressions'. Palmerston had been born a year after George III had recognised the independence of the United States, and had first held office before the War of 1812. He survived to demonstrate his conversion to Confederation by taking George Brown for a celebrated walk in the snow on his Hampshire estate in December 1864.[111] The national disaster of the American War was still only a lifetime away in the 1860s, and many politicians younger than Palmerston had imbibed the same fundamental antipathy towards the United States and its democracy.

We should therefore beware of projecting backwards any modern sense of democratic kinship between Britain and the United States. Even the *Manchester Guardian*, no friend to aristocratic government at home, could argue that the fact that Americans 'enjoy an amount of *political* liberty beyond that which exists in any other country' was 'not, of itself, quite conclusive as to the relative merits of their institutions'. Political liberty was not 'attended by an equal extent of personal freedom and security' and, as a result, 'there is no great deal to choose between Russia and the United States'.[112] Of de Tocqueville's theory that the tendency of all societies was to move towards American-style democracy, the Conservative *Morning Post* retorted in 1840 that the tendency of all mankind was to slide into sin: both were to be resisted.[113] *The Times* was less sure that the American model could be permanently staved off, 'for the parts of England [sic] most like America are Manchester, Liverpool, and Glasgow, and there are many who tell us that the best thing we can all do is to be leavened throughout by these model cities'.[114] Hence Lord Edward Howard's scheme of 1849 to consolidate the provinces into a compact colonial monarchy, 'a so-to-speak European power' which would act as 'a counter-balancing power to democracy'.[115]

There was an artistic linkage in 1867 between the Second Reform Act, which co-opted the urban artisans into the political system to fend off American-style democracy on one side of the Atlantic, and the British North America Act, which secured the Confederation of the North American provinces to create a barrier against the expansion of the American republic on the other. Realistically, few were likely to cherish the notion of replicating merrie England in the constitution of British North America. Lord Derby deplored the concession of an elective upper chamber to Canada in 1854 as ruling out the hope of establishing 'upon that great continent a monarchy free as that of this country, even freer still with regard to the popular influence exercised, but yet a monarchy worthy of the name, and not a mere empty shadow'. Yet even he had to confess that 'perhaps it was only a dream'.[116] While C.R. Ogden had been described by a visiting Irish gentleman in 1834 as 'a most genuine bigoted Tory of the old school',[117] by 1850 even his dream of colonial federation extended no further than 'a form of Government so far Democratic and expansive as to leave nothing to desire that the Americans have, and yet so Conservative as to leave much to envy which the Americans have not'.[118] Very occasionally the provinces provided an opportunity for the British press to sneer at the vaunted superiority of the institutions of the United States: 'notwithstanding the demonstration of its merits which the proximity of the United States has afforded them', *The Times* sardonically noted in 1860 that Canada and New Brunswick held 'unaccountably aloof' from the ballot.[119] Overall, however, British North America would play a more substantial role in resisting the practical, rather than the theoretical challenges of American democracy.

The potential challenge to British power from the United States was two-fold, and in each case British North America could play a key role in checking the danger. First, tariff protection threatened to enable the United States to displace Britain as the world's principal industrial power. Secondly, backed by its growing population and industrial might, an American mercantile marine could provide the foundations for a fighting Navy which would take over command of the seas. Captain Marryat, the spinner of nautical yarns, explained how the existence of a separate British North America would always negate any protectionist policy adopted by the Americans:

Should they increase the tariff ... upon English goods, the Canadas and our other provinces will render their efforts useless, as we have a line of coast of upwards of 2,000 miles, by which we can introduce English goods to any amount by smuggling, and which it is impossible for the Americans to guard against; and as the West fills up, this importation of English goods would every year increase.[120]

'Tariffs are a dream — an utter impossibility, so long as England possesses Upper Canada,' Lord Brougham proclaimed in 1849.[121] Russell was certainly aware of the potential of Canada as a back-door route into the American market, and he wondered how Cobden could fail to 'see that the imposition of a duty of from 30 to 40 per cent. on British manufactured goods from the Mississippi to the St. Lawrence would be a great blow to Manchester & Leeds'.[122] In 1849, it was claimed that British North Americans were six times per capita more valuable as customers to Britain as their American neighbours. It seems likely that some of those goods found their way into the United States. Galt in 1859 was predictably indignant in denying that there was large-scale cross-border smuggling, but Canadian official trade figures routinely added 20 per cent to the value of exports to the United States from inland ports to compensate for under-recording.[123]

Sir William Young, in 1838, appealed to a mercantilist view of naval power which would soon be undermined by the repeal of the Navigation Acts when he claimed that 'our colonial possessions were the nursery of our commercial marine; our commercial marine was the foundation of our royal navy; and it was on our naval supremacy that the pride and majesty of England depended'.[124] None the less, the fact remained that there was a close relationship between a country's ability to recruit a fighting navy and the size of its merchant marine. In the mid-nineteenth century, Britain had the largest merchant fleet, the United States was second — and British North America third. By the mid-1860s, as iron and steam began to challenge wood and wind, British North America was still claimed to rank fourth in world tonnage.[125] Consequently, however small a place held by British North America in other aspects of the British world view, it was an object of policy to prevent the naval resources of the provinces from falling into American hands. 'The extension of the power of the United States to the North Pole I have always considered an event fatal to the maritime superiority of England,' wrote Roebuck.[126] Head considered that Britain's 'moral dignity' would be damaged if British North America were to be lost through 'squabbles' over self-government, but added that it would cause deeper injury 'to allow the force of these Colonies and the advantages of their military position their trade and their shipping to be transferred by any process to the Government of Washington'.[127]

Elgin conjured the ultimate nightmare in typically flamboyant terms: 'Let the Yankees get possession of British North America with the prestige of superior generalship — who can say how soon they may dispute with you the Empire of India and of the Seas?'.[128] He was not alone in his fears. The United States had turned on Britain in 1812, in the last throes of the war against Napoleon. 'Beware, lest when England may be fighting with Russia for Her supremacy, nay for her existence as a great Nation, on the plains of Hindostan, she do not receive a "felon blow" from the power which her indifference and contempt has created in the Western world,' warned C.R. Ogden in 1850.[129] This prophetic linkage of the Russian and American threats — foreshadowing late-Victorian concerns that the future of the world belonged to the great land empires — also underlay Godley's view that building a British North American Confederation as a check on the United States would be a far more valuable national objective than fighting the Crimean War to curb Russia.[130]

At the core of British support for the union of British North America there lay a very simple notion: uniting the provinces would of itself create a barrier against the expansion of the United States. In one sense, this assumption was surprising, since by the late 1840s British opinion seems equally to have discounted the likelihood that the provinces would in fact welcome absorption into the American Union. The Montreal Annexation Movement of 1849 was largely dismissed as an expression of mercenary resentment by protectionists and tories against their loss of commercial and political privilege.[131] By 1856, *The Times* could dismiss the 'misgiving' that Canada was passing through 'a phase in the inevitable transition to independence, or to its almost certain consequence — annexation' as being as likely 'as the similar prospect of England, Ireland, and Scotland being one day added to the United States'.[132] The equation of complete independence with probable annexation did linger on, even beyond Confederation. As late as 1874, Lord Dufferin could report that 'independence both now and for many years to come would quickly result in annexation'.[133] Absorption into the United States thus remained a future danger, at the very least a useful bogey to be invoked by those, like Galt, who sought to postulate a straight choice between federation and annexation: 'every difficulty placed in the way of the former is an argument in favor of those who desire the latter'.[134]

Fears that the transatlantic republic would eventually swallow the whole continent formed only one segment of a range of notions about the future of the United States. At the other end of the spectrum was the belief that it would eventually fracture, at least between North and South, with the West perhaps also going its own way. The views of undergraduate debaters in the Cambridge Union Society may be taken as derivative of the attitudes of the influential classes in Britain: in 1841 they replied in the affirmative to the question, 'Is the present generation likely to witness the dismemberment of the United States of America?', though by a narrow margin.[135] Even in the last months of the American Civil War, the *Daily News* could still deplore the prevalence of the 'old mistake ... of assuming and asserting that the disruption of the Republic is owing to its size'.[136] However, while some believed by the 1850s that the republic would ultimately break up, others found it hard to accept that either secession or civil war were proximate developments. 'If we were to take the people of the United States at their word,' wrote *The Times* during the crisis of 1850, '... we should at once assert that a dissolution of the Union was about immediately to take place'. Since the Union did come close to dissolution, the comment was remarkably dismissive, an attitude explained by the accompanying touch of contempt. With people like the Americans, *The Times* explained, 'talking and writing big words is, in fact, their constitutional safety valve'. Threats of secession were annual events, 'and ought to be viewed simply as a specimen of the bad taste but too prevalent in all the writing and speaking of our American brethren.'[137]

As late as 1858, Head could play down the possibility ('as some people anticipate') that the United States would break up as 'a pure speculation: perhaps a remote contingency'.[138] Even as South Carolina passed its secession ordinance, *The Times* was still adjusting to the 'great effort of mind for any Englishman to enter into a question of national disunion'.[139] Yet if sectional conflict was not regarded as serious enough to destroy the United States, there were periods when it was sufficiently intense to inhibit annexation. 'The southern states would resolutely oppose any such accession of strength to their northern antagonists as must result from the junction of the Canadian provinces,' *The Times* assured its readers in 1849, and should they fail to prevent annexation, 'the weight thus thrown upon the northern extremity of the Union would precipitate the catastrophe so long foreboded, and snap asunder the mighty fabric at its centre'.[140] Edward Ellice in 1838 and Grey in 1848 both consoled themselves with the thought that annexation might lead to the division of the United States, allowing Britain to exercise 'as much power by offensive & defensive alliances as under its Colonial system'.[141]

This range of attitudes to the future of the United States helps to explain the cycles and peaks of British interest in the utility of British North American union. In the 1850s, there seemed no particular urgency about moving towards a regional union of British North America, since the United States was more often than not internally deadlocked over the issue of slavery. The outbreak of the American Civil War did not immediately alter this picture, if only because British opinion clung to the view that the South would eventually succeed in breaking away. In January 1863, for instance, *The Times* dismissed the military case for a railway from Halifax to Quebec — which, it acknowledged, could easily be cut in wartime anyway — by saying that the reunification of the United States was 'contrary to apparent probability', and as late as October 1864, as the Southern Confederacy was being sliced into pieces, *The Times* was sarcastic in its reference to 'some magical process of which we can as yet form no idea' which was to reunite the States 'into one harmonious whole ... for the purpose of subjugating the colonies of Great Britain'.[142] The colonial secretary of the early 1860s, the Duke of Newcastle, seems to have believed in 1861 that Maine would break away from the Union and join British North America,[143] and as late as 1863 he expected that the western states would also separate, and was anxious to co-operate with the plans of a Chicago syndicate interested in the construction of a ship canal from Georgian Bay to the Ottawa River,[144] a scheme which encouraged *The Times* to look to the day when America would 'have a political system of her own, as varied and as complicated as that of Europe'.[145] Thus, until the very eve of Confederation, for some at least in Britain, a united British North America would be only one of a group of states which might emerge from what the colonial enthusiast C.B. Adderley referred to in 1862 as 'the approaching re-formation of Nations in North America'.[146]

The belief that British North American union would prevent annexation was perhaps the most powerful underpinning of British support for Confederation. To understand how it operated, it is necessary to recognise that a union of the provinces, *by itself*, was thought to strengthen them in the face of the United States. As early as 1838, a Canadian correspondent of *The Times* could warn against the easy assumption that through 'a "confederation" of our powers ... we should rear up a new independent government to control the United States'.[147] Union was barely seen as a practical means of improving their local defences. Howick in 1839 and Roebuck in 1849 included co-ordination of militia among the functions to be assigned to a central legislature,[148] but even for the methodical Head in 1851, the matter was almost an afterthought: the cost of military installations 'as well as the expense of organizing the Militia would it is presumed be paid by the Federal Government'. Indeed, Head explicitly stated that the federal government 'would have no Army or Navy to pay'.[149]

The explanation is that British ideas about British North American union were formed in the quarter century before the outbreak of the American Civil War, when the military balance in North America still favoured the empire. The paper strength of the United States Army rarely exceeded 12000 in the two decades before 1861, and it was usually short of recruits. Bouts of Indian warfare could press its effectiveness to the limits. In 1858, Colonel Albert Sidney Johnston at the head of a force of 1500 men was unable to assert more than a shadow of Washington's authority among the Mormons of Utah.[150] When Roebuck warned of the consequences of American expansion to the North Pole, it was because 'the United States would, in fact, have no frontier to defend': his assumption was that in any war with Britain, Americans would be the invaded not the invaders.[151] The Montreal correspondent of *The Times* in 1849 was equally confident that the construction of a railway linking the city to the United States would never provide an invasion route from the south. Even if war came, 'we have far more available troops than the Americans' and 'are more accustomed to military movements and operations'. The 'we' in this statement evidently meant, 'we in the British empire'. It did not occur to the writer that the army of the British empire needed the active support of a colonial militia.[152]

Thus it was that an idea, formed in an era of confidence in British military strength in North America, could play such a reassuring role in the crisis of the mid-1860s — not as a means towards more effective defence, but as a substitute for it. The military balance was already perceived to be tilting before the outbreak of the Civil War, as British garrisons were reduced in order to meet the demands of the war in the Crimea, leaving 'just as many troops in Quebec as are sufficient to keep up the memory and appearance of military occupation, when the reality has passed away for ever'. 'The entire garrison of Canada might be packed in a couple of steamers,' *The Times* remarked in 1861.[153] It took the shock of the *Trent* crisis to begin to bring home the implications of the shift in power, and even then there was a tendency to over-estimate the effectiveness of militia forces in Canada. *The Times* had comforted its readers in 1858 that the volunteer movement was 'popular' in the province and that its militia was 'so complete that all the several arms of the service are forthcoming'. Newcastle in 1862 praised the 'very earnest spirit of volunteering in the whole of these Colonies', while the military historian Sir William Napier reflected a comfortable stereotype in predicting that the Canadian militia would respond better to training than its American counterparts, 'being more accustomed to obedience'.[154] 'Canada armed and on the alert has nothing to fear from invasion,' *The Times* pronounced in June 1861, adding that 'our troops are numerous enough to irritate, but not numerous enough to intimidate or to defend'.[155] Before significant fighting had broken out between North and South, British opinion was already moving half way towards reality: it was accepted that Britain could not defend the provinces against invasion, but it was still assumed that they could protect themselves.

The first year of the American conflict was enough to shatter this illusion. 'It is impossible not to feel that every month the civil war in the States continues the military disparity between them and Canada increases,' Newcastle wrote in April 1862. 'Little more than a year ago they were equal. Now Canada has only an embryo and untrained Militia — the States have a trained army, — and the temptation to aggression whenever the war is brought to a close is proportionately increased.'[156] The answer was for Canada to reform its militia system, and in the spring of 1862 — perhaps indirectly encouraged by overly sanguine reports from the new governor-general, Lord Monck — the British assumed that Canada, the 'model colony', was dutifully rising to the challenge.[157] The news that the Militia Bill had been defeated created shock, expressed in anger against Canada. 'Let her arm by all means, but let her arm, not for our sake, but for her own.'[158] In this painful realisation of the danger facing Britain's transatlantic empire, there was little reference to the union of the provinces: British North American union, in other words, only began to be presented as a measure which would strengthen the defence of the provinces after Confederation had become a practical issue on other grounds. In January 1861, as the secession crisis began, Newcastle had noted that the union of British North America 'is what must eventually be brought about and may be hastened by events arising out of the condition of the rest of the Continent', but he seems to have been drawing on ideas which he had already formed.[159] Similarly, Russell's response to the defeat of the Militia Bill was to revive 'the plan long ago contemplated & then found impracticable, namely that of forming a Federal Union of the British North American Provinces'.[160] If the largest province was condemned as unreliable, then a union of them all was not a very logical deduction from the Militia Bill crisis. Indeed, not a single MP proposed the solution when the Commons irritably debated the affair.[161]

Galt, on a visit to Britain, did not help matters. In a speech in the economy-conscious city of Manchester, he bluntly stated that it had been Britain's 'duty' to defend Canada at the time of the *Trent* crisis, since it was 'impossible' that the province could 'raise an army of 10000 men'. Consequently, *The Times* was in no mood to enter into his political disquisition on the next stage in the development of colonial self-government. The North American and Australian colonies, he mused, should be grouped together, 'arranging the question of self-defence on some fair basis, and not impossibly in the end producing a confederation with Great Britain rather resembling that of Germany than that of America, which now appears to have failed'. *The Times* pointedly misinterpreted his proposal, with a censorious reference to the corruption and ineptitude which characterised Canadian politics, doubting that 'the interests of the North American colonies would indeed be promoted, even if they were to succeed in forming themselves into confederations closely resembling that worst organized of all federal bodies, the Germanic Confederation'.[162] The only commentator who could logically argue for British North American union in the aftermath of the defeat of the Militia Bill was Goldwin Smith, for whom the *Trent* crisis had been a terrible warning that the provinces should be cut loose altogether.[163]

It was the appalling realisation that the North was going to win the Civil War, and emerge from it in no magnanimous mood of forgiveness towards British transgressions, which led British opinion to grasp gratefully at the re-emerging idea of Confederation. 'When the public hear of Canadian defences,' *The Times* confessed in February 1865, 'they experience nothing but a feeling of uneasiness and perplexity.'[164] Canada must be defended; Canada could not be defended. It was to bridge that conundrum that British opinion would turn with some confused desperation to welcome Confederation. In 1858, the *Morning Herald* had seen the federation of the provinces as a device which would 'in time create a counterpoise, through their unity, to the growing power of the United States, which, otherwise, might absorb them severally'.[165] Despite the outbreak of the Civil War, the *Spectator* in 1862 still saw federation as a means of ensuring that 'in a few years' time the British American empire might stand alone, and as one great country defy invasion, and preserve the balance of power in the New World'.[166] Such ideas were simply carried forward, but transmuted into an immediate rather than an eventual nostrum. The *Saturday Review* in October 1864 wrote of 'the floating idea' of 'a great British confederation powerful enough to hold its own even against such a neighbour as the United States'. In June 1865, it assured its readers that the military advantages of Confederation were 'obvious' and that it was impossible to believe that 'an efficient defensive organization will ever be brought about without political amalgamation'.[167] Yet midway between those two statements, the *Saturday Review* had admitted that it was 'not quite true, as has been very generally assumed, that the necessities of military defence were the moving cause of the project of Colonial Federation'. It was rather that the 'threatening attitude of the United States' had been enough 'to infuse into the councils of the colonists an earnestness and unanimity for want of which, at another time, the best-devised scheme of union might have proved abortive'.[168] The accuracy of this analysis needs to be assessed in the light of the fact that it was published just as the reaction against the Quebec scheme was beginning to take effect in the Maritime provinces. The British, in short, were really not sure how Confederation would help solve the frightening problems of Canadian defence, but they grasped at the argument for want of anything better.

Ambiguity about the relationship between Confederation and defence was also evident in the thoughtful study published in 1865 by *The Times* war correspondent, W.H. Russell. Although Russell was not a soldier, his experience of reporting military incompetence in the Crimean War had made him a practical authority on questions of defence, and he was also a keen advocate of British North American union. The evolution of Russell's book, *Canada: Its Defences, Condition and Resources*, partly explains the overlay of his arguments. Originally conceived as a companion to his two volumes on the Civil War, *My Diary, North and South*, it seems to have been intended as a travelogue, spiced with a sharp moral regarding the danger which the provinces faced from a vengeful and militarised neighbour. 'The book was nearly finished when suddenly, as it seemed, the whole of the Provinces, yielding to a common sentiment of danger, sent their delegates to consider the policy and possibility of a great Confederation, which had been strongly recommended in the pages already written.' As a war correspondent, Russell found it natural to link defence with political union, arguing that Confederation 'presents the only means now available, as far as we can perceive, for securing to the Provinces present independence and a future political life distinct from the turbulent existence of the United States'.[169] However, these bold statements, taken from Russell's preface, appear in more complex and contradictory form in his final chapter.[170] It was, he said, 'not surprising that the idea of a Confederation for the purposes of common defence and military collaboration should have arisen'. Yet even in 1865, Russell feared there was 'no sign as yet that the Canadians will quite arouse from a sleep which no fears disturb'. Nor should it 'be supposed that any confederation ... would yield such an increase of force as would enable the collective or several members of it to resist the force of the Republic of the Northern American United States — at least, not just now.' In his realist mode, then, Russell half-recognised that the Canadians did not take their own defence very seriously, and that Confederation would add nothing to the practical strength of the provinces. Indeed, his 'not just now' tailpiece was evidence of the continuing grip of the notion which had been general before the continental crisis of the mid-sixties, that union by and of itself would be enough to create a barrier against the United States.

Russell's supporting arguments were massively unconvincing. The War between North and South showed 'the vast energy and resources of a union of States in war time as compared with the action of States not so joined'. This ignored the inconvenient facts that the Civil War was the result of a rupture of an existing state, and that Northern superiority in industry and population was grinding down the Southern Confederacy which had exceeded the population of British North America. Moreover, Russell's comparison was with 'the action of States not so joined' — France, Britain, Turkey and Sardinia in the Crimean War: 'their power would have been much greater had they acted under a common head'. It was a strained example, and one which Russell presumably used only to buttress a weak argument by implicit appeal to his own experience in the Crimea which had made him a national hero. Russell ignored alternative examples, such as the failure of its ramshackle political union to guarantee military success to the Austrian empire against France in 1859, and the inexplicable success of the unfederated armies of Wellington and Blucher against Napoleon at Waterloo. It is hard to imagine the political structure might have federated Britain, France, northern Italy, the southern Balkans and Asiatic Turkey during the Crimean War.

In fact, buried within Russell's muddled pleading, is a key sentence which demonstrates the extent to which Confederation was a common British vision for the future of the provinces, and the way in which the crisis of the mid-sixties transmuted it into a substitute for a commitment to defend the provinces against invasion which could no longer be discharged. Russell found it 'surprising' that the idea of Confederation 'should have floated about so long' without coming to the point of action. 'I think it is the first notion that occurs to a stranger visiting Canada and casting about for a something to put in place of the strength which distant England cannot, and Canadians will not, afford.' *The Times* made the same admission, in a moment of rueful honesty. 'Conscious as we are of our inability to protect these colonies by land in case of war, we must naturally rejoice at any event which seems to place them in a position in which they would be better able to protect themselves.'[171] The key word in that statement was 'seems'. Confederation was not a solution deduced logically from the threat of American invasion. Rather it was a reassuringly familiar idea almost desperately used to fill a frightening gap.

  This is not to deny that the question of British North American defence became practically entangled with the question of British North American union, but even Creighton, perhaps the most notable exponent of the view of Confederation as an inevitable and logically interlocking event, recognised that in 1864, at least, the two issues appeared to be distinct.[172] It was on their visit to London in 1865, to appeal to Caesar, that the Canadian delegates stressed that 'their powers would be far greater if the Confederation were accomplished than they are now when the Colonies are separate',[173] and at the banquet in the Fishmongers' Hall Cartier breezily implied that all defence problems would be solved once union was achieved.[174] Macdonald's central need in the spring of 1865 was to hold the Great Coalition together, and in particular to prevent George Brown from demanding action on the promise to create a federation of the two Canadas in the wake of the rejection of Confederation in New Brunswick. That meant persuading Brown to undertake a second transatlantic journey within five months as part of the delegation to Britain. Brown saw himself as the voice of Upper Canada, and it was Upper Canada which would be most exposed to invasion if the British decided to pull back their garrisons to strong points at Quebec and Montreal. Thus both to hold together the Canadian ministry and to underline the urgency of their mission in the eyes of the British, it made good sense to conflate the two issues. Insofar as the linkage may have strengthened the cause of Confederation — a possibility which can neither be proved nor disproved — it must be regarded as a contributory cause of the achievement of the union of British North America. However, this should not obscure the reality — which is further discussed in Chapter Seven — that the interconnection lay in the accident of chronology rather than in strict logic. In the event, it is hard to see how in 1865 either issue actually helped the other. As the *Saturday Review* concluded in June 1865, 'the defences wait for the Confederation, and the Confederation waits for New Brunswick'.[175]

  The reasons why the British supported the union of the provinces in the three decades from 1837 to 1867 were characterised by the same imprecision as marked basic British perceptions of British North America and of the concept of federation. There was no firm agreement as to the scope and powers of a central government in British North America, no more than vague consideration of the role to be played by regions and communities, most strikingly the French Canadians, and no clear constitutional target for the eventual relationship between Britain and the colonial state. By contrast, one point stands out in cold and stark clarity: the British did not wish their provinces to form part of the American republic. Well before the outbreak of the Civil War, the British had concluded that the union of the provinces was the best way to prevent their piecemeal annexation to the United States, by creating a common front which would call upon imperial protection to resist both the provocations and the temptations to annexation. Additional arguments were thrown in, but the core motive was resistance to the growth of the United States.

British support for British North American union from 1864 onwards was not something derived from the immediate challenge of defending British North America, not least because the province of Canada was the obvious foundation stone for such a union, and the British were by no means impressed by Canadian zeal for self-defence. During the angry parliamentary debates of 1862, no British politician argued for a union of the provinces, although speeches were made by Roebuck, Lord Bury and Sir Edmund Head's close friend, George Cornewall Lewis.[176] In the summer of 1864, as even Creighton recognised, defence and union were treated in Whitehall as parallel but essentially unrelated issues. It was not as a logical answer but rather as a reassuringly familiar idea which had 'floated about so long'[177] that Confederation was able to fill the gap and become a substitute for a practical defence commitment which could no longer be discharged.

***

It is still necessary to explore one further dimension which helps to explain how Confederation came to be seen as a substitute for the practical defence of British North America. To understand this, it is worthwhile to ask not *why* the British favoured Confederation, but rather *when* did they expect it to be brought about. It will come as no surprise that the union of British North America was seen as something which might happen in the future: the future is a vast reservoir for procrastination and a hopeful storehouse for dreams. The persistence of allusion to the future is none the less impressive and demonstrates that even though the British interested themselves in Canadian events only at intervals, a consistent thread of expectation characterised their thinking, and thereby kept the issue on the agenda for the destiny of British North America. Moreover, at least until the early phase of the Civil War, the British saw the union of the provinces as a future which would have to be worked towards in stages, through a timetable in which certainly an intercolonial railway, and probably the subordinate union of the Maritime provinces, would have to precede the final achievement of Confederation. In this, British notions about the future unification of the provinces were less precise than the contemporary American belief in the 'Manifest Destiny' of the United States to dominate the whole continent. Precisely because Manifest Destiny became a political dogma, nothing was ever done to prepare the way to woo the provinces: to have proposed preliminary steps would in itself have cast doubt on the inevitability of their annexation.

Equally significant was the fact that by the 1860s, the British vision of a future union of the provinces was shared by many British North Americans themselves. This in turn made it easier on both sides of the Atlantic to cope with the terrifying continental crisis caused by the realisation in 1864 of the impending victory of the Northern States, with their mass and apparently insatiable war machine. Confederation had long been seen as the eventual destiny of the provinces. The future had now arrived. In practical terms, political union would achieve very little, but psychologically it seemed to be a response on a scale appropriate to the crisis, and thereby entitled Tilley to warn that rejection of the Quebec scheme 'would be a direct invitation to American aggression'.[178] It is worth remembering that, while such statements may catch the eyes of historians and be gratefully embraced as explanations, they did not necessarily convince contemporaries. Tilley delivered his warning at Sackville, but the surrounding Westmorland County returned anti-Confederation members at both the 1865 and 1866 New Brunswick elections.

When Sir Charles Grey sketched a plan for an internal federation of Lower Canada in November 1836, he expressed the hope that Upper Canada would be included 'at no distant period' and 'ultimately' the other provinces too.[179] James Stephen spoke of federation as 'a forecasting policy'; to Roebuck it was an act of 'forethought'.[180] Among the Whig ministers attempting to respond to the crisis of 1837, Glenelg, ever cautious, described British North American federation as 'a subject for deep and future deliberation', but Russell did not rule it out 'at a fit time'.[181] Peel, in opposition, went considerably further, insisting that Canada 'could not be considered separately from the question regarding all the other colonies of North America', which he wished to see united, 'each province having a domestic Government, but all externally pursuing a common interest, and prepared to defend that interest when involved in difficulty and exposed to danger.' In January 1838 he proclaimed his refusal to 'abandon the hope that such a union may some day be formed'.[182] Edward Ellice urged 'that such a foundation might now be urged as would secure at no distant day the attainment of that desirable end', although it has to be said that Ellice was rarely entirely straightforward, and in this case he was using the argument that 'ultimately' the provinces should be united to argue that no steps should be taken immediately.[183] In August 1838, Sir John Harvey argued that Maritime reluctance 'to connect themselves in any way, with the French population of Lower Canada' pointed to an immediate union of the two Canadas alone, 'leaving it upon the other Provinces of British America to join the Confederation, whenever they become sufficiently sensible of its benefits' — an event which, so far as New Brunswick and Nova Scotia were concerned, 'would not ... be remote'.[184] In 1840, Charles Buller predicted that the union of Upper and Lower Canada 'would be followed by the union of all the other provinces'[185] while Lord Ellenborough claimed that 'every one who considered the condition of our North American provinces would soon be brought to doubt whether it might not ultimately be necessary to adopt some such plan'.[186]

Grey adopted a similar attitude during his term at the Colonial Office in the late 1840s, and it continued to characterise British expectations for the next decade. In June 1847, Grey agreed with Elgin that 'the Union of the Provinces ... was not a matter to be pressed forward in a hurry'.[187] However, when shortly afterwards Elgin reported the small size of the Canadian Assembly made governments vulnerable to the possible defection of disgruntled supporters, Grey drew 'the conclusion that some day or other' a legislative union of all the provinces would 'be highly desirable'. While 'this is a distant vision not to be accomplished within anything like the term to which it is either probable or desirable that my official life should extend', he believed that the likelihood that a wider union would have to be attempted 'at some future time' should not be allowed to fall out of sight. Indeed, it was this sentiment which prompted Grey to declare that he proposed to act as if his successors at the Colonial Office would pursue the same aim.[188] Thus responsible government, like the Union of the Canadas, could be seen as stages on the road to British North American union. Yet in the late 1840s, it remained a distant destination. As Grey cautioned Russell in August 1849, the project was 'for the present at least premature'.[189]

The union of the provinces remained a distant objective for most of the 1850s. Newcastle in 1853 commented that a union of the provinces would 'eventually' solve various problems caused by their small populations.[190] In the same year, the *Morning Herald* reminded its readers that it had 'advocated the union as a thing to be brought about, not immediately, but at no very distant day'.[191] When Manners Sutton warned that the ambitions of New Brunswick politicians logically pointed in the direction of a British North American union, Russell, perhaps recalling Grey's caution, merely observed 'a very natural wish, but premature'.[192] Labouchere was understood to have regarded intercolonial union as something which the British should be ready to accept whenever the provinces requested it.[193] Stanley in 1858 thought federation would be their 'ultimate form' of government,[194] but as late as 1861, while Newcastle saw it as 'an object to prepare for and eventually effect', the time had still not arrived.[195]

A vague sentiment about an eventual development cannot in itself be urged as a major element of historical explanation. What distinguished British perceptions of the timing of a union of the provinces was, first, that it came to be accompanied by some notion of a timetable of preliminary steps and, secondly, that the outline timetable collapsed under the psychological pressure of the American crisis of the early 1860s as the preliminary steps were fused into a single package. The first and obvious step was the construction of a railway from Halifax to Quebec. Without such a line, Grey pointed out to Russell in 1849, 'there was an absence of any sufficient common interests to form the ground work of the union, & there also were physical obstacles to their communication with each other which must render it practically very difficult if not impossible for any description of central authority to work'. Thus if the British seriously wished to encourage the provinces to move towards union, 'the first step to be taken would be to set the railway in operation'. Not merely would its completion overcome physical barriers, but the mere exercise in working together to build it would elevate British North American politics above parochial factionalism.[196] Similarly, in 1855, Merivale commented that railways were 'an essential preliminary' to political union.[197] Edward Watkin recalled that by 1861, Newcastle shared his view that the union of British North America would be 'the necessary, the logical result' of the construction of the Intercolonial railway.[198]

While hopes for its construction were raised on several occasions from 1851 onwards, thanks to the lobbying of colonial delegations in London, the Intercolonial line was in some senses the icing on the cake of railway development in British North America. A burst of construction had given the province of Canada a skeletal railway network by 1860, but by the time of Confederation, New Brunswick and Nova Scotia had only three unconnected lines, totalling 279 miles of track: there was still no Maritime rail system to connect with the Intercolonial.[199] Indeed, the difficulties facing small provinces in financing such large projects pointed to the insertion of a further preliminary step in the overall timetable: the union of the Maritime provinces themselves. Arthur Blackwood actually preferred the smaller union to the larger, since 'the Lower Provinces would be mere tributaries',[200] but Sir Edmund Head favoured keeping both options in play, since Maritime Union 'would not in any way prejudice the future consideration of a more extensive union either with Canada or Newfoundland'.[201] As Newcastle put it in 1859, 'so far from being an impediment to any future Union with Canada it would place such a Measure on a more just footing by rendering it more nearly a union of equals instead of appending three weak Provinces to one strong one and *swamping* the divided interests of the former by the united influence of the latter'.[202]

Newcastle's assumption that Canada would enter a wider union 'united', seems strange given his awareness of the increasing sectional problems of the province. Head, for instance, assumed that British North American union would be accompanied by a re-division of Canada into two. The tenor of references to Maritime Union suggests a vague assumption that the combined population and general weight of the lower provinces would be roughly equal to each of the two Canadian sections. This in turn would help to explain the ambiguous Maritime response to the actual proposal of Confederation in 1864-6. The rapid and continuing growth of Upper Canada shattered any notion of British North American union as a balanced tripod, and faced the Maritimers with the choice between maintaining an isolation which probably could not be sustained indefinitely and entering a union in which they would indeed risk becoming 'mere tributaries'.

Newcastle's own tour of North America in 1860 confirmed him in his belief that although British North American union was 'the object to be aimed at other minor measures must precede it'. Nova Scotia and New Brunswick were 'poor & petty Dependencies' which could not hope to prosper 'struggling on alone', but Maritimers 'will not accede to the wishes of Canada for a federal union because they justly fear that their individual interests would be swamped by the powerful combination of the two Canadas'. There were however reasons to hope that they might be induced to overcome 'local jealousies' and form a Maritime Union 'if there were not the great physical obstacles of want of intercommunication'. Thus a major argument for the Intercolonial was that it would provide the means of 'interlacing them from North to South and preparing them when thus combined into one Province for that more important union with Canada which as a British object ought in my opinion to be always kept in view'.[203]

At the start of 1862, Newcastle was firm in his belief that preliminary steps would be necessary to encourage an eventual union of the provinces. He was evidently less clear about the order in which they should take place. In arguing for cabinet approval of an imperial loan guarantee to finance the Intercolonial, he placed the railway before the union of the Maritime provinces, while implicitly recognising that the railway itself would only make sense if it extended into Canada. Equally, if railways could be argued as the necessary precondition of political union, the equation might also be inverted. Giving evidence to a parliamentary committee on colonial defence a few months earlier, in May 1861, Newcastle had seemed taken aback when asked whether 'a federal union of the North American Provinces would tend to facilitate the arrangements for the more efficient and economical defence of those provinces'. He protested that he was 'rather disinclined' to give any answer which might imply 'the advocacy of a federal union', but added after some further fencing 'that of course any plan which threw the Government of all these countries into a united power would facilitate arrangements for the construction of railways'.[204]

Newcastle's fluid interpretation of the triangular relationship of railway, Maritime Union and Confederation became sharply refined as events unfolded to the south. Even the prospect of civil war in the United States was enough to raise the possibility that the future might be arriving faster than he had expected. His comments in 1861-2 reveal an awareness of the significance of the instability caused by the Civil War, and the implications of the changing balance of power in North America, in bringing Confederation closer.[205] It was in that frame of mind that in June 1862 he responded to Lord Mulgrave's despatch from Nova Scotia reporting Joseph Howe's resolution asking for clarification of imperial policy towards the union of the provinces. 'I have always been of opinion that the necessary preliminary to a Legislative Union if the Lower Provinces is an Intercolonial Railway, and that the completion of *both* these schemes must precede a Union with Canada,' he wrote. Events, however, were moving faster, and the triangle of priorities could no longer be sorted into the neat steps of a long-range timetable. British North American union 'may be hastened by the present condition of the neighbouring Country but I do not expect success to any project which attempts it without first *settling* (if not *accomplishing*) both the smaller Union and the Railway'.[206] The future was already happening. All three steps might be taken in parallel, and tied together in a package. In the event, Confederation and the Intercolonial became too politically intertwined to be disentangled, while Maritime Union was simply by-passed.

A decade earlier, Francis Hincks had believed that there had been more support for a union of the provinces in Britain than in British North America. Gradually, the idea of eventual intercolonial union became implanted on the western side of the Atlantic as well, and the American Civil War was associated with the same foreshortening of the future. When Alexander Morris delivered the first of his landmark 'Nova Britannia' lectures in Montreal in March 1858, he admitted that his vision of a transcontinental union might seem 'the fanciful dream of an enthusiast', although he sounded more confident of the 'probability' of a closer link with the Maritimes.[207] The Canadian ministry's throne speech in August spoke equally cautiously of negotiations to determine 'the principles on which a bond of a federal character, uniting the Provinces of British North America, may perhaps hereafter be practicable'.[208] Although the Canadian initiative of 1858 did not bring that hereafter much closer, by the time Morris delivered a second public lecture on his cherished theme the following winter, he felt able to speak of 'a brilliant future in the distance', and even to predict that if politicians on both sides of the ocean performed their patriotic duty, 'then this dream will be realized, and that perhaps ere the men of this generation have all passed from this fleeting scene'.[209]

In defining British North American union in 1851 as a priority for the future, Head felt that it did not matter 'whether that future be arrived at gradually or suddenly'.[210] In fact, the division in Maritime opinion in and after 1864 represented not so much a split over ultimate aims as a disagreement over whether the future had arrived — and arrived on terms which Maritimers could accept. John Hamilton Gray of Prince Edward Island had dreamed since his earliest years that he would 'be one day a citizen of a great nation extending from the great west to the Atlantic seaboard'[211] and he supported Confederation when the opportunity presented itself. William Annand, on the other hand, recalled that when colonial delegates met for the earlier Quebec conference, to discuss the Intercolonial railway project in September 1862, Confederation had been regarded 'as a matter in the distance'.[212] Newcastle's despatch of 6 July 1862 in response to the Nova Scotian request for clarification of the British government's attitude to intercolonial union had given a broad hint that the provinces themselves might take a lead in discussing the subject, but Annand for one had been content to keep it at arm's length. Joseph Howe was also ambivalent, reporting that the delegates to Quebec in 1862 had preferred to postpone British North American union to 'a more convenient season', which would follow the completion of the Intercolonial.[213] In August 1864, he had claimed to be 'pleased to think the day is rapidly approaching when the Provinces will be united'.[214] Within five months, he had concluded that the day had arrived much too rapidly, that the season was still inconvenient.

Thus the future did not seem to everyone to be approaching at the same speed. While most were aware of the danger to the provinces inherent in the American Civil War, some were reassured that fighting one another gave the Americans enough to do for the time being. 'As long as the Americans fight together, they will leave England alone,' was the hopeful conclusion of Lord Monck's niece — just two weeks before Lee surrendered at Apomattox.[215] As late as January 1865 the *Montreal Gazette* could assure its readers that 'the real subjugation and conquest of the South seem to be almost as distant as ever',[216] while the Halifax journalist P.S. Hamilton a few months earlier had dismissed the United States as 'irrevocably dissolved'.[217] The collapse of the Confederacy came suddenly to those who had clung to the hope that the South would win. Indeed, had it not been for the Fenians, the future might have retreated after April 1865 just as rapidly as it had approached in the year or so beforehand. The risk of formal war between the British empire and the United States was greatly reduced by 1867, but by then the Confederation process had acquired its own momentum.

For Maritimers, the future advanced and retreated in irregular spasms in the early 1860s. In January 1861, the Saint John *Morning News* had revealed a leisurely view of the future unaffected by the developing crisis to the south. Railways were the necessary precondition to bring the Maritimes into real contact with Canada. 'In a dozen years ... it will be time enough to begin to think of federation.'[218] The apparent collapse of the Intercolonial project in 1862 seemed to set the prospect back still further, and certainly did nothing to increase the trust Maritimers might feel in the distant Canadians. In October 1863 the Halifax *Morning Chronicle* could conclude that 'the union of the British North American Colonies, as a group, is no longer a project which men of the present generation can hope to see accomplished'.[219] While in 1861 the Saint John *Morning News* was suspicious of British North American union as 'one of the Tory whims of the day',[220] the Halifax *Witness* three years later could insist that for twenty years past, all Nova Scotian politicians 'be they Tories or Liberals, have seen that a union of some kind is inevitable'.[221] Even T.W. Anglin, an inflexible opponent of Confederation, admitted that he knew of nobody who was 'opposed to union in the abstract'.[222] In 1864, Maritimers had to decide whether the terms of union were right. For many of them, it was not necessary to consider, as if it were a new idea, whether their future lay in a British North American union. It was only necessary to decide whether that future had arrived. The Saint John *Evening Globe* was taken aback by the suddenness with which the revolution in Canadian politics opened up the prospect of general union in the summer of 1864, but it reflected that 'we have all at different times had our dreams of a future when the British possessions in America should become one great nation. For the first time we are being brought face to face with the reality'.[223]

These are not sentiments which can be explained by interpreting Confederation as an unprecedented response which had suddenly emerged from a conjunction of an internal political and an external defence crisis. The sense of crisis explained not the idea of Confederation as the future destiny of the provinces, but the reality that this long-sensed future had actually arrived. At the Halifax banquet in September 1864, George Brown reminded the audience that 'at no time has any Provincial Statesman ever expressed a doubt that the fitting future of these Colonies was to be united under one Government', but he also made it clear that the Canadians could and soon would solve their own internal problems and thereby close the door on the wider scheme. Hence Macdonald's laconic appeal to the sentiment of inevitability. 'Everybody admits that Union must take place sometime. I say now is the time.'[224]

On both sides of the Atlantic, then, British North American union was seen by the 1860s as the ultimate destiny of the provinces. The sentiment that the future had arrived was one which Macdonald both manipulated and fostered, for it represented his only chance of outflanking George Brown in the internal policy rivalry of the Canadian coalition. The arrival of destiny in the form of the Confederation of four provinces in 1867 opened up yet further prospects in a continuing confrontation with an approaching future. W.H. Russell wrote in 1865 of the province of Canada holding 'a heritage of priceless value ... in trust for the great nation that must yet sit enthroned on the Lakes and the St Lawrence, and rule from Labrador to Columbia'.[225] Introducing the British North America bill into the House of Lords, Carnarvon predicted that 'before long' Newfoundland and Prince Edward Island would 'gravitate' towards the union, that the time was 'not far distant when the broad and fertile districts to the west of Canada ... will form part of the Confederation' and even that the day was 'perhaps ... not very far distant' when British Columbia would be incorporated as well.[226] 'There is always something better to be done, something greater to be attained,' as the ever-optimistic

Cartier put it.[227] This is a dimension of the Confederation issue which may illuminate the division of opinion in Nova Scotia, which Jonathan McCully defined as between opponents, who had 'money made', and supporters, who hoped to be 'money making'. In recent decades, several historians have attempted to modify the view of a solid Nova Scotian resistance to the new structure, pointing instead to commercial interests in Halifax and the eastern half of the province which saw potential gains in closer links with the interior of the continent.[228] In the crisis of the mid-sixties, Confederation could be presented both as a desirable end and as an attractive beginning.

The telescoping of time, which enabled Macdonald to equate 'sometime' with 'now', carried with it a telescoping of motive. The first year of the Civil War was enough to persuade Newcastle that the steps which he had previously seen as leading to the union of British North America would have to be incorporated with it. The way in which the package became the political destiny and the practical answer to the continental challenges facing the provinces may also be seen in the evolving attitudes of Lord Mulgrave, who as governor of Nova Scotia in 1858 had reported his province's bleak response to the Canadian federal initiative. Mulgrave argued that a federal system would produce confusion and friction, while legislative union would founder on local jealousies. None the less, he concluded by expressing his own belief 'that ultimately, the British North American Provinces will become one great, and, independent Country, but, I do not think that the time has arrived when they could stand alone, and I should regret to see any step taken which would hasten that event'.[229] In 1863, Mulgrave inherited the title of Marquess of Normanby, and returned home to take up his place in the hierarchy of British public life. He was an obvious target for Joseph Howe to recruit for his campaign against the Quebec scheme. Howe was to be disappointed. Normanby agreed that 'formerly I was always opposed to a union of a Federal character'. If circumstances had 'remained as they were' and the 'internal advancement' of Nova Scotia continued to be his prime object, his opposition would have been unchanged. 'The state of things has however sadly changed during the last two or three years.' The United States was no longer 'a purely Commercial Country' but had 'become a Military a warlike & very aggressive power', so openly hostile to Britain that it was necessary to consider how the provinces could be defended 'in the event of an aggressive movement on the part of the United States' at the conclusion of the Civil War. In Normanby's opinion, Britain could no longer defend the provinces unaided, and had to ask for sacrifices if the imperial link was to be maintained. Half-trained militia forces were no longer enough in the face of the massive numbers of trained troops which the Americans could throw across the border. Nor could Nova Scotia remain aloof, since if Canada were conquered, the other provinces would quickly fall as well. 'I believe the only safety for the Whole is *Union*, the *Intercolonial railroad* & the erection of certain strong fortifications together with a thorough organization of the local forces & then with the assistance which I am sure England would under those circumstances willingly render I believe you might rest in peace & bid defiance to the Yankees.'[230]

The apparent complexity of British motives and expectations may be reduced to a brief summary. In the quarter century before the outbreak of the Civil War, the British thought of the union of British North America as an eventual development which would create a political barrier against the expansionist tendencies of an essentially non-military United States. In the political crisis of the 1860s, they transmuted Confederation from an eventual to an immediate response, from a political device to block annexation to an essential step towards — if not an outright substitute for — improved military defence. In this, their views came to be either shared or parroted by influential political leaders in the provinces themselves, who saw 1864 as the appropriate moment to launch the bid for Confederation. It remains only to examine what role the British actually played in carrying it into effect.

6 The Role of the British in the Launching of Confederation

In seeking to assess the role played by the British in the achievement of Canadian Confederation, it is natural to look to the years of action between 1864 and 1867. Yet it may be that the two most important British contributions had been made well before the delegates gathered at Charlottetown. The British had succeeded, first, in setting the agenda by defining the aim of intercolonial union. Secondly, and arguably even more crucially important, they had found a formula which preserved imperial control over the process of constitutional change while conceding effective autonomy of action to the politicians of British North America.

The British had in effect set the agenda. The legislative compliance of Westminster was required for any form of constitutional change in British North America, thereby virtually compelling the provinces to accommodate their own aims to the imperial target. As Cardwell firmly wrote in discouraging a diversionary move in favour of Maritime Union in 1865, 'I cannot undertake to ask the Imperial Parliament for its sanction of any scheme which does not unite all British North America in one government'.[1] However, while the factor of ultimate British legislative control was crucial in shaping colonial targets in the later stages of the move towards constitutional change, it was potentially also one which could block any local initiation of the issue.

If the scattered provinces of British North America were ever to unite, somebody would have to take a lead in bringing them together. Few who dreamed of a united British North America even tackled the question: with so attractive a vision, it was easier to dwell on the glorious end rather than the technical means, and many projectors simply assumed that their arguments were so overwhelming that parliament would rush to legislate their scheme into reality. Roebuck, for instance, even attempted to tack on an amendment to the Australian Colonies Bill of 1850 incidentally federating British North America.[2] Yet as early as 1822, an attempt by the British government to unite Upper and Lower Canada had foundered partly because of protests from the colonies[3] while, as Francis Hincks later cautioned, parliament had been reluctant to impose Union in 1840 without the appearance of consent from the Canadas.[4] By 1849, a British consensus in favour of an eventual union of British North America had set the aim of Confederation. By the early 1860s, a carefully worded series of despatches from the Colonial Office had cleared the issue of means: although legally British dependencies, the provinces might take the lead in negotiating terms of union.[5] If the British role in setting the target was their greatest contribution to the achievement of Confederation, their success in conjuring away the procedural difficulty of its attainment ranks a close second. The mere fact that the problem would subsequently almost disappear from the historical record is a testimony to the extent of their success.

***

In 1824, William Lyon Mackenzie called for a British act of parliament to establish 'a convention of all the colonies', to be presided over by 'a British nobleman or gentleman of competent knowledge'. Delegates would be elected from each province, with apportionment by population, to prepare 'the outlines' of a constitution, which would 'be sent home for the consideration of the Imperial Parliament'.[6] (Forty years later, at Charlottetown and Quebec, there would be no proconsul in the chair, but neither would there be popularly elected delegates nor representation according to population.) By one of history's ironies, it was the outbreak of rebellions in which Mackenzie was a leading participant which brought to Canada a British nobleman prepared to travel the convention route to federation. The ministerial champion of British North American union, Howick, wished to give 'actual legislative power' to an intercolonial convention, although any structure it might create would not go into effect until it had been laid before both houses of parliament, thus reserving to Westminster 'the complete power of interposing to prevent the adoption of any measures which it might disapprove'.[7]

In fact, parliament deleted the reference to a formal intercolonial convention from the preamble to the instructions shaping Lord Durham's mission to Canada in 1838, although he retained sufficient leeway to attempt the device by summoning an advisory meeting that autumn. On the day that Durham reported the arrival of two delegations from the Maritimes to discuss a British North American solution to the problems of colonial government, he heard that his ordinance banishing rebel leaders to Bermuda had been attacked in parliament. Within a week, he learnt that it had been overruled, and on 22 September, replying to an address of support from the Maritimers, he announced his intention to resign.[8] Charles Buller probably exaggerated the extent to which the idea of a federal union had been welcomed by the Maritimers, but there was no doubting that Durham's fall killed the project.

There was, however, another practical argument against the approach which Mackenzie had proposed and Durham had unconsciously followed. The drama surrounding the end of the Durham mission obscured a more fundamental problem implicit in the open launching of negotiations for a union of the provinces by a British viceroy. It would be difficult to present any such intercolonial meeting as merely exploratory: by the very fact of summoning delegates from the other provinces, especially given the problems of travel, the British government would be implicitly endorsing the importance of British North American union. As Manners Sutton commented in 1858, 'the fact that the appointment of the Commission was authorized by the Secretary of State would give to the report of the Commissioners ... additional weight and authority'. On the other hand, a fruitless outcome might not only set back the cause of British North American union, but damage the standing of the British to support or indeed to shape any subsequent movement.[9] Within a decade, there would be the further complication that the increased measure of self-government in the mainland colonies would make any formal British move seem dangerously like interference in local affairs. Hence the significance of the British official comments — especially from 1859 onwards — on the unripeness of time: they wished to see Confederation brought about, but feared that too overt a British initiative would be counterproductive.

Although it had been Howick who had pressed Durham to call an intercolonial convention, he and James Stephen were converted by the controversy over Durham's instructions to a strategy of federation by stealth. They recognised that representative institutions in the colonies had a tendency to extend their spheres of operation — or, in plain English, to meddle — and they proposed to harness this form of legislative original sin to the evolutionary development of a British North American government which could eventually replace Britain as the central authority for the provinces. This approach had already characterised Stephen's plan of December 1836, which ostensibly aimed at meeting the major Upper Canadian grievance — that customs duties on goods imported into the landlocked province were collected at Lower Canadian ports — by establishing an intercolonial authority which would gradually achieve the 'Euthanasia' of the colonial connection.

In 1836, Stephen had proposed an eleven-member commission to oversee the common interests of the two Canadas, but as a response to the rebellions, the plan was re-cast to include the Maritime provinces as well. Stephen's primary intention was to shift both moral and practical responsibility for the Canadian crisis from Britain to a convention drawn from five provinces, subject to a British veto on fundamental changes in Lower Canada. The convention would also have power 'to regulate those matters in which the provinces are jointly concerned', forming a 'resting place or middle point' between colonial dependence and total separation. The time was 'rapidly approaching' when British North America, already 'a considerable nation', would inevitably 'assume a character very remote from that which it has hitherto borne'. Had such a policy been adopted in an earlier generation, 'the American revolution would never have occurred'.

For cabinet consumption, Howick and Stephen played down this aspect of their ideas. Stephen attempted to dismiss the possibility of a change in the colonial relationship with Britain as 'exceedingly problematical' and 'uncertain and remote'.[10] Howick made it clear that he thought a federal union would be a positive development, but insisted that 'I do not propose at once to effect such a union, but to provide the means of accomplishing it if the inhabitants of British North America desire it'.[11] Their subtlety was ineffective, and the cabinet swung to a union of Upper and Lower Canada, the only structure which could combine an immediate political settlement with some hope of dominating the French.

Unlike most enthusiasts for British North American union, Howick had at least considered not just the end but the means required to achieve it. There were in fact two strands in his proposed strategy: one which looked to the governor-general of the Canadas to fill the intercolonial vacuum and bring the provinces together to discuss common institutions, and the other which assumed that any joint machinery would gradually grow into a central government for the provinces. When he returned to office in 1846, as Earl Grey, he was quick to revive both approaches — and almost as rapidly found neither of them to be productive. One of Grey's first tasks was to select a new governor-general for Canada, to replace Lord Cathcart, a general who had been appointed as a stopgap during the Oregon crisis. Grey was determined that unlike previous imperial representatives in Canada, Elgin should exercise a measure of control over the other provinces.[12] He was also anxious to protect himself against the charge so often thrown at the Whigs, of using government appointments as a source of patronage for their own connections. Instead, he chose for Canada a Scottish peer who had demonstrated 'great ability and success' as governor of Jamaica. Lord Elgin was 'personally altogether unknown to me'. In a brief career in the Commons before inheriting his title, he had made his mark in a speech which had helped bring about the downfall of Lord Melbourne's ministry — 'certainly not one to give him any claims upon us a party', as Grey ruefully commented.[13] As it happened, Elgin undermined the public relations aspect of his appointment by promptly meeting and marrying one of Grey's many nieces, while the colonial secretary found himself dealing with a strong-minded governor-general, whose outstanding success in making responsible government work enabled him virtually to ignore Grey's wider agenda for intercolonial union.

Although it had been a decade earlier, and under very different circumstances, that Stephen and Grey had embraced their gradualist strategy for moving towards a union of British North America, they seem to have independently taken up the idea once again in 1846. When the question of devolving postal services to local control had been raised in September 1846, Stephen had promptly raised the wider issue of intercolonial collaboration, arguing that a British North American postal service implied the creation of 'a Central Authority ... which, when so convened and constituted would rapidly convert its power to other purposes'. As a cautious civil servant, Stephen was reluctant to pursue the implications himself, although he described his prediction as 'a consummation to which my own mind would be very easily reconciled'. Grey then discussed his ideas with his permanent under-secretary[14] — one of the many exchanges which do not survive, even in the rich archives of the mid-Victorian period — and late in December 1846, he drafted a despatch urging the provinces to delegate control over customs duties, postal services and the construction of railways to a central body to be based in Montreal. The model which he had in mind was that of the German Zollverein, a loose commercial union which embraced entirely sovereign states.[15]

In April 1847, as the Canadian parliament was about to meet, Grey attempted to prod Elgin into action. 'I hope one of the first things you will be able to do, will be to bring under their consideration in some shape or other the Union question.' Canadian newspapers had picked up a rumour that intercolonial union might be on the political agenda, and press reaction appeared to be favourable. 'If you find such to be the general disposition of men's minds, it seems to me that it might probably be as good a course as you could adopt, to lay my despatch on this subject before the Legislature,' arranging also for its simultaneous publication in New Brunswick and Nova Scotia.[16] Grey's tentative language suggests that he was feeling his way to some means of jolting the subject into life, but Elgin was trenchant in pointing to practical difficulties. Canadian politics revolved around 'half a dozen parties ... all intent on making political capital out of whatever turns up. It is exceedingly difficult under such circumstances to induce public men to run the risk of adopting any scheme that is bold or novel'.[17] Grey saw his 'Zollverein' scheme as a subtle first step towards enabling the separate colonies to evolve towards the creation of a central government. Elgin, at the front line of Canadian politics, saw no way of persuading 'the free & independant legislatures of British North America ... to grant to delegates even of their own naming such powers as the well drilled bureau ridden councils and diets of Germany confer on their Representatives in the Zollverein'.[18] He might have added that the Germans did trade at least with one another, while Canadians and Maritimers by and large did not. Certainly Grey implicitly accepted that the consent of the colonial legislatures would be required to create any central structure. He still firmly believed 'that *some* bond of union or other ought to be established amongst the different Provinces of North America ... supposing it to be practicable' but 'all that can be done is to throw out the general idea & to endeavour by degrees to lead mens minds in that direction'.[19]

It might have assisted debate on the destiny of British North America had there been a definite agreement that by the late 1840s, the colonies had either the first or the final say over any move towards union. By the end of the decade, responsible government was firmly established in Canada, Nova Scotia and New Brunswick. The rejection in 1849 by both houses of parliament of demands for intervention in the Canadian Rebellion Losses controversy confirmed that it was unlikely that the British would interfere in the purely internal affairs of the provinces, but this in itself did not define the respective colonial and imperial spheres, nor the boundaries between them. Durham in 1839 had proposed a formal division, arguing that there were 'very few' areas over which the British required control.[20] Molesworth in 1850 argued that it was 'necessary carefully to enumerate and accurately to define the powers which ought to be held to be imperial powers'.[21] Ministers, on the other hand, believed that 'the distinction between Local and Imperial legislation ... cannot be drawn'[22] and resisted formal definition. In practice, in place of a formal division of spheres, a spectrum of issues tentatively emerged. At one end, it was unthinkable that the British would intervene in the construction of roads in New Brunswick or the appointment of government clerks in Upper Canada. At the other, nobody expected the colonies to declare war on foreign powers. Between these two extremes, it suited most politicians to avoid precision. Asked at the 1861 parliamentary enquiry on colonial defence if he knew 'anything analogous in the history of the world to our relation with our Colonies', Gladstone sardonically replied that it was 'a novel invention, of which up to the present time we are the patentees, and no one has shown a disposition to invade our patent'.[23]

For most purposes, it made sense to let sleeping problems lie, but in relation to the launching of any move towards British North American union, the ambiguity was a complication. Durham had assumed that the 'constitution of the form of government' was one of the four areas which automatically fell within the imperial sphere[24] and there was no obvious alternative to Westminster as a means of validating any intercolonial structure. Thus the *completion* of any union of British North America almost certainly fell within the British sphere. On the other hand, a *proposal* even to consider the establishment of such a union would come dangerously close to intervention in the internal affairs of a self-governing province — especially in the light of Elgin's warning of the endemic factionalism, 'all intent on making political capital out of whatever turns up'. For most purposes, the reluctance to define boundaries between the imperial and colonial spheres made responsible government work more smoothly by avoiding jurisdictional clashes. British North American union, unfortunately, fell at both ends of the spectrum, since it involved both local autonomy and imperial supremacy. Different commentators emphasised these opposed poles. The *Examiner* in 1849 supported the federation as a means of 'the preservation of the colonies from annexation or independence' but suspected that the 'main obstacle to the success of such a scheme ... will probably arise from the hesitating, reluctant and imperfect manner in which we ourselves are likely to carry it out.'[25] Four years later, recalling the failure of Grey's attempt to fasten an outline federal structure on the Australian colonies, the *Spectator* denied that British North American union 'could properly originate with England; if the Colonies wish it, England can sanction and aid its accomplishment', but 'an official edict' would probably be received in British North America with the same lack of enthusiasm which had greeted the attempt to impose a federal system on the Australian colonies in 1850.[26] In the short term, responsible government complicated the problem. How could self-governing colonies originate a move towards creating common institutions, when they had no common institutions through which to express any such wish? How could an imperial desire to encourage the unification of self-governing provinces be made into reality without interfering in their internal affairs?

Russell had cautioned Grey against acting on the assumption that one and a half million Canadians would think and act as one individual.[27] Elgin had predicted that any proposal to unite the colonies would be caught in the crossfire of local factions. The convention of the British American League at Kingston in 1849 bore out their warnings, and demonstrated that responsible government had not made the problem of initiating a federation movement any easier. The convention proved to be almost the only example of an unofficial gathering which resolved in favour of a union of the provinces. Despite its imposing title, the League was merely a tory front, and moreover composed entirely of delegates from within the province of Canada.[28] Confessing itself 'uncertain as to the sentiments of the sister colonies' regarding a union of the provinces, the Convention called for an intercolonial conference on the subject.[29] Nova Scotia's governor, Sir John Harvey, seems to have jumped to the conclusion that an intercolonial meeting planned for Halifax in September 1849 to discuss harmonisation of tariffs could become the occasion for 'a full & free discussion of the great question of "Federal Union"',[30] but Joseph Howe reflected the deeper British American distaste for revolutionary forms in an open letter to the League's President. 'A confederation of the colonies may be the desire of your convention. If so, the object is legitimate, but it must be pursued by legitimate means.'[31]

It was a fine and proper sentiment — but what were the legitimate means for the pursuit of a union of the provinces? By the 1850s, many were attracted by the vision of a united British North America, but few attempted to consider how it might be made a reality. The attempts which were made by the governor of New Brunswick, Sir Edmund Head, and by two Nova Scotians, Alexander Stewart and Pierce S. Hamilton, between 1851 and 1855 served mainly to highlight the ambiguity of provinces supposedly self-governing but still subject to an undefined imperial suzerainty. The intellectual Head was genuinely interested in solving a problem in political theory. The two Nova Scotians were probably more interested in harnessing the imperial factor in support of a favoured project.

'How would such a measure be laid before the Colonial Governments with any chance of their concurrence?' The final section of Head's 1851 memorandum on British North American federation was not an afterthought, but a 'most important question'. His suggestion was that 'some four or five propositions enunciating the principal features of such a scheme' should be submitted to the colonial legislatures, asking for their outline agreement. If the proposal survived that first hurdle, each colony would then appoint four delegates, two from each house of the legislature, to confer with each other and then with a royal commission — presumably composed of British notables — to draft legislation to be considered at Westminster. In fact, Head's propositions — which within a paragraph had grown to six — would have both constrained the provincial negotiators and sharply limited the freedom of the British parliament. Britain would continue to control defence along with foreign affairs, including commercial relations, while the federal system would be relatively loose, with unenumerated powers remaining with the individual provinces, and all legislation subject to veto by a constitutional court. In 1851, Head had little real knowledge of Canada, and evidently failed to grasp that the largest province was unlikely to accept a minority role in the negotiations. Equally, he envisaged an unrealistically restricted role in the process for colonial politicians, who would be presented with a range of options already narrowed by Head's prescription of loose federalism, and apparently denied any opportunity to ratify the work of the royal commission, let alone submit it to the voters. On the other hand, Head did suggest an amending formula, something which was overlooked in 1867. His constitution might be changed on address from a majority of the provinces, subject to the same process of a delegate meeting conferring with a royal commission, but no amendment would be considered within the first ten years of operation. Head diffidently described his views as 'crude & undigested', perhaps even 'impracticable & visionary'. Apparently it did not occur to him that the refusal by a single province to endorse his outline propositions might set British North American union back indefinitely. Nor did he foresee the danger, which alarmed Manners Sutton in 1858, that any kind of intercolonial commission would transfer effective control of the destiny of British North America from the imperial government to the pace-setting Canadians.[32]

Alexander Stewart displayed a more tough-minded intention to manipulate the imperial factor into overcoming provincial inertia. He had shifted from politics to the bench in 1846, and in 1855 had become a Companion of the Bath, one of the first colonials to be recognised in the British honours system. He was described in a Colonial Office minute in 1855 as 'an able & distinguished man', but one who possessed 'much more of the forwardness, & pushing qualities of the Yankees, than of the "Blue Noses"'. If given encouragement, 'he will not be very easily shaken off'.[33] This verdict may have stemmed from his attempt the previous year to bounce Newcastle into endorsing British North American union. Stewart favoured a union of the provinces, but was convinced that 'nothing but urgent necessity will cause it to originate with the Colonists themselves'. Therefore Britain had a duty 'gently to lead' the provinces 'into a path beneficial to themselves and to the Empire at large'. He counselled the circulation of a confidential despatch to the governors of the various provinces, noting 'that from time to time discussions had arisen in some of the Legislatures and in the Press of the Colonies respecting their being united into one Government'. This would entitle the British government to call for confidential reports from each provincial ministry on the implications of the issue, while at the same time protesting that 'it was by no means their intention to take the initiative in regard to such a union'. Ostensibly to stress the entirely neutral character of the initiative, Stewart proposed that the circular despatch should disclaim all intention either of cutting expenditure or of guaranteeing loans for railway construction. Despite this disclaimer — presumably intended to scotch the association between federation and imperial cost-cutting which had aroused the suspicions of Francis Hincks — Stewart's proposal was disingenuous. By its very nature, a British request for confidential discussion of the implications of a union of the provinces was tantamount to a proposal for its introduction. Moreover, Stewart was well aware that confidentiality was not a hallmark of colonial politics. Indeed, he accepted that it was 'not improbable' that the news would get out, in which case 'the Members of the respective Governments should be permitted to make public the fact, that the Secretary of State had expressed an anxious wish to assent to any measure desired by the Colonists which had a tendency to elevate them socially and politically'.[34]

A few months earlier, Newcastle had hoped that Elgin would take action to encourage a union of the provinces. It seems that he had invited Stewart to put his views in writing. Perhaps he was attracted to the strategy of giving the idea a gentle push under the guise of an uncommitted enquiry: the magnitude of the challenge Britain faced in the east had suddenly been revealed by the Crimean War, and this might justify the British in deftly suggesting a new structure in the west. However, within a fortnight of Stewart's letter, Newcastle left the Colonial Office to become the first secretary of state for War. One of his last acts was to appoint Sir Edmund Head as Elgin's successor, perhaps in the hope that he would lead the minds of Canadian politicians towards a union of British North America.

Stewart's argument was repeated the following year by a fellow Nova Scotian, Pierce Stevens Hamilton, a Halifax editor and an enthusiast not simply for the union of British North America, but for an imperial federation as well. His letter of August 1855 to Sir William Molesworth, one of the fleeting ministers who passed in quick succession through the Colonial Office that year, barely bothered to argue the case for union, but concentrated on a shrewd analysis of the problems inherent in establishing it. The union of the provinces was 'felt to be of great importance by the public men, and indeed by all the better informed classes of British North America', especially in the Maritimes. Ingeniously, Hamilton explained the absence of any move in the provinces towards union by a general belief that 'the initiative should be taken by Great Britain', the more so as it was 'believed that particularly many members of the Cabinet ... are favourable to this union'. In any case, Hamilton pointed out, it would be pointless for the provinces to take the lead without an assurance of British approval, and the separation of the provinces militated against discussion of the issue at colonial level: this was in itself one of the problems which drew attention to the need for central institutions. Furthermore, if one province took a lead, others might react with suspicion. Hamilton was sure that the provinces would eventually take action, unless Britain banned all discussion of the question, but the danger in relying on such inevitability was that the provinces 'may procrastinate such efforts to a period when the consummation of the union would be really more difficult and the possibilities of its successful operation much less, than at the present time'. Everything pointed to a British initiative, timely, disinterested and effective. Nova Scotians 'looked forward as a matter of course' to a union of the provinces, but it was 'considered equally a matter of course that the union must and will take place upon the motion and under the guidance of the Imperial Government'.

Hamilton's plan resembled that of Sir Edmund Head. A scheme of union — not federation — would be sketched in outline in a circular despatch to Canada, New Brunswick, Nova Scotia and Prince Edward Island. Within that framework, the colonies would be left to work out the details, a process which 'could not be of a very onerous, or necessarily protracted character', since any scheme of government for British North America would certainly resemble the existing colonial constitutions. It was not difficult to perceive at least some contradiction, and probably conflict, between Hamilton's breezy confidence in a united response to a British initiative, and his equally firm insistence on provincial involvement. While deferring to British views, the colonies 'would nevertheless expect to be treated as contracting parties'. Not only would each legislature appoint commissioners to negotiate a detailed constitution, but their work would be subject to provincial ratification — a step which had not occurred to Head. Indeed, Hamilton's reference to ratification as 'the last act in effecting a political union of the Provinces' suggests that he did not contemplate any role for the imperial factor once it had initiated the process.[35]

Eighteen months earlier, the suspicious Francis Hincks had grudgingly admitted that 'a federal union might possibly be carried if British influence were thrown into the scale in its favour', although even then he consoled himself with the conviction that 'no scheme could be devised now which would be approved of in the three Provinces'.[36] Hamilton, on the other hand, seemed sure that a British initiative would command unqualified respect and instantaneous compliance. In the patriotic atmosphere of the Crimean War, all obstacles would vanish at once. This could be dismissed as the over-optimism of an enthusiast, but he was shrewd enough in his assessment of the problems of approaching union without British endorsement.

If the *Provinces* take the initiative, and agreeing upon a constitution, afterwards obtain the approval of the Imperial Government, the attainment of the object sought must naturally be very remote; because innumerable propositions and counter-propositions, misunderstandings, and delays, on the part of each and all of those Provinces, must necessarily retard the final arrangement, however desirous all the negotiating parties may be of agreeing.[37]

It is hardly necessary to state that Hamilton hoped to trap the British government into endorsing his own plan for the future of the provinces. Equally, it cannot be doubted that he overestimated the likelihood of a unanimous welcome by the provinces for any British proposal that they should unite, and he certainly underestimated the problems of detail to be solved in the design of a constitution. Yet in other respects, his warnings would be proved correct a decade later. The launching of Confederation in 1864 did come at a time when the continental crisis which, it was argued, made it necessary also complicated its achievement, and attempts to amend or block the project did indeed cause dangerous delays. In short, there was still no answer to the problem inherent in Hamilton's proposal: how could the British government raise the issue of a union of the provinces without dangerously stimulating local factionalism and fatally invading their local autonomy? The question was avoided by Henry Labouchere, who brought some stability if no great energy to the Colonial Office for two years after the frequent ministerial changes of 1855. According to Merivale, Labouchere did not believe that it was the responsibility of the British to take any steps to unite the provinces, but rather that they should await a colonial initiative. However, even Labouchere was prepared to give the issue a gentle shove. Merivale was sure that, during Sir Edmund Head's visit to England in 1857, Labouchere had 'particularly requested him to take it in hand' — but without backing him with any official and recorded instructions on the subject.[38]

The discouraging British response to the Canadian federal initiative of 1858 has been seen by some historians as providing a comparative dimension which points to the importance of the circumstances of 1864 in determining imperial support for, and Maritime acquiescence in, Confederation.[39] In reality, while neither the colonial secretary, Sir Edward Lytton, nor his senior adviser, T.F. Elliot, were enthusiastic about the prospect, the question at issue in 1858 was not so much the end as the means. Too much can be made of Lytton's immediate reaction that Head should be censured for endorsing the Canadian attempt to begin interprovincial negotiations.[40] Lytton was an inexperienced minister in an insecure cabinet. Moreover, he was over-reacting to an expression of royal disapproval from Prince Albert, and responding in ignorance of very recent correspondence between Head and Lytton's predecessor, Lord Stanley. Within days of threatening to recall Head in disgrace, Lytton had satisfied himself that the Canadian initiative had been neither unexpected nor wholly unauthorised.[41] Unfortunately, it was not until the 1970s that historians gained access to Stanley's private papers, which are the key to revealing how ambiguity over the question of means confused the British response to the end sought by the Cartier-Macdonald ministry. Shortcomings in historical description may be pardoned: the evidence simply was not available.

In his letter to Head in April 1858, Stanley had expressed approval of the idea of British North American union, but had not taken a firm grip on the question of how it might be achieved. Indeed, he described it as a question which had 'often been considered in a speculative point of view', and that his 'observations' should be considered 'subject to revisal and reconsideration at a later period'. He ranged around such practical issues as the allocation of provincial debts, the arguments for and against a re-division of Upper and Lower Canada and the question of a federal or a legislative union, but concluded that 'it is one thing to approve generally of a principle, & another to attempt to work it out in detail'. Thus Stanley was imprecise about the process by which a federation movement might be set in motion, although he seemed firm in his support for the end itself. 'If federal Union be practicable & expedient in the interest of the Colonies, England ought to further it by all means in her power.'[42]

Head could not know that by the time his typically thoughtful response could reach London, Stanley would have moved to the India Office, and that his replacement, Lytton, would be unaware of their exchange. As in 1851, Head closed his speculations on the form of union with some firmer ideas about how to proceed towards it. Howe in 1849 had assumed that proposals from 'the Government and Parliament of Canada ... would be treated with deference and respect' in the other provinces.[43] In the same spirit, Head envisaged that Canada's parliament might 'affirm the principle in its vaguest form' and seek 'the views of the English Government & those of the Sister Colonies'. Assuming 'that the other Colonies recognise the object as desirable & that Her Majesty's advisers interpose no obstacle to its consideration', a meeting of commissioners from each province would be the 'next practical step'. They would draw up the headings of a scheme of union, 'which would then have to be submitted to the Queen's advisers & to the several Legislatures and a final commission for the purpose of preparing the draft of the actual measure'. Three years in Canada had educated Head in the realities of colonial politics, and he had moved far beyond the simple ideas about imperial legislation which he had held in 1851. Nor did he share Hamilton's optimism about the process of negotiations. 'A hundred minor difficulties might arise in the course of their discussions & there would necessarily be great difference of opinion as to details.'[44]

It is probable that Head had raised the question of the British attitude to federation because Galt had announced a series of resolutions on the subject in the Canadian Assembly on 8 March. These were debated in July, shortly before the episode of the 'double shuffle'.[45] At one stage during the ministerial upheaval, Head attempted to make Galt premier, a manoeuvre which, though unlikely to succeed, was a deft use of the governor-general's power to boost the standing of a politician — and of the policies he espoused. When the Cartier-Macdonald ministry got itself back into the saddle on 6 August, it was with the reinforcement of Alexander Galt and his policy. Galt's speech to the Assembly in July 1858 had dwelt eloquently on the vision of a general Confederation of the whole of British North America, but only the last of the three resolutions he proposed had dealt with Confederation. The first two resolutions had advocated a federation confined to Upper and Lower Canada, and its expansion to the Hudson's Bay territories. As with George Brown in 1864, so with Galt in 1858: Macdonald needed to form an alliance firmly committed to the larger union in order to prevent his prey from being sucked into any rival grouping committed to the smaller. It was a ploy which would also suit Macdonald's perennial tactic of delay, for by its very magnitude, the project would not commit the ministry to early or dramatic action. On 7 August, Cartier 'announced that the expediency of a federation of the British North American Provinces would be anxiously considered; that communication with the Home Government and the Maritime Provinces on the subject would forthwith be entered into; and that the result would be submitted to Parliament at a future session'.[46]

Sir Edmund Head was a cautious man, and at this point he might well have treated the sudden federal enthusiasm of his ministers as a subject appropriate for formal reference to his superiors in London — as Lytton's under-secretary, Lord Carnarvon, later felt he should have done.[47] Instead he took the plunge, and concluded that the silence which had followed his letter of 28 March constituted consent so far as the launching of federation was concerned: Labouchere had encouraged him 'to take it in hand', and Stanley had been enthusiastic in his certainty that 'England ought to further it by all means in her power'. On 16 August, in a speech closing the parliamentary session, Head took up his ministers' policy in a first-person statement: 'I propose in the course of the recess.... I am desirous ...'.[48]

The frosty response to Head's speech in London is best understood by considering the political problems of the weak ministry. The colonial secretary, Sir Edward Bulwer Lytton, was by no means opposed to Confederation in principle, but he had ample reason for concern at the means the Canadians were adopting in its pursuit. Not only was he utterly without ministerial experience himself, but Lord Derby's government was little more than a suicide mission with a stay of execution. It had come into office after an unexpected factional upheaval had ousted Palmerston six months earlier. Derby had accepted office only because he had been convinced that 'if he refused the Conservative party would be broken up for ever', but he faced 'a majority of two to one against him in the House of Commons' as well as a dearth of administrative talent in his own ranks. As he pleaded to the Queen, 'nothing but the forbearance and support of some of his opponents would make it possible for him to carry on any Government'.[49] In the event, no prominent opponent would agree to serve, and there was little prospect that his ministry would be lightly handled in the Commons. Indeed, Stanley himself was sure that for several years a Derby ministry had been 'the earnest wish of the more advanced Liberals' as a means of uniting 'every section of the Liberal party in opposition'.[50]

Within weeks, the new ministers only just escaped disaster. In May 1858, news arrived in Britain that the governor-general of India, Lord Canning, already much denounced for his policy of 'clemency' in the Mutiny, had issued a proclamation confiscating the property of all but six landowners in the disturbed province of Oude. The government's minister for India, Lord Ellenborough, had already led the ministry into difficulty by proposing an unwieldy scheme for the government of the sub-continent. Now he issued a grandiose and sardonic rebuke to Canning for reversing the usual principles of magnanimity and punishing the many while reprieving the few. Perhaps to recover his own political standing, Ellenborough leaked his despatch to the press. In fact,

Ellenborough had once again miscalculated. There was an outburst of public anger at the humiliation of a proconsul bearing such a terrible responsibility, which was compounded by the Queen's annoyance at Ellenborough's failure to consult her, and the cabinet's embarrassment at Ellenborough's defence that he had handed around a draft of his censure as ministers gathered 'by the fire' at one cabinet meeting, and had been prevented from securing formal approval by pressure of business at another. Whigs, radicals and Peelites prepared to unite and throw out the interloping Tories. At the last moment the Derby ministry was reprieved. Ellenborough blunted the attack by resigning, while it had become known that Canning's policy in Oude was in reality almost the reverse of the official language of his proclamation, being intended to safeguard the peasants who actually tilled the soil by eliminating their overlords.

Canning had sent a private explanation of his policy to Ellenborough's Whig predecessor, Vernon Smith, who had not troubled to pass it on. Vernon Smith was already an unpopular figure, regarded as one of the more arrogant exponents of the Whig belief of their entitlement to rule, and his failure to follow the normal conventions and courtesies between outgoing and incoming ministers undercut the moral outrage of the suddenly reunited opposition. In fine House of Commons management, Disraeli spun the debate out over a whole week, taking advantage of the traditional adjournment for Derby Day, while the prime minister pleaded with the Queen to permit the threat of a general election to be used to stave off defeat. Eventually, the rival Whig leaders, Palmerston and Russell, decided to abandon the motion, which could only be formally withdrawn with Disraeli's permission, and thus in effect upon terms which required the abasement of its proposer. Recalling the high emotions of the Commons during the debate, an observer in 1891 judged that 'nothing like it has occurred since'. To symbolise the breadth of their intended unity, the Whig factions had entrusted the task of moving the censure motion to an 'independent' member, a Peelite untainted by membership of the preceding Palmerston ministry. Disraeli sneered at the selection of 'a gentleman of unimpeachable character' as front man for an unprincipled opposition. The unimpeachable gentleman who moved the motion was Edward Cardwell. Six years later, as colonial secretary, Cardwell would have a powerful motive of self-protection from retaliatory parliamentary attack when he insisted on the British right to shape the movement for Confederation.[51]

The fall of Lord Ellenborough brought Lytton to the Colonial Office, and it was eminently understandable that he should have feared that Sir Edmund Head was to be his Canning. The Derby ministry had unexpectedly survived a ferocious parliamentary onslaught largely because an unpopular opposition politician had not troubled to pass on an important private letter to his Conservative successor. Should it become known that the imperial representative in Canada had been left isolated because one of the lacklustre cabinet's few impressive ministers had omitted to transmit even the substance of his correspondence to his own colleague, a second reprieve would be out of the question. There was certainly never any question that Lytton would dare to carry out his momentary threat to censure Sir Edmund Head: not only would a second Canning affair be a disaster, but Canada's governor-general was a close friend of Cornewall Lewis, chancellor of the exchequer in Palmerston's ministry, and no doubt ready to leap to his defence in the Commons. Lytton was soon to insist that he did not 'wish at this crisis to discredit Sir Edmund Head'.[52] Fortunately, too, when *The Times* rattled Lytton with a thunderous editorial of 15 September, it directed its fire not against Confederation but at the more abstruse issue of the conditions Head had attempted to impose upon George Brown in commissioning him to attempt the formation of a ministry.[53]

The forbearance of *The Times* and the quiescence of the House of Commons avoided ministerial catastrophe but did not in itself solve Lytton's problem that, as Blackwood put it, if ministers did not wish for a confrontation with Canada, 'they have only the shadow of an option'. The episode was 'strikingly illustrative of the little weight which is attached in the present day to the opinions, whichever way they might incline, of the Home Government on Canadian — and British North American domestic policy', with the provincial ministry acting 'just as if the consent of the Queen and Her Government had been formally and previously given'. However, Carnarvon, the parliamentary under-secretary, pointed out that the Canadians 'cannot guard as effectually against the jealousies of the several provinces to be confederated ... as they can against the interposition of the Secretary of State'.[54] There was only one strategy that Lytton could follow. A minority government already out of its depth with the problems of India would not welcome another major imperial project, but any open move to veto Head's 'great indiscretion'[55] would merely be to fight Ellenborough's disastrous battle with Canning on even weaker ground. The only way out was to adopt the lofty position that while Confederation might be a good idea, and was self-evidently a subject in which Canada had 'a very deep interest', it was of such imperial importance that it was 'one which it properly belongs to the Executive Authority of the Empire, and not to that of any separate province, to initiate'.[56] That position, staked out in a despatch as early as September 10, represented the first part of the ministerial exercise in damage limitation. The second would be to use the imperial co-ordinating role to exploit the reluctance of the Maritimes.

While Lytton confided the drafting of a policy statement to Elliot, a new element appeared on the British scene with the arrival of a Canadian delegation, consisting of Cartier — who began a generalised love affair with the London scene — John Ross and Galt. It was Galt, as finance minister, who had the most important practical business to discharge, and it was Galt who was most active and who stayed longest to promote the cause of Confederation. Shortly after their arrival, the delegates submitted to Lytton a private sketch of a possible structure of government, and a public statement which argued the need for a union of British North America, but insisted that all the Canadians were asking was 'that the Imperial Government will be pleased to authorise a meeting of Delegates' from all the provinces 'for the purpose of considering the subject' and reporting through the colonial secretary to their respective legislatures.[57] Elliot noted that it was 'impossible for any one to have made the acquaintance of the three Canadian Ministers ... without sentiments of respect and esteem,'[58] and it is probable that his comment referred principally to Galt, on whom most of the official business fell. He visited Lytton at his Hertfordshire home, where the two men 'had much conversation': Galt was, after all, the son of the then-celebrated 'Ayrshire novelist', while Lytton had set one of his own tales in Canada.[59] In any case, by the end of October, Lytton could afford to be courteous to Galt. The Colonial Office had by now heard from Manners Sutton of New Brunswick, who left no doubt that his province would respond with extreme caution to any move towards union with

Canada. Knowledge of the New Brunswick position, Blackwood noted, 'will largely aid Her Majesty's Government in dealing with the question'.[60]

Elliot argued that since the British government had no official knowledge of the attitude of the Maritime provinces, and no indication that the Canadian parliament would actually support specific proposals for a union of the provinces, it was not entitled to endorse 'so grave a measure as the appointment of delegates to discuss this subject, unless Her Majesty should first be addressed in favour of that course by the Legislatures of the several provinces concerned'. On the positive side, such a stance would both 'adjourn the question' and give the British government 'a much surer basis to act upon'. On the negative side, it might provoke 'undesirable agitation within the provinces', although this had probably become unavoidable.[61] Elliot was critical of Head's ministers, for 'in the endeavour to escape from local and temporary difficulties within the bounds of Canada', they had stirred up 'a question which may compromise the safety of all the interests concerned, Colonial and Imperial'.[62] Lytton not only agreed, but veered even further towards caution. As he told the cabinet, to retreat to the proposition that the British government would not take action 'until addressed by the Legislative bodies in all the provinces' would be to 'invite all the elections in British North America to turn upon this one cardinal point — Federation or not'. Consequently, he preferred to call for confidential reports from the governors on the likely attitudes of each province to a proposal for intercolonial union.[63]

Faced with what Galt's biographer understandably called a 'lukewarm epistle',[64] the governors of the lower provinces had no difficulty in reporting a lack of support for union with Canada, with Lord Mulgrave of Nova Scotia in particular dissecting the whole subject in a devastating rebuttal which Lytton called 'the cleverest despatch we have had upon the subject'.[65] In fact, Lytton had not necessarily intended to rule out all future moves towards intercolonial union. Twenty years earlier, he had stated that 'he should not object if ... they educated the Canadas to that safe and gradual independence which should be the last and crowning boon that a colony should receive'.[66] He had been a radical then, but even when he was startled into threatening to censure Head for embracing Confederation, he insisted that he had 'no prejudice' against the idea itself.[67] His draft despatch contained the statement that the imperial government would have 'no motive for opposition' should Confederation be 'deliberately desired' by all the provinces. It was Derby who struck this out as 'unnecessarily encouraging to a project of very questionable policy'.[68] Derby was one of the few prominent British politicians who never demonstrated any enthusiasm for Confederation. There was irony in the fact that he would be prime minister when it was carried in 1867.

The reluctance of the Maritimers enabled Lytton to play the imperial card to ensure that any early move towards federation was blocked, and their doubts also reinforced his ambivalence on the general issue of its desirability. Even if they responded favourably to the principle, the Maritimers were unlikely tamely to accept a Canadian blueprint for a British North American union without amendment. Almost as soon as he first learnt of Head's proposal for Confederation, Lytton had felt certain that the British could ensure that it would only emerge in a form acceptable to imperial interests.[69] As he assured the cabinet, 'the Crown will retain unimpaired the power so to regulate and guide negotiations as to strip them of those dangers, whether to the connection with the mother-country, or to the internal peace of the provinces' which were to be feared as 'the inevitable result' of losing control of the initiative.[70] Lytton summarised his views to Head: it would be ill-advised of the imperial government to oppose 'a declared & unequivocal desire' on the part of the provinces, 'growing spontaneously out of their wants & interests, to enter into practical negotiations for legislative or federal union', but equally 'it would be unwise ... to do anything to encourage or force on such a project'.[71] Implicit in this attitude — although Lytton probably did not see it — would be an acceptance that the first steps towards Confederation would come from the provinces. Within a very short time, Lytton's insistence on the imperial right to initiate any move towards Confederation had been quietly abandoned. However, his assumption that the British government would retain the right to shape the scheme — either by demanding amendments or through the more technical process of controlling the wording of legislation — was neither asserted nor surrendered.

In June 1859, after the Derby ministry had unsuccessfully appealed to the voters, the opposition factions finally joined under the leadership of Palmerston to install a Liberal government which for several years seemed far more secure. Newcastle went back to the Colonial Office, the post he had left five years earlier to preside over the Crimean disaster. To judge from his earlier attempt to encourage Elgin to take up the issue in 1854, Newcastle would have responded far more positively to the Canadian initiative of 1858. By the time he came back to office, not only had that initiative run into the ground, but it had created a temporary wariness about intruding any British opinion into the re-shaping of the provinces. When Manners Sutton asked for instructions on how to respond to an expected campaign for Maritime Union, Newcastle welcomed the idea as a step towards Confederation, but doubted whether 'the time has come ... to take any active steps for bringing it about'.[72] None the less, while cautioning 'against forming too hasty conclusions', Newcastle professed himself 'ready to entertain favourably any proposals which shall have the concurrence of all the three Provinces'.[73] By November 1859, then, Newcastle had tacitly accepted that — in the Maritimes at least — Lytton's insistence on an imperial right to initiate the discussion of organic change need not apply.

In January 1860, Galt returned to London, accompanied by another Canadian minister, Sidney Smith. They were armed with a request from the Canadian government for information about the replies to Lytton's circular despatch. It was evident that British-Canadian relations could no longer be confined to the rigid protocol of official channels: Newcastle treated the communication from the two Canadians as a private letter, but it triggered a formal circular despatch to all the British North American governors.[74] Their missive was respectful in its wording, but its import verged on the sarcastic, reminiscent of the tongue-in-cheek scorn with which Galt had dismissed the complaints of the Sheffield manufacturers against the Canadian tariff a few months earlier — a rebuke indirectly aimed at Newcastle himself for countenancing the criticism.[75] Boldly, they turned Lytton's policy inside out, and then sweetly hinted that if Newcastle disputed their interpretation, he would be casting doubt on the loyalty and good sense of the people of British North America. Lytton's circular despatch calling for reports from the governors had been 'somewhat misunderstood as indicating a disinclination to entertain the question while it was, we believe, only intended to express the unwillingness of the Imperial authorities to initiate the discussion of a subject which it was conceived, more properly, should proceed from the Colonies themselves'. If this was indeed the view of the imperial authorities, then it constituted 'a further and gratifying proof of the confidence they repose in the local Legislatures and People'. They asked for an assurance that those who saw Lytton's despatch as a ban on discussion of Confederation were mistaken. Indeed, if the British government doubted the wisdom of Confederation, it would be 'very undesireable that the public mind of the Provinces themselves should be agitated by its discussion'.[76]

It was an extremely clever letter. The British government could hardly ignore a request for clarification on its attitude to an obviously important subject, and Galt had ruthlessly supplied the hint that a discouraging response would be taken to imply a lack of confidence in the ability of the provinces to run their own affairs. Equally, while Newcastle had no great opinion of Lytton, 'the great Literary Statesman',[77] there were good reasons for maintaining a bipartisan approach to the maintenance of imperial prerogatives. Much deliberation at the Colonial Office produced a carefully crafted despatch. Its key passage began with a statement that the British government saw 'no reason to depart from the general line of policy which they have hitherto pronounced is their intention to adopt if the occasion should arise. They do not think it their duty to initiate any movement toward such union but they have no wish in any way to impede it.' This was in itself a fine-tuning of Lytton's policy. Furthermore, the draft undertook 'to lend whatever assistance may be requisite from them toward carrying into effect any well considered scheme which may have the concurrence of the people of the Provinces through the Legislatures, assuming of course that it does not interfere with Imperial interests'. This not only went far beyond Lytton, but was too much for Newcastle. Like Derby a year earlier, he insisted on deletion. 'Better not promise any *assistance*,' he wrote in the margin. 'It might be construed into a *suggestion* of the measure.' The key passage was collapsed, to a promise not 'to impede any well considered scheme'. Moreover, governors were forewarned not to appoint delegates to discuss any such scheme 'without previous communication with the Secretary of State'.[78] Head, Mulgrave and Manners Sutton all sent replies confirming that they had no intention of rushing into action.[79] The British government had now renounced its claim to initiate a movement for interprovincial union, but there are indications that

Newcastle remained as interested in encouraging the project as he had been in 1853-4. From its position in his papers, it seems likely that it was at this time that he borrowed from the Colonial Office files — and failed to return — the memorandum on British North American federation prepared by T.W.C. Murdoch in 1849.[80] In 1860, Newcastle accompanied the young Prince of Wales on his transatlantic tour, thus becoming the first colonial secretary ever to visit Canada while in office. The memorandum he submitted to the cabinet in support of the Intercolonial early in 1862 shows not only that he continued to subscribe to Confederation as an aim, but that he was also well aware of the physical barriers to be overcome first.[81]

There are also indications that in 1860, Newcastle hoped to appoint Lord Chandos as governor-general in succession to Sir Edmund Head, with the aim of working towards both the railway and a political union of the provinces. Newcastle did formally offer him the post in August 1861, referring to his 'interest in the affairs of North America last year, and more especially in those of Canada', although by then Chandos had succeeded his father as Duke of Buckingham. Newcastle — a duke himself — was 'certainly not insensible to the great alteration in your position which must influence your decision'.[82] In 1866, Buckingham offered all help to Carnarvon to get Confederation carried through parliament as soon as possible, explaining that 'the interest I took in it in 1861 & 1862 with the late Duke of Newcastle has shewn me the importance of it'.[83] There were good general grounds for grooming Chandos for the post. As the heir to a dukedom, he would bring the social prestige which was undeniably a useful reinforcement of the office of governor-general. He was a Conservative, whose appointment might promise cross-party support, and he had held ministerial office under Derby in 1852. Beyond this there was the qualification — highly unusual in an aristocrat — that he was chairman of a railway company. Chandos had been forced to seek a career because his father had brought the family fortunes to the edge of ruin, despite the old duke's talent — wryly admired by Disraeli — for 'taking swindlers in'.[84] In 1866 Buckingham showed his support for Confederation by inviting Joseph Howe to the first of the house parties at Stowe which were thought to have played their part in sapping Nova Scotian resistance two years later.[85] When Carnarvon resigned over Reform in March 1867, it was

Buckingham who succeeded him at the Colonial Office. In 1860, then, Newcastle seems to have been discussing Confederation with the chairman of the London and North-Western Railway. Early in 1861, a press report predicted that the British government was about to submit a scheme for British North American union to the provinces. Newcastle indignantly dismissed the story as the work of 'an obscure Journal here'.[86] In fact, the *Canadian News* was a weekly publication which even Colonial Office staff found useful for its digests of the Canadian press.[87] Its London base probably made it well placed to pick up rumours, and it may have jumped to this particular conclusion because Sir Edmund Head was on leave in Britain and had recently been the duke's house guest at Clumber.[88] When Sir Fenwick Williams, the acting administrator in Head's absence, forwarded to London a Canadian proposal for a common British North American tariff to simplify the working of the Reciprocity Treaty, both Elliot and Newcastle saw the implied connection with the political union of the provinces.[89] Yet Newcastle maintained a subtle approach.

It was one thing to assure Manners Sutton, a governor who was highly critical of such schemes, that a union of British North America was premature, and in any case would have to be an initiative launched from the provinces themselves.[90] Much more notable was Newcastle's unusual step in writing direct to a Canadian politician, Malcolm Cameron, to deny 'any intention of "compelling" the Provinces of British North America to form a federation or any other Union'. Cameron had spoken enthusiastically of British North American federation at the Reform Convention of 1859, and continued to advocate a transcontinental union — even visiting British Columbia in 1862. A timber exporter from Sarnia, at the western end of the Grand Trunk, he had good locational reasons to argue for expansion both to the prairies and to the Atlantic seaboard. British ministers were usually wary of entering into direct communication with colonial politicians — they could never be sure of the uses their correspondence might be put to. In the circumstances, Newcastle's statement that 'any measure of this kind must originate with the Parties interested' was as much a signal as a disclaimer. Newcastle's insistence that it was 'no part of the business of a British Minister to initiate such schemes either in the Imperial Parliament or the Colonies' did not mean that he ruled out encouragement of British North American union by other means.[91] When it became necessary to replace Sir Edmund Head as governor-general of Canada in the summer of 1861, Newcastle ignored the implied claims to promotion of Manners Sutton, the longest serving governor in the colonial service, and bluntly offered him South Australia instead. Manners Sutton was offended,[92] but it seems fair to speculate that — as in 1854 — Newcastle wanted a governor-general who would seize the opportunity to back Confederation whenever it might arise.

Speculation about Newcastle's intentions perhaps helped to produce a probing resolution on the union of the provinces in the Nova Scotian Assembly in mid-April 1861.[93] When it was eventually forwarded to the Colonial Office a year later, Arthur Blackwood suspected the political machinations of Joseph Howe, who had at long last risen to the premiership of his province.[94] Howe's motives may indeed have been in part political. His hold on office was insecure, and the motion may have been an attempt to recover support from John Tobin, an influential figure among the Irish Catholics, whose support Howe had forfeited in the disastrous sectarian quarrel of recent years. Equally, it may be significant that the motion was seconded by the opposition leader, Charles Tupper, who was already on record as an advocate of British North American union.[95] The fact that Howe took no action on the resolution for over a year adds piquancy to its concluding sentiment that 'the public mind in all the provinces ought to be set at rest' on the question. While the resolution would come to haunt Howe during his campaign against Confederation, in fact it embodied a mild proposal that any scheme for the union either of the Maritimes or of British North America as a whole would require 'mutual consultations of the leading men of the Colonies' as well as 'free communication with the Imperial Government'. Accordingly the governor of Nova Scotia was asked to 'put himself in communication' with the British government and the other provinces 'in order to ascertain the policy of her Majesty's Government, and the opinions of the other colonies'.[96]

Howe's decision to activate this resolution in May 1862 was probably related to a proposed meeting of British North American delegates to discuss the financing of the Intercolonial, which was one of Howe's pet projects. The Nova Scotian ministers were also interested in intercolonial free trade. Lord Mulgrave forwarded the resolution to London, explaining his ministers wanted 'a meeting of the leading men of the different Provinces'. While Mulgrave himself rehashed his earlier doubts about uniting the provinces, he acknowledged that the principle had long been widely supported, but pointed out 'no practical mode of carrying out this Union, has ever been proposed'.[97]

In the Colonial Office, the initial reaction to the resolution was unenthusiastic. Elliot reiterated his support for a union of the Maritime provinces, but doubted 'whether it would be advisable to promote ... their incorporation with Canada', or even to encourage discussion of the question. The parliamentary under-secretary, Chichester Fortescue, felt that the resolution was too vague to justify a detailed response, a point which Newcastle latched on to, adding that to outline British policy in reply to a resolution which had lain dormant for over a year would be inconsistent 'with the intention not to originate here what must first spring from the wishes and interests of the People themselves'.[98] As it happened, the voices urging caution within Newcastle's own administrative team were balanced by advice from the foreign secretary, Lord Russell, that British North American federation should be adopted as government policy in the wake of the defeat of the Militia Bill in the province of Canada — by which in practical terms Russell meant 'adopted so far as public recommendation of it to Canada, Nova Scotia & New Brunswick'.[99] Newcastle had no intention of making any such open declaration, but in formulating his response to the Nova Scotian resolution, his thinking moved forward in two important respects. This was the moment when Newcastle recognised that the staged timetable which had been vaguely envisaged as leading towards British North American union might have to be telescoped — that Maritime Union, the Intercolonial and Confederation could form a single package. Secondly, Newcastle decided to play the Confederation ball firmly into the colonial court. He would not discourage Confederation 'but I would give the Colonists to understand that the movement must come from them although I am well inclined to enter heartily into any well-considered plan which has the concurrence of all Parties concerned'.[100] The resulting despatch of 6 July 1862, which was sent to all the British North American provinces, showed little trace of heartiness, but C.B. Adderley was perhaps disingenuous when he claimed, in 1867, that 'a more calm and colourless answer ... was never sent from any public office'.[101]

The despatch was in fact a crucial document clearing the way for a concerted inter-provincial move towards the union of British North America. It endorsed the view that the union of the provinces was 'a very proper subject for calm deliberation'. It clarified that any proposal either for Maritime Union or for Confederation should 'emanate in the first instance from the Provinces, and should be concurred in by all of them which it would affect'. It specified a means by which the provinces might launch a concerted initiative: there would be 'no objection to any consultation on the subject amongst the leading members of the Governments concerned', and the best means to test public reaction to any resulting proposal of union 'would probably be by means of Resolution or Address, proposed in the Legislature of each Province by its own Government'. Newcastle might have stopped at that point: calmly and colourlessly he had finally resolved the issue of procedure, the issue of 'how?' In fact, he went on, ostensibly declining to offer any definition of British policy in the abstract, but predicting a positive response to any proposal for union which the provinces might support. 'I am sure that the matter would be weighed in this country both by the public, by Parliament, and by Her Majesty's Government, with no other feelings than an anxiety ... to promote any course which might be conducive to the prosperity, the strength and the harmony of all the British Communities in North America.'[102]

The despatch was significant not simply in what it said, but in what it omitted. Fortescue had wished to require colonial legislatures to secure the approval of the Queen before passing any resolutions in support of schemes of union. This provision did not appear in the final despatch. Nor was there any hint of the covering phrase in Newcastle's previous circular despatch of January 1860, which had given the less positive pledge that the British government would not 'impede' any movement towards British North American union, 'assuming of course that it does not interfere with Imperial interests'.[103]

Inside the Colonial Office, the real import of the despatch was clarified early in 1864 in a discussion of procedure adopted to promote Maritime Union, which then seemed a more likely outcome than Confederation. Arthur Blackwood had loftily queried whether Newcastle's encouragement entitled the Maritimers to work out their own destiny and merely report the outcome to

London for ratification. Elliot thought Blackwood was reading too much into the despatch of 6 July 1862. 'Certainly the spirit of it was to let the Provinces follow very much their own inclinations.'[104] This was a far cry from the dark fears of the Elliot of 1858 that even to allow discussion of the subject might be dangerous.[105] Newcastle's approach was continued by his successor, Cardwell, who assured Monck in September 1864 that there was 'no objection at all to a visit of your Ministers, or their friends to the assembled Delegates of the other Provinces, for the purpose ... of ascertaining their wishes and feelings', adding that 'I attach a great deal too much importance to the great questions now involved to be fastidious & precise as to the forms adopted'.[106] It was fortunate that Cardwell was prepared to be so flexible, since the Canadians had actually arrived in Charlottetown a week earlier. When Sir Richard MacDonnell of Nova Scotia requested formal permission to appoint delegates to Quebec, even the habitually rigid Blackwood observed, 'The federation movement is getting beyond the scope of Secretaries of State; & it is of no use to impose restrictions if you can't well enforce them'.[107] None the less, Cardwell insisted that the British would have the last word. When the governor of Newfoundland reported his province had accepted an invitation to be represented at the Quebec conference, Cardwell drily commented that 'the question is one in which the Imperial — as well as the Newfoundland Legislature — will have something to say'.[108] Only gradually did Cardwell recognise the limitations of the British role in the final stages of Confederation.

The significance of Newcastle's despatch of 6 July 1862 is best assessed not by measuring what it achieved, but by asking whether the movement for Confederation would have been disrupted had it never been written. The despatch did not persuade the delegates to the Quebec conference in September 1862 to link the Intercolonial railway with the question of general union, although there is evidence from both Joseph Howe and William Annand that Confederation was discussed, possibly even in a 'full debate'.[109] By May 1864, D'Arcy McGee was enthusiastically attempting to invite himself to the projected Maritime Union conference at Charlottetown 'at least as a spectator', and suggesting to Tilley that 'our proposed Intercolonial Conference' could also take place there 'after your Maritime Conference', in order to 'save time and perhaps, serve both projects'.[110] McGee was already a passionate crusader for British North American union. While we can never know what would have happened had Newcastle never penned his despatch of 6 July 1862, one little-noticed incident at the Quebec conference of 1864 may be indicative. 'What authority from the Home Government have we to consider this subject?' asked the Nova Scotian R.B. Dickey, who was unconvinced of the necessity for political union. John A. Macdonald was quick to produce Newcastle's despatch of 6 July 1862.[111] After 1864, opponents might challenge the principle of Confederation or attack the terms struck at Quebec, but nobody could hide behind the loyal argument that the unification of the provinces would be an invasion of the imperial sphere.

If the British had cleared the way to British North American union in July 1862, they were no more than marking time in the two years that followed. In government circles, attention shifted to Maritime Union, energetically pressed by the governor of New Brunswick, Arthur Gordon, whose rank and political connections gave him a standing in Downing Street capable of withstanding the negative effects of his combative personality.[112] Newcastle approved reports of progress towards Maritime Union, and accepted that events had placed his timetable in disarray. 'I wish the Intercolonial Railway had preceded, but it must follow a Legislative Union. Halifax would no doubt be the Capital & Members of the Legislature must have improved access to it.'[113] The comment was indicative of just how simplistic was the analysis of even a well informed British minister: a railway line from Halifax to Quebec would be of little use to most New Brunswick politicians, and its profitability was unlikely to be enhanced by the journeys of a few dozen local legislators. Maritime Union was a welcome development, but still one from which the British government intended to keep its formal distance. As Blackwood pointed out, open support might 'give offence to Canada',[114] and accordingly in July 1863 Gordon was confidentially instructed to use 'all prudent means, without committing the home Government beforehand' in order to get the project moving.[115] As Newcastle wrote privately to Hastings Doyle, the acting governor of Nova Scotia, in November 1863, 'the Home Government will not initiate any measure with this object, but if the Provinces desire it I shall give every assistance and willing assent'.[116] It was a poignant promise, for within a few months, a fatal illness had forced Newcastle from office.

Throughout the twenty-five years from 1837 to 1862 — and especially from 1849 onwards — British North American union had been consistently discussed in Britain, and a general consensus had developed that it was a desirable end. In 1862, the Duke of Newcastle had found the phrases which deftly located the responsibility for taking the lead towards closer union with the provinces themselves. Yet the record of the next two years is virtually blank. Among British politicians, only the foreign secretary, Lord Russell, seems to have mentioned his hopes for 'some federal tie uniting the whole of British America in a semi-independent connexion with Great Britain'.[117] The absence of any further speculations about British North American union from Newcastle may probably be attributed to his low opinion of the Canadian ministry led by Sandfield Macdonald, which he suspected of being 'secretly and corruptly American'.[118] Newcastle hoped that Monck might be able to get rid of them, perhaps even find an excuse for dismissing them outright, and 'get out of the old routine of jobbing politicians'. By September 1863, he concluded 'that the time is come for the amalgamation of the best men on both sides under some new and honourable man (if indeed such can be found) who is untainted with the old harm'.[119] This was the approach which Monck attempted to adopt in the ministerial crises of both March and June 1864. Neither Newcastle nor Monck linked the political need for a coalition with the opportunity for a new departure in constitutional engineering.

Overall, British North America had temporarily dropped from sight in one of the cycles of national amnesia which characterised Britain's connection with its transatlantic provinces. 'Since the affair of the Trent,' *The Times* commented in June 1864, '... we have had little attention to devote to the position of Canada.' A national uprising in Poland, a confrontation between Prussia and Denmark, and above all the American Civil War had diverted attention from British North America. 'While the banks of the Mississippi have been the scenes of exterminating conflict, the great British river has rolled on its current in peace from the solitudes of Lake Superior to the Atlantic Ocean.'[120] A week later, the first reports arrived of a new Canadian government, with sketchy information that it planned some sort of federal re-structuring of government. *The Times* hoped 'that this union of parties may be as permanent as it is astonishing'.[121] Far from pulling the imperial strings, the new colonial secretary, Edward Cardwell, was taken aback by the sudden revolution in Canadian party politics: 'the question of Federation is so new & so important that I must try to master its bearings before I write to you upon it', he commented to Monck.[122] Within two months, the new Canadian ministers were sailing down the great British river on their way to Charlottetown. After thirty years of speculation about the future of the provinces, circumstances within British North America finally gave the British something to support. There was not a shadow of a doubt that the movement for Confederation commanded British support. However, it is much less obvious that British support could do very much to command the movement for Confederation.

7 The Role of the British in the Achievement of Confederation 1864-1867

Historians have generally regarded the role of the British in the achievement of Confederation between 1864 and 1867 as important, although precisely how the imperial *deus ex machina* managed to overcome opposition in Nova Scotia and New Brunswick in 1865-6 is not fully explained. A collage of phrases captures the prevailing impression created by most studies of the subject: 'Britain overrides resistance' was Brebner's sub-heading, followed by the statement that it took 'two years and the full weight of Britain's resources to get a federation established'. 'The time had now come to invoke the overriding authority of the British government,' wrote McInnis. According to Francis, Jones and Smith, 'Britain now intervened directly to bring about a colonial federation', while McNaught concluded that 'London ... acted decisively'. Finlay and Sprague referred to 'British intervention to break the resistance of Nova Scotia and New Brunswick'. Morton narrowed the allusion to the cabinet, which 'it was clear beyond doubt ... had decided to use all necessary means to carry out the confederation of Canada'. Eldridge concentrated the focus still more, specifying that the colonial secretary, Edward Cardwell, 'was quite prepared to push the Maritime Provinces into joining the confederation'. A detailed study of Cardwell's policy as colonial secretary agrees that he 'was responsible for the weight of the British government behind Confederation'. Judd is almost a lone voice in stressing 'that the new Dominion had grown from Canadian initiatives, not from British pressures'.[1]

The collective product is a huge literary exercise in historical reification: words are used to conjure up a thing that may generally be termed 'British pressure', which was employed by Britain or London or Edward Cardwell to overcome the resistance of the Maritimers to Confederation. Creighton seemed to recognise the emptiness of the term when he refined it to 'British moral pressure': indeed, he recognised that there were few sanctions available to the British. Lower conjured up an alternative monster, 'British financial Imperialism'.[2] By and large, it may be said that historians who habitually emphasise economic factors tend to portray unidentified capitalists whispering in the ears of British ministers in the mid-1860s, urging them to create a united British North America. Insofar as it is defined and analysed, 'British pressure' seems to consist of three elements: first, strongly worded despatches from the Colonial Office; secondly, threats to scale down or even abandon the imperial commitment to defend the provinces; and, thirdly, the carrot of a loan guarantee which would permit the borrowing of money to finance the Intercolonial railway at low rates of interest. As causal factors capable of swinging the destiny of half a continent, these do not stand up to examination. Despatches were paper pellets. There is — to put it mildly — some contradiction in arguing that Confederation was both a price the provinces had to pay to ensure continued imperial protection and a means by which the British could escape from their obligation to defend British North America. There is also some tendency to imply that the British added the Intercolonial loan guarantee as an entirely new element in the package, 'giving the Maritime provinces an additional incentive to unite with the Canadas',[3] overlooking the fact that the guarantee had actually been offered to the separate provinces in 1862, with a five-year deadline which if anything made the more ambitious attempt to link it with political union a reckless diversion.

The British contribution to the achievement of Confederation was important but of a more complex nature. Lower was surely correct in arguing that it 'would have been impossible to bring the colonies together unless the Imperial government had given its blessing'.[4] Beyond that vital precondition, it is easy to exaggerate the role of the Colonial Office and the cabinet, those institutional manifestations of Creighton's imperial Caesar. There is some evidence that Cardwell's minatory despatches may have had a positive impact, but there is also evidence that they were counter-productive.[5] The specific issue of defence came to be intertwined with the question of Confederation not as part of the kind of neat causal package beloved by the authors of textbooks, but more through a combination of a coincidence of passing crises and the political needs of the Canadian and British ministries. To assess the significance of the 'British' role, it is necessary to focus less upon the government, and more upon the wider political community whose support for the idea of Confederation is analysed in Chapter Four.

Brebner was half right when he wrote that 'a benign, if uninformed and uninterested, British public thought it a splendid idea to throw the colonies together and trust to the agglomeration to look after itself'.[6] The point may be put more strongly: the entire British political nation threw its weight behind Confederation. It was supported by both parties, and by all influential sections of the press, to such a degree that potential defectors were blocked off — as *The Times* made clear to Robert Lowe in 1865, and Joseph Howe discovered with some bitterness in 1866-7. Yet it is one thing to write of 'weight' and another to prove that the weight had real bulk. If the British government of itself could do little to force Confederation upon reluctant provinces, it may be riposted that it is hard to see how the opposition and the press could do more.

To appreciate the force of the British consensus, two aspects of the analysis offered in Chapter Four need to be borne in mind. One is that by 1864, British opinion contained a strong thread of uncharitable annoyance towards Canada, although there was some injustice that it should have been Nova Scotia and New Brunswick which felt the backlash of imperial disapproval for their reluctance to trust those same Canadians. When even as perennial an optimist as Joseph Howe encountered difficulties in pushing Nova Scotia's one and only railway ten miles beyond Truro, the Maritimes could not afford the luxury of antagonising opinion in the major international source for investment capital.[7] It was the fortuitous intersection of a thread in British opinion which was not at all benign towards Canada, with a crisis in the distant colony of New Zealand that made the Intercolonial guarantee of 1862 an element in the Confederation issue. In a sense, in buying Confederation to get the Intercolonial, the provinces were forced to pay for something they had already been offered. Insofar as Confederation was a trade-off for the loan guarantee, it was not because the British government had it in its power to confer the boon, but rather because that power seemed temporarily to be slipping away in a phase of political instability which made it necessary that the provinces should appeal not so much to the Caesar of Downing Street as to the wider Senate of the British political nation.

The second important aspect of the wider British attitude was that it embodied a sense of social, educational and metropolitan superiority towards the provinces. In concentrating on the issues of policy discussed, historical accounts of colonial missions to London have largely missed the crucial context of the social relations which surrounded them. The British élite possessed formidable weapons for the demonstration of approval — and disapproval. No colonial visitors had ever been welcomed with the warmth — albeit condescending — which greeted George Brown in December 1864 and the Canadian delegation of 1865. The court, the aristocracy, the cabinet, the intelligentsia — all were mobilised to fête the Canadians and to frown on the dissident Maritimers. Of course, it would be foolhardy to dismiss the tools of the historical trade of explanation, the grand factors of investment and defence, to explain Confederation rather by the smiles of duchesses, and there were limits to the effectiveness of the technique. Galt was uncomfortable with British high society. Albert J. Smith showed a dogged integrity in resisting outright such blandishments. More crucially, George Brown was ambivalent though undoubtedly captivated by his sudden entrée to the world of royalty and of power. For Macdonald and for the cause of Confederation, it was vital to keep Brown tied to coalition and prevented from insisting upon action on its contingent promise to reconstruct the Canadian Union. The flattering of his self-esteem in the drawing rooms of the metropolis seems to have been one factor in maintaining his stance as a statesman of Confederation. Most notably of all, the British élite ruthlessly outgunned Joseph Howe in the winter of 1866-7, patronising him to his face, but damning him as a hypocrite when the British North America bill came before parliament.

Behind this world of superiors unbending to colonials, of the sun of approval and the frown of displeasure, there lay the more basic and ultimately unresolved issue of the scope of imperial power. Newcastle had unambiguously conceded to the provinces the right of initiating any movement towards a union of the provinces, but the imperial parliament retained the power to pass the necessary legislation. There were a few outright threats on the one side and some residual suspicions on the other that in the last resort the

British might impose Confederation outright, but such an imperious exercise of power was out of date by the 1860s, at least in relation to provinces as substantial as British North America. What remained was a sense among the British élite that they were entitled to influence the shape of the scheme, a confidence which drew upon their sense of a superior wisdom which qualified them to insist upon changes of emphasis, to manipulate legislative control with the aim of amending under the guise of codification. It was this aspect of the imperial role which largely explains how the British played a part in securing the adherence of the Maritimes to Confederation.

Metaphor is a dangerous tool for historians, and should only be used accompanied by the scholarly equivalent of a health warning, but it may here point a contrast. Most accounts of Confederation have portrayed the Maritimes as overwhelmingly opposed to any union with Canada. Consequently, a British sledgehammer was required to blast the barrier from the road to Confederation. The fact that Nova Scotia and New Brunswick fell into line provided the evidence that the sledgehammer was effective. If, however, it is assumed that opinion in Nova Scotia and New Brunswick was more evenly divided, with most of the doubts directed at the timing and terms of union with Canada, then 'the weight of the British government' could exercise a crucial influence even if it were no more than a feather on evenly balanced scales. Yet even that image may be misleading if it implies that Maritimers merely responded inertly to external pressures. It is much more likely that Nova Scotia and New Brunswick changed sides in 1866 because enough of their political leaders escaped from the isolationist consequences of their own opposition to the Quebec scheme by appealing to the British to take the lead in producing an amended alternative. Both for the Canadian ministers in 1865 and for a section of the Nova Scotian opposition in 1866, the imperial factor was highly convenient.

***

Far from having master-minded British North America into uniting, Cardwell and the Colonial Office staff did not immediately realise that the Great Coalition seriously intended to make an early move for Confederation.[8] Monck's official account of his new ministry made no mention of Confederation, but merely stated that there were hopes that a compromise would be found to solve the issue of representation by population. Blackwood had been sure that this would mean no more than 'an undoing' of the Union of 1841.[9] He was surprised when Monck began the process of re-writing history in his despatch of 26 August 1864: 'Lord Monck says the second scheme was the *basis* of the Coalition, which is a new statement'.[10] Cardwell had archly noted the lack of official information four weeks earlier, but had approved an unofficial Canadian mission to Charlottetown. 'I have no objection whatever to an union of the whole of British North America in one great & important Province: and I do not anticipate that the Cabinet, or Parliament, will have any.'[11] As encouraging news of progress reached London in the months which followed, so Cardwell returned comments, reassuring to Monck ('here there is but one desire, which is to prosecute to the utmost the work in which you are engaged') and minatory to the suspicious Arthur Gordon of New Brunswick ('It is the earnest desire of the Government that the plan may succeed; & I think public opinion is undivided about it.').[12] 'It seems to be accepted here as a desirable change,' Cobden commented cautiously, while in more extravagant language the *Spectator* recorded that the Quebec scheme had been 'received in England with a sort of rapture of applause'.[13] In December 1864, Cardwell made British support clear when he officially expressed 'the most cordial satisfaction' of the imperial government with the outcome of the Quebec conference.[14]

It is difficult to measure the impact of Cardwell's endorsement, but its importance may be exaggerated. The governor of Nova Scotia, Sir Richard MacDonnell, promptly published the despatch and reported that it had 'given such an additional prestige and weight' to the case for Confederation that opposition had been disarmed and would lack 'any effective organization'.[15] In fact, a few days after MacDonnell's confident if obsequious prediction, Joseph Howe began his devastating 'Botheration' campaign in Nova Scotia, with the magisterial rebuke that 'hereafter we trust to hear no more of Imperial Despatches commanding a Union'.[16] Within two months the Quebec scheme was on its way to rejection by the voters of New Brunswick.

George Brown had a preview of Cardwell's December 1864 despatch during his mission to London. 'It outdoes anything that ever went to any British colony,' he reported, 'praises our statesmanlike discretion, loyalty & so on.'[17] So it did, but it did not say that Confederation would strengthen the defences of British

North America. It was left to a second circular despatch, in June 1865, to state 'the strong and deliberate opinion' of the British government, as the paramount power with overall responsibility for colonial defence, that Confederation was 'an object much to be desired'.[18] As even Creighton, the prince of pattern makers, had observed, in the summer of 1864 British deliberations on the defence of the provinces had seemed to be moving in channels entirely distinct from their comments on the likelihood of Confederation. When Cardwell had urged that the Great Coalition take action on 'the great Question of Defence' in July 1864, he seemed to mean that Canada at last had a ministry strong enough to tackle the issue, not that British North America was about to undertake constitutional change as a necessary precondition. As late as January 1865 he could categorise defence as one of the 'ulterior questions' which would have to 'await the issue of the Scheme for Union'.[19] How, then, did defence and Confederation become intertwined by the spring of 1865?

Defence and Confederation became entangled through the intensity of two short-term crises, and to meet the political needs of Canadian and British ministers. The opening months of 1865 were swept by a particularly severe war scare. The American Civil War seemed to be coming to a close, either through negotiated peace or by conquest, and with it the prospect that the United States would seek to settle accounts with Britain through attacking the provinces. A raid by Southerners from Canadian territory into Vermont in October 1864, followed by an ill-judged 'hot pursuit' order by a Northern general, had underlined the vulnerability of Canada to attack. Even a young American realised how much he disliked 'the prospect of Sherman marching down the St. Lawrence' and — the sardonic dismissals of the *Globe* notwithstanding — the prospect was a great deal more disagreeable to those who might find themselves in the path of Northern revenge.[20] In January, Palmerston warned the Queen of 'the probability that, whenever the Civil war in America shall be ended, the Northern States will make demands upon England which cannot be complied with', leading to an invasion of British North America. In February, Gordon feared that 'the conquest of the South (which appears imminent) will be followed by a war with England'.[21]

In fact, the most intense phase of the scare seems to have passed quickly: by mid-March, Brown noted that the fear of war seemed to have passed, and in early April Russell was 'very sanguine of maintaining peace' with the United States.[22] None the less, the atmosphere was tense, and the American denunciation of the Reciprocity Treaty pointed to a period of bleak relations. This phase coincided with the publication of part of the review of Canadian defences undertaken for the War Office by Colonel Jervois of the Royal Engineers. Jervois had privately concluded that any British military role in North America 'must necessarily be of a defensive rather than an aggressive character', with the 'principal part' of any conflict with the United States falling upon the Navy. In such a war, Britain would need merely to retain control of Montreal and Quebec, thus preventing the Americans from dominating the St Lawrence and by extension the Atlantic coast of British North America.[23] Although Jervois did not favour an immediate concentration of British troops at those two points — not least because the barracks were inadequate to house them — he left no doubt that most of Upper Canada would be overrun if war came. In February 1865, the British government published a digest of the Jervois report. Its effect, according to Macdonald, was to create 'a panic in Western Canada'.[24]

On the political front, for John A. Macdonald March 1865 was a month of supreme crisis for the Great Coalition. New Brunswick had rejected the Quebec scheme. Brown was unabashed: if the larger scheme of British North American union had faltered, the smaller project of a federation of the two Canadas could go ahead in its place, and once again he fought to reconfirm the ministry's commitment to the cosmetically federalised version of representation by population.[25] When the first news of the New Brunswick setback had reached Canada, Macdonald had played the imperial card. Far from abandoning resolutions in support of the Quebec scheme as redundant, he sought to bring to a conclusion the month-long debate in the Assembly to avoid any suspicion of Canadian second thoughts. The British government, he told the Assembly, had already given its 'sanction and approval' and Confederation 'has met, or will meet, with the unmistakable approbation and sanction of the Parliament, the press and the people of England'. The idea that British North America should 'cease to be a source of embarrassment, and become, in fact, a source of strength' had raised the provinces 'in the estimation of the people and Government of England'. Accordingly, a ministerial mission would be sent across the Atlantic to discuss Confederation, defence and Reciprocity, with a view to reporting back to a special session of the legislature in the early summer.[26] The equation between Confederation and defence had moved a stage beyond the after-dinner rhetoric of the previous autumn: it now provided a desperately needed lifeline to keep the coalition in being. Sandfield Macdonald and Dorion pressed hard to be told whether the government would introduce George Brown's 'pet scheme' for an immediate federation of the Canadas.[27] Brown was stung into endorsing John A's argument: the ministerial mission would go 'home' to discuss Confederation and 'other grave matters', defence and Reciprocity.[28]

Mere lip-service was not enough: Macdonald insisted that Brown should join the mission to Britain. As early as the previous August, Brown's unease with his new allies had led him to confess that 'were our visit to the Lower Provinces and to England once over, I would not care how soon a rupture came'.[29] They had stormed the Maritimes and Brown had gone on to conquer the official world of London. Between mid-November 1864 and mid-January 1865, he had spent twenty-three days on the Atlantic. It is not surprising that both his political and personal inclinations were against taking ship for Britain so soon afterwards. Brown's insistence on a reaffirmation of commitment to his 'pet scheme', and Macdonald's demands that Brown travel to Britain to lobby for Confederation, brought the Great Coalition close to collapse on 23 March.[30] The fragile alliance managed to survive, but Brown had still not agreed to travel. While he was considering, Lee surrendered and Lincoln was murdered. Macdonald now played the defence card to prevent Brown from escaping.

'The surrender of Lee & the Close of the War bring matters to a crisis between England & Canada,' he wrote to Brown on 11 April. There was a danger that 'the United States, flushed with success, with their armies full of fight' might force a 'sudden and speedy' crisis. Yet equally, 'we may look for peace for a series of years',[31] for it was just as likely that the Americans would have had their fill of fighting and would concentrate on demobilisation. The defence card, in short, had Brown trumped. The bedrock of his political strength lay not just in Upper Canada, but in the region westward from Toronto, the section of the province which Jervois had so bluntly indicated would have to abandoned in time of war to the armies which had fought under Sherman and Grant. Brown could not refuse to join a mission to Britain to discuss the protection of his people. Yet if he was the voice of Upper Canada, so too was he the friend of economy in government. It might be, as Macdonald speculated, that the burdensome cost of a local defence budget would in fact be unnecessary. Again, Brown could not afford to allow Canada to be sucked into the penury and jobbery all too likely to result from a delegation made up of his political opponents: Galt, notorious for the massive deficit he had created as finance minister; Cartier, who lived in the pocket of the Grand Trunk; and Macdonald, in Brown's eyes capable of any evil. To keep the coalition together, Macdonald had to ensure that Brown went along with its policy by taking part in the delegation to London: left behind in Canada, he would soon find a reason for dissociating himself from Confederation and reclaim his position in the Reform ranks. Hence the Confederation issue had to be tied to the defence crisis.

British ministers also had political reasons for subsuming the defence of the provinces under the heading of Confederation. The cabinet had already discussed the defence of Canada before news arrived in July 1864 of the unexpected change of ministry in the province.[32] Determined to prune government expenditure, Gladstone ingeniously took advantage of Canada's political turnabout to argue for British North American union as an alternative to large-scale works on defence.[33] On 23 July, ministers deliberated for two hours, a 'stiff Cabinet chiefly on Canada Defences'.[34] Cardwell felt that if there had been no British troops in the province, it would have been easy to have refused help until the Canadians provided the necessary fortifications. Unfortunately, the troops were already in Canada, creating the 'dilemma' of whether to pull them out or provide them with proper protection. Since there was no plan to withdraw, there would have to be a programme to upgrade their protection. Gladstone gloomily agreed. His object was to transfer the primary responsibility for colonial defence to the provinces themselves, but 'the Cabinet as a whole is not prepared at the present time, & perhaps never may be prepared, to proceed upon such a basis'.[35] Palmerston tersely cut short ministerial deliberations: the idea of abandoning British North America might make abstract sense, 'but that is not the opinion of England, and it is not mine'.[36]

Gladstone, then, had failed in his initial attempt to make Confederation a substitute for the strengthening of the defences of British North America. In the early summer of 1864, British ministers had little information about the policy of the new Canadian ministry, and no way of knowing whether its project to unite the provinces would be any more fruitful than the 1858 initiative. Far from being interwoven with the issue of Confederation, the question of Canadian defence was one of many factors in the developing fragmentation of domestic politics. Monck had been assured by a member of the cabinet a year earlier that the government's prospects were 'good ... as long as Lord Palmerston lives — but après!'.[37] In 1864, Palmerston was approaching his eightieth birthday, and jockeying for the succession had begun. Gladstone's attempt in May 1864 to nail his colours to the cause of further parliamentary reform had faltered, although it was unlikely that the issue would go away. It was an open secret that Palmerston regarded Gladstone as 'a dangerous man' who should be 'muzzled' and Canada was one the questions on which he found his chancellor 'troublesome and wrong-headed'.[38]

In July 1864, the ministry only just survived a vote of censure on its refusal to support tiny Denmark against warlike Prussia — an issue with uncomfortable parallels to the Canadian problem — and Palmerston's speech showed signs of the toll of passing years. Gladstone briefly thought the censure motion would force a general election, and even dangled a Commons seat under the eyes of Arthur Gordon, who was on leave looking for somebody to marry him. There was something to be said for Gordon's insensitive comment that it would be best if Palmerston 'should drop down dead' before the election came, since his continuing presence at the helm merely meant that nobody could be sure what questions a new parliament would be mandated to tackle and whose eventual leadership the electors were endorsing.[39] The negotiations between the Canadian delegation and British ministers came to a head in the first half of June 1865. The elections took place in July.

It was understandable that Cardwell was nervous about the impact of any delegation from Canada. 'I trust the tone of your Ministers will be reasonable,' he warned Monck, 'for much will depend upon their tone in the effect of their visit on public opinion here.'[40] In a Commons debate in March 1865, there had been 'a strong undercurrent of feeling' supporting the view of Robert

Lowe, who bluntly argued that the province could not be defended at all.[41] Lowe was an influential figure in the House, a former minister and regular leader writer for *The Times*. The *Saturday Review* regarded him as a kind of cathartic safety valve:

> many members probably felt that it was really a very difficult thing to understand how any force we could possibly send to Canada could defend it against the overwhelming strength of the Federal army .... and they were therefore not disinclined to hear Mr. Lowe say broadly that English troops in Canada were altogether useless.[42]

The Canadians recognised that they were dealing with a ministry which was 'very shaky'. Brown felt that in discussion with the British, the delegates invariably had the better of logical argument, 'but then comes the question of what the House of Commons will do, & what will be the effect on the elections & how the Americans may regard such bold measures'.[43]

The political needs of two divided ministries conspired to conflate defence with Confederation through a sleight of hand which has misled many historians. The British did not put pressure on the provinces by threatening to abandon their commitment to their defence, because they could not do so. Cobden's argument that 'the almost intangible thread of political connexion between the new British North American Confederation & the Mother Country should be amicably severed' was simply not practical politics.[44] 'Are we to kick them off?' asked the Duke of Argyll incredulously. 'Would Cobden recommend Cardwell to go down to Parliament and introduce this policy and write out ditto to Monck?'[45]

The negotiations with the Canadian delegation extended over seven weeks. This was deliberate policy on the part of the British. They wished to be 'sure that any Canadian proposals with respect to defence were spontaneous & not mere reflections of imaginary wishes here'.[46] It was also important that the delegates should absorb the feeling of British opinion, for it was in the wider miasma of political discourse that Confederation was beginning to be made the price for continuing support. 'That we cannot pretend to coerce our colonies into union it is needless to say,' admitted *The Times*, '... but it will be open to us to observe that the contributions made from the Imperial treasury towards colonial administration may be regulated by our conceptions of true colonial interests.'[47]

In his first interview with Cardwell, on 26 April, Galt had stated that whereas the previous November the Canadian government had favoured deferring a full defence review until after the expected union of the provinces, subsequent friction with the United States made defence 'much more urgent', so much so that even the construction of fortifications was no answer, since they could not be ready in time. While both British and Canadian ministers spoke of defence and Confederation as interrelated questions, the sharpest arguments focused on Canada alone, for 'no subsequent exertions could ever redeem the disasters that would have fallen upon the people of that Province' in the event of an American invasion.[48] The Canadians demanded a British naval force on the Lakes. Cardwell dismissed this as 'impossible': in peacetime, it was ruled out by the convention of 1817 and 'if that worst of all calamities, a War with the United States shall break out, we must be free to dispose of the Navy & the Army according to the exigencies of that terrible time, unembarrassed by any precise stipulations like these'. The most the British would offer was that gunboats would be placed on the Lakes 'if at any time, on our own responsibility, we think it judicious to do so', and provided that Canada had already taken steps to strengthen local defences.[49] Brown's subsequent jubilation that the delegates had 'received strong assurances that all the troops at England's disposal & the whole Navy of Great Britain will be used for the defence of every portion of Canada in the event of war' seems to have been yet another example of his ability to mislead himself.[50]

Fortunately, by the time the negotiations seemed to have reached a sticking point, it had become clear that the optimists had been right in their belief that victory over the South had for the time being exhausted the desire of the Northern States for conflict. 'All fear of war is supposed to be passed,' Brown noted at the end of May.[51] Brown was very satisfied with the outcome, for Canada's professed willingness to spend its money 'had choked off the cry that we will do nothing towards defence', while in practice the province had been able to escape from any major commitment.[52]

Cardwell summarised the outcome of the negotiations in a despatch which he immediately published. The Canadians had asked for a loan guarantee to pay for defence works to the west of Montreal, and had intimated that if this were not forthcoming, the whole question would probably have to 'await the decision of the

Government and Legislature of the United Provinces'. The British had recognised the merits of the Canadian point of view, but inverted the package, urging that the provincial legislature should formulate its policy before asking for the loan guarantee. However, both sides agreed 'that priority in point of time should be given to the Confederation of the Provinces'.[53] Nor was this an accidental convergence. Gladstone claimed victory in having manoeuvred the delegates 'to place Confederation in the foreground of the whole affair, which is very much what I had wished'.[54] Clarendon had argued that the delegation 'must not be sent home quite empty handed' for fear of the impact upon Canadian public opinion:[55] the promise of unspecified British support to carry Confederation was a cheap substitute. Defence and Confederation had intersected not to provide a cast-iron explanation for historians, but to enable two divided ministries to appear to be responding to a crisis while in reality both had succeeded in avoiding decisive action. It was ironic that British unease about the defensibility of the inland province of Canada should spawn a circular despatch aimed at putting pressure on the Maritimes.

'We should like to be informed as to the steps to be taken to press the Confederation,' the delegates asked as the negotiations reached their awkward phase early in June.[56] Well might they ask, for their own approach was far from clear: Cartier had begun the talks by assuring Cardwell that the Canadians 'in no respect contemplated any thing approaching to an undue interference with the expression of popular opinion' in the Maritimes. Since defence 'was most intimately connected with the Union', the British government 'might properly exercise a very great influence through a decided expression of their views'.[57] Cardwell did not find it easy to answer the question, and sought to discuss 'the feasibilities and prudentialities of putting pressure on New Brunswick' with Cartier and Macdonald after the formal talks. 'I am anxious to turn the screw as hard as will be useful, but not harder.'[58] The metaphor hid British impotence in a fog of words. The *Spectator* doubted whether Britain had any influence over New Brunswick beyond 'force of argument'.[59] The *Saturday Review* doubted whether even that would work. 'The bulk of the voters in New Brunswick will give their suffrages with reference to what they conceive to be the interests of their own little country, rather than with deference to what may seem due to the Mother-country.'[60]

Cardwell's despatch of 24 June 1865 to the governors of the four Atlantic provinces left no doubt that the British government wished 'that all the British North American Colonies should agree to unite in one government'. Moreover, 'the Colonies must recognize a right, and even acknowledge an obligation, incumbent on the Home Government to urge with earnestness and just authority the measures which they consider to be most expedient on the part of the Colonies with a view to their own defence.'[61]

The effect of this despatch is hard to measure. Over the following two years, it probably underscored the rhetorical argument that Confederation would mean stronger defence, and in time of crisis that sort of rhetoric was probably persuasive. In the shorter term, Cardwell's despatch may even have rebounded, stinging Maritime anti-Confederates into resentment against British meddling. On Prince Edward Island, the population of small farmers and 'petty shop and store keepers' talked indignantly of British 'insolence', adopting attitudes which struck a visitor as 'utterly out of proportion to the size and value of the island which they inhabit'. The New Brunswick Executive Council replied in a scorching and sarcastic minute, pointing out that self-government would be 'a mockery if ... the wish of the mother country was in all cases to be followed', in the face of contrary opinions by the local government 'who, being on the spot, and fully conversant with the subject, considered themselves not unable to judge with respect to their own affairs'. Cardwell aloofly dismissed the reply as 'somewhat uncivil' but he may have grasped that waving the big stick could be counterproductive, especially if the stick turned out to be a twig.[62]

Similarly, the threat to end the anomaly by which imperial funds were provided to pay the salary of the governor of Prince Edward Island could only seem bullying and petty. It was not a threat which could be levelled at the other Maritime provinces, which already paid for their own governors, nor was it even credibly timed, since a cost-conscious British government would before long probably seek to excise the item on some other pretext.[63] Certainly Cardwell had seemed to agree when MacDonnell had warned that 'the least semblance of dictation would be most impolitic'.[64] When in the summer of 1866, Governor Musgrave of Newfoundland requested that his colony be officially warned of the consequences of its 'ignorant persistence in the policy of isolation', Arthur Blackwood doubted 'the wisdom of writing such very strong despatches to a weak Colony. They can scarcely fail to be construed as a menace'. Confederation, he argued, would not work if Newfoundlanders felt that it had been 'initiated or forced on them' by the British government. Frederic Rogers agreed: any British threat to reduce its naval and military protection would hardly be credible, since Britain was committed to supporting Newfoundland in the fisheries dispute with France. The incoming colonial secretary, Carnarvon — who a decade later proved himself to be highly interventionist in South Africa — also concluded that there was little that Britain could do to influence Newfoundland opinion. 'Some pressure from home may be necessary: but I doubt that the time for this has yet come.'[65] As the prime minister, Lord Derby, flatly stated in September 1866, 'we are not going to over ride the Local Legislatures but to induce them to concur'.[66]

Far from forcing the half million people of Nova Scotia and New Brunswick to wilt under the terrifying frown of imperial displeasure, one immediate purpose of Cardwell's despatches was to silence New Brunswick's obstinate and wayward governor, Arthur Gordon.[67] Thanks to the lush archival sources which were the hallmark of social eminence in nineteenth-century Britain, a great deal can be reconstructed of government attempts to ensure that Gordon restrained his sharp-tongued dislike for the Quebec scheme — he may even have been the author of the minute rebuking Cardwell[68] — and fell into line in its support. It can only have been embarrassing for the colonial minister of the world's greatest empire to receive messages from New Brunswick's Tilley bluntly urging him to 'communicate his opinions pretty clearly to the Gentlemen who represent Her Majesty out here'.[69] In reality, the entire Gordon episode casts its own light on the hollowness of the 'imperial factor'. It was absurd that any colonial governor should think himself entitled to act as an autonomous policy-maker merely because his father had been prime minister: even cabinet ministers sometimes had to swallow their doubts and follow an agreed line, Cardwell pleaded, and surely the governor of a colony could conscientiously follow instructions?[70] If a major achievement of the might of the British empire was to ensure that a functionary who was — as Cardwell ruefully noted — 'not easily turned'[71] actually obeyed the instructions he had received, it is necessary to re-assess the majesty and effectiveness of imperial power.

Cardwell tried to make his meaning clear when he assured Gordon of his intention 'to avoid all appearance of *undue* pressure, or of dictation, but at the same time to let it be thoroughly understood that this question of Confederation is one in which the Home Government is quite in earnest: & considers that its wishes ought to have & will have great weight with the Provinces'.[72] From Gladstone, there came a terser message, all the more significant because Gordon regarded the chancellor as his mentor — a role which had given Gladstone much reason for vexation.[73] Confederation was 'a great measure: and one which ... it is the right and duty of England to press forward in a special manner'. New Brunswick should 'reflect well on the great effect which her course may produce in regard to our responsibilities for her defence'.[74] Eventually Cardwell lost patience and compelled Gordon to supply a written undertaking that he would obey instructions and support Confederation.[75] The upshot was that the complex Gordon took what was probably unconscious revenge by embroiling himself in an unnecessary constitutional dispute over the exercise of his authority in April 1866, which placed Confederation in jeopardy at just the moment when a number of local politicians were coming round to some form of acceptance.[76]

Overall, it seems likely that despatches from the Colonial Office which argued the case for Confederation 'with just a faint admixture of scolding'[77] were as likely to offend as to persuade Maritimers. The element of pressure lay not in the power of the British government over its colonies, but rather in the possibility that on other matters affecting the provinces, ministers could not command parliament and public opinion, thus again widening the definition of the term 'British' in the manner argued in Chapter Four. It is in this context that the loan guarantee for the Intercolonial railway should be viewed. This was not something which the British threw in as a carrot in 1865, but a promise made three years earlier. It became an incentive for Confederation through a process of hint and bluff, not by the outright mechanisms of bribe and threat.

To understand how this came about, it is necessary first to clarify just what was involved. The British government was not offering to provide money. Rather it was proposing to underwrite Canadian borrowing, promising that should the province default, the money would be repaid by the British taxpayer. 'Canada is poor, and her credit ... does not enable her to borrow on the terms which the English Government can command.' City opinion in 1861 held that Canada was 'likely to have difficulty' in borrowing at any rate of interest 'unless she is supported by the credit of the British Exchequer'. In principle, there was no reason why a loan guarantee should involve any cost to the British Exchequer: however, Gladstone's opposition in 1861-2 was directed against the likelihood that Canada was so badly managed that the province would in fact default and merely sought 'to put her hand into the purse of England'.[78] Newcastle had a stiff fight to secure any form of endorsement from the cabinet, and at one stage despaired of his chances. 'The high Canadian Tariff has raised a host of opponents to any expenditure for the material interest of the Colony'.[79] He was pleasantly surprised — in view of the 'repugnance of a large number in the Cabinet to give *any* aid'[80] — to secure general endorsement by a single vote in a rare instance of a formal ministerial head count.[81] There were, however, two important conditions and one vital contingency. The first condition was that the provinces had to meet terms acceptable to the British government. Gladstone's insistence upon a sinking fund, a commitment to repayment of the capital sum by annual instalments, led to the collapse of the Intercolonial railway talks in the autumn of 1862. Far from relaxing its terms to provide an incentive for Confederation, the Treasury continued to insist upon a sinking fund even after the passage of the British North America Act. The second condition was that agreement had to be secured to implement the loan guarantee by December 1867. It was this provision which enabled George Brown to claim and Henri Joly to object that the money to build the railway was already secured. Cardwell seemed to confirm this interpretation during the negotiations with the Canadian delegation in 1865, telling Cartier and Galt that if Canada wished to use the railway as a lever for winning support in the Maritimes, the province had 'the means of applying the requisite pressure, as the Guarantee depended upon her assent to the terms upon which the Government had undertaken to recommend it to Parliament'.[82]

The crucial contingency of the 1862 promise lay in that last phrase. The cabinet by itself could not promise legislation: as Cardwell reminded Gordon, 'our engagement is that we will ask Parliament to back that guarantee'. When the guarantee finally came before parliament in 1867, Gladstone insisted that it 'was always made clear to the colonial authorities that it was not within our power or inclination to fetter the judgment of the House of Commons'.[83] In strict constitutional terms, this was true, but under normal circumstances, such a promise would be the equivalent of money in the bank, for any ministry introducing enabling legislation to parliament would be implicitly making its passage a question of confidence. The mid-1860s, however, were not normal times: the expected departure of Palmerston and the likely irruption of the Reform question had introduced fundamental elements of instability into politics, to add to cross-currents of unease about colonial issues. Once again, it was sudden coincidence rather than the satisfying neatness of historical explanation that threw doubt upon the Intercolonial loan guarantee.

As outlined in Chapter Four, a powerful strand of British opinion was irritated with Canada between 1862 and 1864. The decision by the city of Hamilton to repudiate its debts damaged Canadian credit,[84] and resentment against Canada's tariff again simmered when Galt's reply to the Sheffield manufacturers was published in 1864. Yet none of this seemed to shake the Intercolonial loan guarantee. Indeed, in one of his last ministerial acts, Newcastle actually added a new dimension to it. The British government agreed that the cost of any line constructed between Truro in Nova Scotia and 'the Bend' (Moncton in New Brunswick) would be retrospectively regarded as covered by the Intercolonial loan guarantee, on the terms previously agreed. This meant that Nova Scotia and New Brunswick could attempt to start construction of the connecting line from their own resources, but that subsidised finance would hinge on subsequent agreement with the province of Canada for the entire project. For Nova Scotians, this tied any early prospect of rail communication with the rest of North America not to Confederation but to a railway line from Moncton to Rivière-du-Loup. Cardwell not only inherited this adjustment of the British offer, but on 25 June 1864 officially forwarded the correspondence to Monck, a clear hint that action was needed to invoke the loan guarantee before the promise expired.[85] How, then, do we find Cardwell warning the governor-general just three weeks later that it was 'doubtful' whether parliament would honour the 1862 promise?[86]

The explanation lay in the fact that ministers had just received a bad fright in attempting to carry similar legislation to underwrite a loan for the delinquent colony of New Zealand. With some reluctance, Cardwell had agreed to propose a bill authorising a loan guarantee of one million pounds, half of which was to enable New Zealand to repay debts it already owed to the British Treasury, with much of the rest to pay for four years of war against the Maori.[87] The wars in New Zealand had shocked humanitarian opinion in Britain, and had already cost the British taxpayer so much that in 1864 Palmerston's government actually cancelled the annual mobilisation of Britain's volunteer cavalry force, the Yeomanry, to cut overall defence costs — the sort of gesture which would have brought a cascade of scholarly censure on the head of a Sandfield Macdonald.[88] One week before the New Zealand loan legislation came before the Commons, news arrived of the disaster later known as the battle of Gate Pa. British troops had stormed a Maori position, only to be overwhelmed by the defenders.[89] It seemed that British lives were being sacrificed in a rapacious war which even the troops themselves lacked the heart to fight.[90] On 14 July, the bill secured a second reading by 92 votes to 55: ministers prudently decided to make concessions to survive the committee stage, where there was another sharp fight to block the measure.[91]

Both sides saw the link between New Zealand and Canada. For the government, Gladstone — no doubt against all his instincts — argued that since a loan had been guaranteed for public works in Canada 'some years back' (in fact in 1842) it would be inconsistent to refuse support to New Zealand. However, Cobden, the grand old man of the free trade cause, criticised colonies for refusing to impose direct taxation to meet their swelling debts and seeking instead to balance their books by the imposition of protectionist tariffs. Thus, helping colonies to borrow money by making loans cheap was actually hitting the British manufacturer, for it was 'very likely that in New Zealand, as in Canada, the Legislature may put an excessive duty upon imports so as materially to interfere with your trade'.[92] It was understandable that Cardwell felt that the promised guarantee for the Intercolonial would 'go bitterly against the grain with Parliament',[93] and the New Zealand episode remained a warning.[94] The British would have been less than human had they not used this evidence of what Monck called 'the abstract disinclination to guarantees which undoubtedly exists in the House of Commons'[95] to get a little blood from the colonial stone. Cardwell sought a more vigorous attitude to defence and a cut in the Canadian tariff.[96] Monck warned Macdonald that 'there would be a fight over the Railway guarantee'.[97]

Thus by sleight of hand, the Intercolonial railway guarantee offered in 1862 was presented to Maritimers as something contingent upon the achievement of Confederation. In Nova Scotia Sir Fenwick Williams 'preached the consequence of one upon the other' on the basis of a conversation with Glyn the banker, who had assured him that 'the money was ready, as soon as we tied the political knot'.[98] Yet when the British North America bill came before the Commons, ministers insisted that the controversial clause 145 merely pledged the provinces to begin work on the Intercolonial within six months of Confederation, and in no way committed parliament to finding the money. There may have been an element of openly recognised charade in this. There was indeed a sharp debate on 26 March 1867, during which Lowe eloquently denounced the Intercolonial guarantee as a bribe to the provinces 'to enter into this Confederation'. However, the procedure adopted was unusual: the substantive debate was held on a resolution in favour of the guarantee, and not on the second reading of the bill itself. By late March, the Reform crisis was at its height, and most members wished to reach a solution, any solution. None the less, some element of collusion may be suspected to provide an opportunity for critics to sound off — and thereby warn the new Dominion, as Gladstone did in unmistakeable terms, that Confederation was intended as a means of shifting the burden of defence to Canada — while ensuring that the legislation itself went through virtually without comment. In fact the second reading debate consisted of a protest by Stephen Gaselee that Adderley had first asked the House 'to assent to the Confederation Bill because it would not bind it to grant the guarantee', but had since announced 'that the guarantee must be given because the Confederation had been sanctioned by Parliament'. His complaint that Adderley had aimed 'to mislead a young Member like himself' suggests a note of humour, since Gaselee was approaching sixty years of age. There was no repetition of the blocking tactics which had been attempted against the New Zealand loan guarantee three years earlier.[99]

To appreciate the British role in the carrying of Confederation, then, it is necessary to focus not on the government's mythical strength in outfacing reluctant colonies but on its relative weakness in relation to parliament and public opinion. Paradoxically, the government's power — such as it was — lay in its ability to hint that without Confederation, the House of Commons might refuse to endorse funding for railway projects, or public opinion take fright at the implications of the commitment to maintain troops and fortifications in the provinces. For these tactics to work, it was vital that politicians like R.S. Aytoun, who objected to the Canadian tariff and opposed the Intercolonial railway guarantee, should nevertheless support Confederation in principle.[100] Similarly, it was crucial that *The Times*, even though it had denounced the Intercolonial, should hold firm in supporting the political unification of the provinces. Not only did the paper roundly denounce the defection of New Brunswick in 1865, but its editor, J.T. Delane, parted company on the issue with Robert Lowe, who had written its colonial leading articles for a dozen years past but was 'against compelling the lesser Colonies to confederate'.[101]

The Times was a respected force on both sides of the Atlantic. Cartier was proud when it quoted one of his speeches. Howe felt the lack of its support. 'The Times, when right, is so useful, and always so influential,' he wrote to Delane in 1866, 'that it is a national misfortune to have it go wrong.'[102] Sir Fenwick Williams, on the other hand, was 'glad to find the "Times" so zealous and talented in supporting the good cause', with beneficial effects on opinion in Nova Scotia.[103] Perhaps most impressive of all was the fact that Confederation had bipartisan support at a time when party identifications seemed to be dissolving on the issue of Reform. As leader of the opposition, Lord Derby made his party's support clear to A.J. Smith of New Brunswick.[104] Cardwell was reassured that Derby's comments 'will put an end to any idea that the English opposition will support him in resisting Confederation'. 'I won many a man to our side by this,' Williams later reported, 'proving that whichever side was "in", the scheme would be persevered in.'[105]

In seeking to explain how this wider British consensus operated, it is understandable that historians have tended to think in terms of the standard imperatives of 'financial imperialism' or military protection. Yet these explanatory strategies can produce a misleading picture. To appreciate the role played by the British, it is necessary to return to their basic sense of their superiority of rank and wisdom over mere colonials. Only rarely is it possible to recapture from the written record the behaviour which in modern parlance is referred to by such terms as interpersonal relations and body language. Take, for example, a discussion in London in December 1864 between George Brown and Sir Frederic Rogers. Brown was responding to Tilley's request that the Colonial Office should compel Arthur Gordon to fall into line in support of Confederation. Gordon's grumbling might not yet seem the open embarrassment it would become after the New Brunswick election a few months later, but on the face of it the Fathers of Confederation had a legitimate concern, even an outright grievance, about the behaviour of an imperial functionary. Rogers was a civil servant, Brown the accredited delegate of a self-governing province of two and a half million people: Rogers in fact regarded him as 'the Canadian Prime Minister'.[106] From a modern point of view, it would be easy to assume that the British civil servant would defer to the Canadian politician, express concern and promise action. In fact, the exchange was very different in tone. Brown avoided naming Gordon, but merely suggested 'that some of the Lieutenant Governors might be troublesome'.[107] ('Mr Gordon is a man who does his own thinking,' Brown diplomatically remarked to Cardwell,[108] who still regarded New Brunswick's governor as a personal friend.) Rogers was anything but deferential. 'He laughed & pooh-poohed it as coolly as you could imagine — said they understood all that sort of thing,' Brown reported to Tilley, '— but the Despatch going out on Saturday would settle it completely — & if not Mr Cardwell would not hesitate to see that the cordial aid of all the Governors was given to the scheme.'[109] Rogers had indeed told Brown what he wanted to hear, but his tone hardly suggested even a relationship between equals. Privately, Rogers wrote of Brown in terms more appropriate to a head footman. 'We have had the principal man here ... to talk it over,' wrote Rogers, in the same sentence in which he identified Brown as Canada's prime minister.[110] Cardwell viewed Brown in much the same light, patronisingly reporting — to the delinquent Gordon of all people — that he was 'much pleased with him'.[111] 'The social force of admitted superiority' which Walter Bagehot believed enabled a British minister to brush aside the objections of his senior civil servants clearly did not extend to visiting Canadian politicians.[112]

Although a Liberal in politics, Bagehot thoroughly approved of 'the *style* of society' in England, of the way in which 'the daily-spoken intercourse of human beings' reverenced rank rather than office or wealth.[113] The aura created by aristocracy was diffused to a broader elite by the public schools and the universities, in a series of widening circles depending on the prestige of individual institutions. By the early nineteenth century, Eton had become by far the most favoured school of the aristocracy and those who sought to join them, not for its educational merits, which were frankly minimal, but through a combination of royal patronage from nearby Windsor Castle and the fact that while convenient to London, it was less accessible to the beguiling wickednesses of a big city than its principal rivals, Westminster and Harrow. Although not an aristocrat by birth, Rogers was a product of Eton and Oriel College, Oxford, the home of the High Church Anglican movement. Carnarvon, Derby, Gladstone and the Duke of Newcastle had all moved from Eton to Christ Church, the most gilded of the Oxford colleges. So had Carnarvon's successor at the Colonial Office, the Duke of Buckingham, and the Duke of Somerset, who presided over the Admiralty when the Canadian delegates pressed for gunboats on the Lakes. Two parliamentary under-secretaries, the Whig Fortescue and the Conservative Adderley, were also Christ Church (or 'House') men. Arthur Blackwood had entered the Colonial Office straight from Harrow, Palmerston's old school. His father had been one of Nelson's vice-admirals at Trafalgar, and his cousin was the Earl of Dufferin. Elliot was related to the Earl of Minto: in 1865, it was natural for him to introduce the Canadian delegates to the leading Conservative politicians at Lady Salisbury's evening party, and then escort them to Lady Waldegrave's rival soirée to meet the Liberals.[114]

Even Cardwell was something of a new type, assimilated from a mercantile background by way of a less fashionable school, Winchester, and Balliol College, not yet the intellectual hotbed of Oxford. Yet Cardwell instinctively felt himself to be an insider in a special cohort of society. Arthur Gordon's problem, he tolerantly remarked, was that he had 'not acquired more experience from the rubs & kicks' of a public school education, for as a boy the frail Gordon had been schooled at home by tutors. Still, Gordon was the son of an earl and had attended Trinity College, Cambridge. Monck and MacDonnell, graduates of Trinity College, Dublin, were slightly marginal figures, although Monck's Irish peerage was an effective ticket to the club: Rogers praised him as 'a thorough gentleman'.[115] Outsiders from the British political world did not easily break into this select band. W.H. Smith, the wealthy newsagent, was blackballed when he sought to join the Reform Club in 1862, and the Reform Club was the unofficial headquarters of the Liberal party. Russell attempted to signal a new political beginning after Palmerston's death by appointing the Bradford merchant W.E. Forster as under-secretary for the colonies. Forster was an open supporter of a wider franchise, and his education had been confined to unfashionable Quaker schools. 'He is certainly a rough diamond, as strange a contrast to Fortescue's polished ... manner as can be well imagined,' wrote Rogers. 'But he seems a clear-headed, thinking, and not wrong-headed man, ready for work and very friendly.'[116] Forster was wealthy, and he had left the Society of Friends to join the Church of England. Yet even rich, Anglican and a minister of the Crown, he was still not a full member of the club.

The unforced sense of natural superiority with which Rogers rebuffed Brown could of course be irksome. Galt in particular was uneasy in London high society: 'I confess I would rather mix with my own class'.[117] Yet to understand the mechanism through which British support for Confederation operated, it is necessary to move away from the protection of red-coated soldiers and the investments of black-coated bankers in order to appreciate the powerful if intangible influences which could be brought to bear upon British North American politicians when a hierarchical élite was mobilised to emphasise a national priority. Colonists had not been notably welcome as visitors to British shores. Philip Vankoughnet commented in 1862 that a Canadian in London 'felt like a cat in a strange garret'[118] and Joseph Howe was outraged by the lack of attention he received as premier of Nova Scotia in London in the winter of 1861-62. The Duke of Newcastle apologised for the oversight, attributing it to the dislocation of official life consequent upon the death of the Prince Consort. Just how easily goodwill could be purchased was demonstrated when the duke invited the Howes to dinner at Clumber, making a point of showing them his family portraits in an after-dinner candle-light tour of the great house.[119] Yet Newcastle did not exactly welcome the presence of colonials in Britain. He responded icily on learning in 1863 that the Canadian ministry contemplated sending 'a Political Agent (a sort of Ambassador)' to reside in London. 'Pray discourage so great a folly', he enjoined Monck.[120]

By contrast, the visit by George Brown to London in December 1864 and the mission of the Canadian delegation from April to June 1865 were lionised with an energy which was intended to convey the political importance of Confederation to the British. 'No amount of wealth would secure the attention we receive,' Galt commented, adding a trifle naively that 'these attentions are given not to us but to our offices, and in compliment to our people.' Although it was obvious that if the Canadians had not been official representatives, 'these people would not bother their heads about one of us', even the uneasy Galt found it 'pleasant to be the recipient of marks of attention'.[121] 'It has always been the complaint of Colonial statesmen that while every other nation was received with distinction in London, the inhabitants of the dominions of the Crown were passed over...' noted *The Times*. It was thus significant that the Canadian ministers had been 'received in London with unusual distinction; they were, in fact, fêted in a most remarkable manner'.[122]

If a crucial precondition for the achievement of Confederation was that George Brown should be kept from bolting from the Great Coalition, then the reception which he received in England between December 1864 and June 1865 should be regarded as an important influence. In announcing Brown's first visit, Monck had commented that he was 'an able and earnest man, but rather impulsive'.[123] Cardwell probably hinted to Brown, as he did to Monck, that Confederation was a subject 'of great interest ... in the highest quarters', a discreet reference to Queen Victoria, who lived in cloistered widowhood.[124] Brown took 'a very warm & natural interest in all that bore upon the Queen's feelings as to the British North American Provinces', and even urged that she should emerge from seclusion to open the first Confederation parliament in person.[125] That Brown should entertain such an unlikely notion was a measure of his romantic attraction to monarchy. The Queen had 'laughed very heartily, saying she was afraid of the sea' to a similar suggestion from Galt in the happier times of 1858. By December 1864 the widow of Windsor insisted that her nerves were '*so* shattered that *any* emotion, *any* discussion, *any* exertion causes much disturbance and suffering to her whole frame' and that even to open parliament at Westminster in person was 'totally out of the question'.[126] Cardwell felt some concern that the impulsive Brown might drag the Queen's name into political debate in Canada, which would be bad form.[127] What was clear was that the sun of British approval was shining on the messenger of Confederation: Brown 'was obviously getting what another age would call the full treatment'.[128] He had 'a wonderfully gracious reception' at the Colonial Office. Gladstone was 'immensely civil'. Cardwell gave a 'grand party' at which Brown 'got on capitally' with two cabinet ministers and an admiral.[129]

Brown lapped up the attention, and probably did not realise how much of it had been orchestrated. For instance, the crowning glory of his mission was a celebrated visit to the prime minister at his country house in Hampshire. Palmerston extended the invitation through Cardwell, expressing a wish to meet 'Mr Brown and make his acquaintance'.[130] 'I feel it would be wrong of me to refuse,' Brown loftily assured his wife, who was waiting for him in Scotland, 'as the result may be very advantageous to Canada'.[131] In fact, it had been Brown who had dropped the hint that he wished to meet Lord Palmerston, and Cardwell had prompted the invitation. Delane of *The Times* was asked to join the party.[132] Snow fell as if to welcome the visitor from Canada, but the doughty octogenarian host was not deterred from sallying forth on to his estate. 'Brown, will you take a walk?' Palmerston asked. 'You don't mind snow, do you?' The significance of the remark lay less in the joke, as in the form of address. The visitor was not 'Mr Brown', a style appropriate to respectable tradesmen, attorneys and the run of colonial politicians, but plain 'Brown' — the man-to-man accolade which conferred temporary membership of the élite. It is no wonder that Brown returned to Canada 'enchanted with his visit'.[133]

If attention was lavished on Brown in December 1864, the Canadian delegation of 1865 was positively drenched in the champagne of social approval. 'Civilities of all kinds continue to pour in upon us,' Brown reported to his wife: 'we are great people — very'.[134] Some allowance must be made for the fact that this time Anne Brown had been left behind, and that her husband wished to cheer her with an account of his exploits, but Brown was enjoying himself. Lord Derby — already twice prime minister — was 'a very agreeable old fellow'. It was 'great fun' to meet Bishop Wilberforce — 'Soapy Sam' to his many detractors — whose mind was closed to all new ideas, even to the extent of asking whether Darwin believed that 'turnips are tending to become men?'. 'I could not have believed that such a specimen of fossilized humanity was to be found in this City of London in the year 1865.'[135] Then there was the Duke of Cambridge, commander-in-chief of the army, and grandson of George III who 'pitched into the Ministry like fun for not doing all we asked at once'.[136]

The high spot was presentation at court along with 'the great notabilities of the Empire'. Much to their 'astonishment & no little alarm', the delegates were told that the Queen wished to receive them first: 'all the Dukes & Duchesses had to give way & open up a passage for us — very much to their astonishment'.[137] They were presented a second time with the diplomatic corps a fortnight later, and then received a command to attend a musical party at Buckingham Palace. Chambermaids crowded on to the balconies of the hotel to watch the delegates set off for the Palace in dress uniform. The Queen chatted informally: Mrs Brown and the baby should come to stay at Balmoral in 1866.[138] The young Prince of Wales also went out of his way to be gracious. The delegates were invited to accompany him to watch the loading of telegraph wire on the *Great Eastern* for the transatlantic cable, and the Prince organised a special Canadian dinner, a reunion for those who had accompanied him on his tour of the province in 1860. 'It seems odd to be visiting on such comparatively easy terms our future King and Queen,' Galt noted, commenting that the Danish-born Princess Alexandra had 'the nicest possible foreign accent'.[139] He was too much the Victorian to add that she was also heavily pregnant, and her appearance at dinner was a compliment to the Canadians. Four days later, she gave birth to her second child. Brown loyally sent his congratulations, and received a message in return that the Princess was one ahead of Anne Brown in the motherhood stakes. 'Not bad that — for a Princess!', Brown reported home.[140] So shrewd and suspicious in colonial politics, Brown does not seem to have guessed that having just given birth to the future George V, Alexandra probably had other matters to consider than matching her fecundity against the wife of a colonial politician.

Brown gradually became tired of 'this magical little circle they call "society"'.[141] The people he met 'are a different race from us, different ideas, different aspirations & however well it may be to see what the thing is like — it takes no hold on your feelings or even of your respect.'[142] Part of him resented 'the cool assumption of superiority over the middle classes', but mostly he revelled in the sense that Confederation was supported by such great personages. 'I know the Queen the Prince of Wales, the Duke of Cambridge, Lord Palmerston, Lord DeGrey the Duke of Somerset the Duke of Argylle & Mr Cardwell are thoroughly with us.'[143]

Galt also noted that 'we have got the Court party on our side, and this will be of the greatest use'.[144] Yet Galt saw the implications which the star-struck Brown had missed. 'We are treated quite as if we were ambassadors and not as *mere Colonists* as we have always been called.' Galt accepted that their reception 'proves how important our mission is considered',[145] but he felt that 'it bodes no good, however flattering it may be'. Brown saw only the astonished faces of the aristocrats ordered to give place to Canada's representatives; Galt was uneasy at being 'treated ... too much as ambassadors'.[146] Cardwell summarised his despatch on the negotiations to Monck: 'it treats Canada as a quasi-independent country, primarily responsible for the measures chiefly necessary for its own defence, though assured of the powerful support of England when doing its duty to itself & to her'.[147] He hoped the point had been noted that 'careful attention' had to be given to the 'growing sensitiveness here' about colonial defence, 'respecting which your very acute & observant advisers must have carried away with them, after their extended intercourse with society here, a very decided impression'.[148] The mobilisation of 'society' gave the Canadian delegates a sense of self-importance — but one which, as Galt sourly recognised, was directed at the work in which they were engaged. It also enabled Cardwell to convey by hint rather than by open threat that a more robust attitude to the local defence of the provinces was overdue.

Similar techniques were employed on anti-Confederate lobbyists who arrived in London, though with less obvious success. Any innate respect which 'Prime Minister Smith' of New Brunswick, as Cardwell sarcastically dubbed him, might have held for the British élite had been badly dented by his experience of its local representative, Arthur Gordon.[149] Self-educated in a small-town law office, Smith had begun his political career by voicing 'deep rooted prejudice' against Fredericton's tiny university, which he saw as a privileged institution catering for the rich. He was twice physically assaulted by political opponents, and he lashed back when Gordon secured his dismissal in 1862 for alleged misuse of the office of attorney-general. When Newcastle upheld his disgrace, Smith in an open letter contrasted the duke's high imperial role with his own humble and provincial status. 'Nevertheless my character and reputation are as dear to me, as yours are to you.'[150]

Cardwell was optimistic that the New Brunswick ministers would be swayed by 'what they see here' and return to seek face-saving changes in the Quebec scheme in order to carry Confederation.[151] Smith was told that Palmerston believed 'that the *pivot* on which the future Defences of Canada by England & themselves turned was *Confederation*'. Sir Fenwick Williams described Smith's visit to Lord Derby as going '*into an enemy's Camp*'.[152] In the short term, Cardwell had to admit defeat: 'the Minister of New Brunswick returns fully impressed with the almost universal feeling of this country, yet I fear he is unshaken in his own determination to oppose to the uttermost'.[153] Cardwell could only hope that the New Brunswick anti-Confederates were 'much impressed ... with the universal wish in this country for the Scheme, and oppressed with the responsibility which attaches to them if they oppose the public policy here, and the majority of their fellow subjects in British North America'.[154] In this, Cardwell partly missed the point that Smith professed himself in favour of a different and closer form of political union although, within a very limited field for manoeuvre, Cardwell hinted that the scheme might be changed. For his part, Smith found the colonial secretary 'an extremely pleasant and agreeable man' and was convinced 'that no attempt will be made to force us into the scheme'.[155] Still, the unanimity and determination of the British created unease in the minds of some opponents. From Newfoundland, Musgrave reported 'a latent conviction' that the island would be legislated into a union whether it liked it or not,[156] while even so robust an opponent as William Annand warned Smith that 'the exertions of the British Government' might make it 'necessary to deal practically with the Union question'[157] — sufficient reason in March 1866 for both men to begin to consider covering their own retreat.

If the unanimity of the British élite had no more than a delayed action upon Smith, it worked on Joseph Howe, if at all, only when Confederation was a *fait accompli* in 1868. The arts of flattery were bungled in 1865, but used more ruthlessly to blunt Howe's attack on the eve of Confederation. In July 1865, with Nova Scotia undoubtedly cool towards the Quebec scheme, Tupper urged that Howe — who was serving as an imperial fisheries commissioner — should be summoned to Britain on official business in the belief that 'he might easily be converted into a supporter of Confederation'.[158] The ploy failed — not least because Howe arrived in August, when high society had abandoned London. Quick to realise that 'they are very anxious to get my support' and probably offended that not even Cardwell was in town to greet him, Howe took the opportunity to enjoy a leisurely holiday on public funds and to draft memoranda against Confederation.[159]

One reason why Howe was relatively ineffective in his campaign against Confederation in Britain the following year was that he attempted to combine his outright opposition to British policy with a wish to cultivate personal contacts with leading politicians. Carnarvon exploited this ambivalence, flattering Howe by inviting his comments, holding out false hopes that ministers might be persuaded to drop Confederation without an all-out public campaign. Sir Frederic Rogers advised Carnarvon to meet Howe and his associates, and convey the view 'that Union was the proper thing for the interests of British North America, and for the interests of this country, and that it was a step which this Country had a right to expect from those who relied on her for defence'. However, Rogers advised a certain detachment, the pose 'of a person who has still to ascertain whether the result which he thinks abstractly best can ... be reduced into practical shape'. It would be preferable to allow ministerial leanings towards Confederation 'to be seen than state it in quotable language'.[160] As Rogers had shown in warning George Brown to back off from criticism of Arthur Gordon, Eton and Christ Church provided a fine training for the conveyance of subtle messages. 'Nothing could be more gracious and kindly than our reception,' Howe wrote of the subsequent interview at the Colonial Office.[161] Carnarvon appeared open-minded, and it seemed that nothing would be decided 'until after the Christmas Holidays'.[162] 'I am glad of the opportunity which has made me acquainted with one who has played so continuous & leading a part in British North America as yourself,' wrote Carnarvon, at the beginning of January 1867, repeating a wish to have Howe's views on Confederation.[163] Howe replied that he was flattered, and asked for a copy of the amended scheme agreed by the delegates at the Westminster Palace Hotel.[164] It transpired that the amended resolutions were not quite complete, not in a convenient form for communication, would be better withheld until the cabinet had considered them.[165]

In short, Howe was being strung along and lured into a trap. 'Remember that just at present Howe does not know exactly what to strike at,' Rogers advised as the delegates worked on their final draft at the Westminster Palace Hotel. 'The moment he sees the extent of change which has been made in the Resolutions, he can organize his campaign. The later he is in a position to do this the better.' Rogers even contemplated the possibility of repeating the strategy of sending 'a spirited kind of despatch' to Nova Scotia, which would openly accuse Howe of wishing to break the link with Britain and make acceptance of Confederation 'a test of genuine Loyalty to the British connexion'.[166] In the absence of a precise target, Howe had succumbed to the temptation to hare off in support of his favourite scheme of imperial federation, which Adderley dismissed as 'futile and visionary' when introducing the British North America bill to the Commons.[167]

It cannot be argued that half a million Nova Scotians and New Brunswickers were brow-beaten into Confederation because a handful of their politicians were cold-shouldered in the fashionable salons of London. The social atmosphere helps to explain how British 'pressure' was conveyed, piecing out official threats by combining a determination to see Confederation carried for its own sake with a degree of uncertainty about the longer-term commitment to support the provinces. It was subtle, it was formidable, but it does not in itself explain why Nova Scotia and New Brunswick swung from apparently fervent opposition to Confederation in 1865 to sullen acceptance a year later. The unquestioning acceptance by most historians of the reality of 'British pressure' has unwittingly contributed to the distortion of the basic description of what was happening in Nova Scotia and New Brunswick between 1864 and 1866. Buckner has asserted that 'no external pressures could have compelled the Maritimes to join Confederation if, ultimately, they had not been convinced that it was in their own interests to do so'.[168] Of course, his claim is not susceptible of scientific proof, but its plausibility is reinforced by a suggestive comparative element. How can it be explained that the British were able to exert effective pressure on the relatively sizeable mainland provinces of New Brunswick and Nova Scotia, but apparently backed off from confrontation with the two insignificant offshore colonies, Prince Edward Island and Newfoundland? The fact that the islands were small and isolated was one factor in the British decision to leave them be for the time being: they would, as Carnarvon put it, 'probably gravitate towards the larger body'.[169] More to the point, opposition in the island provinces was far more united than on the mainland. The hostility of the Prince Edward Island legislature was recognised in the Colonial Office as leaving 'no doubt of the unpopularity of the scheme',[170] while a visitor to the Newfoundland capital sacrificed syntactic accuracy to pungency of expression in noting that opposition to Confederation was 'much more unanimous than in either New Brunswick, Nova Scotia or Cape Breton'.[171]

Historians who have subscribed to the idea that Nova Scotia and New Brunswick were virtually united in their rejection of Confederation in 1865 have found it hard to explain why that opposition suddenly crumbled in 1866. Lower cloaked perplexity with a sneer: the reasons why New Brunswick changed its mind 'are not entirely clear; New Brunswick politics rarely are'.[172] The about-turn in Nova Scotia seemed even more inexplicable, and some historians have resorted to literary technique to mask a huge logical leap: Tupper 'took steps to bring Nova Scotia into line'; Tupper 'was able to get a general resolution through the Nova Scotia Assembly in favour of continued negotiation for a union of British North America'.[173] Tupper, it would seem, had suddenly acquired a remarkable and unexplained ascendancy over Nova Scotia's legislators. Indeed, his success at getting the resolution passed is so mysterious that one recent textbook omits reference to it altogether, leaving the impression that it was only the defiant Howe who spoke for Nova Scotia.[174] Yet since as long ago as 1927, an engaging story has been in print which suggests not that the passage of a unionist resolution was unexpected, but rather that it was a matter of which anti-Confederate would break ranks first.[175]

Historical debate runs in phases and fashions, and the mere fact that recent scholarship has argued for a more even division over Confederation in the Maritimes is not in itself conclusive. What is significant is that in 1865, Edward Cardwell believed that New Brunswick opinion was divided, and furthermore that opposition to the Quebec scheme was itself split into two streams, one opposing any form of closer relations with Canada, the other objecting that the proposed union was not strong enough. Psephology was not an exact science in the nineteenth century. Monck reported calculations 'that the number of votes in New Brunswick *against* the Quebec Scheme exceeded by only a few hundred those in its *favour*'.[176] Gordon replied that 'no such assertion could be made here without exciting ridicule', since Confederation had been beaten by 47000 votes to 29000. Predictably he was offended that the governor-general of Canada 'should not have attached more credit ... to my reports as to simple matters of fact'.[177]

It all depended on whether to add up the raw votes for each candidate, or make an adjustment for the distortion caused by multi-member constituencies. The British were quick to embrace the theory of a narrow result, and to assimilate it to a generally pejorative view of colonial politics. The *Saturday Review* informed its readers that while anti-Confederates 'happen to control two-thirds of the constituencies' they had won 'only a bare majority' of the votes. Then came a remarkable claim that 'the more populous and advanced districts have been out-voted by the scattered settlers, who may scarcely have heard of the project of union until they were summoned to give their votes upon it'.[178] Readers of an influential British periodical were not told that the Quebec scheme had been intensively debated in the New Brunswick press, nor that two of the four counties which returned members favourable to Confederation were in the remote north of the province.[179] A single fact — and a disputed one at that — was seized upon to discredit the New Brunswick vote: 'the majority against the scheme was but 455,' announced *The Times*, ' — a slender balance enough to sway the destinies of half a continent'.[180]

Not merely did it seem that New Brunswick hostility to Confederation was less resolute than first appeared, but it was possible to draw comfort from the nature of the opposition. Cardwell was cheered by Gordon's report 'that the opposition of those, who are against the Scheme altogether, would not have succeeded if it had not been joined by those who wish for a closer union'. This pointed not to the collapse of British North American union, but to the possibility of actually strengthening it.[181] In this can be found another important element in the achievement of Confederation. The British regarded it as a matter of course that they had a legitimate role in shaping any scheme of union. This role came to be accepted by critics of the Quebec scheme in the Maritime provinces as offering either a positive way forward or a face-saving means of escape from their position, for once again there was ambiguity in the British stance. On the one hand, they acted as if confident that they could amend the Quebec scheme and urged the advantages of a closer form of union. On the other hand, they soon came to accept British North American realities, and while hinting at changes preached acceptance of the package on offer.

From the outset, Cardwell insisted that the imperial government must have the power to amend any scheme proposed by the provinces.[182] This would entail giving the delegates who came to London 'formal power to assent' to changes.[183] It was 'natural & reasonable to suppose, that the delegates do not expect us to swallow it whole — and that the amendments which we may suggest will be favourably accepted by the Colonists.'[184] Monck thought it scarcely possible that each province would endorse the Quebec resolutions without amendment, 'and the universal feeling here is that it will be the business of the Home Government and the Imperial Parliament to harmonize their differences and to decide between them where diversities occur'.[185] This eventuality did not occur, since the Quebec scheme was only put to a vote in the Canadian parliament in 1865: thus, in a perverse way, the unpopularity of the Quebec scheme in 1865 left it as the only working basis for agreement a year later.

Cardwell's insistence on the power of amendment did not mean that the British sought to demand a host of minor changes. In his despatch of 3 December 1864, Cardwell pressed for alteration in only two provisions of the Quebec resolutions, and both remained unresolved until the very eve of the introduction of the British North America bill into parliament. The British government was unhappy at placing the power of pardon in the hands of lieutenant-governors. 'Prerogative is tender ground,' Monck had tactfully warned George Brown.[186] The real concern was that with local politicians henceforth to be appointed as lieutenant-governors, the dignity of the office would be tarnished and criminals be able to get out of gaol if they could harness sufficient influence.[187] In December 1866, the delegates gathered in London offered to concede pardon in capital cases to the central government, which hardly met the British concern. Carnarvon retaliated by drafting a bill in which the chief officers of the provinces were to be called 'Superintendents', an echo of the centralising constitution of New Zealand. There followed a 'sham fight' with Macdonald, in which Carnarvon gave way over the terminology in return for the more substantial surrender over the power of pardon.[188]

Cardwell also expressed concern that the provision for life membership of the upper house would make it difficult to resolve any conflict which might arise with the elected chamber.[189] As Carnarvon was to put it, the upper house should be 'strong enough to maintain its own opinion, and to resist the sudden gusts of popular feeling' but not so strong that it would lose touch with popular opinion altogether.[190] This was a difficult balance to strike, and the eventual compromise — an emergency addition of six Senators to the upper house — remained a dead letter for over a century.[191] By the time the issue came to a head, in January 1867, a prolonged constitutional deadlock in the Australian colony of Victoria had underlined the dangers of a rigid second chamber.[192] Carnarvon supported the proposal that the Canadian Senate be debarred from blocking a money bill,[193] but he passed up at least one opportunity to apply pressure. Late in the negotiations, a Nova Scotian delegate, W.A. Henry, wrote to him reporting that the delegates were likely to adopt an unsatisfactory deadlock provision, but would yield if the British government insisted on its point. Carnarvon was unimpressed. 'A curious specimen of British North American morality,' he noted. 'I sent *no* answer.' This was a little unfair to Henry, who had argued for the unrestricted swamping of the upper house to his fellow delegates.[194] Thirty years later, in seeking to influence the shaping of the Australian federal constitution, the British would be less fastidious, even recruiting no less a personage than the premier of New South Wales as their mole in the colonial camp.[195]

It was not that Cardwell sought to tinker with individual provisions of the Quebec scheme, but rather that at first he believed that the imperial factor could be used to strengthen the centre against the provinces. 'Has the Central power complete control over the Local powers?' To Cardwell, that was the 'hinge of the whole matter': if the Quebec resolutions failed to supply a positive answer, 'anarchy is to be apprehended ... sooner or later'. In the autumn of 1864, Cardwell had feared 'that the selfish interests of the men in the smaller Provinces should lead them to insist on *federation*, as against *Union*'. The British would 'be justified in exerting a good deal of firmness in supporting the sound policy of Upper Canada against the unsound policy of the Lower Provinces'.[196] Yet even at that stage, Cardwell was cautious about intervening. In November 1864, for instance, Monck appealed for Cardwell to argue that Upper Canada should be placed under the direct rule of the central government, on the unlikely 'precedent' of the 'district in which Washington is situated'. Monck hoped that 'this Confederation scheme, as it is called' would prove to be 'only a transitional state' and that 'before many years elapse it may become a complete Legislative Union'. This process would be 'hastened if one of the sections, and that the most important and powerful, were already ... directly ruled by the Central authority'. It would also spare the governor-general from 'an anomalous position' by making him 'the principal local Administrator of the member of the Union in which the seat of the Central Government shall be situated'. Cardwell, however, refused to strangle Ontario in the womb. British interference might be unhelpful. Besides, he wanted 'these Local Legislatures to dwindle down towards the Municipal as much as possible' which would mean that 'they would no longer be fitting machines for the Governor-General to work'.[197]

However, the belief that a strand of Maritime opinion also favoured centralisation raised Cardwell's hopes that Britain could steer the new structure away from the pitfalls of provincialism. Through to the spring of 1865, he was hopeful that 'we shall be able to agree on something more closely approaching to a Legislative Union, & not open to the difficulties which apply to the Quebec resolutions'.[198] It was this confidence which led him to play down Gordon's gloomy warnings: 'it *is* a federation, not only in name but in fact'.[199] 'I cannot agree with you in thinking that the reflecting people who wish for a closer Union will wish this occasion to be permitted to pass by unimproved,' Cardwell replied in January 1865. 'When is the Imperial Parliament likely to have a better opportunity of enacting that closer union than now?'[200] Hence Cardwell's belief that he could do business with the ostensibly anti-Confederate ministry in New Brunswick. When Premier Smith argued in July 1865 'that if we were to have a union it should be a legislative one *pure and simple*', Cardwell 'agreed with us'.[201]

In fact, Cardwell's dream of bolting British North America into an imperially engineered unitary structure had vanished in a cold touch of Canadian reality. The Canadian delegation had been unable to persuade the British to place a ring of steel around the upper province, but they were evidently more successful in conveying the political facts of life about Lower Canada. In common with most British observers, Cardwell regarded the existence of a French-speaking community in Canada as at most a passive element, simply one of the deep background factors in British North America. His response to the Quebec scheme was to assert that 'it would have been possible to recognize more pointedly the difficulties about Lower Canada: & to provide in express terms for the autonomy of the French population', in the way that Scotland's distinct ecclesiastical and legal system had been protected within the Union of 1707.[202] Much as Cardwell might have yearned to strike a deal with New Brunswick's Smith in the summer of 1865, he had come to realise that French Canadian intractability would have to be placed before Maritime perfectionism. 'My best chance with him would have been to offer some variation from the Scheme of Quebec in the sense of a closer & more complete union,' Cardwell reported to Monck after his talks with Smith. 'I had, however, the fear of Lower Canada before me, — and took care not to go back upon the advance which has already been made.'[203] Cardwell still hoped that the union of the provinces might 'be made complete', with guarantees for the 'specialties' of Lower Canada within an imperial act, but this was now a matter for the provinces themselves to settle. 'I have not ventured ... to depart from the Quebec platform,' he assured Monck in September 1865, 'lest I should be opening floodgates, which it might be beyond my power to close.'[204] In contrast with his earlier talk of firmness and improvement, he now counselled Gordon that 'any amendment ... however desirable in itself, must be weighed with a view to its effect on the success of the whole Measure'.[205]

Once Cardwell had abandoned any serious notion of an independent imperial contribution to the shaping of Confederation, the illusion of a British role became little more than another element of hint and bluff within which the real terms of union were struck. It made sense, for instance, to emphasise the idea of imperial pressure, if only to disguise the real truth that if Maritimers wanted any form of union, they had to accept Canadian terms. As Cardwell enjoined Monck, there was 'great jealousy of Canada' in the Maritimes, and 'while Imperial influence may be pressed, Canadian predominance must be *sup*-pressed.'[206] He regretted his inability to offer an alternative scheme of union to the New Brunswickers, since they could 'with less appearance of inconsistency or discomfiture accept it'.[207] Yet this was little more than a ploy designed to persuade Maritimers that if they wished for any form of union, they must accept Canadian supremacy. Lord Derby told Smith that 'they were moving in a wrong direction, that Legislative Union was out of the question, for the Lower Canadians are already swamped by the Upper Canadians, & would be still more so, if the New Brunswickers & Nova Scotians were added to such an assembly'.[208] The *Westminster Review* agreed that the existence of a French-speaking community 'sensitively tenacious of its national distinctions' meant that there was 'no choice in the matter. Federation forms the only possible principle upon which British America can now be united'.[209] When a New Brunswick anti-Confederate gained access to the columns of *The Times* to explain why Confederation had been defeated at the polls, his arguments were denounced in a leading article which concluded that 'even an imperfect Federation is better than none at all'.[210]

It is only possible to begin to understand the change of front in New Brunswick and Nova Scotia in 1866 by appreciating that however great the distrust of Canadian motives and dislike for Canadian terms, a powerful strand of Maritime opinion recognised that some form of intercolonial union was necessary. 'The colonies cannot, in the very nature of things, always continue as they are,' mused William Annand's *Morning Chronicle* in January 1866.[211] Timothy Anglin knew of nobody 'opposed to union in the abstract'.[212] 'Intelligent people are by no means wedded to isolation', conceded the New Brunswick anti-Confederate correspondent of *The Times*.[213] The image of small but proud provinces dragooned into Confederation has captured the historical imagination, but it is not the whole story. Resentment continued to simmer in New Brunswick after the legislature formally accepted Confederation in June 1866, but it is significant that there was no continuing agitation as in Nova Scotia.

In Nova Scotia, too, the furious sound of Joseph Howe's campaign may also be overestimated. Naturally, it suited superior British legislators to throw doubt on the signatures claimed for the petitions against Confederation, and to dismiss them as a put-up job. Howe was no amateur: of course he orchestrated the arguments designed for transmission to Britain. Carnarvon ran very little risk in publishing both the petitions and Howe's own letter of protest: the duplications were evident in the first, while the loyal and florid rhetoric of the second was badly dated by the mid-sixties and probably read as embarrassing blather.[214] Yet even Howe's long experience of political stage-management could not conjure anger where there was at most apathy. There were no petitions at all from the eastern half of Nova Scotia: Howe ingeniously boosted Hugh McDonald from Cape Breton as 'able to speak for the Eastern Counties' in London.[215] Equally, opposition in Halifax was nothing like as vehement as Howe would have liked: '1500 names out of 30000 are too few', he complained.[216] In the first Dominion election in September 1867, Halifax city voted narrowly in favour of candidates supporting Confederation, but opposition in the surrounding district swung the riding the other way. The anti-Confederate sweep of Nova Scotia in that election — carrying eighteen of the nineteen seats — masked divisions both on the issue and on how to respond to it. Almost forty per cent of voters supported candidates pledged to Confederation, and with uncharacteristic humility, Tupper would later admit that as premier he had lost support through his handling of railway and schools questions.[217] Some of the most extreme statements against Confederation came from Yarmouth, the south-western port with its trading access to New England and the West Indies, but even there Thomas Killam pledged to fight for low tariffs and the interests of fishermen, an implicit admission that his first plank, Repeal, might be unattainable.[218] It may be better to think of the Nova Scotian block elected to Ottawa in 1867 less as a secessionist movement and more as a regional party: it is surely significant that with such an apparently strong mandate, they actually *went* to Ottawa, where Howe showed a remarkably Canadian spirit in declining to accept the formal role of leader of the opposition on the grounds that he did not speak French.[219]

The assertion of general laws in Canadian history is a risky business, but it may be suggested that the broader a coalition in British North American politics, the more likely it was to be disrupted from within. Canada's coalition held together because only by pursuing the British target of Confederation could they secure any change in their system of government. Nova Scotia's less structured anti-Confederation movement split twice, in 1866 and again in 1868-9, and in each case the refusal of the British to endorse their aims was, if not a causal factor, then certainly a means of escape. As opposition to Confederation in New Brunswick cracked early in April 1866, William Miller warned his fellow Cape Breton representative Samuel Macdonnell that Nova Scotian politicians would soon follow, and that the two of them 'had better get into line or ... lose all chance of obtaining any of the good positions'.[220] Miller's defection was Tupper's cue to introduce resolutions into both houses of the legislature stating that it was 'desirable that a Confederation of the British North American Provinces should take place' but authorising the appointment of 'delegates to arrange with the Imperial Government a scheme of union which will effectually ensure just provision for the rights and interests of this Province'.[221] Nova Scotia's governor, Sir Fenwick Williams, had Cardwell's secret permission to pack the Legislative Council to secure a favourable vote, but this was not necessary and certainly would have been of no use had the Assembly not fallen into line.[222] Tupper's resolution recognised that any new negotiations under the auspices of the imperial government would include the Canadians, and it was obvious that both the Canadians and the British were committed to the Quebec scheme. The precise reasons why the majority of Nova Scotia's legislators fell into line on the road to Confederation in 1866 may never be reconstructed. However, it seems safe to dismiss the notion that they were marching to British orders. Rather, the imperial factor and the language of loyalty to Britain provided a discreet cover for accepting Canadian terms.

***

The British North America Act passed through Westminster in the very midst of the sharpest political crisis between the repeal of the Corn Laws in 1846 and the Irish Home Rule episode of 1886. That it should have been passed at such a time with such firm support from all sides in politics is further evidence that Confederation was a generally accepted objective, but even so, its passage was not without hazards. The events of July 1866 provided the first indication of the problems which might arise in ratifying a constitution for Canada during a Reform crisis in Britain.

In June 1866, Russell's Liberal government was defeated in its attempt to carry a Reform bill. The Queen commissioned Lord Derby to form a ministry on 27 June, but the new Conservative cabinet was not sworn in until 6 July. For his part, Cardwell left office happy in the belief that 'the now, I trust, secure & certain union' of mainland British North America would go ahead, regretting only that he would not himself 'clinch those nails',[223] a metaphor anti-Confederates might have found interesting. For the outgoing prime minister, resignation was a more solemn event, since it was unlikely that he would hold office again, and his final seven-month term would look very much like an inconsequential tailpiece to the supremacy of Palmerston. It was perhaps a combination of personal vanity and a sense of his place in history which led Russell to propose immediate cross-party action on Confederation. 'Lord Russell asked me today if I thought the new government would carry Confederation through this year,' Cardwell wrote to the incoming colonial secretary, Carnarvon, on 6 July. 'I told him ... that I thought you could not reasonably be expected to do so. To this Lord Russell replied that perhaps you would wish to do so, as it is a very important measure, & it is impossible to say what accidents might occur if months were permitted to elapse: — & that with our assistance you would have no difficulty in carrying it.'[224]

Carnarvon decided to make the attempt, but a flurry of exchanges through the next three weeks steadily proved that the exercise was doomed.[225] At one point, Carnarvon did indeed announce his abandonment of any hope of early legislation, only to revive the idea again three days later.[226] There was a marked deterioration in the relations between the young and excitable Carnarvon and his austere and more experienced predecessor as the episode progressed. However, its most serious problems lay not in personalities but in the exercise itself. Parliament rarely sat for long into August. It was of 'cardinal importance', as Cardwell insisted, that legislation should be approved in advance by the delegates from the provinces, and it was not clear when, or indeed, whether they would arrive.[227] In the event, on learning of the change of ministry, the Canadians had decided not to cross the Atlantic, enabling Macdonald to spin out — so it would seem — the final stages of planning for the new structure.[228]

One result of Carnarvon's headlong rush was that his proposed legislation could only be an outline measure, leaving most of the details to be settled by Order in Council. Cardwell was uneasy about this. His despatch of 3 December 1864 had 'left an opening' for a conference of delegates in London to 'obviate any imperfections' in the Quebec scheme, but the Canadians had 'proceeded on the understanding that the Quebec Resolutions constitute the scheme', while Nova Scotia and New Brunswick hoped for a 'closer Union'. Carnarvon, in short, was leaving himself open to a charge of bad faith in sweeping aside everything that had been debated in the previous two years, although it seems that he resented having the danger pointed out to him.[229] Rather, on 20 July he pressed Cardwell to guarantee opposition support for his bill before even taking it to the cabinet. Cardwell thought this was 'putting the cart before the horse', an objection which Carnarvon dismissed as 'one of form'.[230] Then, on 24 July, Gladstone reminded Cardwell that the late ministry had agreed to recommend to parliament a loan guarantee for the Intercolonial railway, and it did not seem fair to spring this matter on an exhausted House of Commons so late in the session.[231] It would thus be necessary to separate the railway question from Confederation, and this would require the agreement of the delegates, which would pose a problem for the Maritimers.

Thus it was already unlikely that a Confederation bill could be carried in the summer of 1866 when on 22 July a march by the Reform League was turned away from Hyde Park on government orders. The crush of the crowd forced the railings to give way, and an assemblage of working men engaged in dignified protest against their exclusion from the rights of citizenship turned into a rioting mob.[232] For several days, the West End of London was the scene of a Saturnalia which teetered on the verge of revolution. Ministers called in the cavalry, but good sense restrained them from ordering troops to open fire. The Hyde Park riots formed the one episode in 1866-7 which recalled the threat of anarchy which had hung over the Reform crisis of 1831. The disturbances were almost certainly responsible for generating a new threat to Carnarvon's already doomed attempt to legislate. Carnarvon had contemplated uniform franchise qualifications for the united provinces. Gladstone and Russell now disagreed, insisting that each province should retain its existing regulations until the new central legislature decided for itself. This might sound like a technical disagreement, but it is more likely that it represented the refusal of the opposition front bench to endorse voting qualifications for Canada which might be thrown back in their faces in the British debate over Reform.[233]

The long parliamentary recess meant that no legislation could be proposed until February 1867, although the pressure for Reform remained strong, and by the autumn the Derby government had decided to add to the hazards of its perennial minority status by attempting to tackle the question itself. The late arrival of the Canadians also left the field largely clear for Joseph Howe, who had arrived in Britain in July. In fact, Howe proved to be a poor tactician, refusing for instance to attempt to counter pro-Confederation articles in *The Times* because to do so would 'have frittered away our case' in a series of 'small wars'.[234] Instead, Howe concentrated on the circulation to MPs and editors in mid-September of a pamphlet attacking the scheme.[235] The explosion in journalism consequent upon the repeal of the Newspaper Stamp Duty in 1855 made pamphlets much less effective than perhaps Howe realised, although Gladstone certainly read it.[236] Carnarvon privately described Howe's criticisms as 'plausible',[237] but by and large Howe failed to capitalise on his early start. By September, both Tupper and McCully were actively contesting his claim to speak for Nova Scotia. In October, Howe caused considerable alarm by propagating stories that John A. Macdonald was a heavy drinker.[238] Howe's intention was to label the Quebec scheme as the product of befuddlement; Carnarvon was more alarmed by the fact that Macdonald was Canada's minister of militia, and was 'occasionally so drunk as to be incapable of all official business for days together'. If British soldiers were killed by Fenians as a result of a failure of support from the militia, 'Parliament would hardly absolve us'. Yet 'in spite of this notorious vice' Macdonald was 'the ablest politician in Upper Canada' and if he were forced to resign the coalition would collapse, which 'would absolutely destroy Confederation, & even lead to more serious effects.'[239] Yet Howe pulled away from this damaging line of attack, believing that it was 'more dignified ... to take high ground and enlarge rather than narrow the boundaries of discussion'.[240]

Instead of concentrating on the vices both of Confederation and of its authors, Howe circulated a second pamphlet arguing for the 'Organization of the Empire', his cherished plan to convert the British empire into a world-wide federation. It is hard to see how anybody could regard this scheme as 'a diversion ... that may be fatal to Confederation'.[241] Howe's belief that Westminster should impose taxes on the whole empire to pay for defence cut the ground under Nova Scotian objections to being subjected to the distant rule of Ottawa. The suggestion that members of parliament from the colonies be admitted to the British House of Commons had enjoyed some support in earlier decades,[242] but its time had passed — and no radical seeking a louder voice for the British cities would be likely to champion the cause of Nova Scotia if such support implied Bluenose MPs at Westminster. 'We shall do nothing further until the Canadian men are here,' Howe reported in the first week in November,[243] thereby writing off another three weeks of potential activity. For all his brave talk that he could afford to wait for the world once again to swing to his support,[244] Howe was tired. Once Confederation was carried, he did nothing to block the Intercolonial railway guarantee, even though one prominent opponent, R.S. Aytoun, sought his help. 'I would have thrown over the Railroad to defeat Confederation but as the measure had to pass we might as well have the road.'[245]

The Canadians finally arrived in late November, and Confederation was hammered into its final form at a series of conferences which continued into January. Despite Macdonald's 'notorious weakness', Rogers 'was very greatly struck by his power of management and adroitness'. In negotiations, Macdonald was surrounded by suspicious colleagues who watched him 'as eager dogs watch a rat hole; a snap on one side might have provoked a snap on the other, and put an end to the accord'. Macdonald put his points 'with cool, ready fluency' but it was always obvious that 'every word was measured, and that while he was making for a point ahead, he was never for a moment unconscious of any of the rocks among which he had to steer'.[246] In conference, Macdonald could hold the discordant delegates in harness. The House of Commons would be a different matter. The under-secretary, C.B. Adderley, insisted on having Macdonald close at hand,[247] a prudent and humble recognition of his shortcomings as a parliamentary performer which drove Carnarvon to distraction.[248] Yet if MPs took a snap at a key provision of the bill — for instance at Section 145 which seemed to imply that the British would underwrite the costs of the Intercolonial — the whole structure might tumble at the last minute.

Important issues remained unsettled at a very late stage. F.S. Reilly, the Lincoln's Inn barrister who drafted the actual legislation, complained that he could not get hold of the delegates to clarify important matters: as February began, he was still estimating three full days of work, adding testily, 'I can't make bricks without clay, to say nothing of straw'.[249] It was tacitly recognised that the united provinces would be called 'Canada'. Adderley held out for 'British North America' as 'in the large spirit of the age', but Blackwood recommended accepting Monck's recommendation: 'as one of the objects of the Confederation must be to make British North America better known to the inhabitants of this kingdom', it made sense to adopt a familiar name.[250] Yet on 5 February, as the new parliamentary session began, the Queen was seeking confirmation that 'Canada' really was the choice of the delegates, and Carnarvon had to assure her that the Maritimers had taken the lead in arguing that it would 'be for the political advantage of the Confederation that it should be known by a name which is at once familiar and important'.[251] The rank and style of the new structure was more of a problem. As late as 2 February, the draft bill spoke of 'the Kingdom of Canada', but the foreign secretary, Stanley, objected that a monarchical style 'would wound the sensibilities of the Yankees'.[252] The delegates then pressed for 'Viceroyalty', which Carnarvon thought 'open to grave objection', before retreating to 'Dominion' which was 'somewhat in opposition to the institutions on the other side of the border', but not offensively so.[253] Derby thought the term 'rather absurd', perhaps thinking of Psalm 72, which spoke of 'dominion also from sea to sea and from the river unto the ends of the earth'.[254] Not even British Columbia was that far away.

With so much still being settled at the eleventh hour, there was a risk that somewhere along the line, somebody would find something to attack in parliament. 'The difficulties, the suggestions, the amendments during the last week have been almost endless,' wrote Carnarvon as he struggled to get the measure into legislative form.[255] Three potential dangers threatened the British North America bill as it passed through Westminster in February and March 1867. Specifically, MPs might block the funding of the Intercolonial — which would render Confederation virtually untenable in the Maritimes — or they might pause and insist on confirmation that the apparently unhappy Nova Scotians really did wish to join with Canada.

More generally, brooding over the whole political scene was the general uncertainty that the ministry might be defeated and resort to a general election. In mid-January, before the parliamentary session had begun, Galt feared the 'dangerous delays' which might arise if the 'most precarious' government failed to get its Reform policy right in the Queen's speech. Should ministers simply resign, 'our Bill will pass in good time', but if an election were called, all pending legislation would automatically lapse and have to start afresh in a new parliament, 'and in the meantime, an election must take place in Nova Scotia, which will certainly be adverse to Confederation'. Galt could only hope that even if ministers were forced into an election, 'they may induce the House to pass certain measures first, of which ours may be one'.[256] That such a hope could be entertained was an indication that Confederation was seen to be a generally supported aim in Britain.

None the less, it was a tense time. The British North America bill was debated in the Lords on 19 and 26 February, and reached the Commons two days later. On 25 February, the cabinet came to the verge of 'breaking up' when Carnarvon threatened to resign over Reform.[257] The breach was only averted by the adoption of a hasty compromise proposal known — from the time of its gestation — as the 'Ten Minutes Bill', which in turn promptly collapsed in the face of parliamentary hostility.[258] Three ministers, one of them Carnarvon, resigned on 2 March. It was not without significance that one of his objections to the proposed Reform measure was that it would reduce franchise qualifications even below those applied in the colonies.[259] The unscathed passage of a colonial constitution right in the midst of this political crisis is a remarkable indication of the strength and breadth of British support for the union of British North America.

Yet if Confederation emerged unscathed, it did not pass unchallenged. What requires to be explained is why the issue of Nova Scotia did not become entangled with the question of reform. There was some latent sentiment — or sentimentality — favouring the 'loyal Bluenoses'.[260] Moreover, Nova Scotia had much the same population as Manchester, and might have been seized upon as a symbolic battle ground by Reformers seeking a voice for industrial Britain especially since — as Galt was so well aware — the province was due to elect a new Assembly within a few months. Joseph Howe was surely justified in wondering why 'those who so highly prize the franchise and are seeking to extend it' should refuse to delay Confederation for a few months until 'a kindred people' with more than a century's experience of representative government had been given the opportunity to express their opinion at the polls.[261] The Nova Scotia issue was contained through the combination of a bizarre coincidence of British and Nova Scotian political issues with the blatant manipulation of British ignorance.

Towards the close of 1866, Howe's campaign had seemed to be effective in winning the support the *Daily News* and the *Morning Star*,[262] journals close to the radical giant, John Bright — the voice of the one section of the political spectrum which did not share the assumptions of the enclosed world of the élite. Moves were rapidly made to contain the threat, and here sheer coincidence played a part. Nova Scotia had adopted universal adult male suffrage in 1854, an experiment which it soon came to regret. Although a Liberal, Howe held to an old-fashioned belief that the franchise was not a right but a privilege to be earned, and as premier in 1863 he had carried legislation 'to purge our constitution, and purify our electoral system' by imposing qualifications based on wealth and property. However the upper house amended Howe's legislation so that the new franchise would not take effect until after the general election of 1863.[263] Once Tupper, the Conservative, spread the word that Howe, the Liberal, had rolled back the franchise in Nova Scotia, the *Star* went into reverse.[264]

It was probably the same issue that undermined the attempt by Lord Campbell, in the House of Lords on 26 February, to delay Confederation until after the forthcoming Nova Scotian general election. Campbell's age and background creates a suspicion that the malign hand of Arthur Gordon might be detected in his intervention.[265] He was unsympathetic to Reform at home,[266] and based his argument squarely on the failure of universal suffrage in Nova Scotia. The Assembly which had sent delegates to Charlottetown in 1864 and assented to union in 1866 was 'a body whose foundation is condemned'. Why not wait for a few weeks to receive 'the judgment of a body whose foundation is unquestioned'?[267] Carnarvon deflected the attack by pointing to its knock-on effect: Canadians were due to go to the polls shortly after Nova Scotians, and the delay could be indefinite.[268] It is striking that in the hereditary chamber which was the bulwark against the rashness of democracy, not one peer came to Campbell's support, and indeed not merely did he withdraw his motion but he seemed almost to apologise for it. Twenty-four hours after the Conservative government had proposed a broad extension of the franchise in

Britain, few were willing to endorse the curtailment of the right to vote in a colony.

Howe's embarrassing record of having restricted the franchise probably explains why leading radicals backed away from supporting the Nova Scotian opponents in parliament. John Bright, for instance, was obviously unhappy at the way in which the province was being treated, but he professed no more than a vague awareness of the existence of petitions against the bill.[269] At the very least, in the midst of a political crisis over Reform, most had other fish to fry. John Stuart Mill conceded to Howe's associate, William Garvie, that 'Confederation was being pushed through with disgraceful haste and disregard of Nova Scotia wishes, but he added he could not spare a moment to fight our battle'. Garvie would have found this easier to bear had Mill not been simultaneously 'so anxious to have even women entitled to vote on public affairs'.[270] There were brief hopes that another Liberal, George Hadfield, would agree to move a delaying amendment which Howe drafted, 'but Cardwell got at him and cajoled him to withdraw it'.[271]

Howe was forced to turn to opponents of Reform, whose motives would be suspect, but with as little success. Robert Lowe, for instance, explained 'that it was of no use to speak at all in a cause which would be lost through both sides following their leaders'.[272] Howe's last hope lay with Edward Horsman, a Whig who had taken a leading part in the malcontent group nicknamed 'the Cave of Adullam' which had ousted Russell's ministry by defeating his Reform bill the previous year. Horsman accepted custody of the petitions Howe wished to have formally presented to the House of Commons, but after due consideration concluded that he would have to state that he disagreed with them, which would undoubtedly prejudice the case. Horsman returned the petitions 'in order that you may place them in better hands', but unfortunately not until 3 March, after the bill had passed its second reading in the Commons.[273]

Howe was unfortunate in the way events conspired against him, but the most potent force against him was not bad luck, but the fundamental British ignorance about the provinces, which was manipulated to discount opposition even to the point of outright falsehood. In his maiden speech in the House of Lords, Monck claimed that the Nova Scotian opposition was 'entirely got up by a few energetic individuals',[274] while Carnarvon insisted that it was no business of parliament to challenge the decisions of Nova Scotia's Assembly and Legislative Council: 'really, if this House is to go into all the intricacies and details of colonial government there can be no end to the matter'.[275] The tone was dismissive, but both comments fell within the legitimate bounds of partisan debate. Markedly less honourable was the statement by Normanby, speaking with the authority of a former governor of Nova Scotia, that the leading opponent of Confederation had formerly supported the idea, 'so that his arguments could not be accounted of much worth'.[276] This transparent allusion to Howe was unfair: he had been ambivalent towards intercolonial union, but neither in 1854 nor in 1861 had he committed himself when the subject came before the Assembly.

The most blatant distortion of all was supplied by Edward Watkin in the House of Commons. John Bright, although formally keeping the Nova Scotian opposition at arm's length, had made the damaging assertion that Confederation had never been placed before the people of the province.[277] Matters were not much helped by an inept speech in which Sir John Pakington replied that the Nova Scotian Assembly had voted 'in favour of a union of the Provinces' in 1862 — both the date and the interpretation were incorrect — that there had been an election in 1863 'and again in 1864, we find the representative body still favourable to the union'.[278] Watkin had risen from his place and walked across to the enclosure for distinguished visitors which adjoined the Commons benches: Howe and his dissident associates were exiled to the gallery. Thus it had been easy for Watkin to ask Tupper how to reply to Bright's challenge. Tupper did not specialise in apologies, but there would be a note almost of embarrassment in his subsequent explanation of the terrible misunderstanding which had ensued. He had replied by mentioning the 1861 resolution, alluded to the fact that he was a known supporter of a union of the provinces, and added that victory in the 1863 election had enabled him to carry Confederation by a large majority. It seemed that nobody was more embarrassed than Tupper himself when Watkin misunderstood the import of their hurried consultation, and melded these three entirely distinct statements into a single explanatory package. Tupper, Watkin assured the House, 'went through the country preaching this Confederation of the Provinces' during the 1863 election campaign. 'It was brought under the notice of the electors at every polling-booth, and at every hustings the issue was distinctly raised.' The Assembly had then endorsed the plan 'by an enormous majority', thereby mandating the delegates who negotiated on their behalf. Watkin's account was a travesty. It was also in striking contrast to the assumption of the *Saturday Review* that the voters of New Brunswick had not even heard of the issue when they voted in 1865. Tupper — according to his own account — turned to his neighbour, Galt, 'and remarked how difficult it was to make parties understand, when they were not familiar with the history of a question'.[279] He might equally have commented on how easy it was to hoodwink the British when they were already determined on a course of action.

It was one thing to blot out Nova Scotian doubts because Confederation was a generally approved British aim. The danger, in an all-engulfing political crisis, was that the same insistence upon domestic priorities might brush aside a constitution for distant provinces altogether. Creighton believed that by the time of Carnarvon's resignation, 'his measure was through in safety'.[280] In fact, on 4 March, the day on which Carnarvon explained to the Lords why he had left the cabinet, there was an attempt to challenge Confederation in the Commons. It was, as Disraeli confessed, 'a bad night' for the government. He buried the Ten Minutes Bill, but could offer only the lame promise of a further measure in two weeks' time. MPs were 'sulky', not least because Carnarvon's speech in the upper house had not been matched by a full explanation in the Commons. Ministers were forced to put off discussion of the Army Estimates. 'Nothing can be more insolent, bullying, and defiant, than they are,' Disraeli wrote irritably of the honourable members.[281] It was not a propitious moment for Bernal Osborne to attempt to block the committee stage of the British North America bill on the grounds that it was high time ministers announced their policy on Reform.[282]

Bernal Osborne was a prominent MP who had the ear of the House. He had held office in the 1850s, and sat for Nottingham, one of the under-represented industrial towns. Above all, he had a reputation as a Commons wit, even if the jealous Disraeli thought his style laboured and out of date.[283] At that moment, on 4 March 1867, the fate of Confederation was in the balance. If Osborne managed to block the committee stage, the bill would fall back in the parliamentary timetable — and the Commons was anything but an efficient legislative body — perhaps become caught up in the Reform controversy and maybe crash altogether should the cowed ministry be forced into an election. Certainly, on that March Monday evening, there was nothing that ministers could do, for they had lost control over the House. Rather, it was Gladstone, the increasingly towering figure on the Liberal benches, who saved the day. He spoke, generally on Reform, in a tone which was 'not exactly violent ... but marked by a good deal of his customary vehemence of delivery' and with 'an undercurrent of bitterness'.[284] Yet he did not go for the kill. In fact, he appealed to Osborne not to press his point, enigmatically stating that Confederation was 'a matter which appertains — I will not say to the security, but to the dignity of the Empire'. Equally striking was his direct appeal to R.S. Aytoun not to proceed with his announced intention to delete Section 145, the Intercolonial clause, from the British North America bill. There would be a chance, Gladstone pleaded, to discuss this issue when enabling legislation subsequently came before the House. Given Gladstone's stature among the Liberals, Aytoun had little choice but to agree.[285]

Gladstone's intervention is further evidence of the significance of a general British consensus in favour of British North American union. It may also be some testimony to the activity of the Canadians themselves. Macdonald and Watkin had toyed in February with the idea of lobbying Cardwell and Gladstone in the hope of delaying discussion of Reform in order to get Confederation through. Carnarvon had not forbidden such an approach, but had sought to convey the feeling that doubt had been placed on his competence.[286] On 4 March, the day of Osborne's attempt to block the committee stage, Gladstone had received a visit from 'Mr Galt (Canada)'.[287] It seems very likely that Galt, who had 'a league, offensive & defensive' with Watkin and the Grand Trunk,[288] had come to beg Gladstone's intervention to stop Aytoun from upsetting the deal which the Fathers of Confederation had so carefully put together.

Macdonald's subsequent annoyance that the British North America Act had been passed at thinly attended sessions by largely indifferent members just as if it had been 'a private Bill uniting two or three English parishes'[289] was another example of colonial sensitivity towards metropolitan pretensions. There was justification for Westminster's low-key approach, and Macdonald would have been the last person to rejoice had British MPs started to pick apart his carefully crafted constitution. It was true that the House of Commons 'got livelier and better filled' after the second reading of the British North America bill as members raised questions about the dog tax.[290] This was not necessarily a sign that MPs were indifferent to Confederation, but rather (as McGee put it) that 'it was quite evident to the members of the Imperial Parliament that the adoption of the measure was a foregone conclusion, and they are not apt in England to debate matters already decided'.[291] On the other hand, MPs could and did point out that the home for 'Destitute Dogs' in London could not possibly pay tax on its three thousand inmates.[292] Of course it suited Carnarvon to argue that the bill was 'of the nature of a treaty' negotiated by the provinces themselves, a strategy which the *Daily News* dismissed as disingenuous. Confederation was not 'a merely intercolonial project, and Ministers know it: hence their language is inconsistent, and their arguments do not hang together'.[293] Yet Carnarvon's formula was ideal in reconciling the outward pageantry of imperial supremacy with the actual reality that Confederation was the achievement of the provincial politicians themselves, even if they had framed their scheme to conform with a British sentiment in favour of a union of the provinces.

Angry at his inability to get the grievances of Nova Scotia heard, William Garvie raged at the recollection of a thinly attended House of Commons 'rushing through a disagreeably dull measure which did not affect anybodys seat' with 'lazy contempt'. At the committee stage, the clerk 'gabbled on *not* the clauses even but the *numbers* of the clauses ... and they passed sure enough, without anybody worrying himself about their contents'. Yet the supremacy of the imperial parliament was upheld. The MP for Salisbury, Edward Hamilton, 'had been in Australia' Garvie commented sourly, 'and therefore wanted to drag himself into notice as a great Colonial authority'.[294] Hamilton's sharp eyes spotted a problem. The British North America bill embodied the principle which the opposition had insisted upon the previous summer: until the Dominion parliament decided otherwise, the existing provisional franchise provisions would remain in force. However, in the remote district of Algoma, property values had little meaning, and accordingly Section 41 proposed that there 'every Householder otherwise qualified except in respect of Real Property' should have the vote. Hamilton asked 'whether it was intended to give the franchise to females, or confine it to males?' For the government, Adderley hastily agreed to a clarifying amendment which inserted the word 'male'. It was almost certainly one of the few amendments which Westminster could insert without any implications for domestic political discord.[295]

  Hamilton's amendment saved the eldest daughter of the empire from the perils of female suffrage, but its insertion meant that the British North America bill had to return to the Lords for their formal agreement to the change, which was given without discussion on 12 March. The measure passed into law on receiving the royal assent on 29 March, two days after the token division of strength in the House of Commons had demonstrated that the Intercolonial loan guarantee would go through safely. Writing from his official residence at Quebec to his son at Oxford on 27 June, Lord Monck mentioned that he would be 'obliged to go to Ottawa tomorrow for a few days for some business'. The 'business' was the proclamation, on 1 July 1867, of the union of the provinces as 'One Dominion under the Name of Canada'.[296]

Conclusion

The chief shortcoming of the Quebec resolutions, in the opinion of Frederic Rogers, was that so many interests had to be accommodated in a British North American union that the proposed scheme of government was 'rather wanting in neatness and scientific character'.[1] Historians should certainly beware of implying neatness and scientific precision in attempting to explain why Confederation occurred in the 1860s. In the end, politicians in Canada, New Brunswick and Nova Scotia were able to put together majorities in favour of union. Various motives, different cocktails of incentive, played their part in each province, perhaps even in each individual. Arguments were advanced to state the case in as many different ways as possible in order to appeal to people who thought in many different ways. Some arguments were plausible and effective, some merely effective, others were tried but discarded when no roof resounded with appreciative cheers. To carry Confederation by majorities was to carry Confederation by coalitions, and coalition armies march to a cacophony of drumbeats. Historians can reconstruct the cut-and-thrust of debate and note that in 1867 those who favoured Confederation overcame those who opposed it, in the mainland provinces at least. Yet it can never be proved that Confederation triumphed on account of any one of those arguments, or of all of them woven into a package.

The story was told in the 1860s of the principle on which one of the members for the New Brunswick county of Charlotte always decided to cast his vote. 'When a bill's before this house I always asks whats it going to do for Charlotte. I ain't got anything to do with the Province — I sits here for Charlotte and if they tells me it'll do good to the Province but do harm to Charlotte then says I "I go in for Charlotte". And if they tells me that it'll harm the Province but do good to Charlotte then too says I "I go in for Charlotte"'.[2] British North America was composed of many Charlottes, not all of them represented by such frank legislators. Yet the story is not just a cameo of localism but also a reminder of expectations. It is relatively easy to reconstruct why supporters of Confederation claimed that it was the right answer to the problems of the 1860s, but much harder to reconstruct where they thought British North America might be ten or twenty years ahead. Cobden felt that they did not know themselves, that Confederation was 'a device of the Canadian politicians for escaping from themselves into a new & enlarged political arena ... few of the prominent actors look beyond this immediate object'.[3] Cobden was habitually unsympathetic in his assessments of Canadian motives. It is much more likely that the prominent actors had notions about the future which were shifting, imprecise but none the less in large measure shared. Galt was unusual in believing — as he admitted two years later — that Confederation 'must ultimately lead' to independence from Britain, although this did not prevent him from accepting a knighthood.[4] Others envisaged an early expansion into a transcontinental union, although the enthusiasm which enticed British Columbia into Confederation in 1870-1 was not fully matched by a determination to keep it in the decade which followed.

Yet it would be ungenerous for historians to abuse the luxury of hindsight by damning the politicians of British North America for their failure to foresee the future, and still less for their inability to find solutions which could impose themselves fully on events. As premier of Nova Scotia, Joseph Howe once justified a piece of legislation as 'framed on the principle, if you can't do all the good you wish, do all you can'.[5] The novelist E.M. Forster once waspishly described the attraction of becoming a historian as like being 'transferred from an office where one is afraid of a sergeant-major into an office where one can intimidate generals'.[6] Historians have no right to censure past politicians for supporting projects which did not solve every difficulty, but might eventually help to solve some — especially if the alternative would be to blame them for inactivity. Yet equally it is important to avoid the trap of assuming that merely because those past politicians advanced large claims in support of any particular project, it must have been the answer to all their problems and prayers.

By the 1860s, the idea of a British North American union had come to be seen not as a distant vision but as a vehicle by which more specific aims might be realised. In 1849, Grey had described federation as an 'old idea'[7] but dismissed it as a practical proposition because of 'an absence of any sufficient common interests to form the ground work of the union'.[8] Thirteen years later, the *Saturday Review* could also describe it as an 'idea, which so far from being novel, has long attracted the attention of Imperial and colonial statesmen' but significantly it had now become something which might facilitate other changes, 'holding out a prospect, however remote, of the reconstruction on a basis more equal, and therefore more likely to be lasting, of those bonds which connect us with our Transatlantic fellow-subjects'.[9]

A few historians have considered the role of Confederation as an idea. Brebner baldly excluded 'the quite natural, if impractical' proposals of earlier times in order to confine the movement for Confederation to the nine years between the depression of 1857 and the departure of delegates for London in 1866.[10] Morton, on the other hand, acknowledged that the 'sudden and dramatic' Canadian mission to Charlottetown could only be 'explained by the long years of germination of the idea of British North American union,' which had 'recurred steadily and rhythmically' at least since the annexationist talk of 1849.[11] Yet the predominant tendency has been to assume that Confederation was deduced from the immediate circumstances of 1864. Upton complained that Canadian history tended to be presented as a pedestrian saga of pragmatic problem-solving, 'so that it often appears that our present form of government was devised overnight by one or two politicians. John A. Macdonald and George Brown, we might be excused for believing, went to Charlottetown in 1864 and placed their daring innovation before an astonished group of lesser men quite unprepared to cope with such intellectual giants.'[12] Put in that form, it becomes comprehensible that some historians have regarded the outcome as miraculous.

Contemporaries were aware that the idea had a prehistory, although they had their own motives for emphasising its existence. The *Westminster Review*, for instance, sought to dismiss the notion that 'the scheme of confederation is the offspring of fear' since its origins could be 'traced much further back than the civil war in the United States'.[13] 'We know that the idea exists in a defined form', the *Daily Telegraph* wrote in 1864, 'but we cannot point to the time or place of its first existence.'[14]

The task of the historian is thus not so much to explain why British North American union was seized upon as the answer to the challenges facing the provinces in 1864 — indeed in some respects it was not a very obvious answer at all — but rather why an idea which, as the *Westminster Review* put it in 1865, had 'never been extinct in any of the provinces, although it has taken Rip van Winkle slumbers' — should suddenly flare into life in 1864.[15] 'Colonists are the last people in the world to do or suffer anything for an idea,' lamented *The Times* in September 1865 as Confederation seemed to be slipping away, 'and must have something more solid to reward them for their devotion.'[16] The precise origin of the idea is of less importance than the fact that it had come to take so firm a hold on the British mind in the quarter century before Charlottetown. To say this is not to attempt an imperial recolonisation of Canadian history by seizing the credit for the birth of the Canadian state. The *Edinburgh Review* was surely right in asserting that 'the mainspring of the Federative Movement must be sought not in any past or present impulse from Imperial authorities, but in the political circumstances, necessities, and instincts of the provinces',[17] although as the details emerged, both *The Times* and the *Saturday Review* expressed surprise at the active involvement of the imperial factor.[18]

Fundamentally, Confederation was the creation of a vigorous and confident Upper Canada, which saw it as the best way of escaping from the political log-jam of the existing province, and as an acceptable framework for the prosecution of other projects. Without that dynamic Upper Canadian push, the British would no doubt have continued to wait in the wings for something in British North America to support. Yet equally, without the pre-existing British support for a union of the provinces, vague and illogical though it may have been, there is no reason to suppose that it would have made sense for the ambitious Upper Canadians to have adopted the Confederation of all the provinces as their way forward in 1864. When Canadian politicians recognised in June 1864 that the reconstruction of their province could no longer be postponed, their best chance of securing the legislative compliance of Westminster lay in pursuing the aim of British North American union. For Macdonald, the adhesion of the Maritimes offered a chance of a balancing element which might save him from being trampled under foot in the unavoidable shift of electoral power towards the

Grits and Reformers of Upper Canada. In an age of slow communications, the involvement of the British gave him the precious factor of time. In a province and an era permeated by the rhetoric of loyalty, British support would give him an asset intangible in itself but embarrassing by its absence to his opponents. The involvement of the British also exposed the complex Brown to the intimidating magic of a social élite, for long enough to inhibit him from demanding action on a purely Canadian reform project instead of Confederation. Perhaps the homilies and reproaches of the British rattled Nova Scotians and New Brunswickers — but not their island neighbours — into doubting their own rejection of the Quebec scheme, but perhaps too Maritime politicians who recognised that their provinces were too small to endure in a world of big battalions found it more convenient to seem to bow the knee to the distant imperial Caesar rather than to their fellow centurions from Canada. *The Times*, of course, was wrong to allege that colonists would not make sacrifices for an idea. In a sense, Confederation itself was a form of sacrificial gesture to British opinion. Galt assured Cardwell in April 1865 that the motive of the Canadian government in pressing for Confederation was 'not in any way to weaken the connection with the Mother Country, but rather to remove those causes which now afforded many parties in England arguments for asserting that the connection was mutually disadvantageous'.[19] Visiting London that autumn, Monck concluded that 'the anti Colonial party' were 'for the moment, choked off by the proposal for our Union, but if that fails I believe they will return to the charge with redoubled energy'.[20] The strategy could only work if British North American union was not simply a generally accepted British aim, but one which was seen as a forerunner, substitute or just plain nostrum for solving all the problems of the colonial relationship.

Two elements need to be woven into the march of events and the cavalcade of politicians along the road to Confederation. One is the idea of British North American union, and the other is the imperial factor. Both were pervasive but diffuse rather than precise. The idea of intercolonial union, for instance, took many forms, creating the complication that some of the argument in the middle years of the 1860s was not about the end itself but rather the version which had come to the fore, with some Lower Canadians objecting that Confederation would destroy local autonomy, and a strong strand of Maritime opinion fearing that it was not centralised enough. Similarly, the imperial factor should be considered in the broader but less grandiose terms of a general consensus of British opinion. D'Arcy McGee's role in the opening of the Confederation debates in the Canadian Assembly was to combine an overview of the issue with some oratorical spice. Like Brebner, he was content to 'dismiss the antecedent history of the question' and focus rather on the events since 1858 which had given 'importance to the theory in men's minds', but he traced the idea back to the days of Durham and beyond. 'If we have dreamed a dream of union ... it is at least worth while remarking that a dream which has been dreamed by such wise and good men, may ... have been a sort of vision, a vision foreshadowing forthcoming natural events in a clear intelligence.'[21] Stripped of its oratorical ornament, McGee's point was that the relationship between events and ideas was not merely one-way: the first and original cause of Confederation was the idea of Confederation itself. Once the basic importance of the idea is recognised, then it is possible to see the British role not as one of pressure and command but rather context and support. As *The Times* commented in reporting the first meeting of the Dominion parliament in November 1867: 'Empire never spoke with so small and still a voice as when England humbly suggested and gently aided the idea of a Canadian Confederation'.[22]

Note on Sources

In keeping with modern practice, there is no full bibliography. An outline of the principal works on the causes of Confederation may be found in Notes 2, 4, 5, 6 and 60 of Chapter 1. Academic debate as it stood around 1980 is reviewed in D.A. Muise, 'Confederation' in D.A. Muise (ed.), *A Reader's Guide to Canadian History*: i, *Beginnings to Confederation* (Toronto, 1982) pp. 237-48.

Publication details for books are given in full at first citation. Short title is used for second citation, and *op. cit.* thereafter, except where confusion may occur. Articles, essays and chapters are given in full at first citation, and then in short form thereafter. Abbreviations are used for frequently cited sources; a list follows this Note. For occasional footnote excursions into classic novels, citations are given by chapter to avoid tying the reference to any one edition.

The status of the sources used varies greatly. Statements in numbered despatches of the various 'CO' series may be regarded as expressions of that mysterious entity called 'policy', because their publication could be called for by parliament. On the other hand, the 'minutes' which were scrawled across such documents were for internal consumption in the Colonial Office. Private letters often fill out the real intentions of ministers and governors but, despite their refreshing immediacy, they do not always tell their own story in full: few people wrote letters when they could exchange views direct. Similarly, statements of fact in newspapers and other publications were not necessarily accurate, and are often given to illustrate the frailty of British perceptions. Nor is it implied that any published statement of opinion was influential: some of the more choice viewpoints are quoted only to demonstrate that wayward ideas were in circulation.

Some sources conform more closely to the demands of modern scholarship than others in their rendering of quoted material. Older biographies in particular are open to suspicions of having cleaned up private correspondence, the originals of which may now have disappeared. In most cases, I have relied on the readings of other scholars; once or twice, variant readings have been suggested in the Notes. At the very least, it would seem that differences of opinion over transcription are minor.

Eavesdropping on nineteenth-century discussions of the shaping of the world can be a beguiling experience. It is worth pointing out that there have been subtle but important changes in the structure and vocabulary of the English language. In the mid-nineteenth century, 'quite' meant 'absolutely' and never — as in slipshod modern usage — conveyed the sense of 'partly'. When an office-holder used 'I wish', he was conveying an instruction not expressing a dream.

I have tried to combine my discussions of attitudes and policies with recognition of the individuality and sometimes idiosyncrasy of the politicians through whom viewpoints were expressed and events were acted out. I have relied upon two invaluable reference sources. One is the *Dictionary of Canadian Biography*, especially volumes 7 to 11, created under the general editorship of Francess G. Halpenny and published by the University of Toronto Press (these volumes between 1975 and 1982). The other is its far older inspiration, the multi-volume *Dictionary of National Biography*, which Oxford University Press began over a century ago. My debt to the *DCB* and *DNB* is usually a silent one, with specific citations reserved for direct quotations or major points of interpretation.

In the Notes and References, I try to make some acknowledgement where material has been quoted by other scholars, and to indicate alternative viewpoints or discussions of related issues which bear upon the subject. Such citation does not imply agreement with the views so signposted. Equally, the absence of such allusion does not prove (although it may be the case) lack of familiarity on my part with the work of others. I have tried to resist the temptation to burden the Notes and References with asides, but some additional material has crept in.

Abbreviations

Sample references are given for archival sources.

Beck, *Howe*: J.M. Beck, *Joseph Howe* (2 vols, Kingston and Montreal, 1962- 63), i: *Conservative Reformer 1804-1848*; ii: *The Briton Becomes Canadian 1848-1873*.

BPP: *British Parliamentary Papers*. Individual papers are cited by year, volume and short title: full original citations are given in M.I. Adam, J. Ewing and J. Munro, *Guide to the Principal Parliamentary Papers Relating to the Dominions 1812-1911* (Edinburgh, 1913), pp. 25-28. Many libraries hold the material in volumes 23-25 of the *Canada* series of reprints produced in 1969 by the Irish University Press.

Brebner: J.B. Brebner, *Canada; A Modern History* (Ann Arbor, Mich., 1960).

Broadlands NE/88/3 Southampton University Library, Broadlands MSS, General Correspondence, NE/88/3.

Brown: J.M.S. Careless, *Brown of the Globe* (2 vols, Toronto, 1959- 63), i: *The Voice of Upper Canada 1818-1859*; ii: *The Statesman of Confederation 1860-1880*.

Brown 5: Ottawa, National Archives of Canada, Brown Papers, MG24, B40, vol. 5.

Browne: G.P. Browne (ed.), *Documents on the Confederation of British North America* (Toronto, 1969).

Burpee: L.J. Burpee (ed.), 'Joseph Howe and the Anti-Confederation League', *Transactions of the Royal Society of Canada*, section ii, series iii, March 1917, pp. 409-473.

CD: *Parliamentary Debates on the Subject of the Confederation of the British North American Provinces* (Quebec, 1865).

CHR: *Canadian Historical Review* .

Cardwell 6/39: London, Public Record Office, Cardwell Papers, PRO 30/48/6/39.

Careless, *Union of the Canadas*: J.M.S. Careless, *The Union of the Canada*: *The Growth of Canadian Institutions 1841-1857* (Toronto, 1968).

Carnarvon 6/139: London, Public Record Office, Carnarvon Papers, PRO 30/6/139.

Chisholm: J.A. Chisholm (ed.), *The Speeches and Public Letters of Joseph Howe* (2 vols, Halifax, 1908).

CO 42/640: London, Public Record Office, Colonial Office series, CO 42/640.

Colony to Nation: Arthur R.M. Lower, *Colony to Nation: A History of Canada* (5th ed., Toronto, 1977, first published 1946).

Critical Years: W.L. Morton, *The Critical Years: The Union of British North America 1857-1873* (Toronto, 1964).

DCB: *Dictionary of Canadian Biography*.

Dominion of the North: D.G. Creighton, *Dominion of the North*: *A History of Canada* (rev. ed., Toronto, 1962, first published 1944).

Durham 19: Ottawa, National Archives of Canada, Durham Papers, MG24 A27, vol. 19.

Elgin A-396: Ottawa, National Archives of Canada, Elgin Papers, microfilm A-396.

Elgin-Grey Papers: A.G. Doughty (ed.), *The Elgin-Grey Papers 1846-1852* (4 vols, Ottawa, 1937).

Galt 7: Ottawa, National Archives of Canada, Galt Papers, MG27 I D7.

Gladstone 44136: London, British Library, Gladstone Papers, Additional Manuscript 44136.

Grey Papers: University of Durham, Grey Papers.

Hansard: *Hansard's Parliamentary Debates* (3rd series).

HCC 2028: Aberystwyth, National Library of Wales, Harpton Court Collection, C/2028.

Howe 5: Ottawa, National Archives of Canada, Joseph Howe Papers, MG24 B29.

Hughenden He/5: Bodleian Library, Oxford, Hughenden MSS, B/XX/He/5.

JICH: *Journal of Imperial and Commonwealth History*.

Kingdom of Canada: W.L. Morton, *The Kingdom of Canada: A General History from Earliest Times* (2nd ed., Toronto, 1969, first published 1963).

Knox, *JICH*, 1976: B.A. Knox, 'The British Government, Sir Edmund Head, and British North American Confederation, 1858' *Journal of Imperial and Commonwealth History*, iv (1975-76), pp. 206-17.

Life and Times: P.B. Waite, *The Life and Times of Confederation 1864-1867: Politics, Newspapers, and the Union of British North America* (Toronto, 1963).

Lucas: C.P. Lucas (ed.), *Lord Durham's Report on the Affairs of British North America* (3 vols, Oxford, 1912, first published 1839).

Lytton 01: Hertford, Hertfordshire County Record Office, Lytton Papers, D/EK/01.

Macdonald: D.G. Creighton, *John A. Macdonald* (2 vols, Toronto, 1952-55), i: *The Young Politician*; ii, *The Old Chieftain*.

Macdonald 75: National Archives of Canada, Macdonald Papers, MG26a, vol. 75.

C. Martin, *Foundations*: Chester Martin, *Foundations of Canadian Nationhood* (Toronto, 1955).

Ged Martin (ed.), *Causes*: Ged Martin (ed.), *The Causes of Canadian Confederation* (Fredericton, 1990).

McInnis: E. McInnis, *Canada: A Social and Political History* (4th ed., Toronto, 1982, first published 1968).

McNaught: K. McNaught, *The Pelican History of Canada* (rev. ed, London, 1978, first published 1969).

Monck A-755: Ottawa, National Archives of Canada, Monck Papers, microfilm A-755.

Monck Letters and Journals: W.L. Morton (ed.), *Monck Letters and Journals 1863-1868*; *Canada from Government House at Confederation* (Toronto, 1970).

NAC: Ottawa, National Archives of Canada.

Newcastle 11413: University of Nottingham, Newcastle Papers, NeC 11413.

Pope (ed.), *Confederation*: J. Pope, (ed.), *Confederation: Being a Series of Hitherto Unpublished Documents Bearing on the British North America Act* (Toronto, 1895).

Pope, *Memoirs*: J. Pope, *Memoirs of the Right Honourable Sir John Alexander Macdonald G.C.B. First Prime Minister of Canada* (Toronto, 1930 ed., first published 1894).

PRO: London, Public Record Office.

Russell 31: London, Public Record Office, Russell Papers, PRO 30/22/31.

Stanmore 1: University of New Brunswick, Harriet Irving Library, Stanmore Papers, microfilm 1.

Structure of Canadian History: J.L. Finlay and D.N. Sprague, *The Structure of Canadian History* (2nd ed., Scarborough Ont., 1984, first published 1979).

Whelan: E. Whelan (comp.), *The Union of the British Provinces ... Together with a Report of the Speeches Delivered by the Delegates from the Provinces on Important Public Occasions* (Summerside, PEI, 1949, first published 1865).

Notes and References

PREFACE

1. W.H. Russell, *My Diary North and South* (2 vols, London, 1863) i, p. v.
2. Henry Fielding, *Tom Jones* (first published 1749), ch. 2.
3. E.M Wrong, *Charles Buller and Responsible Government* (Oxford, 1929) p. v.

1 BRITISH NORTH AMERICA ON THE EVE OF CONFEDERATION

1. The preamble to the British North America Act (1867) is given in Joseph Pope (ed.), *Confederation*, p. 249 and Browne, p. 302.
2. These issues are also discussed in Ged Martin, 'An Imperial Idea and Its Friends: Canadian Confederation and the British, 1837-1864' in Gordon Martel (ed.), *Studies in British Imperial History: Essays in Honour of A.P. Thornton* (Basingstoke, 1986) pp. 49-94; and Ged Martin, 'Launching Canadian Confederation: Means to Ends', *Historical Journal*, xxvii (1984) pp. 575-602. The present study also draws upon G.W. Martin, 'Britain and the Future of British North America, 1837-1867' (PhD thesis, Cambridge, 1972).
   Various studies discuss the idea of Confederation in the decades before 1867. Older works which remain useful are R.G. Trotter, *Canadian Federation : Its Origins and Achievements. A Study in Nation-Building* (Toronto, 1924) and W.M. Whitelaw, *The Maritimes and Canada before Confederation* (Toronto, 1934). Chester Martin, *Foundations of Canadian Nationhood* (Toronto, 1955) is valuable in placing Confederation in a longer perspective, but its usefulness is reduced by the absence of any citation of sources. For the Loyalist

pedigree of Confederation, see Peter J. Smith, 'The Ideological Origins of Canadian Confederation', *Canadian Journal of Political Science*, xx (1987) pp. 3-31; Peter J. Smith, 'The Dream of Political Union: Loyalism, Toryism and the Federal Idea in Pre-Confederation Canada', in Ged Martin (ed.), *Causes*, pp. 148-71. Other essays and articles include James A. Gibson, 'The Colonial Office View of Canadian Federation, 1856-1867', *CHR*, xxxv (1954), pp. 279-313; L.F.S. Upton, 'The Idea of Confederation, 1754-1858' in W.L. Morton (ed.), *The Shield of Achilles* (Toronto, 1968); Bruce A. Knox, 'The Rise of Colonial Federation as an Object of British Policy, 1850-1870', *Journal of British Studies*, xi (1972), pp. 92-112; Ged Martin, 'Confederation Rejected: the British Debate on Canada, 1837-1840', *JICH*, xi (1982), pp. 33-57; and Ged Martin, 'Britain and the Future of British North America, 1841-1846', *British Journal of Canadian Studies*, ii (1987) pp. 74-96.

3.   Phillip A. Buckner, 'The Maritimes and Confederation: A Reassessment', *CHR*, lxxi (1990) p. 21n.

4.   The three most authoritative modern studies are D.G. Creighton, *The Road to Confederation: The Emergence of Canada 1863-1867* (Toronto, 1964) [cited as *Road to Confederation*]; W.L. Morton, *The Critical Years: The Union of British North America 1857-1873* (Toronto, 1964) [cited as *Critical Years*]; and P.B. Waite, *The Life and Times of Confederation 1864-1867: Politics, Newspapers, and the Union of British North America* (Toronto, 1962) [cited as *Life and Times*]. These should be supplemented by two giant biographies of leading politicians: D.G. Creighton, *John A. Macdonald: The Young Politician* (Toronto, 1952) [cited as *Macdonald*, i] and J.M.S. Careless, *Brown of the Globe*, i: *The Voice of Upper Canada 1818-1859* (Toronto, 1959) and ii: *Statesman of Confederation 1860-1880* (Toronto, 1963) [cited as *Brown*].

5.   Arthur R.M. Lower, *Colony to Nation: A History of Canada* (5th ed., 1977, first published 1946), pp. xiii, 471. Other general works referred to include J.B. Brebner, *Canada: A Modern History* (Ann Arbor, 1960) [cited as Brebner]; J.M.S. Careless, *Canada: A Story of Challenge* (rev. ed., Toronto, 1974); D.G. Creighton, *Dominion of the North: A History of Canada* (rev. ed., Toronto, 1962) [cited as *Dominion of the North*]; J.L. Finlay and D.N. Sprague, *The Structure of Canadian History* (2nd ed., Scarborough, Ont., 1984) [cited as *Structure of Canadian History*]; R. Douglas Francis, R. Jones and D.B. Smith, *Origins: Canadian History to Confederation* (Toronto, 1988); Edgar McInnis, *Canada: A Social and Political History* (4th ed.,

Toronto, 1982) [cited as McInnis]; Kenneth McNaught, *The Pelican History of Canada* (rev. ed., London, 1978) [cited as McNaught]; Desmond Morton, *A Short History of Canada* (rev. ed., Edmonton, 1983); W.L. Morton, *Kingdom of Canada: A General History from Earliest Times* (2nd ed., Toronto, 1969) [cited as *Kingdom of Canada*]. For a selection of articles, see Ramsay Cook (ed.), *Confederation* (Canadian Historical Readings, no. 3, Toronto, 1967).

6. J.H. Dales, *The Protective Tariff in Canada's Development* (Toronto, 1966) pp. 145-9. Dales quoted Innis, Creighton, Brebner, Easterbrook and Aitken but exempted Lower and Chester Martin from his 'historians' stereotype'.

7. Buckner argues that opposition to Confederation in the Maritimes has been exaggerated, 'The Maritimes and Confederation', pp. 1-30, esp. 5-7, reprinted in Ged Martin (ed.), *Causes*, pp. 86-113. See also D.A. Muise, 'The Federal Election of 1867 in Nova Scotia: An Economic Interpretation', *Collections of the Nova Scotia Historical Society*, xxxvi (1968), pp. 327-51, and Brian D. Tennyson, 'Economic Nationalism, Confederation and Nova Scotia', in Ged Martin (ed.), *Causes*, pp. 130-41.

8. *Colony to Nation*, ch. 23 ('The Miracle of Union').

9. Ronald L. Watts, 'An Overview', in R.L. Watts and D.M. Brown (eds), *Options for a New Canada* (Toronto, 1991) p. 12; Robert C. Vipond, *Liberty and Community: Canadian Federalism and the Failure of the Constitution* (Albany NY, 1991) p. 17; D.J. Bercuson and B. Cooper, *Deconfederation: Canada Without Quebec* (Toronto, 1991) p. 75.

10. E.W. Watkin, *Canada and the States: Recollections 1851 to 1886* (London, 1886) pp. 2, 65b.

11. Watkin's role was seized upon as early as 1924 by R.G. Trotter, *Canadian Federation*, ch. xiii ('Introducing a Promoter of Empire') and enshrined in *Cambridge History of the British Empire*, vi: *Canada and Newfoundland* (1930) pp. 443-4, 462. Watkin also appears in Brebner, pp. 282-4; Careless, *Canada: A Story of Challenge*, pp. 241-2; *Dominion of the North*, pp. 292-3; *Colony to Nation*, p. 317; McInnis, pp. 344, 363; and *Kingdom of Canada*, p. 312. This is one of several examples which call to mind the term 'historians' consensus', as used by Dales. Watkin also figures large in an important economic interpretation, Stanley B. Ryerson, *Unequal Union: Roots of Crisis in the Canadas, 1815-1873* (2nd ed., Toronto, 1973) pp. 322-3, 343. An important attempt to interpret the financial aspect of the British role is D.W.

Roman, 'The Contribution of Imperial Guarantees for Colonial Railway Loans to the Consolidation of British North America 1847-1865', (DPhil. thesis, Oxford, 1978).

12. Francis, Jones and Smith, *Origins*, p. 390.

13. Watkin, *Canada and the States*, p. 2.

14. They were published in *British Parliamentary Papers* [cited as *BPP*], 1866, lxxiii, *Colonial Trade Statistics*, pp. 126-81.

15. *Life and Times,* ch. 17.

16. J.M.S. Careless, *The Union of the Canadas: The Growth of Canadian Institutions* (Toronto, 1967).

17. Margaret A. Banks, 'Upper and Lower Canada or Canada West and East?', *CHR*, liv (1973) pp. 473-80.

18. *Monck Letters and Journals*, p. 175.

19. *Critical Years*, pp. 2-3.

20. United States figures from *Historical Statistics of the United States: Colonial Times to 1957* (Washington DC, 1960).

21. British figures from B.R. Mitchell with P. Deane, *Abstract of British Historical Statistics* (Cambridge, 1962).

22. *CD*, p. 763. The speaker was John Macdonald, Reform Member for Toronto West, not to be confused with the better-known John A. Macdonald and John Sandfield Macdonald.

23. Quoted in Monck A-755, Cardwell to Monck, private, 1 September 1865. For Newfoundland and the Ipswich election, *Hansard*, lxiii (26 May 1842) col. 875.

24. As argued by R.C. Nelson, W.C. Soderlund, R.H. Wagenberg and E.D. Briggs, 'Canadian Confederation as a Case Study in Community Formation', in Ged Martin (ed.), *Causes*, pp. 50-85, esp. 59-60, 75-6. Compare S.A. Saunders, *The Economic History of the Maritime Provinces* (Fredericton, 1984) pp. 98-100.

25. *Punch*, 30 March 1861, p. 134.

26. Grey Papers, Ashburton to Howick, 10 April 1838.

27. R.W. Fogel and S.L. Engermann, *Time on the Cross* (2 vols, London, 1974) i, p. 250; ii, p. 163. Sharp differences in per capita commodity income by region in 1870 are demonstrated by the maps in Kris Inwood and James Irwin, 'Canadian Regional Commodity Income Differences at Confederation' in Kris Inwood (ed.), *Farm, Factory and Fortune: New Studies in the Economic History of the Maritime Provinces* (Fredericton, 1993) pp. 99-100.

28. Lucas, ii, p. 212; A. Trollope, *North America* (2 vols, London, 1968 ed., first published 1861) i, p. 55.

29. Douglas McCalla, 'Railways and the Development of Canada West, 1850-1870' in A. Greer and I. Radforth (eds), *Colonial Leviathan: State Formation in Mid-Nineteenth-Century Canada* (Toronto, 1992) pp. 192-229.

30. HCC 1543, Head to Lewis, 20 October 1855.

31. Perceptions of the Maritimes are discussed in Chapter Four. There is some emerging difference of emphasis among economic historians about the dependence of the province of Canada on imported British capital. For an effective summary of the view that British governments manipulated the colonial need for access to capital to sustain a British North America separate from the United States, see P.J. Cain and A.G. Hopkins, *British Imperialism: Innovation and Expansion 1688-1914* (London, 1993) pp. 258-73. Douglas McCalla has argued that much of the capital required for the development of Upper Canada was locally generated, and that comparison with adjoining American states suggests that larger projects could have been financed independently of the colonial connection. While accepting that Canada benefited from indirect British subsidies, notably through expenditure on garrisons, McCalla also suggests that the three largest British-financed transportation projects were of limited benefit. The Rideau Canal, a defence project, quickly became irrelevant. The Grand Trunk Railway was 'neither the only nor even the best possibility for completing the core Canadian railway system'. Most notably, the enlargement of the Welland Canal, financed by the loan which the British government used as a carrot for securing Upper Canadian acquiescence in the Union of 1841, was an 'inappropriate strategy', creating a waterway which rarely functioned above 15 per cent of its capacity. (Douglas McCalla, *Planting the Province: The Economic History of Upper Canada 1784-1870* (Toronto, 1993) esp. pp. 202, 126.) What McCalla terms the 'overbuilding' of the Welland as a ship canal is of some importance in this discussion, since Cain and Hopkins revealingly talk of the 'St. Lawrence Seaway as a conduit for trade between Britain and the mid-west of America'. (Cain and Hopkins, *British Imperialism: Innovation and Expansion*, p. 259.) The Seaway was opened in 1959, and the *Oxford English Dictionary* cites the earliest use of the term from 1921.

32. C. Dickens, *Pictures from Italy and American Notes* (London, 1859 ed.) p. 205. The description was of Halifax in 1842.

33. Gladstone 44136, Cobden to Gladstone, 24 February 1865, fos 275-8.

34. *The Times*, 26 January 1850.

35. For the evolution of colonial self-government, see Phillip A. Buckner, *The Transition to Responsible Government: British Policy in British North America 1815-1850* (Westport, Conn., 1985); Ged Martin, 'The Canadian Rebellion Losses Bill of 1849 in British Politics', *JICH*, vi (1977) pp. 3-22.

36. J. Pope, *Correspondence of Sir John Macdonald* (Garden City NY ed., 1921) p. 29n.

37. Careless, *Union of the Canadas*.

38. Brown, i, esp. chs 6-8.

39. The resolutions are given in O.D. Skelton, *Life and Times of Sir Alexander Tilloch Galt* (ed. G. MacLean, Toronto, 1966) pp. 283-4.

40. *Critical Years*, pp. 16-20; *Macdonald*, i, pp. 261-70; *Brown*, i, pp. 254-80.

41. Pope, *Memoirs*, pp. 216-17; *Canadian Presbyter*, September 1858, quoted R.W. Vaudry, *The Free Church in Victorian Canada* (Waterloo, Ont., 1989) p. 76.

42. *Brown*, ii, p. 47.

43. For the *Trent* crisis and its political implications, see W.L. Morton, *Critical Years*, ch. 6, and R.W. Winks, *Canada and the United States: The Civil War Years* (rev. ed., Montreal, 1971) ch. 6. For the military problems, see Kenneth Bourne, *Britain and the Balance of Power in North America* (London, 1967) ch. 7, and J. Mackay Hitsman, *Safeguarding Canada 1763-1871* (Toronto, 1968) ch. 8.

44. For example, Newcastle 11413, Monck to Newcastle, private, 8 March 1862.

45. Bruce W. Hodgins, *John Sandfield Macdonald 1812-1872* (Toronto, 1971).

46. *Critical Years*, pp. 121-5.

47. *Ibid.*, p. 125.

48. *Ibid.*, pp. 128-9; *Brown*, ii, pp. 92-5.

49. Newcastle 10887, Newcastle to Monck (copy), private, 18 September 1863, pp. 47-52; Monck to Henry Monck, 28 March 1864, in *Monck Letters and Journals*, pp. 42-3.

50. *Brown*, ii, pp. 127-9.

51. J. Young, *Public Men and Public Life in Canada: The Story of the Canadian Confederacy* (2 vols, Toronto, 1912) i, pp. 197-8.

52. Macdonald to Lindsey, confidential, 24 September 1858; same to same, 14 June 1860, in J.K. Johnson and C.B. Stelmack (eds), *The Papers of the Prime Ministers: The Letters of Sir John A. Macdonald 1858-1861* (Ottawa, 1969) pp. 84, 214.

53. Young, *Public Men and Public Life,* i, p. 201.

54. *Ibid.,* i, p. 211. Young claimed to have had the story from Brown.

55. *Brown,* ii, pp. 129, 124.

56. For an attempted revision of the politics of the Great Coalition, see Ged Martin, *Faction and Fiction in Canada's Great Coalition of 1864* (Sackville, New Brunswick, 1993). For examples of emphasis upon the aim of British North American union, see McNaught, p. 122 and *Structure of Canadian History,* p. 174.

57. *Road to Confederation,* chs 3-7; *Critical Years,* pp. 151-70; *Life and Times,* chs 4-7.

58. *Road to Confederation,* pp. 234-7; A.I. Silver, *The French-Canadian Idea of Confederation 1864-1900* (Toronto, 1982) ch. 2. A selection of *The Confederation Debates in the Province of Canada 1865* (Toronto, 1963) was edited by P. B. Waite. Citations in this work are to the full edition of 1865 (*CD*).

59. *Road to Confederation,* chs 7-8; *Critical Years,* pp. 170-81; Beck, *Howe,* ii, ch. 9.

60. W.M. Baker, *Timothy Warren Anglin 1822-1896: Irish Catholic Canadian* (Toronto, 1977) pp. 69-79; A.G. Bailey, 'Railways and the Confederation Issue in New Brunswick, 1863-1865', *CHR,* xxi (1940) pp. 367-83, and 'The Basis and Persistence of Opposition to Confederation in New Brunswick', *CHR,* xxiii (1942) pp. 374-97; J.K. Chapman, 'Arthur Gordon and Confederation', *CHR,* xxxvii (1956) pp. 142-57.

61. Macdonald Letter Book, 8, Macdonald to Watkin (copy), private, 27 March 1865.

62. *Road to Confederation,* ch. 9.

63. Baker, *Anglin,* ch. 7; J.K. Chapman, *The Career of Arthur Hamilton Gordon, First Lord Stanmore 1829-1912* (Toronto, 1964) ch. 2, esp. pp. 36-7.

64. The British role is discussed in Chapter Seven.

65. Baker, *Anglin,* ch. 7; *Road to Confederation,* chs 10-12; *Critical Years,* ch. 10.

66. *Road to Confederation,* ch. 14; *Critical Years,* ch. 11; Beck, *Howe,* ii, pp. 202-18.

67. For example, *Critical Years*, p. 149; *Structure of Canadian History*, p. 171.
68. G.P. de T. Glazebrook, *A History of Transportation in Canada* (2 vols, Toronto, 1964 ed.) i, p. 172.
69. *Colony to Nation*, p. 316.
70. Francis, Jones and Smith, *Origins*, p. 379.
71. For example, McNaught, pp. 125-6, but compare the note of doubt in *Dominion of the North*, p. 301.
72. Desmond Morton, *Short History of Canada*, p. 71.
73. *Colony to Nation*, p. 323.
74. *Critical Years*, p. 149.
75. McNaught, p. 122.
76. *Dominion of the North*, p. 305.
77. For an example of pride in the achievement of Confederation: Careless, *Canada: A Story of Challenge*, pp. 230, 245.
78. *Kingdom of Canada*, p. 317.

2   CANADIAN CONFEDERATION AND HISTORICAL EXPLANATION

1. Knox, *JICH*, 1976.
2. This section draws on Ged Martin, *History as Science or Literature*: *Explaining Canadian Confederation 1858-1867* (Canada House Lecture, no. 41, London, 1989).
3. Arthur Marwick, *The Nature of History* (London, 1970) p. 99. The classic statement of history as a science was made by J.B. Bury in 1903, in H. Temperley (ed.), *Selected Essays of J.B. Bury* (Cambridge, 1930), pp. 3-22, and contested by G.M. Trevelyan, *Clio: A Muse and Other Essays* (2nd ed., London, 1930) pp. 143-9. See also Lee Benson, *Toward the Scientific Study of History: Selected Essays* (Philadelphia, 1972).
4. Baker, *Anglin*, p. 115. But Buckner hazards the opinion that some form of union might well have come in the next decade. 'The Maritimes and Confederation', p. 21.
5. Gwyn Macfarlane, *Alexander Fleming: The Man and the Myth* (London, 1984) p. 246.
6. Chester Martin, *Foundations*, pp. 297-8.
7. W.H. Russell, *Canada: Its Defences, Condition and Resources* (London, 1865) p. 311.

8. *Canadian Encyclopedia* (3 vols, Edmonton, 1985), i, p. 399. This statement was sufficiently attractive to be quoted in Francis, Jones and Smith, *Origins*, p. 378. However, Waite has subsequently abandoned the metaphor. Peter Waite, 'Between Three Oceans: Challenges of Continental Destiny (1840-1900)' in C. Brown (ed.), *The Illustrated History of Canada* (Toronto, 1987), p. 314.

9. Brebner, p. 277.

10. David Hackett Fischer, *Historians' Fallacies: Towards a Logic of Historical Thought* (New York, 1970), pp. xxi-xxii.

11. Bruce A. Knox, 'Rise of Colonial Federation as an Object of British Policy, 1850-1870', *Journal of British Studies*, xi (1972) pp. 92-112.

12. C.F. Goodfellow, *Great Britain and South African Confederation 1870-1881* (Cape Town, 1966) p. 47.

13. *Road to Confederation*, ch. 9.

14. John Morley, *The Life of William Ewart Gladstone* (3 vols, London, 1903) i, p. 192.

15. W.F. Monypenny and G.E. Buckle, *The Life of Benjamin Disraeli Earl of Beaconsfield* (6 vols, London, 1910-20) iv, p. 173.

16. J.L. Granatstein, *Canada's War: The Politics of the Mackenzie King Government, 1939-1945* (Toronto, 1975) p. 372.

17. Speech at Halifax, 13 August 1864, in Chisholm, ii, p. 433; Beck, *Howe*, ii, p. 182.

18. F.W.P. Bolger, *Prince Edward Island and Confederation* (Charlottetown, 1964) pp. 85-6.

19. Francis Palgrave, *Quarterly Review*, lxxiii (1843) p. 557. I owe this quotation to Sandra Kaiser.

20. *CD*, p. 9.

21. As Joly inconveniently pointed out, *ibid.*, pp. 357-8, and compare pp. 1000-1.

22. Speech at Quebec, 15 October 1864, in Whelan, p. 76.

23. *CD*, p. 6.

24. *Ibid.*, p. 483.

25. *Globe*, 12 May 1865, reporting speeches in London, 26 April.

26. Speech at Halifax, 12 October 1864, in Whelan, p. 26.

27. *Ibid.*, pp. 38-9.

28. *Globe*, 6 August 1864

29. *Ibid.*, 15 May 1865.

30. Brebner, p. 273.

31. *The Times*, 4 April 1857.

32. *Brown*, i, p. 239.

33. *The Times*, 1 September 1858.

34. Memorandum by T.F. Elliot, 4 November 1858, in R.G.Trotter, 'The British Government and the Proposal of Federation in 1858', *CHR*, xiv (1933) pp. 285-92, esp. p. 290.

35. *Kingdom of Canada*, p. 309

36. *Structure of Canadian History*, p. 170

37. HCC 2028, Herman Merivale to G.C. Lewis, 23 September 1858.

38. *Colony to Nation*, p. 299.

39. *Ibid.*, p. 321.

40. For mild verdicts, see *Structure of Canadian History*, p. 202 and *Kingdom of Canada*, p. 346. The 'nation building' aspect of the episode has been criticised by A.A. den Otter, 'Nationalism and the Pacific Scandal', *CHR*, lxix (1988) pp. 315-39. In some respects, Macdonald's fall in 1873 was evidence that pre-Confederation political instability had survived 1867. There are, for instance, estimates of Macdonald's majority in the House of Commons after the 1872 election which vary from 8 to 53. J.M. Beck, *Pendulum of Power: Canada's Federal Elections* (Scarborough, Ont., 1968) pp. 19, 21; Dale C. Thomson, *Alexander Mackenzie: Clear Grit* (Toronto, 1960) p. 144; *Critical Years*, p. 271.

41. *Colony to Nation*, p. 365.

42. *Ibid.*, p. 300.

43. *Dominion of the North*, p. 290.

44. As George Brown explained to Richard Cobden in 1862. Gladstone 44136, Cobden to Gladstone, 14 February 1865, fos 248-59.

45. Creighton (*Macdonald*, i, pp. 329-33) and Morton (*Critical Years*, pp. 108-12) both touched on the issue. See also C.P. Stacey, *Canada and the British Army 1846-1871* (2nd ed., Toronto, 1963) p. 135.

46. *Kingdom of Canada*, p. 428; *Critical Years*, p. 125.

47. Howe to C.B. Adderley, 24 December 1862 (open letter) in Chisholm, ii, p. 403.

48. Spencer Walpole, *The Life of Lord John Russell* (2 vols, London, 1889) ii, pp. 13-30, esp. p. 25.

49. D. Southgate, *'The Most English Minister': The Policies and Politics of Palmerston* (London, 1966) pp. 308-10; Goldwin Smith, *The Empire: A Series of Letters Published in The Daily News, 1862, 1863* (Oxford, 1863) p. 115.

50. R.C. Brown and R. Cook, *Canada 1896-1921: A Nation Transformed* (Toronto, 1974) p. 210; and compare R.S. Churchill, *Winston S. Churchill*, ii: *Young Statesman 1901-1914* (London, 1967) pp. 665-66.

51. J.L. Granatstein et al., *Twentieth Century Canada* (2nd ed., Toronto, 1986) p. 64.

52. For the Canadian militia in the 1860s, see *Critical Years*, pp. 126-8; Hodgins, *Sandfield Macdonald*, pp. 87-8; Richard A. Preston, *Canada and 'Imperial Defense'* (Durham, N.C., 1967) pp. 46-7, 59-62.

53. *Critical Years*, p. 128.

54. *Ibid.*, p. 146.

55. Preston, *Canada and 'Imperial Defense'*, pp. 46-7.

56. *Ibid.*, pp. 60-1. There is no mention of this episode in *Critical Years*, nor in *Macdonald*, ii.

57. Trotter, *Canadian Federation*, p. 51.

58. Quoted, F.H. Underhill, *The Image of Confederation* (Toronto, 1964) p. 19.

59. *Critical Years*, pp. 121-5.

60. *Ibid.*, p. 124.

61. *Ibid.*, p. 123.

62. Goldwin Smith, *My Memory of Gladstone* (London, 1904), pp. 43-4. Paul Knaplund, *Gladstone and Britain's Imperial Policy* (London, 1927) pp. 91-2, was at pains to discredit the story, but unconvincingly.

63. Peter M. Toner, 'New Brunswick Schools and the Rise of Provincial Rights', in Bruce W. Hodgins, Don Wright and W.H. Heick (eds), *Federalism in Canada and Australia: The Early Years* (Waterloo, Ont., 1978) pp. 125-35, esp. p. 135; Paul Crunican, *Priests and Politicians: Manitoba Schools and the Election of 1896* (Toronto, 1974) esp. p. 322.

64. *Brown*, ii, p. 64.

65. Goldwin Smith, *Reminiscences* (New York, 1910), p. 436.

66. *Critical Years*, pp. 112-13.

67. *Ibid.*, p. 112.

68. *Ibid.*, pp. 464, 491, and compare the contrast with Meighen, pp. 455-56.

69. Pope, *Memoirs*, p. 373.

70. Creighton mentioned Sandfield Macdonald as premier of Ontario in *Macdonald*, ii, p. 4, with no mention of how he was appointed, which leaves the reader unprepared for Sir John A's regret at his defeat in 1872 on p. 114. Sandfield's premiership is not mentioned at all in *Dominion of the North, The Story of Canada* (London, 1959) nor in *Canada's First Century 1867-1967* (Toronto, 1970). W.L. Morton was more explicit in *Kingdom of Canada*, p. 328 than in *Critical Years*, p. 218. Here, as on other points, Desmond Morton, *Short History of Canada*, p. 80, perceives a significance which many accounts miss.

See also Robert Bothwell, *A Short History of Ontario* (Edmonton, 1986) pp. 76-8.

71. *Colony to Nation*, p. 307.

72. Compare M. Larkin, *France Since the Popular Front: Government and People 1936-1986* (Oxford, 1988) pp. 34-62, 396.

73. *Colony to Nation*, p. 308. The following would generally be recognised as premiers: Louis LaFontaine (1842, 1848-51), Robert Baldwin (1842, 1848-51); Francis Hincks (1851-4); Augustin Norbert Morin (1851-4); Allan Napier MacNab (1854-6); Etienne Paschal Taché (1856-7, 1864-5); George Etienne Cartier (1857-8, 1858-62); John A. Macdonald (1857-8, 1858-62); John Sandfield Macdonald (1862-4); Louis Victor Sicotte (1862-3); Antoine-Aimé Dorion (1863-4); Narcisse Belleau (1865-7). Most historians would now add to the list William Henry Draper (1843-8) and it would be churlish to omit George Brown, for two days co-premier with Dorion in 1858. The basis of Lower's count is obscure.

74. *Colony to Nation*, p. 311.

75. J.C. Dent, *The Last Forty Years: Canada Since the Union of 1841* (2 vols, Toronto, 1881) ii, p. 439.

76. *Globe*, 18 June 1864; Brown, ii, p. 131.

77. An Irish political commentator wrote of 'structural deadlock'. Vincent Browne, ed., *The Magill Guide to Election 82* (Dublin, 1982) p. 4.

78. Quoted, McNaught, p. 308.

79. *CD*, p. 586.

80. *Ibid.*, p. 543.

81. *Ibid.*, p. 797.

82. *Ibid.*, p. 358.

83. *Kingdom of Canada*, p. 315; McInnis, p. 343.

84. McNaught, p. 121; *Kingdom of Canada*, p. 315.

85. *Colony to Nation*, p. 313; P.G. Cornell, *The Great Coalition* (Canadian Historical Association Booklet, no. 19, 2nd ed., 1971) p. 17.

86. Speech at Halifax, 12 September 1864, Whelan, p. 28.

87. Goldwin Smith, *Canada and the Canadian Question* (ed. C. Berger, Toronto, 1971, first published 1891) p. 114.

88. Careless, *Canada: A Story of Challenge*, p. 233; Cornell, *Great Coalition*, p. 17. Other historians have spoken of 'kaleidoscopic' factionalism: C. Martin, *Foundations*, p. 300; McNaught, p. 120.

89. *Structure of Canadian History*, p. 174; Francis, Jones and Smith, *Origins*, p. 269.

90. Ryerson is one of the few historians to have used the 'log-jam' image: *Unequal Union*, p. 342.

91. W. Ormsby, *The Emergence of the Federal Concept in the Province of Canada 1839-1845* (Toronto, 1969) p. 125; *Road to Confederation*, p. 45; *Kingdom of Canada*, p. 317.

92. Two members, John Jones Ross and John Le Boutillier, are hard to classify, and I am indebted to Professor Kenneth Munro for discussion on this point. It may seem symbolic that Le Boutillier entertained the Canadian delegates on their way to Charlottetown, *Brown*, ii, p. 153.

93. Canada Union Act, 1840, 3 & 4 Vic., cap. 35, clauses 26, 12, in F. Madden (ed.), *Imperial Constitutional Documents, 1765-1965: A Supplement* (Oxford, 1966) p. 21. For the repeal of sec. 26, see *United Kingdom Public General Statutes*, 17 & 18 Vic., cap. 118, sec. 5; C. Martin, *Foundations*, p. 300.

94. Sir Edmund Head's memorandum on the seat of government, 1857, quoted D.G.G. Kerr, with J.A. Gibson, *Sir Edmund Head: A Scholarly Governor* (Toronto, 1954) p. 173. Head expressed a similar view in a memorandum apparently dating from 1858, C. Martin, 'Sir Edmund Head and Canadian Confederation 1851-1858', *Canadian Historical Association Annual Report*, 1929, p. 13, also quoted in C. Martin, *Foundations*, p. 302.

95. C. Martin, *Foundations*, p. 303.

96. *Brown*, ii, pp. 42, 62, 97.

97. *CD*, p. 28.

98. J. Cauchon, *L'Union des Provinces de l'Amérique Britannique du Nord* (Quebec, 1865), p. 18.

99. C. Martin, *Foundations*, p. 301.

100. *Brown*, ii, p. 120; *Globe*, 15 March 1864.

101. Hodgins, *Sandfield Macdonald*, p. 68.

102. *CD*, p. 624 (Perrault).

103. Compare the comments of J.W. Dawson, Principal of McGill University, *Life and Times*, p. 135.

104. Dorion's signals were detected by C. Martin (*Foundations*, p. 301) and by Waite (*Life and Times*, p. 139), and referred to by George Brown in *CD*, p. 92.

105. D. Morton, *Short History*, pp. 72-3.

106. A. Mackenzie, *The Life and Speeches of Hon. George Brown* (Toronto, 1882) pp. 88-94.

107. McNaught, p. 122 and see also *Structure of Canadian History*, p. 174.

108. For memoranda of the negotiations, see Pope, *Memoirs*, pp. 680-7 and Mackenzie, *Life and Speeches of Brown*, pp. 88-94. For a more detailed discussion, see Ged Martin, *Faction and Fiction*, pp. 15-18.

109. Pope, ed., *Memoirs*, p. 684.

110. *Macdonald*, i, p. 357.

111. Brown to Holton, 29 January 1858, quoted in *Brown*, i, p. 253. For other expressions of Brown's view that federation would not be an early development, *Brown*, i, pp. 315, 321. For similar views from the *Globe*, in 1860 and 1863, see *Brown*, ii. pp. 23, 111, and *Globe*, 27 June 1864.

112. *Brown*, ii, pp. 142-4; *Globe*, 23 June 1864, reporting ministerial explanations of 22 June.

113. *Globe*, 24 June 1864.

114. Speech at Halifax, 12 September 1864, in Whelan, p. 24.

115. Quoted, Pope, ed., *Confederation*, p. 55.

116. Gordon to Cardwell, private, 30 January 1865, quoted Chapman, *Gordon*, p. 28.

117. *Monck Letters and Journals*, pp. 158-9. Howe made effective use of such reports in England in 1866.

118. Macdonald Letter Book, 8, Macdonald to Watkin (copy), private, 27 March 1865.

119. *CD*, p. 657.

120. Brown to Anne Brown, 8 March 1865, quoted *Brown*, ii, p. 190.

121. Correspondence and memoranda in Pope (ed.), *Memoirs*, pp. 700-6.

122. *Road to Confederation*, pp. 312-15.

123. Brown to Cartier, 19 December 1865, quoted *Brown*, ii, pp. 217-18, and with slight variation in Pope (ed.), *Memoirs*, pp. 708-9.

124. *Road to Confederation*, p. 339.

125. Annand's version of a conversation in November 1865, quoted *Life and Times*, pp. 220-1.

126. *BPP*, 1867, xlviii, *Correspondence*, Minute of New Brunswick Executive Council, 12 July 1865, p. 100.

127. This section draws on Ged Martin, 'The Case Against Canadian Confederation, 1864-1867' in Ged Martin (ed.), *Causes*, pp. 19-49.

128. As Article 45 of the British North America Act, Pope (ed.), *Confederation*, p. 282. Gordon objected to this as unnecessary, but Tilley desperately needed the assurance during the 1865 election campaign. Compare also the comment of Luther Holton. CO 188/143, Gordon to Cardwell, no. 23, 27 February 1865, printed in

BPP, 1867, xlvii, *Correspondence*, pp. 88-9; Bailey, 'Basis and Persistence', pp. 378-9; *CD*, p. 17.

129. Newcastle's despatch of 6 July 1862 is discussed in Chapter Six.
130. *CD*, pp. 103, 356.
131. Speech at Halifax, 12 September 1864, in Whelan, p.38.
132. Frequently quoted, e.g. Bailey, 'Basis and Persistence' p. 379, also in Cook (ed.), *Confederation*, p. 75. W.S. MacNutt, *New Brunswick A History: 1784-1867* (Toronto, 1984 ed.) p. 428 attributes the couplet to G.L. Hatheway.
133. Tilley to Gordon, 27 February 1863, in P.B. Waite, 'A Letter from Leonard Tilley on the Intercolonial Railway, 1863', *CHR*, xlv (1964), p. 128.
134. *CD*, p. 230.
135. *Ibid.*, p. 233 (John Simpson).
136. *Ibid*, p. 196. Compare *DCB*, xi, pp. 315-16.
137. Galt to Lytton, 17 November 1858, in Skelton, *Life and Times of Galt* (ed. MacLean) pp. 99-100.
138. Speech at Halifax, 12 September 1864, in Whelan, p. 45.
139. *Colony to Nation*, p. 315; Saint John *Evening Globe*, 8 September 1865, quoted Bailey, 'Basis and Persistence', p. 390.
140. *CD*, pp. 863 (Eric Dorion), 355 (Joly).
141. *Ibid.*, p. 99.
142. *Ibid.*, p. 356.
143. *Critical Years*, p. 144.
144. N.Rogers, 'The Confederate Council of Trade', *CHR*, vii (1926), 277-86. The Council is mentioned in *Critical Years*, p. 188 and *Life and Times*, pp. 216-17. Its importance is recognised in *Road to Confederation*, pp. 307-8.
145. Monck A-755, Cardwell to Monck, private, 16 July 1864.
146. K.G. Pryke, *Nova Scotia and Confederation 1864-74* (Toronto, 1979) pp. 63-4, and see also *CD*, p. 188 (Letellier de St Just).
147. *CD*, p. 179 (L.A. Olivier).
148. C.Mackay, 'A Week in Prince Edward Island', *Fortnightly Review*, v (1866) pp. 143-57. See also the comments of Shea and Whelan, in W.G. Ormsby, 'Letters to Galt Concerning the Maritime Provinces and Confederation', *CHR*, xxxiv (1953) pp. 167-8.
149. Bolger, *Prince Edward Island and Confederation*, p. 68.
150. *CD*, p. 524.
151. D.G. Creighton, 'Economic Nationalism and Confederation', in Cook (ed.), *Confederation*, p. 8. A.A. den Otter argues that the 1859

tariff foreshadowed the idea of a continental economy, but perhaps exaggerates in terming it 'an embryo National Policy'. A.A. den Otter, 'Alexander Galt, the 1859 Tariff, and Canadian Economic Nationalism', *CHR*, lxiii (1982) pp. 151-78, esp. p. 152.

152. *CD*, p. 99: *Globe*, 27 June 1864.

153. P.B. Waite, *Canada 1874-1896: Arduous Destiny*, p. 76.

154. *Critical Years*, p. 6; J.M.S. Careless, *Toronto to 1918: An Illustrated History* (Toronto, 1984) p. 76.

155. Waite, *Arduous Destiny*, pp. 76-7.

156. *Ibid.*, p. 57.

157. *The Times*, 9 December 1861.

158. Bourne, *Britain and the Balance of Power*, pp. 218-47. One officer missed his sailing in St John's Newfoundland because his cat had vanished down a town drain. The celebrated incident of the diversion of officers' baggage through Portland merely added a note of farce, although the propaganda coup handed to the Americans infuriated British officials. *Monck Letters and Journals*, p. 201; Bourne, *op. cit.*, p. 232n; J.Mackay Hitsman, 'Winter Troop Movements to Canada, 1862, *CHR*, xliii (1962), 127-35; R.W. Winks, *Canada and the United States: The Civil War Years* (Montreal, 1971 ed.) pp. 105-10; CO 42/636, minutes by Elliot and Newcastle, 6, 8 February 1862, fos 52, 71-2.

159. *CD*, pp. 257 (Dorion), 750 (Thomas Scatcherd).

160. Russell, *Canada*, p. 229.

161. *Hansard*, clxxxvi, 26 March 1867, col. 758.

162. *CD*, p. 883.

163. Goldwin Smith, *Canada and the Canadian Question*, p. 111.

164. Speech at Montreal, 29 October 1864, in Whelan, pp. 122-23.

165. Gladstone 44753, fos 128-41, printed in P. Knaplund, *Gladstone and Britain's Imperial Policy*, pp. 228-42.

166. *Road to Confederation*, p. 88.

167. *The Times*, 11 July 1864. Cardwell had heard the news on the afternoon of 7 July: Monck A-755, Cardwell to Monck, private, 7 July 1864. Gladstone began his paper on 11 July. He asked Arthur Gordon, who was then in Britain, for his 'opinion orally, or in writing if you would like to give it, on British North American Federation' in a letter dated 12 July but probably written the day before. H.C.G. Matthew (ed.), *The Gladstone Diaries*: vi, *1861-1868*, pp. 288-9; Gladstone to Gordon, 12 July 1864, in P. Knaplund (ed.),

Gladstone-Gordon Correspondence, 1851-1896 in *Transactions of the American Philosophical Society*, new series, li, iv (1961), pp. 44-5.

168. *CD*, p. 40.

169. *Ibid.*, p. 355.

170. CO 43/153, Newcastle to Monck, 21 August 1862, quoted Gibson, 'The Colonial Office View of Canadian Confederation', p. 304n.

171. For example, *CD*, p. 229 (P.H.Moore); speech by Howe, 22 May 1867, in Chisholm, ii, p. 512, and see also protest from Digby County, Nova Scotia, in *BPP*, 1867, xlviii, *Correspondence*, pp. 69-70.

172. J.H. Gray to Tupper, 7 January 1865, and see *Islander*, 6 January 1865, quoted *Life and Times*, pp. 183, 186.

173. *Newfoundlander*, 12 January 1865, quoted *Life and Times*, p. 167; J.K. Hiller, 'Confederation Defeated: The Newfoundland Election of 1869' in J. Hiller and P. Neary (eds), *Newfoundland in the Nineteenth and Twentieth Centuries: Essays in Reinterpretation* (Toronto, 1980) p. 83.

174. *CD*, pp. 176 (Olivier).

175. *CD*, pp. 123 (Sanborn), 256 (Dorion); Bailey, 'Basis and Persistence', p. 380.

176. *CD*, p. 796 (O'Halloran).

177. *Ibid.*, p. 46 (James Currie) and see also pp. 223 (P.H. Moore) and 763 (J.Macdonald).

178. Quoted, J. Schull, *Laurier: The First Canadian* (Toronto, 1966), p. 57.

179. *CD*, p. 55.

180. *Ibid.*, p. 354.

181. *Ibid.*, p. 796, and see also p. 223 (Moore).

182. Whelan, p. 46.

183. *CD*, p. 55.

184. Macdonald 188, Brown to Macdonald, private and confidential, 22 December 1864, also printed in Pope, *Memoirs*, pp. 289-90.

185. *CD*, p. 107.

186. CO 217/235, MacDonnell to Cardwell, separate, 22 November 1864, fos 187-212.

187. Minute by Palmerston, 29 July 1864, quoted *Macdonald*, i, p. 361.

188. Russell 97, Russell to Lyons, copy, 20 October 1864.

189. Watkin, *Canada and the States*, p. 16.

190. Undated letter of 1865 from Rogers to Taylor, in *Autobiography of Henry Taylor* (2 vols, London, 1875) ii, pp. 241-2.

191. Gladstone 44118, Gladstone to Cardwell, copy, private, 23 May 1865, fos 187-90, printed in Knaplund, *Gladstone's Imperial Policy*, p.

243. See also the 1869 speech by Cardwell in the House of Commons, quoted Hitsman, *Safeguarding Canada*, p. 214.

192. *The Times*, 24 November 1864; *Road to Confederation*, p. 215.

193. Quoted, Creighton, *Macdonald*, ii, p. 277.

194. *BPP*, 1861, xiii, *Report of Select Committee on Colonial Military Expenditure*, Q. 2619.

195. *The Times*, 2 September 1861, 20 March 1865.

196. Clarendon to Cowley, 29 November 1861, quoted Bourne, *op. cit.*, p. 247.

197. Broadlands NE/88/3, Newcastle to Palmerston, 3 September 1861.

198. *CD*, p. 107.

199. *Macdonald*, i, p. 361.

200. Diary of Frances Monck, 19 December 1864, in *Monck Letters and Journals*, p. 186.

201. *CD*, p. 795.

202. Quoted in Chisholm, ii, pp. 487, 489. One of Howe's sons had served in the Northern armies.

203. Speech at Halifax, 12 September 1864, in Whelan, p. 26. Compare A. Smith, 'Old Ontario and the Emergence of a National Frame of Mind', in F.H. Armstrong, H.A. Stevenson and J.D. Wilson (eds), *Aspects of Nineteenth-Century Ontario* (Toronto, 1974) pp. 194-217.

204. *CD*, p. 60.

205. Speech at Quebec, 14 October 1864, in Whelan, p. 77.

206. *CD*, p. 45.

207. *Ibid.*, pp. 748, 208. *Hansard*, lcxxxv, 28 February 1867, cols 1177-8.

208. *Hansard*, clxxxv, 28 February 1867, cols 1177-8.

209. Nelson et al., 'Canadian Confederation as a Case Study in Community Formation', in Ged Martin (ed.), *Causes*, esp. p. 85; MacNutt, *New Brunswick: A History*, p. 447.

210. *The Nation*, 26 February 1875, quoted Underhill, *The Image of Confederation*, p. 20. In 1893, the prime minister of Canada could say that 'this country ought to be a nation, will be a nation, and please God we will and shall make it a nation' but that in the face of the overwhelming power of the United States, independence would be 'absurdity, if not treason'. P.B. Waite, *The Man from Halifax: Sir John Thompson Prime Minister* (Toronto, 1985) p. 357.

211. *Structure of Canadian History*, p. 171.

212. *CD*, p. 763 (John Macdonald) and see also p. 353 (Joly).

213. *Ibid.*, p. 263.

214. Pope (ed.), *Confederation*, p. 52.

215. *CD*, p. 453 (T.C. Wallbridge).

216. Pope (ed.), *Confederation*, p. 59.

217. Macdonald to Watkin, 27 March 1865, in Pope (ed.), *Memoirs*, pp. 396-7.

218. *Colony to Nation*, p. 295.

219. Brydges to Macdonald, 24 February 1864, quoted *Macdonald*, i, p. 349; see also *Brown*, ii, pp. 116-17.

220. *Saturday Review*, 10 June 1865, p. 687.

221. *Kingdom of Canada*, p. 317.

222. Bailey, 'Basis and Persistence', p. 378.

223. D. Owram, *Promise of Eden; The Canadian Expansionist Movement and the Idea of the West, 1856-1900* (Toronto, 1980) pp. 38-58; *Brown*, i, pp. 211-14.

224. Brydges to Macpherson, 11 March 1872, in Glazebrook, *History of Transportation*, ii, pp. 49-50. For Watkin, see his letter of 13 November 1860, in Watkin, *op. cit.*, pp. 12-15 and J.S. Galbraith, *The Hudson's Bay Company as an Imperial Factor 1821-1869* (New York, 1977 ed.) pp. 381-2.

225. Tilley to Gordon, 2 February 1863, in Waite, 'A Letter from Leonard Tilley on the Intercolonial', p. 128.

226. Speech at Halifax, 12 September 1864, in Whelan, p. 45.

227. *Ibid.*, p. 26, and see also the comments of David Reesor in *CD*, p. 164.

228. *CD*, pp. 54-5 (Cartier).

229. Taché used it in conversation with Whelan, who was a Prince Edward Islander. *Life and Times*, p. 102.

230. For two surveys of French Canadian opinion, see *Life and Times*, pp. 134-60; Silver, *The French-Canadian Idea of Confederation*, pp. 33-50.

231. Cauchon, *L'Union des Provinces*, p. 46.

232. *CD*, p. 250 (Dorion); Macdonald to M.C. Cameron, quoted in *DCB*, xii, p. 599.

233. Carnarvon 6/137, Connolly to Carnarvon, 18 January 1867, fos 148-9; Toner, 'New Brunswick Schools'.

234. *CD*, p. 624 (Perrault).

235. Browne, p. 133.

236. Speeches at Quebec, 14 October 1864, by Abraham Joseph and Tupper, Whelan, pp. 63, 68.

237. Chisholm, ii, p. 489.

238. A.R. Stewart, 'The State of Maine and Canadian Confederation', *CHR*, xxxiii (1952), pp. 148-64.

239. Buckner, 'The Maritimes and Confederation', p. 14.

240. *Kingdom of Canada*, p. 317.
241. Macdonald to M.C. Cameron, 3 January 1872, in Pope (ed.), *Correspondence*, p. 161.
242. John Willison, *Reminiscences: Political and Personal* (Toronto, 1919) p. 177.
243. *Globe*, 28 June 1864.
244. *Ibid.*, 24, 29 June 1864.
245. *The Times*, 21 July; *Globe*, 6 August 1864.
246. Macdonald 188, Brown to Macdonald, private and confidential, 22 December 1864, printed in Pope (ed.), *Memoirs*, pp. 289-90.
247. Speech at Oxford, 2 January 1865, *The Times*, 7 January 1865.
248. Rogers to Miss Rogers, 23 December 1864, in Marindin (ed.), *Letters of Blachford*, pp. 252-3, and recollection, p. 226.
249. Monck A-755, Cardwell to Monck, private and confidential, 3 December 1864.
250. Quoted, Southgate, *'The Most English Minister'*, p. 528.
251. *Brown*, i, p. 348.
252. R. Shannon, *Gladstone: i, 1809-1865* (London, 1982), pp. 506-12.
253. *CD*, pp. 186-7.
254. F.B. Smith, *The Making of the Second Reform Bill* (Melbourne, 1966) p. 16.
255. Quoted, G. Kitson Clark, *The Making of Victorian England* (London, 1965 ed.) p. 209.
256. C. Seymour, *Electoral Reform in England and Wales* (New Haven, Conn., 1915) pp. 335-46; Smith, *Second Reform Bill*, p. 225.
257. Newcastle 10886, Newcastle to Monck, copy, private, 14 June 1862 (another copy in Newcastle 11211).
258. Monck 755, Cardwell to Monck, private, 27 July 1865.
259. *Hansard*, 1867, clxxxv, 28 February 1867, col. 1166.

3   THE ORIGINS OF BRITISH SUPPORT FOR CONFEDERATION

1. See the studies cited in Chapter 1, note 2.
2. Perhaps the classic exposition is C. Martin, 'British Policy in Canadian Confederation', *CHR*, xiii (1932) p. 4. Compare also D.G. Creighton, 'The United States and Canadian Confederation', *CHR*, xxxix (1958) pp. 209-22.
3. *Daily News*, 24 December 1864.

4. The first five of these questions are outlined in Ged Martin, 'An Imperial Idea and its Friends'; the sixth in Ged Martin, 'Launching Canadian Confederation: Means to Ends, 1836-1864', *Historical Journal*, xxvii (1984) pp. 575-602. (For a similar approach, see *Rudyard Kipling's Verse: Definitive Edition* (London, 1940) p. 605.)

5. P.J. Smith, 'The Dream of Political Union: Loyalism, Toryism and the Federal Idea in Pre-Confederation Canada', and 'The Ideological Origins of Canadian Confederation'; G.W. Spragge, 'John Strachan's Connexion with Early Proposals for Confederation', *CHR*, xxiii (1942) pp. 362-73.

6. Robert Gourlay, *General Introduction to Statistical Survey of Upper Canada Compiled with a View to a Grand System of Emigration in Connexion with a Reform of the Poor Laws* (London, 1822) pp. cccxxxviii-cccl.

7. Trotter, 'Early Proposal', pp. 151-2; Robert Gourlay, *An Appeal to the Common Sense, Mind and Manhood of the British Nation* (London, 1826) pp. 149-50; Upton, 'Idea of Confederation', p. 190.

8. CO 537/137, secret minute by Stephen, 20 December 1836, fos 144-69 (copy 170-95); *ibid.*, epitome of proposed Canada Act, 19 January 1837, fos 196-202; Grey Papers, journal, 18, 23, 26 January, 2 February 1837 for cabinet discussions. Compare Ged Martin, 'Confederation Rejected', pp. 37-9.

9. CO 537/137, minute by Stephen, 2 November 1837, fos 210-15.

10. *Hansard*, xxxvii, 14 April 1837, cols 1209-29.

11. *Examiner*, 21 January 1838, pp. 32-3; *Sun*, 18 December 1837, and compare *Spectator*, 3 February 1838, pp. 97-8; *Eclectic Review*, n.s., iii (January 1838), pp. 235-8. Peter Burroughs discusses British press reactions to the rebellions in J.E. Flint and G. Williams (eds), *Perspectives of Empire* (London, 1972) pp. 54-92.

12. Compare Grey Papers, Russell to Howick, 31 December 1837. No letter from Kempt survives, but Russell referred to his discouraging response in *Hansard*, xlvii, 3 June 1839, col. 1264 and cv, 24 May 1849, cols 955-6, and in Russell 31, Russell to Newcastle, copy, confidential, 12 June 1862, fos 97-8.

13. Grey Papers, Colonial Papers, nos.99 (Stephen), [28 December 1837], 100 (Howick) (and compare draft, no. 101), 29 December 1837. For Stephen's contribution, see *ibid.*, Stephen to Howick, 28 December 1837, partly quoted in H.T. Manning, 'Who Ran the British Empire 1830-1850?', *Journal of British Studies*, v (1965) pp. 99-100, and see also Grey journal, 29 December 1837.

14. *Ibid.*, Melbourne to Howick, 2 January 1838.
15. *The Times*, 11 January 1838. The letter was signed 'R.B.S.' [? R.B. Sullivan].
16. Grey Papers, Melbourne to Howick, 2 January 1838.
17. Lucas, ii, pp. 304-5.
18. Durham to Melbourne, 17 July 1838, in S.J. Reid (ed.), *Life and Letters of the First Earl of Durham, 1792-1840* (2 vols, London, 1906) ii, pp. 222-6.
19. For example, Durham to J.B. Robinson, confidential, in C.R. Sanderson (ed.), *The Arthur Papers* (3 vols, Toronto, 1957-59) i, p. 274.
20. Memorandum by Sullivan, [1 June 1838], *ibid.*, i, pp. 178-81; Baldwin to Durham, 23 August 1838, in A.G. Doughty (ed.), *Report of the Public Archives for the Year 1923* (Ottawa, 1924) pp. 326-8.
21. Durham 18, confidential memorandum by Harvey, 16 August 1838, fos 378-90; Trotter, 'Early Proposal', pp. 152-3.
22. C0 42/283, Durham to Glenelg, no. 58, 13 September 1838, fos 162-3.
23. Compare National Library of Scotland, Ellice Papers, E5, Buller to Ellice, 29 September 1838, fos 16-21 with *Edinburgh Review*, lxxxv (1847) pp. 390-1. For Maritime reactions, see J.S. Martell, 'Some Editorial Opinions from the Newspapers of the Maritime Provinces in the 1830s', *CHR*, xix (1938) p. 55; D.C. Harvey, 'Nova Scotia and the Durham Mission', *CHR*, xx (1939) pp. 165-71.
24. *Globe* (London), 8, 10 October; *Morning Post*, 9 October; *Morning Herald*, 20, 22 October and see also *The Times*, 11 October and *Spectator*, 20 October 1838, pp. 988-9.
25. Melbourne to Russell, 25 August 1838, in L.C. Sanders (ed.), *Lord Melbourne's Papers* (London, 1889) pp. 432-3.
26. *Morning Chronicle*, 17 October 1838. Ellice's hand was recognised: *The Times*, 18 October 1838; Russell 8B, Russell to Melbourne (copies), 18, 24 October 1838, fos 715-16, 724-5. For Ellice's influence, see D.E.T. Long, 'The Elusive Mr Ellice', *CHR*, xxiii (1942) pp. 42-57 and J.M. Colthart, 'Edward Ellice and the Decision for Self-Government, 1839', *Canadian Historical Association Annual Papers*, 1975, pp. 113-33.
27. *Hansard*, xlvii, 3 June 1839, col. 1264 (Russell) and lv, 30 June 1840, col. 234 (Melbourne).
28. Durham 19, Durham to Arthur (copy), no. 11, 9 October 1838, fos 815-19.
29. Lucas, ii, pp. 304-23.

30. *Edinburgh Review*, lxxxv (1847) pp. 390-1; Durham 28, memorandum by Buller [February 1839] fos 194-9.

31. Lucas, ii, p. 306; Russell 3C, memorandum, 28 March 1838, fos 998-1001.

32. *Hansard*, liv, 29 May, col. 725 (Gladstone); lv, 30 June 1840, cols 259-62 (Ashburton); PRO, Ellenborough Papers, PRO 30/12/24/10, untitled fragment on Canadian Union; *Examiner*, no. 1692, 9 July 1840, pp. 417-18.

33. CO 880/1, iii, Ellice to Melbourne, private, 24 February 1838, fos 12-14.

34. *Hansard*, liv, 29 May 1840, col. 740.

35. *Ibid.*, liii, 13 April 1840, col. 1065.

36. PRO, Ellenborough Papers, PRO 30/12/24/11, memorandum, 30 June 1840.

37. Ged Martin, 'Britain and the Future of British North America 1841-1850', p. 76. For the events of this period, Careless, *Union of the Canadas*, chs 1-6; Ormsby, *Emergence of the Federal Concept*; W.P. Morrell, *British Colonial Policy in the Age of Peel and Russell* (Oxford, 1930) chs 2-3.

38. Cambridge University Library, Graham Papers, microfilm 40, Charles Arbuthnot to Graham, private, 7 September 1840; British Library, Aberdeen Papers, Add. MS 43062, Peel to Aberdeen, 16 May 1842, fos 48-55, printed in C.S. Parker, *Sir Robert Peel from his Private Papers* (3 vols, London, 1899) iii, pp. 388-90. For the crisis of 1842, see G.P. de T. Glazebrook, *Sir Charles Bagot in Canada: A Study in British Colonial Government* (Oxford, 1929).

39. N. Gash, *Sir Robert Peel: The Life of Sir Robert Peel After 1830* (London, 1972) chs 15-17; Careless, *Union of the Canadas*, ch. 6; Morrell, *British Colonial Policy*, chs 8-10.

40. J.M. Ward, *Colonial Self-Government: The British Experience 1759-1856* (London, 1976) chs 7-9; Buckner, *Transition to Responsible Government*, chs 7-8; P. Burroughs, 'The Determinants of Colonial Self-Government', *JICH*, vi (1978) pp. 313-29.

41. Careless, *Union of the Canadas*, ch. 7.

42. G.H. Francis, *Orators of the Age* (London, 1847) pp. 180, 178, 176.

43. Grey Papers, Russell to Grey, 4 August 1846. Entries in Grey's journal for December 1845 show that he was hurt by the criticism of his actions and forced to question his own motives.

44. Francis, *Orators of the Age*, p. 180.

45. CO 188/97, minute by Stephen, 12 November 1846, fos 52-5, quoted P. Knaplund, *James Stephen and the British Colonial System* (Madison, Wisc., 1953) p. 277; CO 42/536, minute by Stephen, 12 September 1846, pp. 131-2.

46. CO 42/534, Grey to Elgin (draft), no. 10, 31 December 1846, fos 369-79, copy in Elgin A-396.

47. *Elgin-Grey Papers*, Grey to Elgin, 2 February 1847 (copy), i, pp. 10-12.

48. *Ibid.*, Elgin to Grey, 26 April 1847, i, pp. 33-4.

49. *Ibid.*, Elgin to Grey, private, 7 May 1847, i, pp. 34-7.

50. *Edinburgh Review*, lxxxv (1847) p. 397.

51. *The Times*, 23 January 1847.

52. *Elgin-Grey Papers*, i, pp. 47-8, Grey to Elgin (copy), 16 June 1847.

53. Ged Martin, 'The Canadian Rebellion Losses Bill'.

54. *The Times*, 11 January 1849.

55. *Ibid.*, 11 May 1849.

56. J.A. Roebuck, *The Colonies of England: A Plan for the Government of Some Portion of our Colonial Possessions* (London, 1849) p. 188. For the debate, *Hansard*, cv, 24 May 1849, cols 928-43.

57. *Morning Chronicle*, 24 May; *Morning Herald*, 25 May; *Daily News*, 25 May; *Globe* (London), 25 May; *Examiner*, 26 May 1849, pp. 323-5.

58. *Hansard*, cv, 24 May 1849, cols 954-8.

59. *Ibid.*, cols 943-9, 961-2. Murdoch's memorandum of 23 May 1849 is in Newcastle 11276.

60. *The Times*, 6 August 1849; Grey Papers, Russell to Grey, 6 August 1849; *Elgin-Grey Papers*, Grey to Elgin (copy), 8 August 1849, i, pp. 437-8.

61. Grey Papers, Russell to Grey, 9 April 1849.

62. *Ibid.*, Russell to Grey, 3 July 1849.

63. *Ibid.*, Russell to Grey, 6 August 1849.

64. Russell 8A, Grey to Russell, 8 August 1849, fos 62-5.

65. *Elgin-Grey Papers*, Grey to Elgin (copy), 8 August 1849, i, pp. 437-8.

66. *Ibid.*, Elgin to Grey, private, 6 August 1849, i, pp. 440-4.

67. *Ibid.*, Grey to Elgin (copy), 22 September 1849, ii, pp. 470-1.

68. John M. Ward, *Earl Grey and the Australian Colonies 1846-1857: A Study of Self-Government and Self-Interest* (Melbourne, 1958) pp. 33-4, 107-96; Grey to Sir Harry Smith, cancelled draft despatch, January 1851, quoted Goodfellow, *Great Britain and South African Confederation*, p. 14.

69. Grey Papers, Grey to Hincks, copy, private, 17 September 1849.
70. *Elgin-Grey Papers*, Grey to Elgin, private, 1 August 1851, ii, pp. 850-1.
71. Elgin A-398, Head to Elgin, private, 27 May 1848.
72. HCC 1512, Head to Lewis, 9 September 1849; Lewis to Head, 24 April 1850, in G.F. Lewis, ed., *Letters of the Right Hon. George Cornewall Lewis to Various Friends* (London, 1870) pp. 221-4.
73. Journal, 25 February 1858, in J. Vincent (ed.), *Disraeli, Derby and the Conservative Party: Journals and Memoirs of Edward Henry, Lord Stanley 1849-1869* (Hassocks, 1978) p. 159. As Merivale recalled, there were seven ministers or acting ministers within a single year, 1855. *BPP*, 1861, xiii, *Colonial Military Expenditure*, Q. 2205.
74. C. Martin, 'Sir Edmund Head's First Project of Federation, 1851', *Canadian Historical Association Annual Report, 1928*', pp. 14-28; D.G.G. Kerr, 'Edmund Head, Robert Lowe and Confederation', *CHR*, xx (1939) pp. 409-20; A.R. Stewart, 'Sir Edmund Head's Memorandum of 1857 on Maritime Union: A Lost Confederation Document', *CHR*, xxvi (1945) pp. 406-19.
75. *Fraser's Magazine*, xlvii (February 1853), pp. 189-90; *Morning Chronicle*, 12 September 1853; *Standard*, 1 November 1853; Godley to Adderley, 25 August 1854, in *Extracts from Letters of J.R. Godley to C.B. Adderley* (London, 1863) pp. 214-16.
76. *Morning Herald*, 3 November 1853; *The Times*, 15 November 1855, 4 April 1857; *Blackwood's Magazine*, lxxxii (1857) p. 188.
77. J.B. Conacher, *The Aberdeen Coalition 1852-1855: A Study in Mid-Nineteenth-Century Party Politics* (Cambridge, 1968); F.D. Munsell, *The Unfortunate Duke: Henry Pelham, Fifth Duke of Newcastle, 1811-1864* (Columbia, Mo., 1985) ch. 7.
78. *The Times*, 27 December 1852.
79. CO 188/119, minutes by Blackwood and Newcastle, 24 May, 7 June 1853, fos 273-4. Newcastle's minute is quoted by Gibson, 'Colonial Office View', p. 297.
80. CO 42/591, minute by Newcastle, 30 September 1853, fo. 336.
81. Newcastle A-308, Hamilton to Newcastle, private, 3 November 1853.
82. Newcastle 11260, memorandum [early 1862].
83. *Spectator*, 17 September 1853, p. 885.
84. Elgin A-309, Hincks to Bruce, 10 December 1853. The *Montreal Gazette* commented favourably on the report on 11 October.

85. Newcastle 10888, Newcastle to Gordon (copy), 28 November 1863, pp. 37-41.

86. Queen Victoria to King Leopold, 3 December 1863, in G.E. Buckle (ed.), *The Letters of Queen Victoria: Second Series. A Selection from Her Majesty's Correspondence and Journal between the Years 1862 and 1878* (2 vols, London, 1926) i, pp. 130-1; Lord Stanley's journal, 30 November 1863, 11 June 1864, in Vincent (ed.), *Disraeli, Derby and the Conservative Party*, pp. 202, 219. Newcastle died in October 1864.

87. Elgin A-401, Elgin to Lady Elgin, 'Sunday' [?late 1853].

88. Rogers to Lady Rogers, 17 June 1860, in Marindin (ed.), *op. cit.*, pp. 227-8.

89. For Elgin's belief in imperial federation, see Ged Martin, 'Empire Federalism and Imperial Parliamentary Union, 1820-1870', *Historical Journal*, xvi (1973) p. 68n., and his speech at Glasgow, 4 January 1856, *The Times*, 7 January 1856.

90. Stewart, 'Sir Edmund Head's Memorandum of 1857', p. 416.

91. HCC 1543, Head to Lewis, 20 October 1855; Kerr, *Scholarly Governor*, pp. 146-7.

92. Stewart, 'Sir Edmund Head's Memorandum of 1857', p. 417.

93. CO 42/603, Head to Labouchere, no. 20, 30 January 1856, fos 137-8, quoted Kerr, *Scholarly Governor*, p. 164.

94. NAC, RG7, G9, vol. 32, Head to Labouchere, copy, private and confidential, 3 September 1856, quoted Kerr, *Scholarly Governor*, p. 167.

95. CO 188/124, Manners Sutton to Russell, private and confidential, 20 April 1855, and minute by Merivale, 10 May 1855, fos 251-3; CO 42/608, minute by Merivale, 18 January 1856, fos 10-11.

96. CO 188/124, Manners Sutton to Russell, private, 12 June 1855, enclosing copy of address from St Stephen, and undated minute by Russell, fos 405-13.

97. CO 217/220, Le Marchant to Labouchere, no. 41, 16 June 1857, and minute by Blackwood, 29 June 1857, fos 163-70.

98. CO 42/614, minute by Merivale, 31 August 1858, fos 295-6, quoted Gibson, 'Colonial Office View', p. 281; Whitelaw, *op. cit.*, p. 121n, Kerr, *Scholarly Governor*, p. 180.

99. Bodleian Library, Oxford, Clarendon Deposit, C-70, Labouchere to Clarendon, private, 30 September 1857.

100. NAC, RG7, G10, Head to Labouchere, copy, separate, 29 July 1857, quoted Stewart, 'Sir Edmund Head's Memorandum of 1857', p. 408.

101. Stewart, 'Sir Edmund Head's Memorandum', p. 419.

102. *Ibid.*, pp. 414, 417.

103. HCC 1546, Head to Lewis, private, 9 June 1856, quoted Kerr, *Scholarly Governor*, p. 150.

104. HCC 2028, Head to Lewis, 23 September 1858.

105. Head to Stanley, 28 April 1858, printed in Knox, *JICH* (1976), pp. 212-15. (Original in Liverpool City Library, Derby Papers, 920/DER/7/130/1.)

106. NAC, John Charles Dent Papers, Head to Hincks, 31 October 1858, enclosed with Hincks to Dent, 12 January 1883.

107. Head to Stanley, 28 April 1858, in Knox, *JICH* (1976) p. 213.

108. *Critical Years*, pp. 60-1, 68-9; C. Martin, *Foundations*, pp. 268-70. This view has been convincingly challenged by B.A. Knox, 'Conservative Imperialism 1858-1874: Bulwer Lytton, Lord Carnarvon, and Canadian Confederation', *International History Review*, vi (1984) pp. 333-57.

109. Robert Blake, *Disraeli*, (London, 1966), pp. 326, 437-8, 419; J. Vincent (ed.), *op. cit.*, p. xii.

110. *The Times*, 6 November 1855.

111. The episode of the Greek throne has been exaggerated. Compare Derby journal, 7 December 1862, in Vincent (ed.), *op. cit.*, p. 192 with Blake, *Disraeli*, p. 419. For Stanley's interest in becoming governor-general of Canada, see his journal, 21 February 1858, Vincent (ed.), *op. cit.*, p. 157.

112. Ged Martin, 'Empire Federalism', p. 67.

113. Disraeli to Malmesbury, 13 August 1852, in Monypenny and Buckle, *Life of Benjamin Disraeli, Earl of Beaconsfield*, iii, p. 385. The remark was an expression of irritation, not a statement of policy. S.R. Stembridge, 'Disraeli and the Millstones', *Journal of British Studies*, v (1965) pp. 122-39.

114. Stanley to Head (copy), private, 7 April 1858, in Knox, *JICH* (1976) p. 210. (Original in Liverpool City Library, 920/DER/7.)

115. *Critical Years*, pp. 16-17; C. Martin, *Foundations*, pp. 262-3.

116. CO 42/614, minute by Merivale, 31 August 1858, fos 295-6, quoted Whitelaw, *op. cit.*, p. 121n; Kerr, *Scholarly Governor*, p. 180.

117. Stanley to Head (copy), private, 7 April 1858, in Knox, *JICH* (1976), p. 210. (Original in Liverpool City Library, 920/DER/7.)

118. Journal, 21 February 1858, Vincent (ed.), *op. cit.*, p. 157.

119. Stanley to Head, (copy), private, 7 April 1858, in Knox, *JICH* (1976) p. 211.

120. Head to Stanley, private, 28 April 1858, in Knox, *JICH* (1976) pp. 212-15.

121. Liverpool City Library, Derby Papers, 920/DER/5/1, Derby to Stanley, 29 May 1858, p. 11; Blake, *op. cit.*, pp. 382-5; Shannon, *Gladstone*, pp. 354-8.

122. Galt D8/1, Galt to Amy Galt (typed copy), 8 October 1858, pp. 8-9. (Original at D8/7, pp. 2390-2404.)

123. Rogers to K. Rogers, 8 November 1858, in Marindin (ed.), *op. cit.*, p. 182.

124. Liverpool City Library, Derby Papers, 162/1, Lytton to Derby, confidential, 16 December 1858. Lytton submitted his resignation again on 4 April and 3 May 1859.

125. Rogers to K. Rogers, 8 November 1858, in Marindin (ed.), *op. cit.*, p. 182.

126. W.P. Morrell, *British Colonial Policy in the Mid-Victorian Age: South Africa, New Zealand, the West Indies* (Oxford, 1969) p. 23.

127. Blake, *op. cit.*, p. 385.

128. Liverpool City Library, Derby Papers, 162/1, Lytton to Derby, private and confidential, 4 April 1859.

129. CO 42/614, minutes by Blackwood, Merivale, Carnarvon and Lytton, 30, 31 August, 1 September and undated, fos 295-6.

130. Lytton 01, Lytton to Prince Albert (copy), 9 September 1858. (Original in Royal Archives, RA/M54/102.)

131. Merivale to Stanley, 8 September 1858, and note by Stanley, in Knox, *JICH* (1976) p. 215. (Original in Liverpool City Library, Derby Papers, 920/DER/7/130/1.)

132. Royal Archives, RA/M54/106, Lytton to Prince Albert, 11 November 1858. 133. *Canadian News*, 15 September 1858, p. 258. Blackwood had a high opinion of the publication, CO 42/645, minute, 8 February 1864, fos 65-6.

134. CO 194/154, Bannerman to Lytton, no. 83, 11 October 1858, fos 380-1.

135. Galt D8/1, Galt to Amy Galt (typed copy), 8 October 1858, pp. 8-9.

136. CO 42/614, minute by Lytton, undated [September 11858] fos 295-6.

137. Lytton to Derby, 7 September 1858, printed in B.A. Knox, 'Sir Edward Lytton and Confederation 1858', *CHR*, liii (1972), pp. 110-11.

138. *The Times*, 4 April 1857; 13 August, 3 September 1858.

139. Blake, *op. cit.*, pp. 380-1.

140. *Spectator*, 2 October 1858, p. 1026; *Morning Herald*, 6 September; *Morning Post*, 4 September 1858; Galt D8/7, Galt to Amy Galt, 30 September 1858, pp. 2382-5.

141. Cartier, Ross and Galt to Lytton, 23 October, and Galt to Lytton, 22 November 1858, in Skelton, *op. cit.*, pp. 93-6, 99-100. The draft of the first letter indicates that Galt was the principal author, *ibid.*, p. 93.

142. C. Martin, *Foundations*, p. 270. Lytton indicated to the cabinet that Elliot had ignored the arguments for Confederation, see memorandum, 'most confidential', 10 November 1858, in Trotter, 'The British Government', p. 285.

143. Lytton 025, Head to Lytton, confidential, 15 November 1858; 027, Lytton to Head (copy), confidential, 12 December 1858.

144. Trotter, 'The British Government'; CO 188/131, Manners Sutton to Lytton, private and confidential, 2 October 1858, fos 428-42.

145. Southgate, *op. cit.*, chs 24-7.

146. Recollections of Rogers, Marindin (ed.), *op. cit.*, pp. 225-6. Gladstone had also seen Newcastle as future leader, but had changed his opinion after 1859. Gladstone to Gordon, 29 January 1869, in Knaplund (ed.), *Gladstone-Gordon Correspondence*, p.49, printed with excisions in Morley, *Gladstone*, ii, pp. 255-56.

147. CO 188/132, minutes by Merivale and Newcastle, 21, 23 October 1858, fo. 362, printed in Whitelaw, *op. cit.*, p. 142.

148. CO 537/137, minute by Newcastle, 26 March 1860, fo. 306.

149. CO 188/132, minute by Merivale, 21 October 1859, fo. 362.

150. CO 42/619, draft of circular despatch, 27 January 1860, fos 375-6, versions printed in Browne, p. 30 and Gibson, 'Colonial Office View', p. 296.

151. Watkin, *op. cit.*, p. 65b.

152. Newcastle 11276, memorandum by T.W.C. Murdoch, 23 May 1849.

153. Newcastle 11260, memorandum on Intercolonial railway, 1862.

154. CO 42/626, minute by Elliot, 9 March 1860, fos 16-21; CO 217/230, minute by Elliot, 14 June 1862, fo. 254, quoted Whitelaw, *op. cit.*, p. 178.

155. CO 42/626, minute by Newcastle, 13 March 1861, fos 22-24.

156. Newcastle 10885, Newcastle to Manners Sutton (copy), private, 8 March 1861, pp. 41-5.

157. CO 217/230, Newcastle to Mulgrave (draft), 6 July 1862, fos 251-61. The importance of this despatch is discussed in Chapter Six.

158. Newcastle 11260, memorandum on Intercolonial railway, 1862.

159.   Newcastle 11257, memorandum by Gladstone, 14 December 1861, printed in Matthew (ed.), *Gladstone Diaries*, vi, pp. 80-3; Watkin, *op. cit.*, p. 84.

160.   Letters of 15, 16 April 1879 in A.T. Bassett, ed., *Gladstone to his Wife* (London, 1936), p. 225. One of the Sèvres vases had previously been smashed and painstakingly reconstructed. Goldwin Smith, *Reminiscences*, (ed. A. Haultain, New York, 1910), p. 191.

161.   Newcastle 11260, memorandum on Intercolonial railway, 1862.

162.   Bourne, *op. cit.*, pp. 216-18; Munsell, *Unfortunate Duke*, p. 260; Newcastle 10890, Newcastle to Palmerston (copy), 30 August [?9 September] 1861, and Newcastle to Lewis (copy), 24 September 1861, pp. 69-72, 68-9.

163.   Conacher, *Aberdeen Coalition*, pp. 477-8; Munsell, *op. cit.*, pp. 186-7. The contractors were Peto and Betts.

164.   Newcastle 11260, memorandum on Intercolonial railway, 1862.

165.   G. Smith, *The Empire*, pp. 101-2.

166.   Trollope, *North America*, ii, p. 105.

167.   Walpole, *Life of Lord John Russell*, i, p. 11.

168.   Russell 31, Russell to Newcastle (copy), confidential, 12 June 1862.

169.   CO 217/230, minute by Newcastle, 22 June 1862, fos 255-6.

170.   *Spectator*, 23 August 1862, p. 933.

171.   Buckner, 'The Maritimes and Confederation', p. 21n.

172.   *Montreal Transcript*, 23 November 1850, in *Elgin-Grey Papers*, ii, p. 759.

173.   Newcastle 9552, Hincks to Bruce, 10 December 1853.

174.   CO 217/216, P.S. Hamilton to Molesworth, 15 August 1855, fos 224-7.

175.   Galt D8/7, Galt to Amy Galt, 30 September 1858, pp. 2382-5.

4   THE BRITISH AND THEIR PERCEPTIONS

1.   Compare Ged Martin, 'An Imperial Idea and its Friends'.

2.   For an example, see the interpolation by Gibson ('Colonial Office View', p. 281) in Merivale's description of Labouchere's view Confederation was not 'a thing to be urged from this side, but that we [the Colonial Office] ought to be prepared for its proposal and rather encourage it than otherwise'. Merivale's allusion to 'this side' suggests a much wider British consensus.

3.   Goodfellow, *op. cit.*, p. 47.

4. For the building, see H.L. Hall, *The Colonial Office: A History* (London, 1937) pp. 48-9; D.M.L. Farr, *The Colonial Office and Canada, 1867-1887* (Toronto, 1955) p. 28; Lytton 026, Manners to Lytton, 14 December 1858; *Autobiography of Henry Taylor*, ii, p. 34.

5. W. Baillie-Hamilton, 'Forty-Four Years at the Colonial Office', *Nineteenth Century and After*, lxv (1909) pp. 603, 601.

6. Hughenden He/5, Carnarvon to Disraeli, private, 9 October 1866. For Colonial Office administration, see Hall, *Colonial Office*, chs 2-3; R.B. Pugh, 'The Colonial Office', *Cambridge History of the British Empire*, iii (Cambridge, 1959) pp. 711-68; R.C. Snelling and T.J. Barron, 'The Colonial Office and its Permanent Officials, 1801-1914' in G. Sutherland (ed.), *Studies in the Growth of Nineteenth-Century Government* (London, 1972), pp. 139-66; J.C. Sainty (ed.), *Colonial Office Officials (Office-Holders in Modern Britain*: vi, London, 1976) pp. 1-7; D.B. Swinfen, *Imperial Control of Colonial Legislation 1813-1865* (Oxford, 1970) ch. 3; J.W. Cell, *British Colonial Administration in the Mid-Nineteenth Century: The Policy-Making Process* (New Haven, 1970) ch. 1.

7. Baillie-Hamilton, 'Forty-Four Years', pp. 602-3.

8. E.G. Wakefield, *A View of the Art of Colonization* (London, 1849) p. 146.

9. *Autobiography of Henry Taylor*, ii, p. 34.

10. C. Buller, *Responsible Government for the Colonies* (1840), reprinted in Wrong, *Charles Buller and Responsible Government*, pp. 162, 160. For Carnarvon's complaint about the state of the furniture in 1858, Cell, *British Colonial Administration*, p. 4.

11. *Hansard*, civ, 16 April 149, col. 321 (speech by Francis Scott, MP for Berwickshire).

12. *The Times*, 6 May 1850. Molesworth's speech of 6 May 1850 is printed in H.E. Egerton (ed.), *Selected Speeches of Sir William Molesworth on Questions Relating to Colonial Policy* (London, 1903) pp. 365-92.

13. Lewis to Head, 6 August 1848, in Lewis (ed.), *Letters of George Cornewall Lewis*, pp. 179-84.

14. Monck A-755, Newcastle to Monck, 11 August 1864.

15. R. Robinson and J. Gallagher with A. Denny, *Africa and the Victorians: The Official Mind of Imperialism* (London, 1965).

16. Carnarvon 6/146, Carnarvon to Howe (copy), 2 February 1867, fos 1695-6.

17. CO 42/595, fo. 214, undated minute by Merivale, 1855 ('I may be hypercritical...')
18. Grey Papers, Russell to Grey, 16 March 1848. For Stephen's admiration of Russell, Cambridge University Library, Add. MS 7511, diary of James Stephen, 22 January 1846.
19. Cambridge University Library, Add. MS 7511, Stephen diary, 6 March 1846.
20. Grey Papers, Stephen to Howick, 11 January 1836.
21. CO 537/137, confidential minute, 30 April 1836, fos 29-49.
22. Russell 3D, Normanby to Russell, 2 September 1839, fos 1245-52.
23. CO 537/137, confidential minute, 30 April 1836, fos 29-49.
24. Royal Archives, Melbourne Papers, 7/76, Howick to Melbourne, private, 27 December 1837.
25. CO 42/552, minute by Elliot, 20 September 1848, fo. 76. His opposition to British North American union was argued in a confidential memorandum of 4 November 1858, Trotter, 'The British Government', pp. 287-97.
26. Newcastle 11276, memorandum by Murdoch for Hawes, 23 May 1849.
27. CO 42/582, minute by Merivale, 11 September 1852, fo. 250; Elgin A-397, Newcastle to Elgin, 7 January 1853.
28. Elgin A-396, Elgin to Newcastle (copy), 28 January 1853. (Original, marked private, in Newcastle 9552).
29. Lytton 01, memorandum by Merivale, 6 September 1858.
30. Sydenham to Russell, 24 November 1840, in P. Knaplund (ed.), *Letters from Lord Sydenham Governor-General of Canada 1839-1841 to Lord John Russell* (London, 1931) pp. 103-6.
31. British Library, Peel Papers, Add. MS, Stanley to Peel (27 May 1842) fos 202-3.
32. *Elgin-Grey Papers*, Elgin to Grey, private, 27 March 1848, i, p. 139.
33. *Hansard*, civ, 4 May 1849, cols 1250-5.
34. Carnarvon 6/134, Monck to Adderley, 20 July 1866, enclosed in Adderley to Carnarvon, undated, fos 31-6. For Monck's friendship with Adderley, which crossed party lines, see *Monck Letters and Journals*, p. 29.
35. For the argument that the Elgin-Grey correspondence was three-cornered, see G.W. Martin, 'Britain and the Future of British North America', p. 18n.
36. These are outlined in Chapter Three and discussed in Chapter Six.
37. Lytton 01, memorandum by Merivale, 6 September 1858.

38. Description of the role of governor-general by Lord Dufferin in 1874, C.W. de Kiewiet and F.H. Underhill (eds), *Dufferin-Carnarvon Correspondence 1874-1878* (Toronto, 1955) pp. 74-5.

39. The essential continuity in the exercise of power is argued by N. Gash, *Reaction and Reconstruction in English Politics 1832-52* (Oxford, 1965). For Burke's definition of a political nation of 400000 people, see R.B. McDowell (ed.), *The Writings and Speeches of Edmund Burke*, ix (Oxford, 1991) pp. 223-24. The term 'political nation' is used by G.H. Guttridge, *English Whiggism and the American Revolution* (Berkeley, 1963 ed.), p. 31. I am obliged to Professor Peter D. Marshall for his guidance on Burke.

40. Elgin A-397, Grey to Elgin, 23 December 1846.

41. Cambridge University Library, Add MS 7511, Stephen Diary, 16 March 1846. For his (pardonable) dislike of Buller, *ibid.*, 16 May, 12 July 1846. Stephen's attitude to Buller is discussed in T.J. Barron and K.J. Cable, 'The Diary of James Stephen, 1846', *Historical Studies Australia and New Zealand*, xiii (1967-9) pp. 512-13.

42. Watkin, *op. cit.*, pp. 7-8.

43. Quoted, Farr, *Colonial Office and Canada*, p. 23.

44. G.C. Lewis, *An Essay on the Influence of Authority in Matters of Opinion* (London, 1849) pp. 342-50. Lewis was delighted when the book sold 'nearly 200 copies'. Lewis (ed.), *Lewis Letters*, pp. 207-8.

45. Marindin (ed.), *op. cit.*, pp. 112-15.

46. Palmerston to Delane, 14 December 1864, in A.I. Dasent, *John Thaddeus Delane Editor of 'The Times': His Life and Correspondence* (2 vols, London 1908) ii, p. 135; *The History of The Times*, ii (London, 1939) p. 131.

47. Lewis, *Influence of Authority*, pp. 342-50.

48. J. Vincent, *The Formation of the Liberal Party 1857-1868* (London, 1966) pp. 59-60.

49. Anthony Trollope, *Phineas Redux* (1874) ch. 5.

50. Cobden to Hargreaves, 16 February 1861, in J.Morley, *The Life of Richard Cobden* (London, 1903 ed.) p. 886; speech at Holmfirth, *The Times*, 5 February 1853.

51. Speech of 12 November 1855, in Knaplund, *Gladstone and Britain's Imperial Policy*, pp. 185-227.

52. *The Times*, 15 November 1855.

53. Lytton 01, memorandum by Merivale, 22 September 1858.

54. Comment by Greville, 12 July 1854 in *A Journal of the Reign of Queen Victoria from 1852 to 1860: The Greville Memoirs (Third Part)* (2 vols, London, 1887) i, p. 74.

55. The *Daily News* in 1849 was unusual in stressing the advantages of British North American union to the Maritimes.

56. Quoted, Morley, *Gladstone*, i, p. 138.

57. *Sun*, 16 July 1840. For circulation figures, A.P. Wadsworth, *Newspaper Circulations, 1850-1954* (Manchester Statistical Society, 1955) esp. p. 9. The *Morning Advertiser*, which certainly ranked second in circulation, may even have rivalled *The Times*. Its editor argued in 1858 that it was mainly distributed in towns, and accordingly was distributed by railway and not through the post. Consequently, its circulation was under-reported through newspaper stamp duty statistics. However, the *Morning Advertiser* circulated almost entirely in public houses, as the official organ of the Licensed Victuallers, and lacked discernible political influence. Perhaps this was for the best. In 1849, its New York correspondent reported that Lord Elgin's secretary had married a French Canadian heiress who had suborned both men into supporting 'the banishment of everything Anglo-Saxon' (*Morning Advertiser*, 7 May 1849).

58. Greville to Reeve, 19 October 1855, in A.H. Johnson (ed.), *The Letters of Charles Greville and Henry Reeve 1836-1865* (London, 1924) p. 248.

59. Clarendon to Reeve, 14 October 1849, in H. Maxwell (ed.), *The Life and Letters of George William Frederick Fourth Earl of Clarendon* (2 vols, London, 1912) ii, p. 292. See also B.K. Martin, *The Triumph of Lord Palmerston: A Study of Public Opinion in England before the Crimean War* (London, 1924) p. 87.

60. Cobden to F.W. Cobden, 4 November 1851, in Morley, *Cobden*, p. 565.

61. Stanley journal, 24 March 1853, in Vincent (ed.), *op. cit.*, p. 104; Anthony Trollope, *The Warden* (1855) ch. 7, in which *The Times* is thinly disguised as *The Jupiter*; Shaftesbury journal, 27 June 1855, quoted B. Harrison, 'The Sunday Trading Riots of 1855', *Historical Journal*, viii (1965) p. 231.

62. W.H. Russell, *My Diary North and South*, i, p. 57.

63. *Dublin University Magazine*, xxv (1850) p. 161.

64. Speech at Halifax, 28 August 1861, in Chisholm, ii, p. 369.

65. Journal, 15 October 1864, in *Monck Letters and Journals*, pp. 153-4.

66. Hayward to Young, 14 September, 1853, in H.E. Carlisle (ed.), *A Selection from the Correspondence of Abraham Hayward Q.C. from 1834 to 1884* (2 vols, London, 1886) i, pp. 187-90.

67. Disraeli to Lord Bath, 30 March 1854, in Monypenny and Buckle, *op. cit.*, iii, pp. 503-4.

68. C. Mitchell, *Newspaper Press Directory* (3rd ed., London, 1851) p. 133.

69. Minute by James Lowther, 20 April 1874, quoted Robinson and Gallagher, *Africa and the Victorians*, p. 31.

70. *North British Review*, xvii (1852) p. 27.

71. Mitchell, *Newspaper Press Directory*, p. 71. For Palmerston's link with the *Morning Post*, see B.K. Martin, *Triumph of Lord Palmerston*, pp. 88-9; *Greville Memoirs 1851-1860*, i, pp. 1-2.

72. *North British Review*, xvii (1852), p. 27.

73. Mitchell, *op. cit.*, p. 133.

74. Howe to Stairs, 23 November 1866, in Burpee, pp. 443-4.

75. *Globe* (London), 2 January 1838; *The Times*, 5 January, reporting meeting at the 'Crown and Anchor', 4 January 1838. I am obliged to Dr J.L. Sturgis for pointing out that Hume was a notoriously dull speaker. The *Northern Star*, 6, 13 January 1838, tried without much success to whip up a Chartist campaign in support of the Canadian rebels.

76. *Eclectic Review*, n.s., iii (1838) pp. 235-8.

77. W.H. Russell, *Canada*, p. 57.

78. Nelson et al., 'Canadian Confederation as a Case Study', in Ged Martin (ed.), *Causes*, pp. 68, 70.

79. *BPP*, 1867, xlviii, Bishop James Rogers to E. Williston, (April 1866) pp. 107-8. Rogers was Bishop of Chatham, in Northumberland County, which elected Confederates. However, the immediately adjoining counties of Kent and Gloucester held out against Confederation. No doubt Catholic Acadians did not regard England as their 'mother'. See map in *Road to Confederation*, p. 387. T.W. Anglin balanced Irish opposition to unjust government in their homeland against loyalty to the self-governing institutions of British North America. Baker, *op. cit.*, pp. 51-2.

80. Howe blurred the facts a little in 1851 in stating that his forebears had originated 'in the southern counties of England', but he was speaking in Southampton at the time. Chisholm, ii, p. 156.

81. Watkin, *op. cit.*, p. 499.

82. The connections are discussed in Chapters Three and Six.

83. *DCB*, xi, pp. 369-71; speech at Saint John, 14 September 1864, in Whelan, p. 54.

84. Bolger, *op. cit.*, p. 24.

85. Poulett Thomson's description of the British press, Thomson to Russell, private, 13 March 1840, in Knaplund (ed.), *Sydenham-Russell Letters*, pp. 50-5.

86. H.S. Tremenheere, *Notes on Public Subjects Made During a Tour of the United States and Canada* (London, 1852) p. 174; Tremenheere to Elgin, 18 December 1853, in E.L. and O.P. Edmonds, *I Was There: Memoirs of H.S. Tremenheere* (Windsor, 1965) pp. 91-3.

87. *Sunday Times*, 27 May 1849.

88. *The Times*, 25 November 1837.

89. Macdonald 74, Monck to Macdonald, private, 22 December 1866; Howe to Stairs, 13 July 1866, in Burpee, pp. 425-6.

90. Mrs Gaskell, *Mary Barton* (first published 1848, many editions) ch. 38.

91. Captain Ballantine of the *Peruvian*, quoted in journal of Frances Monck, 21 July 1864, *Monck Letters and Journals*, pp. 93-4.

92. *Ibid.*, 16 January 1865, p. 206; *DCB*, xii, pp. 1100-1.

93. Grey Papers, journal, 3 June 1836.

94. Hitsman, *Safeguarding Canada*, p. 173; Howe to Stairs, 15 March 1867, in Burpee, pp. 456-9.

95. Thomson to Russell, 28 May 1840, in Knaplund (ed.), *Sydenham-Russell Letters*, pp. 69-72.

96. *The Times*, 3 September 1865.

97. *Saturday Review*, 16 July 1864, p. 75.

98. *Morning Herald*, 5 May 1849.

99. *Sun*, 26 June 1849; *Elgin-Grey Papers*, Grey to Elgin (copy), private, 13 June 1851, ii, pp. 824-5.

100. *Manchester Guardian*, 25 August 1849.

101. Stanley to Head (copy), 7 April; Head to Stanley, 28 April 1858, in Knox, *JICH* (1976) pp. 210, 212.

102. Watkin, *op. cit.*, pp. 16-17.

103. Newcastle 11260, memorandum on Intercolonial railway 1862.

104. *Westminster Review*, xxvii (1865) p. 554.

105. *Morning Herald*, 5 May 1849.

106. *The Times*, 9 July 1858.

107. *Hansard*, cv, 24 May 1849, cols 961-2.

108. *The Times*, 22 July 1858.

109. Head to Lytton, confidential, 9 September 1858, printed in G.P. de T. Glazebrook, 'A Letter on the West by Sir Edmund Head', *CHR*, xxi (1940) pp. 58-9.

110. Quoted, Chisholm, ii, p. 271.

111. *Saturday Review*, 28 October 1865, p. 538.

112. *BPP*, 1861, xiii, *Colonial Military Expenditure*, Q. 2961 (Earl Grey), and compare Merivale, Q. 2221.

113. CO 42/656, minute by Blackwood, 20 September 1866, fos 367-8.

114. For example, *The Times*, 18 April 1859.

115. CO 42/590, minute by Merivale (1854) fo. 377.

116. Mackay, 'A Week in Prince Edward Island', p. 143; *Saturday Review*, 26 November 1864, p. 651.

117. *Examiner*, 22 October 1864, pp. 673-4.

118. *Hansard*, cli, 8 July 1858, col. 1120 (Francis Crossley, MP for Halifax).

119. For example, T.C. Haliburton, *Sam Slick's Wise Saws and Modern Instances* (2 vols, London, 1853) ii, p. 221.

120. *The Times*, 22 October 1844; Chapman, *op. cit.*, p. 6.

121. CO 42/616, minute by Blackwood, 25 May 1858, fo. 582.

122. Quoted, Beck, *Howe*, ii, p. 156.

123. 11 October 1864, in Pope (ed.), *Confederation*, p. 55.

124. *The Times*, 6 January 1860.

125. W. Monsell MP, quoted Morrell, *British Colonial Policy in the Mid-Victorian Age*, p. 364.

126. *The Times*, 22 December 1856. 'Canada West' was the term widely used for Upper Canada at this period.

127. Letter of William Garvie, 13 March 1867, in Burpee, p. 463.

128. Gordon to Gladstone, private, January 1864, in Knaplund (ed.), *Gladstone-Gordon Correspondence*, p. 42.

129. Grey Papers, Grey to Head, copy, 27 November 1851; CO 188/131, Manners Sutton to Blackwood, private, 30 October 1858, fos 453-8.

130. CO 188/139, Gordon to Newcastle, Most Confidential, 28 September 1863, fos 58-63; CO 217/233, minute by Elliot, 9 December 1863, fo. 78. Tupper received his medical training at Edinburgh.

131. *Elgin-Grey Papers*, Elgin to Grey, 26 April 1847, i, pp. 33-4; *Standard*, 27 October 1864.

132. Royal Archives. RA/M54/106, Lytton to Albert, 11 November 1858.

133. Speech at Niagara, 18 September 1862, Chisholm, ii, p. 375.

134. CO 880/6, 52, October 1868, fos 55-7.

135. Stewart, 'Sir Edmund Head's Memorandum of 1857', p. 414.

136. *Brown*, i, p. 2.

137. *The Times*, 16 June 1852, letter from Rev. Edward Hincks, p. 6; Elgin A-398, Head to Elgin, 8 September 1852.

138. *The Times*, 12 July 1854.

139. *BPP*, 1864, xli, *Customs Duties (Canada)*, Report by Galt, 25 October 1859.

140. CO 42/624, minute by Fortescue, 17 May 1860, fos 230-3.

141. Speech at Manchester, 25 September, *Daily News*, 26 September 1862.

142. Newcastle 10886, Newcastle to Monck (copy), private, 12 April 1862.

143. *The Times*, 4 and 11 February, 6 June, 19 August, 28 July 1862.

144. Newcastle 10886, Newcastle to Monck (copy), private, 26 July 1862.

145. *Hansard*, clxxiv, 28 April 1864, cols 1770-1.

146. *The Times*, 12 July 1864.

147. *Hansard*, clxxxv, 28 February 1867, col. 1180.

148. *The Times*, 26 August 1865. Cardwell had taken office on 7 April. The Commons ordered the papers to be printed on 17 June 1864.

149. C.A. Bodelsen, *Studies in Mid-Victorian Imperialism* (London, 1924); J.S. Galbraith, 'Myths of the "Little England" Era', *American Historical Review*, lxvii (1961), reprinted in A.G.L. Shaw, *Great Britain and the Colonies, 1815-1865* (London, 1970) pp. 27-45; Ged Martin, '"Anti-Imperialism" in the Mid-Nineteenth Century and the Nature of the British Empire, 1820-1870' in R. Hyam and G. Martin, *Reappraisals in British Imperial History* (London, 1975) pp. 88-120.

150. *Examiner*, 22 October 1864, pp. 673-4.

151. *Saturday Review*, 4 October 1862, p. 397.

152. *Westminster Review*, xxvii (1865) p. 537.

153. Dent, *Last Forty Years*, ii, p. 426. There were some harsh comments in both Houses of Parliament, *Hansard*, clxvii, 12 June, cols 627-9; clxviii, 18 July 1862, cols 479-98. In a speech at Toronto in November 1864, George Brown made 'a firm protest' against being lectured by the British on the duty of self-defence, Whelan, pp. 199-200.

154. 'Preface' by G.M. Grant to J.W. Bengough, *A Caricature History of Canadian Politics* (1886, ed. D. Fetherling, Toronto, 1974) p. ix.

155. *Punch*, 16 February 1867, p. 63. The Northern rout at First Bull Run was portrayed as a move to 'take Canada'.

156. *The Times*, 2 June 1863. Hooker had just been pushed back across the Rappahannock after the bloody battle of Chancellorsville.

157. Grey Papers, Russell to Grey, 16 March 1848.

158. *The Times*, 20 November 1849.

159. *Ibid.*, 22 December 1856.

160. *Morning Chronicle*, 5 April 1849.

161. *The Times*, 10 March 1837, 15 January 1838.

162. CO 42/546, minute by Stephen, 3 September 1847, fo. 217.

163. *The Times*, 11 April 1849.

164. *Ibid.*, 27 December 1837.

165. HCC 1542, Head to Lewis, private, 20 July 1855.

166. *Elgin-Grey Papers*, Elgin to Grey, private, 22 November 1850, ii, p. 745.

167. Grey Papers, Lord Edward Howard to Russell, 7 August 1849, enclosed in Russell to Grey, 19 August 1849.

168. Gladstone 44136, Cobden to Gladstone, 24 February 1865, fos 275-8.

169. 'Union' in *The Times*, 5 April 1865.

170. Lucas, ii, p. 308.

171. *Colonial Gazette*, 6 January 1844, pp. 1-2.

172. Head to Stanley, 28 April 1858, in Knox, *JICH* (1976) p. 213.

173. *The Times*, 23 March 1849.

174. P.S. Hamilton, *Observations upon a Union of the Colonies of British North America* (Halifax, 1855) p. 25.

175. Lucas, ii, p. 304. See also G.M. Craig (ed.), *Lord Durham's Report* (Toronto, 1963) p. 158, with variation in capitalisation.

176. [T.C. Haliburton], *A Reply to the Report of the Earl of Durham* (London, 1839) pp. 30-1, reprinted from *The Times*, 18-25 February 1839.

177. H.Bliss, *An Essay on the Re-Constitution of Her Majesty's Government in Canada* (London, 1839) p. 101. For Bliss, see *The Times*, 20 January 1838; *Simmonds's Colonial Magazine*, x (1846) p. 308; *DCB*, x, pp. 71-2.

178. Grey Papers, Stephen to Howick, 28 December 1837.

179. *Ibid.*, journal, 29 December 1837; Colonial Papers, 100, 101 (draft) 29 December 1837.

180. Grey Papers, Palmerston to Howick, 4 January 1838.

181. Russell 20/11, memorandum, 30 June 1840.

182. Russell 8A, Grey to Russell, 8 August 1849, fos 62-5.

183. *Elgin-Grey Papers*, Elgin to Grey, private, 3 September 1849, ii, pp. 463-6.

184. *Ibid.*, Elgin to Grey, private, 7 May 1847, i, pp. 34-7.

185. C. Martin, 'Sir Edmund Head's First Project', p. 23.

186. *Globe* (London) 8 October 1838.

187. Goldwin Smith, *The Empire*, p. 200.

188. Bliss, *Essay*, pp. 97, 105.

189. *Elgin-Grey Papers*, Elgin to Grey, private, 7 May 1847, i, p. 34.

190. Newcastle 9552, Hincks to Bruce, 10 December 1853.

191. *The Canadian Crisis and Lord Durham's Mission* (London, 1838) p. 42.

192. Lucas, ii, pp. 322, 302.

193. *Elgin-Grey Papers*, Grey to Elgin (copy), private, 16 June 1847, i, pp. 47-8.

194. *Ibid.*, Grey to Elgin (copy), 22 September 1849, ii, p. 471.

195. Head to Stanley, 28 April 1858, in Knox, *JICH* (1976) pp. 213-14.

196. *The Times*, 3 September 1858.

197. Head to Stanley, 28 April 1858, in Knox, 'The British Government, 1858', pp. 213-14.

198. Lytton to Derby, 7 September 1858, in Knox, 'Sir Edward Lytton and Confederation', pp. 110-11.

199. *Life and Times*, pp. 37n-38n, and see also *Critical Years*, pp. 207-8.

200. Monck A-755, Cardwell to Monck, private, 16 July 1864.

201. Gladstone 44118, Cardwell to Gladstone, 27 October 1864, fos 176-9.

202. Cardwell 6/39, Cardwell to Gordon, copies, private, 14 October, 12 November 1864, fos 3-6, 15-16. (Originals in University of New Brunswick, Stanmore Papers, microfilm 1.)

203. CO 42/643, Cardwell to Monck (draft), no. 84, 2 November 1864, fo. 132.

204. Monck A-757, Williams to Monck, private, 24 March 1866.

205. Monck to Carnarvon, confidential, 7 September 1866, in W.M. Whitelaw, 'Lord Monck and the Canadian Constitution', *CHR*, xxi (1940) pp. 299-306. (Original in CO 42/656, fos 360-6.)

206. CO 880/4, confidential print, vii, fos 51-7.

5   MOTIVES AND EXPECTATIONS OF THE BRITISH

1. Compare Ged Martin, 'An Imperial Idea and its Friends', pp. 67-78.

2. Howe to Normanby, private, 22 November 1866, in Burpee, p. 444.

3. Ged Martin, '"Anti-Imperialism" in the Mid-Nineteenth Century', pp. 101-6.

4. See the entertaining discussion by M.E. Chamberlain, 'Canada's International Status, 1867-1919', in C.C. Eldridge (ed.), *From Rebellion to Patriation: Canada and Britain in the Nineteenth and Twentieth Centuries* (Canadian Studies in Wales Group, 1989) pp. 82-

90. Chamberlain nominates 28 June 1919, the date of the Treaty of Versailles, but Lower (*Colony to Nation*, p. 489) plumps for 11 December 1931, the passage of the Statute of Westminster.

5. *Hansard*, xl, 26 January 1838, cols 557-8.

6. Lucas, ii, pp. 305, 312.

7. Grey Papers, Russell to Grey, 6 August 1849.

8. C. Martin, 'Sir Edmund Head's First Project', p. 24.

9. Head to Stanley, 28 April 1858, in Knox, *JICH* (1976) p. 214.

10. *The Times*, 3 September 1858.

11. Watkin, *op. cit.*, p. 23.

12. Newcastle 11276, memorandum by Murdoch, 23 May 1849.

13. Russell 8A, Grey to Russell, 8 August 1849, fos 62-5.

14. CO 188/97, minute by Stephen, 12 November 1846, fos 52-5.

15. Memorandum by Elliot, confidential, 4 November 1858, in Trotter, 'The British Government', p. 289.

16. CO 42/626, Williams to Newcastle, no. 2, 2 January 1861, fos 8-10.

17. *Elgin-Grey Papers*, Elgin to Grey, private, 7 May 1849, i, p. 34.

18. CO 217/ 221, Mulgrave to Lytton, confidential, 30 December 1858, fos 556-76.

19. HCC 1516, Head to Lewis, 2 March 1850.

20. Howe to Normanby, private, 22 November 1866, in Burpee, p. 444.

21. *The Times*, 3 October 1863.

22. C. Martin, 'Sir Edmund Head's First Project', pp. 92,93.

23. Stewart, 'Sir Edmund Head's Memorandum of 1857', p. 418.

24. Stanley to Head (copy), 7 April 1858, in Knox, *JICH* (1976) p. 211.

25. Monck A-755, Cardwell to Monck, private, 6 August 1864.

26. Newcastle 9552, Hincks to Bruce, 10 December 1853.

27. CO 537/137, secret minute by Stephen, 20 December 1836, fos 144-69.

28. *Ibid.*, epitome of the proposed Canada Act, 19 January 1837, fos 196-202.

29. As Russell recalled, Russell 31, Russell to Newcastle, copy, confidential, 12 June 1862, fos 97-8.

30. Royal Archives, Melbourne Papers, 7/56, Howick to Melbourne, private, 2 January [1838].

31. Arthur's views may be deduced from Colborne to Arthur, 25 June 1838, in Sanderson (ed.), *Arthur Papers*, i, pp. 205-6.

32. NAC, Roebuck Papers, MG 24 A19, 2/8, Roebuck to Melbourne (draft) [29 December 1837].

33. Roebuck's memorandum to Durham [1838], in Roebuck, *Colonies of England*, pp. 192-220, esp. p. 194.

34. Melbourne to Russell, 11 December 1838, in Sanders (ed.), *Lord Melbourne's Papers*, pp. 441-2.

35. Durham 28, memorandum by Buller, 28 March 1839, fos 998-1001.

36. Memorandum by Sullivan, [1 June 1838], in Sanderson (ed.), *op. cit.*, i, pp. 178-81.

37. *Elgin-Grey Papers*, Elgin to Grey, 26 April 1847, i, pp. 33-4.

38. New York correspondent of *The Times*, 16 August 1849.

39. *Elgin-Grey Papers*, Elgin to Grey, private, 6 August 1849.

40. Roebuck, *op. cit.*, pp. 175, 224.

41. C. Martin, 'Sir Edmund Head's First Project', pp. 24-5.

42. Russell 31, Russell to Newcastle (copy), confidential, 12 June 1862, fos 97-8.

43. Stanley to Head (copy), 7 April 1858, in Knox, *JICH* (1976) p. 211.

44. Ged Martin, 'Imperial Idea and its Friends', p. 64.

45. Roebuck, *op. cit.*, pp. 177-85.

46. Cartier, Ross and Galt to Lytton, 23 October 1858, in Skelton, *op. cit.*, pp. 239-42.

47. CO 217/221, Mulgrave to Lytton, confidential, 30 December 1858, fos 556-76.

48. CO 42/536, minute by Stephen, 12 September 1846, fos 131-2; CO 217/202, Harvey to Grey, private, 16 August 1849, fos 204-5.

49. Memorandum by Elliot, confidential, 4 November 1858, in Trotter, 'The British Government', p. 293.

50. CO 188/124, Manners Sutton to Russell, private and confidential, 20 April 1855, fos 251-3, quoted Whitelaw, *op. cit.*, p. 109.

51. CO 188/131, Manners Sutton to Blackwood, private, 30 October 1858, fos 453-8, quoted Whitelaw, *op. cit.*, pp. 134-5, who reads 'cork' as 'case'.

52. Ged Martin, '"Anti-Imperialism" in the Mid-Nineteenth Century'.

53. *Hansard*, xl, 25 January 1838, col. 484.

54. Roebuck, *op. cit.*, pp. 170, 188.

55. *The Times*, 7 and 21 March 1865.

56. Melbourne to Durham, 22 July 1837, in Reid, *Life and Letters of the First Earl of Durham*, ii, pp. 137-8.

57. Grey Papers, Russell to Grey, 19 August 1849.

58. Palmerston to Lewis, 2 December 1861, quoted in N.B. Ferris, *The Trent Affair: A Diplomatic Crisis* (Knoxville, 1977) p. 63.

59. Gourlay, *General Introduction*, pp. cccxxxviii-cccl; *DCB*, ix, p. 492; *The Times*, 27 August 1863 (McGee); for Cartier, speech at Halifax, 12 September 1864, Whelan, p. 26. For Queen Victoria, Buckle, ed., *Letters of Queen Victoria* (second series) i, p. 250.

60. *Saturday Review,* 15 February 1862, p. 176.

61. *Leeds Mercury,* 5 November 1864.

62. Trollope, *North America,* i, pp. 105-6.

63. 'Our Lady of the Snows' (1897), *Kipling's Verse,* p. 182. The poem was written to celebrate a preferential tariff.

64. G. Smith, *The Empire*, pp. 114-19, 155-6.

65. *Hansard*, cviii, 8 February 1850, col. 567.

66. *Elgin-Grey Papers,* Elgin to Grey, private, 23 March 1850, ii, pp. 608-9.

67. Grey Papers, Russell to Grey, 19 April 1850.

68. CO 537/137, secret minute by Stephen, 20 December 1836, fos 146-69.

69. Grey Papers, Stephen to Howick, 28 December 1837. In 1850, Stephen summarised British policy towards Canada as one of 'substituting a federal for a colonial relation', C.E. Stephen, *The First Sir James Stephen* (Gloucester, 1906) p. 144. The starting point in Stephen's use of the term would have been the Latin 'foedus', meaning a treaty, league or compact.

70. Russell 3C, memorandum by Russell, 28 March 1839, fos 998-1001.

71. *Hansard*, xl, 16 January 1838, col. 41.

72. Grey Papers, Russell to Grey, 6 August 1849.

73. Lucas, ii, p. 310.

74. CO 42/570, Ogden to Grey, 25 October 1850, fos 244-50.

75. C. Martin, 'Sir Edmund Head's First Project', pp. 18, 17.

76. Lytton to Derby, 7 September 1858, in Knox, 'Lytton and Confederation', p. 111.

77. Viscount Bury, *Exodus of Western Nations* (2 vols, London, 1865) ii, pp. 488-93. For Bury's enmity towards Head, HCC 2028, Merivale to Lewis, 27 September 1858.

78. H. Thring, *Colonial Reform: Provisions Intended as Suggestions for a Colonial Bill* (London, 1865, 2nd ed., 1903).

79. Broadlands NE/89/1, Newcastle to Palmerston, 11 November 1861.

80. For example, Ged Martin, '"Anti-Imperialism" in the Mid-Nineteenth Century', pp. 91-3.

81. Brown to Macdonald, private and confidential, 22 December 1864; Pope, *Memoirs*, p. 290.

82. Howe to Stairs, 15 March 1867, in Burpee, p. 457.

83. Brown to Macdonald, private and confidential, 22 December 1864, Pope, *Memoirs*, p. 290.

84. Letter of William Garvie, 15 March 1867, in Burpee, p. 461; *Dictionary of National Biography*, xlii, p. 143.

85. For Ludlow, see *Spectator*, 5-26 January 1867; Monck A-755, F.Bruce to Monck, private, 18 September 1866.

86. *The Times*, 9 January 1865; *Saturday Review*, 17 December 1864, p. 739.

87. *Westminster Review*, xxvii (1865), p. 532.

88. *Saturday Review*, 2 September 1865, p. 289.

89. *Edinburgh Review*, cxxi (1865), p. 183, also printed in B.W. Hodgins and R. Page (eds), *Canadian History Since Confederation: Essays and Interpretations* (2nd ed., Georgetown, Ont., 1979), p. 5.

90. *The Times*, 4 February 1862.

91. *Punch*, 2 March 1867, p. 84.

92. C. Martin, 'Sir Edmund Head's First Project', p. 17.

93. HCC 1531, Head to Lewis, 29 December 1853. Head was using the now-archaic subjunctive.

94. D. Brymner, *Report of the Public Archives for 1884* (Ottawa, 1885) pp. xxvii-lix.

95. CO 537/137, confidential minute by Stephen, 30 April 1836, fos 29-49.

96. *Hansard*, xxxvii, 14 April 1837, cols 1229-49.

97. Roebuck, speaking at the bar of the House, *Hansard*, xl, 5 February 1838, col. 770.

98. *Ibid.*, 18 January, cols 214-15 (Brougham), 25 January 1838, col. 484 (Warburton).

99. Lucas, ii, p. 309.

100. *Morning Post*, 9 October 1838.

101. Roebuck, *op. cit.*, pp. 188, 175.

102. *The Times*, 31 October 1849.

103. Grey Papers, Russell to Grey, 6 August 1849.

104. Godley to Adderley, 25 August 1854, in *Extracts from Letters of Godley*, pp. 214-16.

105. Grey Papers, Russell to Grey, 19 August 1849; Cobden to Combe, 8 February 1849, in Morley, *Cobden*, pp. 506-7.

106. H.C. Allen, *The Anglo-American Relationship Since 1783* (London 1959) p. 95.

107. Russell, *Diary*, ii, p. 37, and see also ii, pp. 6, 372-3.

108. *The Times*, 10 October 1860; 1 February 1862.

109. Trinity College, Cambridge, Whewell Papers, D.18.E1/59, Everett to Whewell, 3 September 1849.

110. Trollope, *Phineas Finn*, ch. 56.

111. Villiers to Bright, 25 January 1862, in B. Jenkins, *Britain & the War for the Union* (2 vols, London, 1974) i, p. 83.

112. *Manchester Guardian*, 27 October 1849.

113. *Morning Post*, 31 December 1840.

114. *The Times*, 1 August 1853.

115. Grey Papers, Howard to Russell, 7 August 1849, enclosed in Russell to Grey, 19 August 1849.

116. *Hansard*, cxxxiv, 29 June 1854, col. 844.

117. Quoted R.F. Foster, *Charles Stewart Parnell: The Man and his Family* (Hassocks, 1979), p. 47.

118. CO 42/570, Ogden to Grey, 25 October 1850, fos 244-50.

119. *The Times*, 7 April 1860.

120. F. Marryat, *A Diary in America with Remarks on its Institutions* (*Part Second*, 3 vols, London, 1839) iii, p.6.

121. *Hansard*, cvi, 19 June 1849, col. 481.

122. Grey Papers, Russell to Grey, 19 August 1849.

123. *Manchester Guardian*, 7 April 1849, lecture by John Dunmore Lang of New South Wales; *BPP*, 1864, xli, *Customs Duties*, report by Galt, 25 October 1859, pp. 11-18. McCalla, *Planting the Province*, p. 165, agrees with Galt in discounting smuggling into Canada.

124. Speech at Aylesbury, *The Times*, 19 January 1838. Young was Conservative MP for Buckinghamshire.

125. So Haliburton told the House of Commons in 1860, see V.L.O. Chittick, *Thomas Chandler Haliburton ('Sam Slick'): A Study in Provincial Toryism* (New York, 1924), p. 622. Howe in 1862 and Bury in 1865 placed British North America fourth, behind Britain, the United States and Russia: Chisholm, ii, p. 382; Bury, *Exodus of Western Nations*, ii, p. 398. Cardwell expected a united British North America to become 'the fourth Naval Power in the world', Monck A-755, Cardwell to Monck, private, 4 March 1865. There was some sparring about these claims in the Canadian Assembly in 1865, with Luther Holton insinuating that they were based on tonnage built — much of which was immediately sold overseas — rather than tonnage operated. *CD*, p. 100.

126. Roebuck, *op. cit.*, p. 188.

127. C. Martin 'Sir Edmund Head's First Project', p. 17.

128. *Elgin-Grey Papers*, Elgin to Grey, private, 18 May 1849, i, pp. 166-7.

129. CO 42/570, Ogden to Grey, 25 October 1850, fos 244-50.

130. Godley to Adderley, 25 August 1854, in *Extracts from Letters of Godley*, pp. 214-16.

131. For example, *The Times*, 29 November, *Daily News*, 3 November ('the expression of individual spite'), *Liverpool Mercury*, 9 November, *North British Daily Mail*, 15 November 1849. The *Nonconformist* (31 October 1849, pp. 866-7) listed the annexation manifesto among 'the less striking events' of the week, ranking it below the assassination of the Governor of Macao.

132. *The Times*, 22 December 1856.

133. Dufferin to Carnarvon, no. 22, private, 23 April 1874, in de Kiewiet and Underhill (eds), *Dufferin-Carnarvon Correspondence*, pp. 26-8.

134. Galt to Lytton, 22 November 1858, in Skelton, *op. cit.*, p. 104.

135. *Cambridge Union Society Annual Report* (Cambridge, 1841) p. 6 (6 February 1841).

136. *Daily News*, 24 December 1864.

137. *The Times*, 16 December 1850.

138. Head to Stanley, 28 April 1858, in Knox, *JICH* (1976) p. 212.

139. *The Times*, 5 December 1860.

140. *Ibid.*, 22 August 1849.

141. Russell 3A, memorandum by Ellice, 7 January 1838, fos 40-2; *Elgin-Grey Papers*, Grey to Elgin (copy), private, 27 July 1848, i, pp. 206-8. Compare Winks, *Canada and the United States*, pp. 28-9.

142. *The Times*, 26 January 1863, 15 October 1864.

143. Watkin, *op. cit.*, p. 65c; Newcastle 10885, Newcastle to Head (copy) private, 12 January 1861, and see cutting from *Montreal Gazette*, 12 January 1861 in Newcastle 11347b. See also Bourne, *op. cit.*, pp. 241-2; *Canadian News*, 27 February 1861, pp. 65-6, 68.

144. Newcastle 10887, Newcastle to Monck (copy), private, 21 March 1858, pp. 127-33.

145. *The Times*, 29 April 1863.

146. Monck A-755, Adderley to Monck, 29 August 1862.

147. Letter of 'R.B.S.' [?Sullivan], *The Times*, 11 January 1838.

148. Howick to Durham, 7 February 1839, in Doughty, *Report of the Public Archives for 1923*, pp. 338-40; Roebuck, *op. cit.*, pp. 176-8.

149. C. Martin, 'Sir Edmund Head's First Project', p. 23.

150. S.E. Morison, H.S. Commager and W.E. Leuchtenburg, *The Growth of the American Republic* (7th ed., 2 vols, New York, 1980) i, p. 536.

151. Roebuck, *op. cit.*, p. 188. Compare Bliss, *Essay*, pp. 11-12.

152. *The Times*, 16 August 1849.

153. *Ibid.*, 12 December 1854, 10 June 1861.

154. *Ibid.*, 16 September 1858. Newcastle praised the volunteer spirit in Canada in his memorandum on the Intercolonial, Newcastle 11260. For Napier, see Bourne, *op. cit.*, p. 194n.

155. *The Times*, 17 June 1861.

156. Newcastle 10886, Newcastle to Monck (copy), private, 12 April 1862, pp. 107-12.

157. *The Times*, 1 February, 26 May 1862. Compare CO 42/632, Monck to Newcastle, no. 24, 2 February 182, fos 163-7, and Newcastle 11413, Monck to Newcastle, private, 28 March 1862.

158. *The Times*, 6 June 1862.

159. CO 42/626, minute by Newcastle, 13 March 1861, fos 22-4.

160. Russell 31, Russell to Newcastle, copy, confidential, 12 June 1862.

161. *Hansard*, clviii, 25 July 1862, cols 843-76.

162. For Galt's speech, *Daily News*, 26 September, and see his letter and condemnatory leading article in *The Times*, 1 October 1862.

163. G. Smith, *The Empire*, pp. 104-46.

164. *The Times*, 21 February 1865.

165. *Morning Herald*, 6 September 1858.

166. *Spectator*, 23 August 1862, p. 933.

167. *Saturday Review,* 15 October 1864, p. 469; 10 June 1865, p. 687.

168. *Ibid.*, 11 February 1865, p. 159.

169. Russell, *Canada*, p. vi. It is possible that Russell simply exploited the interest in British North America created by the move to unite the provinces to capitalise on the success of his two volumes on the United States published in 1863. The title page labels the book 'a third and concluding volume of "My Diary, North and South"'. *The Times* management had not been happy with Russell's excursion north of the border: 'Delane doesn't like letters from Canada when he wants them from the Potomac'. J.B. Atkins, *The Life of Sir William Howard Russell* (2 vols, London, 1911) ii, p. 96.

170. The quotations from W.H. Russell in this paragraph and the next are taken from his *Canada*, pp. 311-12.

171. Russell, *Canada*, p. 312; *The Times*, 15 October 1864.

172. *Macdonald*, i, p. 361.

173. Gladstone 44603, confidential memorandum, fo. 94.

174. Speech of 26 April, *Globe*, 12 May 1865.

175. *Saturday Review*, 24 June 1865, p. 751.

176. *Hansard*, clviii, 25 July 1862, cols 843-76.

177. Russell, *Canada*, p. 311.
178. Speech, January 1865, quoted *Road to Confederation*, p. 230.
179. *BPP*, 1837, xxiv, report of Sir Charles Grey, 17 November 1836, pp. 246-8.
180. CO 537/137, confidential minute by Stephen, 30 April 1836, fos 29-49; *Hansard*, xxxvii, 14 April 1837, fos 1209-29 (Roebuck).
181. *Hansard*, xl, 2 February, col. 484 (Glenelg); 16 January 1838, col. 41 (Russell).
182. *Ibid.*, 16, 26 January 1838, cols 73, 557-8 (Peel).
183. *Ibid.*, 26 January 1838, col. 560.
184. Durham 18, confidential memorandum by Harvey, 16 August 1838, fos 378-80.
185. *Hansard*, l, 29 May 1840, col. 740.
186. *Ibid.*, lv, 9 July 1840, col. 562.
187. *Elgin-Grey Papers*, Grey to Elgin (copy), private, 2 June 1847, i, p. 37.
188. *Ibid.*, Grey to Elgin (copy), private, 16 June 1847, i, pp. 47-8.
189. Russell 8A, Grey to Russell, 8 August 1849, fos 62-5.
190. CO 188/119, minute by Newcastle, 7 June 1853, fo. 274.
191. *Morning Herald*, 3 November 1853.
192. CO 188/124, undated minute by Russell [1855], fos 251-3.
193. CO 42/614, minute by Merivale, 31 August 1858, fos 295-6.
194. Stanley to Head, 7 April 1858, in Knox, *JICH* (1976) pp. 210-11.
195. Newcastle 10885, Newcastle to Manners Sutton (copy), private, 8 March 1861, pp. 41-5.
196. Russell 8A, Grey to Russell, 8 August 1849, fos 62-5.
197. CO 188/124, minute by Merivale, 3 July 1855, fos 205-15.
198. Watkin, *op. cit.*, p. 56b.
199. Glazebrook, *History of Transportation*, i, p. 152.
200. CO 188/131, minute by Blackwood, 20 October 1858, fo. 442.
201. NAC, RG 7, G10, 2, Head to Labouchere, copy, separate, 29 July 1857.
202. CO 217/220, minute by Newcastle, 22 June 1862, fos 255-6.
203. Newcastle 11260, memorandum on Intercolonial railway, 1862.
204. *BPP*, 1861, *Colonial Military Expenditure*, Q. 2968.
205. Minutes by Newcastle, CO 42/626, 13 March 1861, fos 22-4; CO 217/230, 22 June 1862, fos 251-6; Newcastle 10886, Newcastle to Monck (copy), private, 12 April 1862, pp. 107-12.
206. CO 217/230, minute by Newcastle, 22 June 1862, fos 251-6.
207. A. Morris, *Nova Britannia: Or, Our New Canadian Dominion Foreshadowed* (Toronto, 1884) p. 4, and see also p. 47 (18 March 1858).

208. Quoted, Whitelaw, *op. cit.*, p. 128.

209. Morris, *Nova Britannia*, pp. 53, 90 (late 1858).

210. C. Martin, 'Sir Edmund Head's First Project', p. 17.

211. Speech at Quebec, 15 October 1864, in Whelan, p. 74.

212. Quoted, *Life and Times*, p. 50. The recollection was in 1865.

213. Quoted, Beck, *Howe*, ii, p. 162, and see also J.M. Beck (ed.), *Joseph Howe: Voice of Nova Scotia* (Toronto, 1964) pp. 171-2, for Howe's explanation in 1867.

214. Speech, 13 August 1864, Chisholm, ii, pp. 432-4.

215. Journal of Frances Monck, 24 March 1865, in *Monck Letters and Journals*, p. 248.

216. *Montreal Gazette*, 20 January 1865, quoted in *Road to Confederation*, p. 274.

217. P.S. Hamilton, *Union of the Colonies of British North America* (1864) p. 6, quoted *Life and Times*, p. 29.

218. Saint John *Morning News*, 7 August 1861, quoted Whitelaw, *op. cit.*, pp. 177-8.

219. *Morning Chronicle* (Halifax), 27 October 1863, quoted *Road to Confederation*, p. 25.

220. Saint John *Morning News*, 7 August 1861, quoted Whitelaw, *op. cit.*, pp. 177-8.

221. Halifax *Witness*, 24 December 1864, quoted *Globe*, 4 January 1865.

222. Speech of 7 April 1865, quoted Baker, *op. cit.*, p. 103.

223. Saint John *Evening Globe*, August 1864, quoted *Life and Times*, p. 63.

224. Speeches at Halifax, 12 September 1864, in Whelan, pp. 29-30, 46.

225. Russell, *Canada*, p. 225.

226. *Hansard*, clxxxv, 19 February 1867, col. 558.

227. At the Quebec Conference, 10 October 1864, in Browne, p. 129.

228. Muise, 'The Federal Election of 1867 in Nova Scotia'; Buckner, 'The Maritimes and Confederation' and Tennyson, 'Economic Nationalism, Confederation and Nova Scotia'.

229. CO 217/221, Mulgrave to Lytton, confidential, 30 December 1858, fos 556-76.

230. Howe 5, Normanby to Howe, 17 February 1865, pp. 263-78.

6   THE ROLE OF THE BRITISH IN THE LAUNCHING OF
      CONFEDERATION

1. Monck A-755, Cardwell to Monck, private, 27 July 1865.
2. *Hansard*, cx, 13 May 1850, col. 1426.
3. K.L.P. Martin, 'The Union Bill of 1822', *CHR*, v (1924) pp. 42-54.
4. Newcastle 9552, Hincks to Bruce, 10 December 1853.
5. Compare Ged Martin, 'Launching Canadian Confederation'.
6. *Colonial Advocate*, 24 June 1824, quoted C. Lindsey, *The Life and Times of Wm. Lyon Mackenzie* (2 vols, Toronto, 1862) i, p. 58.
7. Russell 3A, Howick to Russell, private, 2 January 1838, fos 15-16.
8. CO 42/283, Durham to Glenelg, no. 58, 13 September 1838, fos 162-3; Chester W. New, *Lord Durham: A Biography of John George Lambton First Earl of Durham* (Oxford, 1929) chs 19-20.
9. Manners Sutton to Lytton, private and confidential, 2 October 1858, in Browne, pp. 5-13. Lytton warned in 1858 that a botched British initiative would reduce subsequent imperial influence, Trotter, 'The British Government', p. 287.
10. CO 537/137, secret minute, 20 December 1836, fos 144-9; Grey Papers, Stephen to Howick, 28 December 1837; Colonial Papers, no. 99.
11. Royal Archives, Melbourne Papers, Howick to Melbourne, private, 2 January 1838.
12. Elgin A-397, Grey to Elgin, 23 December 1846.
13. Earl Grey, *The Colonial Policy of Lord John Russell's Administration* (2 vols, London, 1853) i, p. 207.
14. CO 42/536, minutes by Stephen and Grey, 12, 14 September 1846, fos 131-2.
15. CO 42/534, Grey to Elgin (draft), no. 10, 31 December 1846, fos 369-79, copy in Elgin A-396.
16. Elgin A-397, Grey to Elgin, copy, private, 2 April 1847.
17. *Elgin-Grey Papers*, Elgin to Grey, 26 April 1847, i, pp. 33-4.
18. *Ibid.*, Elgin to Grey, private, 7 May 1849, i, p. 34.
19. *Ibid.*, Grey to Elgin, (copy), private, 2 June 1847, i, p. 37.
20. Lucas, ii, p. 282, and see also Ged Martin, *The Durham Report and British Policy* (Cambridge, 1972) pp. 54-60.
21. Speech, 8 February 1850, in Egerton (ed.), *Molesworth Speeches*, pp. 302-3.
22. CO 885/1, vii, confidential minute by Hawes, 5 January 1850.
23. *BPP*, 1861, *Colonial Military Expenditure*, Q. 3875.

24. Lucas, ii, p. 282.
25. *Examiner*, 26 May 1849, pp. 323-5.
26. *Spectator*, 17 September 1853, p. 885. For the failure of an imperial scheme for federation in Australia, see Ward, *Earl Grey and the Australian Colonies*, ch. 7.
27. Grey Papers, Russell to Grey, 16 March 1848.
28. Delegates were listed by *Montreal Gazette*, 28 July 1849, in *Elgin-Grey Papers*, i, pp. 445-6.
29. *Ibid.*, i, pp. 441n-443n.
30. CO 217/202, Harvey to Grey, private, 16 August 1849, fos 204-5.
31. Howe to Moffat, 8 May 1849, in Chisholm, ii, p. 25.
32. C. Martin, 'Sir Edmund Head's First Project', pp. 25-6.
33. CO 217/217, minute by Blackwood, 13 October 1855, fos 425-7.
34. Newcastle 9631A, Stewart to Newcastle, 26 May 1854.
35. CO 217/216, Hamilton to Molesworth, 15 August 1855, fos 224-7.
36. Newcastle 9552, Hincks to Bruce, 10 December 1853.
37. CO 217/216, Hamilton to Molesworth, 15 August 1855, fos 224-7.
38. CO 42/614, minute by Merivale, 31 August 1858, fos 295-6, quoted in Gibson, 'Colonial Office View', p. 281.
39. For example, C. Martin, 'British Policy in Canadian Confederation'.
40. CO 42/614, minute by Lytton (September 1858), fos 295-6, quoted Whitelaw, *op. cit.*, p. 131.
41. Lytton 01, Lytton to Albert (copy), 9 September 1858.
42. Stanley to Head, 7 April 1858, in Knox, *JICH* (1976) pp. 210-11.
43. Howe to Moffat, 8 May 1849, in Chisholm, ii, p. 25.
44. Head to Stanley, 28 April 1858, in Knox, *JICH* (1976) p. 215.
45. *Critical Years*, pp. 16-20.
46. Quoted in Skelton, *op. cit.*, p. 93. Galt's resolutions are printed at p. 283. It is not always noted that they pointed to a federation of Canada as well as to Confederation of all the provinces.
47. Carnarvon 6/132, memorandum, 22 September 1858, fos 21-2.
48. Quoted in Whitelaw, *op. cit.*, p. 128.
49. Memorandum by Prince Albert, 21 February 1858, in A.C. Benson and Lord Esher (eds), *The Letters of Queen Victoria (First Series, 1837-1861)* (3 vols, London, 1908 ed.), p. 267.
50. Journal, 21 February 1858, in Vincent (ed.), *op. cit.*, pp. 155-6.
51. Blake, *op. cit.*, pp. 381-3, Monypeny and Buckle, *op. cit.*, iv, pp. 145-54.
52. Quoted in Gibson, 'Colonial Office View', p. 287.

53.   *The Times*, 15 September 1858, and see the reassuring comments by Merivale, 22 September 1858, Lytton 01.

54.   CO 42/615, minutes by Blackwood and Carnarvon, 22 September 1858, fos 64-5.

55.   *Ibid.*, minute by Lytton (September 1858) fo. 296.

56.   CO 42/614, Lytton to Head (draft), no. 55, 10 September 1858, fos 297-300, quoted in Browne, p. 2; Gibson, 'Colonial Office View', pp. 288-9.

57.   Cartier, Ross and Galt to Lytton, 23, 25 October 1858, in Skelton, *op. cit.*, pp. 93-6. The letters were in fact written on the same day, and both were the work of Galt.

58.   Confidential memorandum by Elliot, 4 November 1858, in Trotter, 'The British Government', p. 287.

59.   Galt to Amy Galt, 29 October 1858, in Skelton, *op. cit.*, p. 100. Lytton had set his 1849 novel, *The Caxtons*, partly in Canada. A.T. Galt's father, John Galt, had been a successful novelist before becoming involved with the British American Land Company.

60.   CO 188/131, Manners Sutton to Lytton, private and confidential, 2 October, and minute by Blackwood, 20 October 1858, fos 428-42.

61.   Confidential memorandum by Elliot, 4 November 1858, in Trotter, 'The British Government', p. 296.

62.   CO 188/131, minute by Elliot, 25 October 1858, fo. 442.

63.   Most Confidential memorandum by Lytton, 10 November 1858, in Trotter, 'The British Government', pp. 285-6.

64.   Lytton's despatch of 26 November 1858 is in Skelton, *op. cit.*, pp. 104-5, and Browne, pp. 27-8.

65.   CO 217/221, Mulgrave to Lytton, confidential, 30 December 1858, and minute by Lytton, 14 January 1859, fos 556-78.

66.   *Hansard*, xl, 23 January 1838, col. 398 (Lytton was then known as E.L. Bulwer).

67.   CO 42/614, minute by Lytton (September 1858) fo. 296.

68.   As pointed out by Knox, *JICH* (1976) p. 208.

69.   Lytton to Derby, 7 September 1858, in Knox, 'Sir Edward Lytton', pp. 110-11.

70.   Most Confidential memorandum by Lytton, 10 November 1858, Trotter, 'The British Government', p. 286.

71.   Lytton 027, Lytton to Head (copy), confidential, 12 December 1858.

72.   CO 188/132, minute by Newcastle, 23 October 1859, fos 368-72.

73.   Newcastle to Manners Sutton, 5 November 1859, in Whitelaw, *op. cit.*, p. 143.

74. Newcastle 11230, Galt and Smith to Newcastle, 18 January 1860, unsigned copy in CO 42/622, fos 90-1.

75. *BPP*, 1864, xli, *Customs Duties*.

76. Newcastle 11230, Galt and Smith to Newcastle, 18 January 1860.

77. Newcastle 10889, Newcastle to Ellice (copy), 31 October 1859, pp. 55-59.

78. CO 42/619, draft of circular despatch, 27 January 1860, fos 375-6. Extracts quoted, with minor variations, Browne, p. 30; Gibson, 'Colonial Office View', p. 296; Whitelaw, *op. cit.*, p. 147.

79. CO 42/622, Head to Newcastle, confidential, 16 February, fos 92-3; CO 188/133, Manners Sutton to Newcastle, confidential, 20 February, fos 92-3; CO 217/226, Mulgrave to Newcastle, confidential, 1 March 1860, fos 164-81.

80. Newcastle 11276.

81. Newcastle 11260.

82. Newcastle 10890, Newcastle to Buckingham (copy), private, 14 August 1861. There had been an earlier ducal governor-general of Canada: Richmond in 1818-19.

83. Carnarvon 6/135, Buckingham to Carnarvon, 16 July 1866, fos 204-5.

84. Blake, *op. cit.*, p. 400.

85. Monck A-755, Adderley to Monck, 22 April 1868.

86. *Canadian News*, 16 January 1861, pp. 25-6; Newcastle 10885, Newcastle to Manners Sutton (copy), private, 8 March 1861, pp. 41-5.

87. CO 42/645, minute by Blackwood, 8 February 1864, fos 65-6.

88. *Canadian News*, 3 January 1861, p. 3.

89. CO 42/626, Williams to Newcastle, no. 2, 2 January, and minutes by Elliot and Newcastle, 9, 13 March 1862, fos 8-10, 16-24.

90. Newcastle 10885, Newcastle to Manners Sutton (copy), private, 8 March 1861, pp. 41-5, quoted in J.A. Gibson, 'The Duke of Newcastle and British North American Affairs, 1859-1864', *CHR*, xliv (1963) p. 153.

91. Newcastle 10888, Newcastle to Malcolm Cameron (copy), private, 25 March 1861, pp. 192-4, quoted Gibson, 'Newcastle and British North America', p. 154; *DCB*, x, pp. 124-9.

92. Manners Sutton's letter does not survive, but its contents may be deduced from Newcastle 10885, Newcastle to Manners Sutton (copy), 23 August 1861, quoted Gibson, 'Newcastle and British North America', pp. 147-9. Newcastle had probably raised Manners

Sutton's hopes through an infelicitous allusion to his seniority in the colonial service, Newcastle 10885, Newcastle to Manners Sutton (copy), private, 28 June 1861.

93. The timing of the resolution may have been coincidence: Howe did not mention Newcastle when he explained the background to the resolution in 1867, Beck (ed.), *Joseph Howe*, pp. 171-2.

94. CO 217/230, Mulgrave to Newcastle, no. 47, 21 May, and minute by Blackwood, 13 June 1862, fos 251-3.

95. Beck, *Howe*, ii, p. 152.

96. The resolutions are in Chisholm, ii, pp. 368-9 and Whitelaw, *op. cit.*, p. 175.

97. CO 217/230, Mulgrave to Newcastle, no. 47, 21 May 1862.

98. CO 217/230, minutes by Elliot, Fortescue and Newcastle, 14, 19, 22 June 1862, fos 254-6, quoted Whitelaw, *op. cit.*, pp. 178-9.

99. Russell 31, Russell to Newcastle (copy), confidential, 12 June 1862.

100. CO 217/230, minute by Newcastle, 22 June 1862, fos 255-6, quoted Whitelaw, *op. cit.*, pp. 178-9 and Browne, p. 30.

101. *Hansard*, clxxxv, 19 February 1867, col. 1166.

102. CO 217/230, Newcastle to Mulgrave (draft), no. 182, 6 July 1862, fos 259-61. The despatch was printed in *BPP*, 1865, xxxvii, *Correspondence*, pp. 13-14, to establish the legitimacy of the Quebec Conference, also in Pope (ed.), *Confederation*, pp. 303-4 and Browne, pp. 30-1.

103. CO 42/619, draft of circular despatch, 27 January 1860, fos 375-6.

104. CO 226/100, minutes by Blackwood and Elliot, 29 March 1864, fo. 116.

105. Confidential memorandum by Elliot, 4 November 1858, in Trotter, 'The British Government', p. 293.

106. Monck A-755, Cardwell to Monck, private, 9 September 1864.

107. CO 217/235, MacDonnell to Cardwell, 15 September, and minute by Blackwood, 27 September 1864, fos 55-61.

108. *Ibid.*, minute by Cardwell, 11 October 1864, fo. 7.

109. Beck, ed., *Joseph Howe*, pp. 171-2; *Life and Times*, p. 50.

110. University of New Brunswick, Harriet Irving Library, Tilley Papers, MG H10, McGee to Tilley, 9 May 1864.

111. 11 October 1864, Pope (ed.), *Confederation*, p. 59; Browne, p. 98.

112. Chapman, 'Arthur Gordon and Confederation'; G.W. Martin, 'Britain and the Future of British North America', pp. 256-66.

113. CO 188/138, minute by Newcastle, 30 July 1863, fo. 429.

114. *Ibid.*, minute by Blackwood, 21 July 1863, fo. 429.

115. *Ibid.*, Newcastle to Gordon (draft), confidential, 31 July 1863, fo. 429.
116. Newcastle 10888, Newcastle to Doyle (copy), private, 28 November 1863.
117. Russell 97, Russell to Lyons, copy, 4 July 1863.
118. Newcastle 10887, Newcastle to Monck (copy), private, 20 June 1863, pp. 172-6.
119. *Ibid.*, Newcastle to Monck (copy), private, 18 September 1863, pp. 47-52.
120. *The Times*, 29 June 1864.
121. *Ibid.*, 12 July 1864.
122. Monck A-755, Cardwell to Monck, private, 7 July 1864. Cardwell received the first news of the change of ministry that afternoon.

7 THE ROLE OF THE BRITISH IN THE ACHIEVEMENT OF CONFEDERATION 1864-1867

1. Brebner, p. 288; McInnis, p. 353; Francis, Jones and Smith, *Origins*, p. 390; *Structure of Canadian History*, p. 180; *Critical Years*, p. 182; C.C. Eldridge, *Victorian Imperialism* (London, 1978), p. 88; P.B. Waite, 'Edward Cardwell and Confederation', *CHR*, xliii (1962) pp. 17-41, esp. p. 41; D. Judd, *The Victorian Empire* (London, 1970), p. 29. Ronald Hyam also refers to Cardwell's 'fairly ruthless pressure' in R. Hyam, *Britain's Imperial Century 1815-1914: A Study of Empire and Expansion* (London, 1976), p. 194.
2. *Road to Confederation*, p. 303; *Colony to Nation*, p. 316.
3. Francis, Jones and Smith, *op. cit.*, p. 390.
4. *Colony to Nation*, p. 322.
5. Compare the comments of James Brown of Charlotte County, New Brunswick with the anger noted by Charles Mackay in Prince Edward Island, MacNutt, *op. cit.*, pp. 435-6; Mackay, 'Week in Prince Edward Island', p.147.
6. Brebner, p. 288.
7. Beck, *Howe*, ii, p. 148.
8. *Hansard*, clxxvi, 19 July 1864, cols 1708-9, reply by Cardwell to Sir John Walsh MP. *The Times*, 11 July 1864, had put Canadian federation first, with 'the probable ultimate union of all British North America under one general legislature'.
9. CO 42/641, Monck to Cardwell, no. 97, 30 June 1864, fos 422-5, with memoranda, fos 426-37. Monck also sent a copy of his speech

proroguing parliament, *ibid.*, no. 98, fos 437-42. There are no minutes on these despatches, but Blackwood commented on a crank letter, CO 42/646, minute of 3 August 1864, fo. 305. Chester Martin noted the lack of response, and argued that it implied a 'reversal of British policy' soon afterwards. C. Martin, 'British Policy', p. 9.

10. CO 42/642, Monck to Cardwell, no. 124, 26 August 1864, and marginal note by Blackwood [10 September 1858], fos 153-4.

11. Monck A-755, Cardwell to Monck, private, 16 July 1864.

12. *Ibid.*, Cardwell to Monck, private, 26 November 1864; Stanmore 1, Cardwell to Gordon, private, 10 December 1864, printed in Browne, p. 172.

13. Cobden to Cole, 20 March 1865, in Morley, *Cobden*, pp. 934-5; *Spectator*, 15 April 1865, p. 402.

14. Cardwell to Monck, no. 93, 3 December 1864, (copies circulated to all North American governors) in Browne, pp. 168-71; *BPP*, 1865, *Correspondence*, pp. 11-12. (Draft in CO 42/643, fos 232-40.)

15. MacDonnell reported the publication of the despatch on 23 December 1864, and assessed its impact on 5 January 1865, *BPP*, 1867, *Correspondence*, pp. 53-54.

16. Attributed to Howe, *Life and Times*, p. 212, and see also Beck, *Howe*, ii, pp. 184-8.

17. Brown 5, Brown to Anne Brown, 5 December 1864, pp. 1104-6.

18. Cardwell's circular despatch of 24 June 1865 is in *BPP*, 1867, *Correspondence*, pp. 79-80, 118-19, 136, 155-6.

19. *Macdonald*, i, p. 361; Monck A-755, Cardwell to Monck, private, 16 July 1864, 28 January 1865.

20. Henry Adams, 20 December 1864, quoted Winks, *op. cit.*, p. 320, and see *ibid.*, chs 14-15 and *Road to Confederation*, chs 7-8. Even the *Globe* was shaken from its usual confidence that there would be no war, Andrew Robb, 'The Toronto Globe and the Defence of Canada, 1861-1866', *Ontario History*, lxiv (1972), pp. 74-6.

21. Buckle, ed., *Letters of Queen Victoria*, i, pp. 248-9, and see the Queen's fears of war, 12 February 1865, *ibid.*, p. 250; Gordon to Gladstone, 27 February 1865, in Knaplund (ed.), *Gladstone-Gordon Correspondence*, p. 46, and see also Cardwell 6/39, Gordon to Cardwell, 8 February 1865, fos 58-61: 'War *here* will very speedily follow peace *there*.'

22. Brown 5, Brown to Anne Brown, 17 March 1865, pp. 1206-9; Broadlands RU/897, Russell to Palmerston, 6 April 1865.

23. Quoted, Bourne, *op. cit.*, p. 278. The Jervois report was published in *BPP*, 1865, *Defence of Canada*.

24. Macdonald to Gray, private, 27 March 1865, in Pope, *Memoirs*, pp. 296-8.
25. *Brown*, ii, p. 190.
26. *CD*, p. 649 (6 March 1865).
27. *Ibid*, pp. 650-7.
28. *Ibid.*, p. 663.
29. Quoted, *Brown*, ii, p. 152.
30. *Ibid.*, ii, p. 192.
31. Brown 6, Macdonald to Brown, private, 11 April 1865, also quoted in *Road to Confederation*, p. 275.
32. Monck A-755, Cardwell to Monck, private, 13 May 1864.
33. Gladstone 44753, fos 125-41; Knaplund, *Gladstone and Britain's Imperial Policy*, pp. 228-42.
34. Matthew (ed.), *op. cit.*, vi, 291.
35. Gladstone 44118, Cardwell to Gladstone, 27 July 1864, fos 170-1; *ibid.*, Gladstone to Cardwell, copy, 28 July 1864, fos 166-9.
36. Quoted in *Macdonald*, i, p. 361.
37. Monck A-756, de Grey to Monck, private, 28 August 1863.
38. Quoted, Shannon, *op. cit.*, p. 544; Buckle, ed., *op. cit.*, p. 248.
39. Matthew (ed.), *op. cit.*, vi, p. 288; Gladstone to Gordon, 5 July 1864, in Knaplund (ed.), *Gladstone-Gordon Correspondence*, p. 44; Gordon to Bishop of Oxford (copy) [1865].
40. Monck A-755, Cardwell to Monck, private, 15 April 1865.
41. *Ibid.*, Cardwell to Monck, private, 18 March 1865.
42. *Saturday Review*, 18 March 1865, p. 304.
43. Brown 6, Brown to Anne Brown, 13 May 1865, pp. 1250-5.
44. Gladstone 44136, Cobden to Gladstone, 14 February 1865, fos 248-59.
45. Argyll to Gladstone, 24 February 1865, in Jenkins, *Britain and the War for the Union*, ii, p. 377.
46. Gladstone to Gordon, 11 July 1865, in Knaplund (ed.), *Gladstone-Gordon Correspondence*, p.46.
47. *The Times*, 21 March 1865.
48. Macdonald 161, memorandum of interview with Cardwell, 26 April 1865, pp. 65221, 65225. Documents relating to the negotiations are also in Gladstone 44603.
49. Monck A-755, Cardwell to Monck, strictly confidential, 27 May 1865.
50. Brown 6, Brown to Anne Brown, 3 June 1865, pp. 1282-6.
51. *Ibid.*, Brown to Anne Brown, 25 May 1865, pp. 1269-72.

52. *Ibid.*, Brown to Anne Brown, 3 June 1865, pp. 1282-6.

53. *BPP*, 1865, Papers, Cardwell to Monck, no. 95, 17 June 1865.

54. Gladstone to Argyll, 27 May 1865, quoted Jenkins, *op. cit.*, ii, p. 391.

55. Quoted in *ibid.*

56. Macdonald 161, Observations, 2 June 1865, p. 65254.

57. *Ibid.*, memorandum, 26 April 1865, pp. 65213-4.

58. Monck A-755, Cardwell to Monck, private, 17 June 1865.

59. *Spectator*, 24 June 1865, p. 688.

60. *Saturday Review*, 2 September 1865, p. 288.

61. *BPP*, 1867, *Correspondence*, pp. 79-80, 118-19, 136, 155-6.

62. Mackay, 'Week in Prince Edward Island', p. 147; *BPP*, 1867, *Correspondence*, minute of Executive Council, 12 July 1865, pp. 99-100; Monck A-755, Cardwell to Monck, private, 11 August 1865.

63. *Road to Confederation*, p. 292.

64. CO 217/232, MacDonnell to Cardwell, confidential, 15 February, and minute by Cardwell, 2 March 1865, fos 150-2.

65. CO 194/174, Musgrave to Cardwell, no. 104, 15 May, and minutes by Blackwood, Rogers and Carnarvon, 31 July, 1, 11 August 1866, fos 195-9.

66. Carnarvon 6/138, Derby to Carnarvon, private, 5 September 1866, fos 91-3.

67. Chapman, 'Gordon and Confederation'.

68. So Anglin claimed in 1866, Baker, *op. cit.*, pp. 86-7.

69. Brown 5, Tilley to Brown, private and confidential, 21 November 1864. Macdonald continued to believe that Gordon's open opposition was largely responsible for the defeat of Confederation in New Brunswick. Pope, *Memoirs*, p. 504.

70. Stanmore 1, Cardwell to Gordon, private, 7 January 1865.

71. Monck A-755, Cardwell to Monck, private, 26 January 1865.

72. Stanmore 1, Cardwell to Gordon, private, 13 May 1865.

73. Knaplund (ed.), *Gladstone-Gordon Correspondence*, pp. 5-39. Typically, Gordon could write, 'I do not know that I have anything to thank him for', Stanmore 4, Gordon to Bishop of Oxford, 12 September 1864. This was a strange comment from a man who had asked Mrs Gladstone to propose on his behalf to her own daughter.

74. Gladstone to Gordon, 11 July 1865, p. 46.

75. Chapman, *op. cit.*, pp. 36-7.

76. MacNutt, *op. cit*, pp. 446-7.

77. *Saturday Review*, 2 September 1865, p. 288.

78. *Saturday Review*, 24 June 1865, p. 752; memorandum by Gladstone, 14 December 1861, in Matthew, (ed.), *op. cit.*, vi, p. 81.
79. Newcastle 10886, Newcastle to Gordon (copy), private, 5 April 1862, pp. 100-3. (Original in Stanmore 1.)
80. *Ibid.*, Newcastle to Monck (copy), private, 12 April 1862.
81. Matthew (ed.), *op. cit.*, vi, p. 114. The vote, by 8 to 7, took place on 10 April 1862. One constitutional authority regards majority voting in cabinet as a development which began in 1880. I. Jennings, *Cabinet Government* (3rd ed., Cambridge, 1965), p. 261, but compare J.P. Macintosh, *The British Cabinet* (2nd ed., London, 1968) pp. 317-20.
82. Treasury Minute, 26 March 1867, in *BPP*, 1867, *Intercolonial Railway*, p. 19; Macdonald 161, memorandum, 26 April 1865, p. 65216.
83. Stanmore 1, Cardwell to Gordon, private, 18 March 1865 (copy in Cardwell 6/39); *Hansard*, clxxxvi, 26 March 1867, col. 751.
84. Newcastle 10887, Newcastle to Monck (copy), private, 29 May 1863; *BPP*, 1863, *Hamilton*.
85. *BPP*, 1864, *Intercolonial Railway*, Cardwell to Monck, no. 31, 25 June, enclosing Rogers to Treasury, 11 March 1864, pp. 42-46.
86. Monck A-755, Cardwell to Monck, private, 16 June 1864.
87. Morrell, *British Colonial Policy in the Mid-Victorian Age*, pp. 300-4.
88. Palmerston to Gladstone, 16 March 1864, in P. Guedella (ed.), *Gladstone and Palmerston* (London, 1928) pp. 277-8.
89. James Belich, *The New Zealand Wars and the Victorian Interpretation of Racial Conflict* (Auckland, 1986) pp. 178-96.
90. *The Times*, 7 July 1864, was shocked by the high proportion of officers among the casualties, suggesting a lack of enthusiasm (or worse) among the other ranks.
91. Morrell, *British Colonial Policy in the Mid-Victorian Age*, p. 304.
92. *Hansard*, clxxvi, 14 July 1864, cols 1476 (Gladstone), 1515-16 (Cobden).
93. Monck A-755, Cardwell to Monck, private, 2 September 1864.
94. *Ibid.*, Cardwell to Monck, private, 21 January 1865.
95. Macdonald 51B, Monck to Macdonald, private, 28 February 1867, pp. 20397-403.
96. Monck A-755, Cardwell to Monck, private, 16 July, 2 September 1864.
97. Macdonald 51B, Monck to Macdonald, private, 31 December 1866.
98. Carnarvon 6/158, Williams to Carnarvon, private, 27 September 1866, fos 226-7.

99.   *Hansard*, clxxxvi, 26 March, cols 736-64, esp. col. 760 (Lowe), and 2 April 1867, col. 973 (Gaselee). Gaselee had been elected for Portsmouth in July 1865, having unsuccessfully opposed Monck there ten years earlier.

100. *Ibid.*, 28 February 1867, col. 1180.

101. *The History of The Times*, ii, p. 131, and see *The Times*, 5 April 1865.

102. *Monck Letters and Journals*, p. 193; Howe 9, Howe to Editor of *The Times* (copy), private, 17 September 1866, pp. 135-7 (partly quoted in Beck, *Howe*, ii, p. 206, who reads 'natural misfortune').

103. Carnarvon 6/158, Williams to Carnarvon, private, 30 August 1866, fos 213-18.

104. As reported in Monck A-755, Cardwell to Monck, private, 22 July 1865.

105. *Ibid.*, Cardwell to Monck, private and confidential, 15 July 1865; Carnarvon 6/158, Williams to Carnarvon, private, 17 August 1866, fos 207-12.

106. Marindin (ed.), *op. cit.*, p. 253.

107. University of New Brunswick, Harriet Irving Library, Tilley Papers, MG10 H8, Brown to Tilley, private and confidential, 8 December 1864.

108. Quoted, Stanmore 1, incomplete letter, Cardwell to Gordon, 10 December 1864.

109. University of New Brunswick, Harriet Irving Library, Tilley Papers, MG10 H8, Brown to Tilley, private and confidential, 8 December 1864. The despatch was that of 3 December 1864, referred to above.

110. Marindin (ed.), *op. cit.*, p. 253.

111. Stanmore 1, incomplete letter, Cardwell to Gordon, 10 December 1864.

112. W. Bagehot, *The English Constitution* (ed. R.H.S. Crossman, London, 1963), p. 112.

113. *Ibid.*, pp. 122-3.

114. Skelton, *op. cit.*, p. 164.

115. The Colonial Office had been obliged to censure Lord Monck for the mistakes of his ministers in handling the extradition of Lamirande, a swindler from France. Carnarvon 6/154, Rogers to Carnarvon, 24 December 1866, fos 201-3.

116. Marindin (ed.), *op. cit.*, pp. 258-9.

117. Galt to Amy Galt, 4 May 1865, in Skelton, *op. cit.*, p. 164.

118. Speech at inaugural meeting of British North American Association, 30 January, in *The Times*, 31 January 1862, and see also Wakefield, *A*

View of the Art of Colonization, pp. 147-9: 'When a distinguished colonist comes to London ... he prowls about the streets, and sees the sights until he is sick of doing nothing else, and then returns home disgusted with his visit to the old country'.

119. Beck, *Howe*, ii, p. 157; Newcastle 10890, Newcastle to Howe (copy), private, 24 January 1862, pp. 124-37.

120. Newcastle 10887, Newcastle to Monck (copy), private, 23 June 1863, pp. 63-5.

121. Galt to Amy Galt, 4 May 1865, in Skelton, *op. cit.*, pp. 164-5.

122. *The Times*, 30 August 1865.

123. Royal Archives, RA/P22/97, Monck to Cardwell, copy with omissions, 14 November 1864, enclosed with Cardwell to Queen Victoria, 11 December 1864, RA/P22/94.

124. Monck A-755, Cardwell to Monck, private, 3 December 1864.

125. *Ibid.*, Cardwell to Monck, 'Quite Private', 6 January 1865.

126. The 1858 suggestion was made by John Ross, Skelton, *op. cit.*, p. 101; Queen Victoria to Russell, 8 December 1864, in Buckle (ed.), *op. cit.*, pp. 244-5.

127. Monck A-755, Cardwell to Monck, private, 3 December 1864. Brown was aware of the rule, *CD*, p. 664.

128. Comment by Careless, *Brown*, ii, p. 180.

129. Brown 5, Brown to Anne Brown, 3, 6, 10 December 1864, pp. 1100-1, 1107-10, 1118-19.

130. *Ibid.*, Palmerston to Cardwell, 14 December 1864, pp. 1129-30.

131. *Ibid.*, Brown to Anne Brown, 16 December 1864, pp. 1131-2.

132. Monck A-755, Cardwell to Monck, private and confidential, 24 December 1864; Palmerston to Delane, 14 December 1864, in Dasent, *Delane*, ii, p. 135.

133. Frances Monck's account, 19 January 1865, *Monck Letters and Journals*, pp. 208-9.

134. Brown 6, Brown to Anne Brown, 13 May 1865, pp. 1250-5.

135. *Ibid.*, Brown to Anne Brown, 17 May 1865; P. Appleman, W.A. Madden and M. Wolff (eds), *1859: Entering an Age of Crisis* (Bloomington, Ind., 1959) p. 56.

136. Brown, 6, Brown to Anne Brown, 17 May 1865.

137. *Ibid.*, Brown to Anne Brown, 18 May 1865, pp. 1257-61.

138. *Ibid.*, Brown to Anne Brown, 3 June 1865, pp. 1282-6.

139. Galt to Amy Galt, 30 May 1865, in Skelton, *op. cit.*, pp. 168-9.

140. Brown 6, Brown to Anne Brown, 3 June 1865, pp. 1282-6.

141. *Ibid.*, Brown to Anne Brown, 1 June 1865, pp. 1278-81.

142. *Ibid.*, Brown to Anne Brown, 27 May 1865, pp. 1274-7.

143. *Ibid.*, Brown to Anne Brown, 1 June, 20 May 1865, pp. 1278-81, 1265-6.

144. Galt to Amy Galt, 30 May 1865, in Skelton, *op. cit.*, pp. 168-9.

145. Galt to Amy Galt, 17 May 1865, in *ibid.*, p. 166.

146. Galt to Amy Galt, 25 May 1865, in *ibid.*, pp. 168-9.

147. Monck A-755, Cardwell to Monck, private, 17 June 1865.

148. *Ibid.*, Cardwell to Monck, private, 1 September 1865.

149. *Ibid.*, Cardwell to Monck, private, 11 August 1865. 'High birth and lofty position, a cocked hat and gold lace did not make the man,' was Smith's comment on Gordon. C. Wallace, 'Albert J. Smith, Confederation and Reaction in New Brunswick, 1852-1882', *CHR*, xliv (1963) p. 293.

150. *DCB*, xi, p. 829.

151. Monck A-755, Cardwell to Monck, private and confidential, 8 July 1865.

152. Stanmore 2, Williams to Gordon, private, 12 January 1866.

153. Russell 26, Cardwell to Russell, 15 August 1865, fos 71-2.

154. Monck A-755, Cardwell to Monck, private, 25 August 1865.

155. Stanmore 4, Smith to Gordon, 7 July 1865.

156. CO 194/174, Musgrave to Cardwell, no. 65, 19 August 1865, fos 239-40.

157. Annand to Smith, 20 March 1866, in *Life and Times*, pp. 226-7.

158. Russell 26, Cardwell to Russell, 15 July 1865.

159. Beck, *Howe*, ii, pp. 191-3.

160. Carnarvon 6/154, Rogers to Carnarvon, 12 December 1866, fos 175-6, and see Elliot to Howe, 16 August; Howe to Stairs, 12 October; Howe to Hay, 12 November; Howe to Stairs, 21 December 1866, in Burpee, pp. 429, 434-5, 437-9, 447-8.

161. Howe to Stairs, 21 December 1866, in Burpee, pp. 447-8.

162. *Ibid.*

163. Howe 3, Carnarvon to Howe, private, 29 December 1866, 1 January 1867, pp. 261-3 (copies in Carnarvon 6/146, fos 164-6).

164. Carnarvon 6/146, Howe to Carnarvon, private, 21 December 1866.

165. *Ibid.*, Carnarvon to Howe, 4 January 1867, fo. 173.

166. *Ibid.*, Rogers to Carnarvon, 2 January 1867, 21 December 1866, fos 216-18, 195-8.

167. *Ibid.*, Rogers to Carnarvon, 26 December 1866, fos 206-8; *Hansard*, clxxxv, 28 February 1867, col. 1172.

168. Buckner, 'Maritimes and Confederation', p. 20.

169. *Hansard*, clxxxv, 19 February 1867, col. 558.

170. CO 226/101, minute by Blackwood, 24 April 1865, fo. 109, and see also marginal annotation '& size' added to reasons given by Governor Dundas why the Island's refusal to join would not matter, CO 226/100, Dundas to Cardwell, confidential, 30 December 1864, fos 463-6.

171. 1865 comment, quoted by J.K. Hiller, 'Confederation Defeated: The Newfoundland Election of 1869' in Hiller and Neary, eds., *Newfoundland in the Nineteenth and Twentieth Centuries*, p. 70.

172. *Colony to Nation*, p. 321.

173. McInnis, p. 354; *Kingdom of Canada*, p. 323.

174. Francis, Jones and Smith, *op. cit.*, p. 388.

175. G. Patterson, 'An Unexplained Incident in Confederation in Nova Scotia', *Dalhousie Review*, vii (1927), pp. 442-6. I am grateful to John Stanton for his help with this point.

176. As reported in Stanmore 1, Cardwell to Gordon, private, 13 May 1865, and see *Road to Confederation*, pp. 259-60; *Life and Times*, p. 246.

177. Stanmore 3, Gordon to Monck (copy), private, undated (1865) and see also Cardwell 6/39, Gordon to Cardwell, private, 5 June 1865, fos 89-92.

178. *Saturday Review*, 29 April 1865, p. 498. This interpretation may have stemmed from the final paragraphs of the anti-Confederation letter from 'Union' in *The Times*, 5 April 1865.

179. See map of the 1865 election in *Road to Confederation*, p. 261.

180. *The Times*, 28 April 1865.

181. Stanmore 1, Cardwell to Gordon, private, 1 April 1865.

182. Monck A-755, Cardwell to Monck, private, 18 November 1864.

183. *Ibid.*, Cardwell to Monck, private, 3 December 1864.

184. Stanmore 1, Cardwell to Gordon, private, 7 January 1865.

185. Royal Archives, RA/P22/104, Monck to Cardwell, copy, private, 24 December 1864.

186. Brown 5, Monck to Brown, confidential, [November 1864], pp. 1085-6. Monck assured Cardwell that Resolution 44, on pardon, would be abandoned, and Cardwell passed this assurance to the Queen. Royal Archives, RA/P22/95, Monck to Cardwell, private, 11 November 1864.

187. CO 188/141, Gordon to Cardwell, Confidential, 21 November 1864, fos 385-92.

188. Pope (ed.), *Confederation*, pp. 107, 150; Arthur Hardinge, *The Life of Henry Howard Molyneux Herbert Fourth Earl of Carnarvon 1831-1890* (3 vols, Oxford, 1925) i, pp. 303-4.

189. In his despatch of 3 December 1864, in Browne, pp. 168-71.

190. *Hansard*, clxxxv, 19 February 1867, col. 560.

191. Compare E. Forsey, 'Alexander Mackenzie's Memoranda on the Appointment of Extra Senators, 1873-1874', *CHR*, xxvii (1946) pp. 189-94.

192. A.B. Keith, *Responsible Government in the Dominions* (3 vols, Oxford, 1912 ed.) ii, pp. 599-604.

193. Carnarvon 6/134, undated note by Carnarvon on Adderley to Carnarvon, 29 January 1867, fos 82-3. (Adderley argued that the lower house should be empowered to override the upper house by a two-thirds majority, and wished the definition of money bills to include 'everything remotely bearing on revenue — such as questions of Protection'.)

194. *Ibid.*, Henry to Carnarvon, 29 January 1867, and undated note by Carnarvon, fos 227-8.

195. B.K. de Garis, 'The Colonial Office and the Commonwealth Constitution Bill', in A.W. Martin (ed.), *Essays in Australian Federation* (Melbourne, 1969), pp. 98-100.

196. Monck A-755, Cardwell to Monck, private, 18 November 1864; Gladstone 44118, Cardwell to Gladstone, 27 October 1864, fos 176-9. There is a slight mystery about the date of this letter. It appears to be a reply to Gladstone's letter of 25 October, quoted in Knaplund, *Gladstone and Britain's Imperial Policy*, pp. 92-3, but it contains the statement: 'If Maclellan had carried the Presidency....' The presidential election did not take place until 8 November 1864, and the result of course did not reach Britain immediately. However, McLellan's chances of defeating Lincoln had been widely discounted by early October. As evidence of Cardwell's attitudes late in 1864, the letter does not require precise dating, but the element of uncertainty is another reminder of the insecurity of historical evidence.

197. Gladstone 44600, Monck to Cardwell, private, 21 November 1864, fo. 56; Monck A-755, Cardwell to Monck, 16(?) December 1864. Monck agreed that Cardwell had made the right decision, Royal Archives, RA/P22/105, Monck to Cardwell, copy, private, 2 January 1865.

198. Monck A-755, Cardwell to Monck, private, 1 April 1865.

199. Cardwell 6/39, Gordon to Cardwell, undated fragment (?December 1864), fos 21-5, and see CO 188/141, Gordon to Cardwell, Confidential, 21 November 1864, fos 385-92.

200. Cardwell 6/39, Cardwell to Gordon (copy), private, 7 January 1865, fos 37-40. (Original in Stanmore 1.)

201. Stanmore 2, Smith to Gordon, 7 July 1865.

202. Monck A-755, Cardwell to Monck, private, 18 November 1864.

203. *Ibid.*, Cardwell to Monck, private, 11 August 1865.

204. *Ibid.*, Cardwell to Monck, private, 19 September 1865.

205. Stanmore 1, Cardwell to Gordon, 15 September 1865.

206. Monck A-755, Cardwell to Monck, private, 30 June 1865. Compare Cardwell 6/39, Gordon to Cardwell, private, 5 June 1866, fos 89-92.

207. *Ibid.*, Cardwell to Monck, private, 11 August 1865.

208. *Ibid.*, Cardwell to Monck, private, 22 July 1865, report of Sir Fenwick Williams.

209. *Westminster Review*, xxvii (1865) p. 552.

210. *The Times*, 5 April 1865.

211. *Morning Chronicle* (Halifax), 24 January 1866, quoted *Life and Times*, p. 221.

212. Speech of 7 April 1866, quoted Baker, *op. cit.*, p. 103.

213. 'Union' 13 March, in *The Times*, 5 April 1865. There is a version (draft or copy?) of this letter in Stanmore 3, suggesting that Gordon was in some way involved in writing it. A possible author is J.C. Allen.

214. *BPP*, 1867, *Correspondence* and *Letter to the Earl of Carnarvon*. Although Howe is not named, it is clear that it was his florid style which *The Times* had dismissed ten years earlier as 'one of the most extraordinary specimens of Transatlantic eloquence that it has yet been our lot to see'. *The Times*, 7 January 1856.

215. Howe to Stairs, 21 December 1866, in Burpee, p. 447.

216. Howe to Stairs, 18 August 1866, *ibid.*, p. 428.

217. Speech of 8 November 1867, in *House of Commons Debates First Session 1867-1868* (ed. P.B. Waite, Ottawa, 1967), pp. 15-16. I am grateful to John Milloy for his help with this point.

218. Muise, 'The Federal Election of 1867', pp. 345-6.

219. Speech, 8 November 1867, *House of Commons Debates*, p. 10.

220. Patterson, 'An Unexplained Incident', p. 445.

221. The resolution is in *BPP*, 1867, *Correspondence*, p. 62, and see also *Life and Times*, pp. 268-71 and *Road to Confederation*, pp. 366-9.

222. Pryke, *Nova Scotia and Confederation*, p. 28. Cardwell recognised that this was a high-risk strategy. Waite, 'Cardwell and Confederation', p. 34.

223. Cardwell 6/40, Cardwell to Williams (copy), private, 7 July 1866, fos 19-20.

224. Carnarvon 6/136, Cardwell to Carnarvon, private, 6 July 1866 (copy in Russell 16B, fos 1333-4). For attempts to persuade Russell to face facts and announce his retirement, see J. Prest, *Lord John Russell* (London, 1972) pp. 415-17.

225. Some of the correspondence between Cardwell and Carnarvon is undated, and Cardwell insisted that one letter had been backdated, with the implication that he was made to seem dilatory. The episode is partly unravelled in G.W. Martin, 'Britain and the Future of British North America', pp. 312-19 and see also *Road to Confederation*, p. 396.

226. Cardwell 6/40, Carnarvon to Cardwell, private, 16 July, confidential, 19 July 1866, fos 26, 35-6.

227. Carnarvon 6/136, Cardwell to Carnarvon, 20 July 1866, fos 716-18, and see also Browne, p. 180. Carnarvon actually wrote to Macdonald on 27 July, welcoming him to England, on the expectation that the delegates would arrive the next day; Howe had recognised as early as the 20th that there would not be sufficient time for legislation before the session ended. Carnarvon 6/149, fos 5-6; Burpee, p. 426.

228. Cardwell 6/40, Monck to Cardwell, 12 July 1867, fos 93-4. Monck had come close to accusing Macdonald of wasting time in an exchange of letters late in June. Pope, *Memoirs*, pp. 316-21. Macdonald also made it clear that he would brook no criticism from the Maritimers: their 'failure' to ratify the Quebec agreement in 1865 'perilled the existence' of the Great Coalition. 'Even had we sailed on the 21st of July, I do not believe that Confederation could have been carried.' Macdonald to Tilley, 8 October 1866, *ibid.*, pp. 323-6. Gordon alleged that the New Brunswick delegates had been hurried to London by their wives. Carnarvon 6/142, Gordon to Carnarvon, private, 30 July 1866.

229. Carnarvon 6/136, Cardwell to Carnarvon, 20 July 1866, fos 716-18, and see also Browne, p. 180; Cardwell 6/40, Carnarvon to Cardwell, 20 July 1866, fos 41-2.

230. Memoranda of a meeting, in Cardwell 6/40, fos 47-55.

231. Cardwell 6/40, Cardwell to Russell (copy), 24 July 1866, fos 57-60, probably reflecting discussion at a meeting between Cardwell and Gladstone that day; Matthew (ed.), *op. cit.*, vi, p. 454.

232. Smith, *Second Reform Act*, pp. 128-32.

233. Carnarvon 6/136, Cardwell to Carnarvon, 27 July 1866, fos 726-9.

234. Howe to Stairs, 10 September 1866, Burpee, p. 431.

235. Burpee, p. 432.

236. Vincent, *Formation of the Liberal Party*, pp. 59-60, argues that pamphleteering was 'killed dead' by the cheap press. The *Saturday Review* discussed and dismissed the pamphlet on 20 October 1866 (p. 477), calling its author 'Mr Home': the historian is reassured to find that the Victorians had problems reading their own writing. Howe could only retaliate by adopting Bright's nickname, the *Saturday Reviler*, Burpee, p. 450. Gladstone read Howe on 24 September, Matthew (ed.), *op. cit.*, vi, p. 466.

237. Carnarvon 6/138, Carnarvon to Derby (copy), private, 11 October 1864, fos 105-7.

238. CO 42/661, Howe and Annand to Carnarvon, printed letter, 3 October 1866, fos 462-7. Rogers hoped the Canadians 'would now have the good sense' to keep Macdonald 'on the other side of the Atlantic', *ibid*., minute of 5 October. Carnarvon asked for an urgent report from Monck, Carnarvon 6/151, Carnarvon to Monck (copy), private and confidential, 7 October 1866, fos 962-3. Howe claimed that the *Daily Telegraph* had broken the story and 'we thought the matter might be improved'. Compare Burpee, p. 435. Macdonald, who was not named by Annand and Howe, eased the problem by re-marrying in February 1867.

239. Carnarvon 6/138, Carnarvon to Derby (copy), private, 12 October 1866.

240. Howe to Stairs, 12 October 1866, Burpee, p. 434.

241. Howe to Stairs, 9 November 1866, in *ibid*., p. 436.

242. Ged Martin, 'Empire Federalism and Imperial Parliamentary Union'.

243. Howe to Stairs, 8 November 1866, Burpee, p. 435.

244. Howe to Normanby, 22 November 1866, Burpee, pp. 439-42.

245. Howe 3, Aytoun to Howe, 7 March 1867, pp. 293-7; Howe to Stairs, 29 March 1867, Burpee, p. 461.

246. Recollections, 1885, Marindin (ed.), *op. cit.*, pp. 301-2.

247. Macdonald 51A, Adderley to Macdonald, 27 February 1867, pp. 20394-6.

248. Carnarvon 6/134, Carnarvon to Adderley (copy), 1 August 1866, fos 25-6; *ibid.*, 6/39, Carnarvon to Derby (copy), private and confidential, 7 January 1867, fos 20-2. Carnarvon's offer to resign to make way for a colonial secretary in the Commons may not have been entirely disinterested. If the priority was to place the British North America bill in competent hands in the lower house, the most plausible candidate (from thinly talented ranks) was the foreign secretary, Stanley. Carnarvon may have had an inkling that the Queen had favoured his own appointment to the Foreign Office the previous June. Buckle, ed., *op. cit.*, pp. 352-3. When Derby decided to place Commons management of the bill in the hands of a cabinet minister without any change in portfolios, Carnarvon's concern about Adderley's incompetence sharply diminished, and he advanced the unusual argument that Cardwell, from the opposition benches, would support the weak junior minister. Carnarvon 6/139, Carnarvon to Derby (copy), private and confidential, 22 February 1867, fos 42-4. As a result, Adderley and Cardwell acted together, to the disgust of Nova Scotian opponents, 'as if both were wet nurses for a foundling bill'. Burpee, p. 462.

249. Carnarvon 6/154, Reilly to Graham, 1 February 1867, fos 26-7. The man who produced the actual text of Canada's constitution deserves to be better commemorated. Francis Savage Reilly was born in Dublin in 1825, went to school in Dungannon and graduated from Trinity College Dublin in 1847. He was called to the English Bar in 1851 and was a member of Lincoln's Inn. He specialised in arbitration and insurance cases, and was knighted in 1882 for his services to the Foreign and Colonial Offices. He died at Bournemouth in 1883. I owe this information to David Parris. From the testy tone of his letters, Reilly seems to have regarded the British North America bill as an unwelcome burden.

250. CO 42/656, Monck to Carnarvon, confidential, 7 September, and minutes by Blackwood and Adderley, 20 and 28 September 1866, fos 360-70.

251. Buckle (ed.), *op. cit.*, pp. 392-4.

252. Pope (ed.), *Confederation*, p. 159, and see also p. 181; Macdonald to Knutsford, 18 July 1889, in Pope, *Memoirs*, p. 332.

253. Carnarvon 6/139, Carnarvon to Derby (copy), 6 February 1867, fos 30-1, quoted *Critical Years*, pp. 212-13.

254. *Ibid.*, Derby to Carnarvon, 7 February 1867, fos 42-4. The Queen also approved, Buckle (ed.), *op. cit.*, p. 394.

255. Carnarvon 6/139, Carnarvon to Derby (copy), 6 February 1867, fos 30-1.

256. Galt D8/3, Galt to Amy Galt (copy), 14 January 1867, p. 1153.

257. The foreign secretary's phrase, Vincent (ed.), *op. cit.*, p. 290. For the crisis, see Blake, *op. cit.*, pp. 456-63; Smith, *Second Reform Act*, pp. 148-61.

258. Blake, *op. cit.*, p. 459.

259. Hardinge, *Carnarvon*, i, pp. 349-59.

260. In 1868, *Punch* regretted parliament's refusal to hear the Nova Scotian case: 'The Blue Noses are very loyal Blue Noses, and do not deserve a wipe of this kind'. (*Punch*, 27 June 1868, p. 275.)

261. Howe to Russell, February 1867, in Burpee, p. 455.

262. Howe to Stairs, 28 September 1866, *ibid.*, p. 433.

263. Beck, *Howe*, ii, pp. 169-70.

264. Howe to Stairs, 9 November 1866, in Burpee, p. 437; Carnarvon 6/134, Adderley to Carnarvon, 26 September 1866, fos 53-4.

265. Unusually, Campbell had inherited peerages from both his parents, and sat in the Lords as Baron Stratheden and Campbell. Like Gordon, he was a Scot who studied at Trinity College, Cambridge. Each became President of the Union, and although Campbell was five years older, he had sat as MP for the borough of Cambridge during Gordon's undergraduate years.

266. This is a deduction from an obscure motion he moved on the subject, *Hansard*, clxxxv, 21 February 1867, cols 701-10.

267. *Ibid.*, 26 February 1867, cols 1011-17, esp. col. 1011.

268. *Ibid.*, cols 1017-20.

269. *Ibid.*, 28 February 1867, cols 1180-5.

270. Report by Garvie, 15 March 1867, in Burpee, p. 462.

271. *Ibid.*, and see also Howe 3, Hadfield to Howe, 1 March 1867, p. 285. Hadfield expressed his unhappiness at the speed with which Nova Scotia was being pushed into Confederation in *Hansard*, clxxxv, 28 February 1867, col. 1195.

272. Report by Garvie, 15 March 1867, in Burpee, p. 462.

273. Howe 3, Horsman to Howe, 3 March 1867, pp. 289-91.

274. *Hansard*, clxxxv, 19 February 1867, cols 579-80. Monck was making his maiden speech after receiving a British peerage (in addition to his Irish title) which entitled him to sit in the Lords. (Palmerston, another Irish peer, sat in the Commons throughout his career.)

275. *Ibid.*, 26 February 1867, col. 1018.

276. *Ibid.*, 19 February 1867, col. 578, and see also Beck, *Howe*, ii, p. 215. But D'Arcy McGee claimed that at Quebec in 1862, Howe had made 'an ardent appeal ... to take up the Union question conjointly with the railroad'. Speech of 14 November 1867, *Debates of the House of Commons*, p. 68.

277. *Hansard*, clxxxv, 28 February 1867, cols 1180-5.

278. *Ibid.*, col. 1187.

279. *Ibid.*, col. 1188, and see also explanation by Tupper, *Debates of the House of Commons*, 8 November 1867, p. 19. 'If ever there was just & adequate evidence of legitimate popular consent it was in this case,' wrote Gladstone two years later. Gladstone to Granville, 8 January 1869, in A. Ramm (ed.), *The Political Correspondence of Mr Gladstone and Lord Granville 1868-1876* (2 vols, London, 1952) i, p. 8.

280. *Road to Confederation*, p. 429.

281. Disraeli to Derby, 4 March 1867, in Monypeny and Buckle, *op. cit.*, iv, p. 513.

282. *Hansard*, clxxxv, 4 March 1867, col. 1310.

283. Monypeny and Buckle, *op. cit.*, p. 451.

284. Stanley diary, 4 March 1867, in Vincent (ed.), *op. cit.*, p. 293.

285. *Hansard*, clxxxv, 4 March 1867, cols 1311-15 (Gladstone); 1320 (Aytoun).

286. Macdonald 161, Watkin to Macdonald, private, [February 1867]; Carnarvon 6/149, Macdonald to Carnarvon, private, 21 February 1867, fo. 41; Macdonald 51B, Carnarvon to Macdonald, private, 21 February 1867, pp. 20383-5.

287. Matthew (ed.), *op. cit.*, vi, p. 504.

288. Galt 3, Galt to Amy Galt (copy), 14 January 1867, p. 1153.

289. Macdonald to Knutsford, 18 July 1889, in Pope, *Memoirs*, p. 332. A fairer example might have been the *Hansard* heading for the 1862 Commons debate on miscellaneous matters in which members criticised the defeat of the Militia Bill: 'Defence of Canada — Captain Grant's Cooking Apparatus', clxvii, 15 July 1862, cols 843-76.

290. Burpee, p. 463.

291. *Debates of the House of Commons*, p. 71.

292. *Hansard*, clxxxv, 28 February 1867, col. 1198.

293. *Ibid.*, 19 February 1867, col. 582; *Daily News*, 22 February 1867.

294. Garvie's report, 15 March 1867, in Burpee, pp. 462-3. Garvie's anger remains vivid, but it is also an example of the shortcomings of contemporary evidence. Within a fortnight, he had managed to

confuse the second reading debate of 28 February with the committee stage on 4 March. Moreover, there was nothing unusual, still less improper, in the handling of the bill at committee stage. Garvie had arrived in London a few months earlier to study law, and was observing Commons procedure for the first time. *DCB*, x, p. 300.

295. *Hansard*, 4 March 1867, col. 1316, and see the alteration between the final draft and the British North America Act, Pope (ed.), *Confederation*, pp. 221, 257.

296. Monck to Henry Monck, 26 June 1867, *Monck Letters and Journals*, pp. 324-5. Monck insisted to Macdonald that the inauguration of the Dominion should be a low-key affair, confirming McGee's earlier frustration that the governor-general set his face against displays of 'heartiness and public *eclat*'. However, Monck reported to Abraham Hayward shortly afterwards that 1 July 1867 had been 'a holiday all through the country, and if the feelings of the people towards the measure of Union are to be interpreted by the manner in which they welcomed its advent, it must be pronounced eminently popular'. Macdonald 51A, Monck to Macdonald, 26 June 1867, pp. 20538-40; *ibid.*, 231, McGee to Macdonald, 19 December 1866, pp. 99992-5; Monck to Hayward, 19 July 1867, in Carlisle (ed.), *op. cit.*, ii, pp. 159-60.

CONCLUSION

1. Rogers to Miss Rogers, 23 December 1864, in Marindin (ed.), *op. cit.*, pp. 252-3.

2. Story told in Gordon to Gladstone, January 1864, in Knaplund (ed.), *Gladstone-Gordon Correspondence*, pp. 42-3.

3. Gladstone 44136, Cobden to Gladstone, 26 February 1865, fos 275-8.

4. Galt to Sir John Young, 15 May 1869, in Skelton, *op. cit.*, pp. 221-2.

5. Quoted, Beck, *Howe*, ii, p. 169.

6. Quoted, R. Fitzhenry (ed.), *The Fitzhenry & Whiteside Book of Quotations* (Toronto, 1981) p. 134.

7. *Elgin-Grey Papers*, Grey to Elgin (copy), 8 August 1849, i, p. 437.

8. Russell 8A, Grey to Russell, 8 August 1849, fos 62-5.

9. *Saturday Review*, 4 October 1862, p. 397.

10. Brebner, p. 283.

11. *Kingdom of Canada*, p. 317.
12. Upton, 'Idea of Confederation', p. 184.
13. *Westminster Review*, xxvii (1865) p. 536.
14. *Daily Telegraph*, 25 November 1864.
15. *Westminster Review*, xxvii (1865) p. 540.
16. *The Times*, 14 September 1865.
17. *Edinburgh Review*, cxxxi (1865) p. 184.
18. *The Times*, 9 January 1865; *Saturday Review*, 14 January 1865, p. 37, both commenting on Cardwell's despatch of 3 December 1864.
19. Macdonald 161, report of Galt's statement to Cardwell, p. 65222.
20. Galt 3, Monck to Galt, 26 October 1865, pp. 1057-61.
21. *CD*, pp. 126.
22. *The Times*, 22 November 1867.

Index